Protecting Information Assets and IT Infrastructure in the Cloud

This book is a second edition. The last one reviewed the evolution of the Cloud, important Cloud concepts and terminology, and the threats that are posed on a daily basis to it. A deep dive into the components of Microsoft Azure were also provided, as well as risk mitigation strategies, and protecting data that resides in a Cloud environment.

In this second edition, we extend this knowledge gained to discuss the concepts of Microsoft Azure. We also examine how Microsoft is playing a huge role in artificial intelligence and machine learning with its relationship with OpenAI. An overview into ChatGPT is also provided, along with a very serious discussion of the social implications for artificial intelligence.

Ravi Das is a technical writer in the cybersecurity realm. He also does cybersecurity consulting on the side through his private practice, RaviDas.Tech, Inc. He also holds the Certified in Cybersecurity certification from the ISC(2).

Protecting Information Assets and IT Infrastructure in the Cloud

Second Edition

Ravi Das

CRC Press
Taylor & Francis Group
Boca Raton London New York

CRC Press is an imprint of the
Taylor & Francis Group, an **informa** business

Designed cover image: © Shutterstock, Stock Photo ID 1931270681, Photo Contributor Tada Images

Second edition published 2024
by CRC Press
2385 NW Executive Center Drive, Suite 320, Boca Raton FL 33431

and by CRC Press
4 Park Square, Milton Park, Abingdon, Oxon, OX14 4RN

CRC Press is an imprint of Taylor & Francis Group, LLC

© 2024 Ravi Das

First Edition Published by Taylor & Francis 2019

Library of Congress Cataloging-in-Publication Data
Names: Das, Ravindra, author.
Title: Protecting information assets and IT infrastructure in the Cloud / Ravi Das.
Description: Second edition. | Boca Raton, FL : CRC Press, 2024. |
    Includes bibliographical references and index.
Identifiers: LCCN 2023031644 (print) | LCCN 2023031645 (ebook) |
    ISBN 9781032605104 (hbk) | ISBN 9781032605401 (pbk) | ISBN 9781003459569 (ebk)
Subjects: LCSH: Cloud computing—Security measures. | Computer networks—
    Security measures. | Artificial intelligence—Social aspects.
Classification: LCC QA76.585 .D37 2024 (print) | LCC QA76.585 (ebook) |
    DDC 004.67/82—dc23/eng/20230822
LC record available at https://lccn.loc.gov/2023031644
LC ebook record available at https://lccn.loc.gov/2023031645

ISBN: 978-1-032-60510-4 (hbk)
ISBN: 978-1-032-60540-1 (pbk)
ISBN: 978-1-003-45956-9 (ebk)

DOI: 10.1201/9781003459569

Typeset in Times
by Apex CoVantage, LLC

This book is dedicated to my Lord and Savior, Jesus Christ, the Grand Designer of the Universe, and to my parents, Dr. Gopal Das and Mrs. Kunda Das.

This book is also dedicated to:

Richard and Gwenda Bowman

Jaya Chandra

My loving cats, Fifi and Bubu

Contents

Acknowledgments

I would like to thank Ms. Gabrielle Williams, my editor, who made this book into a reality.

1 Introduction to the Cloud Computing Environment

EVOLUTION TO THE CLOUD: THE MAINFRAME

The term *information technology* (IT) has certainly evolved over the last few decades. As a society, we first started out using the largest mainframes ever known. Of course, the main programming languages at the time were COBOL and Job Control Language (JCL).

These types of computers were used in the 1950s and the 1960s at the major research centers worldwide, and even in the corporate setting, if such a large system could fit into the place of business or corporation.

For example, mainframes were also used heavily by the National Aeronautics and Space Administration (NASA) in the space program to land humans on the moon. The same type of technology was also used in both Apollo space capsules, but of course on a much smaller scale so that they could fit and work easily in both the Command Module (CM) and the Lunar Excursion Module (LEM).

In fact, the mainframes that were used in the Apollo flights were designed, built, manufactured, and implemented by IBM. The primary one that was used was known as "System/360." The price ranged from $133,000 all the way up to $5.5 million. In just over a short 2-month timespan, over 2000 units were sold, and NASA was a prime customer.

The following quoted excerpt summarizes just how crucial System/360 was:

> Apollo flights had so much information to relay that their computers had to report in an electronic form of shorthand.... Even in shorthand, however, it took a circuit capable of transmitting a novel a minute to get the information to NASA's Manned Spacecraft Center—now the Johnson Space Center—in Houston, Texas. Receiving this enormous amount of data was a powerful IBM computer whose sole task was to translate the shorthand into meaningful information for Apollo flight controllers. The IBM System/360 computer absorbed, translated, calculated, evaluated, and relayed this information for display. It was one of five System/360 machines used by NASA for the Apollo 11 mission. The same System/360 computer that processed the data for the first lunar landing from 240,000 miles away in Houston also calculated the liftoff data needed by astronauts Neil Armstrong and Edwin "Buzz" Aldrin to rendezvous back with the command module piloted by Michael Collins for the flight back to Earth.
>
> *(https://arstechnica.com/information-technology/2014/04/50-years-ago-ibm-created-mainframe-that-helped-bring-men-to-the-moon/)*

The replacement for System/360 was System/370, which was introduced in the early 1970s. Even to this day, IBM significantly dominates the mainframe market; the latest

DOI: 10.1201/9781003459569-1

model is known as "System z." This technology is even backward-compatible with System/360.

Apart from landing a human on the moon, other primary uses for System/360 and System/370 also involved bulk data processing, such as the census, industry, and consumer statistics; enterprise resource planning; and transaction processing. Even before System/360 was built, IBM had developed a much more primitive mainframe computer that was known as the *automatic sequence-controlled calculator* (ASCC).

The ASCC consisted primarily of thousands of vacuum tubes, in which the primary purpose was to solve mathematical addition and multiplication problems. In between the ASCC and System/360, IBM had developed the RAMAC 305 computing system, which was a crucial technological component in developing the first series of the random-access memory (RAM) module chips.

It should be noted that during this timeframe, IBM was not the only player in the mainframe market. There were others as well. For example, another mainframe model that came out was known as the "Universal Automatic Computer" (UNIVAC). It took 4 years just to develop one model of this brand, and it was finally completed on March 31, 1951.

This mainframe cost well over \$1,000,000; it occupied an area of 352 ft^2, and consisted of 5400 vacuum tubes. The launch customer for the UNIVAC was the United States Census Bureau; in fact, it was even used to predict the outcome of the 1952 presidential election. This laid the groundwork for the technological development of predictive tools that were used in subsequent presidential elections.

Another competitor to the System/360 was known as the "CRAY-1," which was developed by Seymour Cray. It first debuted in 1976. This technology was deemed to be more of a supercomputer. For instance, it could process well over one hundred million arithmetic operations per second. The cost of the CRAY-1 ranged anywhere from \$5 million to \$8 million, and this model produced a massive amount of heat during its processing cycles. For this reason, the use of Freon was introduced as a cooling mechanism, which added further expense to the hardware.

The term *mainframe* simply refers to the way the machine has been built up from scratch. All the relevant units (processing, communication, etc.) were hung into a frame, and the primary computer was built into it.

In fact, the original manufacturers of mainframe computers were known colloquially as "IBM and the Seven Dwarfs." This included IBM, Burroughs, UNIVAC, NCR, Control Data, Honeywell, General Electric, and RCA.

After the departure of General Electric and RCA, this group of mainframe manufacturers became known as the "IBM and the BUNCH." When mainframes made their debut, they were (and, in fact, still are) characterized less by a raw single-task computational speed [typically defined as a *million instructions per second* (MIPS) or a *million floating-point operations per second* (FLOPS)].

Other characteristics of the mainframe include the following:

- Redundant internal engineering that yields high reliability and security.
- Extensive input/output (I/O) facilities capable of offloading to separate engines.

- Strict backward compatibility with older and other various types of software.
- High hardware and computational utilization rates through virtualization to support massive throughput.
- Extremely high levels of reliability, availability, and serviceability (collectively known as "RAS").
- Higher levels of security than even some present-day computing systems. In fact, the National Institute of Standards (NIST) vulnerabilities database, US-CERT, rates traditional mainframes such as IBM z Series, Unisys Dorado, and Unisys Libra as among the most secure with vulnerabilities in the low single digits when compared with the thousands for Windows, UNIX, and Linux.
- Functionalities of what is known as "virtual machines." This technique allows applications to run as if they were on physically distinct computers. In this role, a single mainframe can replace higher-functioning hardware services that are available to conventional servers.
- Ability to add or hot-swap system capacity without disrupting system function, with specificity and granularity to a level of sophistication not even available in today's server technology.
- Design enabling very high-volume input/output (I/O) to be handled, with an emphasis on throughput computing.
- Execution integrity characteristics for fault-tolerant computing.

The technical characteristics of the modern mainframe include the following:

- It has 16 central processing units (CPUs) or greater.
- It has at least 8 terabytes (TB) of available RAM.
- Its processing power is well over 550 megabytes per second Mbps.
- It has subcabinets for the following:
  - Data storage
  - I/O processes
  - The RAM module chips
- It can process separate, heavy applications such as
  - Task management
  - Program management
  - Job management
  - Serialization
  - Interlinear address spacing
  - Deep-level Internet communications

When mainframes were first introduced in the 1950s, they had only a rudimentary interactive interface, which was the console, and they used sets of punched cards, paper tape, or magnetic tape to transfer data and programs. They operated pretty much in what was known as a "batch mode" to support back-office functions such as payroll and customer billing.

The next step up from this was the *interactive user terminal*. This was used almost exclusively for booking types of applications (e.g., airline or train booking), rather than for software application or other types of program development projects.

During the 1970s, many of the existing mainframe computers were operating as timesharing computers, which literally supported hundreds of users simultaneously along with batch processing. Another feature that was added during this timeframe was the specialized text terminal cathode-ray tube (CRT) displays coupled with integral keyboards.

In the 1980s and 1990s (especially during the "Internet bubble"), mainframe technology was supported by graphic display terminals, and terminal emulation. Then, at the beginning of the 21st century, modern mainframes were entirely phased out (the classic "green screen" terminal access) in favor of the intuitive and easy-to-follow web-style user interfaces.

The demand for and growth of mainframes started to pick up even further into the mid-1990s with the explosion of the Internet bubble and e-commerce. There was still a need for high-end processing capability, given the sheer number of online stores that were proliferating.

Also, another factor that increased mainframe usage within this timeframe was the development of the Linux operating system, which arrived on IBM mainframe systems in 1999 and is typically run in scores or up to approximately 8000 virtual machines on a single mainframe. Linux allows users to take advantage of open-source software combined with mainframe hardware RAS.

At the beginning of this (21st) century, rapid expansion and development in emerging markets, particularly the People's Republic of China, spurred major mainframe investments to solve exceptionally difficult computing problems, such as providing unified, extremely high-volume online transaction processing databases for 1 billion consumers across multiple industries (banking, insurance, credit reporting, government services, etc.).

Finally, in 2012, NASA shut down the last mainframe computer that it purchased from IBM as the Space Shuttle program ended. Even to this day, IBM is still the dominant player in the mainframe market, although it is shrinking rapidly given the explosion of Cloud infrastructure.

With this timeframe, IBM has shifted its strategy. For example, it has its own large research and development (R&D) team devoted exclusively to designing new, homegrown CPUs, including mainframe processors such as the 5.5-GHz six-core zEC12 mainframe microprocessor developed in 2012.

There are still some smaller players in the mainframe market (when compared to the gargantuan size of IBM) such as BMC, Compuware, and CA Technologies. Also included in this list are Fujitsu and Hitachi, as both continue to use custom S/390-compatible processors, as well as other CPUs (including POWER and Xeon) for their lower-end mainframe systems.

NEC uses Xeon processors for its low-end ACOS-2 mainframe line but develops the custom NOAH-6 processor for its high-end ACOS-4 mainframe series. Finally, Unisys produces code-compatible mainframe systems that range from laptops to cabinet-sized mainframes that utilize homegrown CPUs as well as Xeon processors.

There is often confusion between supercomputers and mainframes. The former are used primarily for scientific and engineering problems (high-performance computing) that crunch numbers and data, while the latter focus on bulk transaction processing. Other technical differences include the following:

- Mainframes are built to be reliable for transaction processing. A *transaction* is typically defined as a set of operations including disk read/writes, operating system calls, or some form of data transfer from one subsystem to another.
- Supercomputer performance is measured in floating-point operations per second (FLOPS), or in traversed edges per second (TEPS) metrics that are not very meaningful for mainframe applications. Floating-point operations are mostly addition, subtraction, and multiplication (of *binary* floating point in supercomputers).

EVOLUTION TO THE CLOUD: THE PERSONAL COMPUTER

The last section provided an overview of the history of the mainframe computer, and in certain instances, how the development of this technology has helped lead to development of Cloud infrastructure. One area where this has happened is in the creation of virtual machines, as reviewed above.

There is yet another aspect in the computing world that has led to the development of Cloud infrastructure. This is the growth of the personal computer (PC). Probably the main reason for this is that the vast majority of the global population use the Cloud for personal objectives just as they would with their own PCs.

One of the biggest areas in which Cloud infrastructure has been utilized in this regard is for the storage of personal information and data, with the ability to access the data on demand (as well as other types and kinds of software applications) when and where this access is needed or required.

Although this is a very simple task to achieve with just a few clicks of the mouse, there is a lot of history and technological development with regard to the personal computer that has made this possible.

Therefore, in this section, we will provide an overview of the development of the personal computer, and how it has lent itself to the creation of Cloud infrastructure as we see it today. We will begin with a chronological history of the key milestones in PC development, followed by further details in some other areas as well.

CHRONOLOGICAL HISTORY OF KEY MILESTONES IN PERSONAL COMPUTER DEVELOPMENT

1. **From 1971 to 1973:**
   The Intel 4004 chip: This has been deemed as the first-ever true "microprocessor." It heralded the dawn of the personal computing age. The Intel 4004 had an initial clock speed of 108 kHz and 2300 individual transistors compared to 3.9GHz and 1.4 billion transistors on the latest chips.

The Xerox Alto: The Xerox Alto was the first computer with a graphical user interface (GUI)—complete with desktop, folders, and icons—and was the first to be controlled by a mouse. It was never sold to the public, however.

2. **1975 to 1977:**

The Altair 8800: This was widely regarded as the first personal computer; the Altair 8800 was groundbreaking. It was sold in an assembly kit form, containing four separate circuit boards and many different parts. Microsoft was founded to supply a Beginner's All-purpose Symbolic Instruction Code (BASIC) interpreter for the Altair.

APPLE II: This was considered to be the first commercially successful PC. It launched with an integrated QWERTY keyboard, color graphics, and a cassette tape deck for loading programs. The first model sported a 1-MHz processor and 4 kB of RAM.

3. **From 1980 to 1981:**

The Creation of MS-DOS: In July 1980, IBM approached Microsoft to provide an operating system for a forthcoming personal computer, code-named "Chess." Microsoft acquired the rights to 86-DOS from Seattle Computer Products and adapted it to IBM's needs. The Microsoft *Disk Operating System* (DOS) was thus born.

Birth of the IBM PC: "Chess" was eventually unveiled as the IBM 5150 PC in August 1981. It used an Intel 8088 CPU running at 4.77 MHz and up to 64 kB of RAM. Its impact was such that, in 1982, *Time* magazine declared the home computer as its "Person of the Year."

The GRiD Compass: Debate continues over what was the first "laptop," but credit has been officially given to the GRiD Compass. It cost up to $10,000 and was used by NASA.

The Rise of the Clones: Using both a combination of Intel processors and the MS-DOS platform, several manufacturers created IBM PC-compatible computers. Companies such as Compaq and HP created so-called clones that could run the same software as IBM's machines, but were often much cheaper.

4. **From 1984 to 1985:**

The MacIntosh Computer: Although Xerox Alto had introduced such concepts more than a decade earlier, MacIntosh became the first mass-market computer to ship with a graphical user interface and a mouse.

The Rise of the Micromachines: Although not IBM compatibles, the so-called micromachines such as ZX Spectrum, Commodore 64, and BBC Micro became the first personal computers that were launched in Europe.

5. **From 1985 to 1990:**

Windows 1.0: This was deemed the forefather of the Windows Operating System that is used on most of today's PCs. Windows 1.0 replaced MS-DOS typed commands with point-and-click "windows," including drop-down menus, scrollbars, and more.

Microsoft Word: This was initially released for MS-DOS back in 1983. Microsoft Word has become one of the most widely used applications of all time. It, of course, formed part of the first Office suite, alongside with both Excel and PowerPoint in 1990.

6. **From 1990 to 1993:**

Windows 3.x: The 1990 launch of Windows 3.0 and the subsequent 1992 arrival of Windows 3.1 created a steep upswing in PC ownership. Concepts such as the Program Manager and File Manager were introduced for the first time. These are also some very key components of Cloud infrastructure.

Netscape Navigator (Mosaic): Mosaic, later renamed "Netscape Navigator," was the first popular web browser. In 1994, it accounted for 90% of overall web usage, but by 2002, Internet Explorer had 95% of the market share.

Windows 95: The personal computer came of age with Windows 95, which sold 7 million copies in its first 5 weeks. It introduced the "Start" button as well as the "desktop" that are still in use today. There is no doubt that this is the most influential operating system ever made.

The iMac: Windows-based personal computers dominated the 1990s, but Apple introduced the most iconic computer of the decade, the all-in-one iMac, which launched a year after Steve Jobs returned to Apple.

7. **From 2001 to 2009:**

Windows XP: This particular operating system that made Windows so stable that Microsoft is still having to convince companies to part with it today, 13 years after its initial release.

Windows 7: Windows 7 has been of the most widely used operating systems in the world today. It greatly improved on Windows XP's reliability and performance.

8. **From 2009 to Present:**

The Apple iPad: Windows 7 offered touch controls, but touchscreen tablets really took off with the launch of Apple's iPad. The iPad transformed mobile as well as Cloud computing and paved the way for tablets running a variety of operating systems.

Windows 8, 9, and 10: Windows 8 gave birth to dozens of new laptop, hybrid, and desktop designs. Windows 8.1 and 10 have all made key refinements to the overall Windows-based architecture.

OTHER KEY MWILESTONES

Apart from the other milestones listed in the last section, others as well have led to the Cloud computing infrastructure as we know it today. Here are some of these noteworthy developments:

1. **TRS-80:**

There were three models of TRS-80, known as the models I, II, and III. Model I combined the motherboard and keyboard into one unit, in which the monitor and the power supply were separate components. Model I employed a Zilog Z80 processor clocked at 1.77 MHz (the later models were shipped with a Z80A processor). Model I originally shipped with 4 kB of RAM and subsequently with 16 kB. This allowed for the RAM expansion of a total of 48 kB. Its other unique features were its full-stroke QWERTY keyboard, small size, as well as the Microsoft floating-point BASIC programming language and the inclusion of a monitor and tape deck. Over 1.5 million units of model I were sold before they were canceled in 1981, when models II and III took over.

2. **The Atari 400/800:**
   The Atari computing system was a well-known brand in the late 1970s, because of its popular arcade games such as Pong, as well as the Atari VCS game console. Within this timeframe, the Atari computing systems offered what was then much higher performance than the contemporary designs, as well as numerous unique graphics and sound features.

3. **The CD-ROM:**
   In the early 1990s, the CD-ROM became an industry standard, and was built into almost all desktop computers. Initially, the CD-ROM was utilized for audio-based files. Another popular use of CD-ROMs was for multimedia files.

4. **P2P File Sharing:**
   "Peer to peer" (also known as P2P) file-sharing networks such as Napster, Kazaa, and Gnutella were used almost exclusively for sharing music files.

5. **The 64-Bit Microprocessor:**
   In 2003, AMD shipped its 64-bit microprocessor line. Also in 2003, IBM released the 64-bit PowerPC 970 for Apple's high-end Power Mac G5 systems. Intel, in 2004, reacted to AMD's success with 64-bit processors, releasing updated versions of their Xeon and Pentium 4 lines. Initially, 64-bit processors were common in high-end systems, such as servers and workstations.

6. **Local-Area Networks:**
   The invention of local-area networks (LANs), notably the Ethernet, allowed PCs to communicate with each other and with shared printers.

7. **Multiprocessing:**
   In May 2005, AMD and Intel released their first dual-core 64-bit processors, the Pentium D and the Athlon 64 X2, respectively.

EVOLUTION TO THE CLOUD: THE WIRELESS NETWORK

Just as much as the mainframe and the personal computer have been crucial in laying the foundation for Cloud infrastructure, the next critical component has been the evolution of wireless networks, and the devices that are associated with them, such as the tablets, smartphones, and notebooks. A primary reason for this is the fact that many applications from the Cloud are downloaded and used through wireless technology. In fact, many of the software applications that reside in Cloud infrastructure are now available as mobile applications that can be downloaded and installed instantaneously onto a wireless device.

Besides applications, another key role between wireless networks and Cloud infrastructure is that of communications. Many businesses and corporations as well as individuals and society as a whole are now highly dependent on Cloud infrastructure for instantaneous communication at a fraction of the time and cost that would normally be required with a traditional landline carrier.

In fact, these statistics outline just how dependent wireless networks are on Cloud infrastructure:

1. The total number of wireless Cloud users worldwide grew rapidly to just over 998 million in 2014, up from 42.8 million in 2008, representing an annual growth rate of 69%.
2. The global market for wireless Cloud computing is expected to grow from $40.7 billion in 2011 to more than $241 billion in 2020, and the total size of the public Cloud market is expected to grow from $25.5 billion in 2011 to $159.3 billion in 2020.
3. The global Cloud IP traffic (fixed and mobile) has increased by 66% per annum and reached 133 exabytes per month in 2015.
4. The global mobile data traffic (including both Cloud and non-Cloud traffic) grew by 113% in 2011 and is predicted to grow at 78% per annum. In 2016 data traffic reached 10.8 exabytes per month, with wireless Cloud services (cellular and Wi-Fi) accounting for 71% (7.6 exabytes per month) of this traffic.
5. The Cloud-based mobile applications market grew by 88% per annum between 2009 and 2014.

(http://ceet.unimelb.edu.au/publications/
ceet-white-paper-wireless-cloud.pdf)

Therefore, it is also important to provide an overview as to how the wireless networks have actually developed and, given their sheer importance to Cloud infrastructure, what is being planned for them in the future.

1. **In 1970:**
   Professor Norman Abramson invented the "Alohanet," which is considered to be the forerunner of the present-day Ethernet and the wireless LAN. Radio communications were specifically utilized for the transmission of the high-speed data packets.
2. **In 1979:**
   The first-generation (1G) wireless network was launched. Its first application was for the analog cellular phone (cellphone) carrier known specifically as "Nippon Telegraph and Telephone," based in Japan.
3. **In 1995:**
   The second-generation (2G) wireless network appeared, introduced by Sprint.

4. **In 2000:**
   The third-generation (3G) wireless network is launched by SK Telecom, based in South Korea.
5. **In 2009:**
   The fourth-generation (4G) wireless network was launched.
6. **In 2014:**
   The 40 billionth mobile application was downloaded from the Apple Store, which resides in Cloud infrastructure.

MAJOR CHANGES FROM THE 3G NETWORK TO THE 4G NETWORK

1. **In 1998:**
   The 3G wireless network now has functionalities for the following:
   • Sending and receiving email
   • GPS connectivity
   • Social media and social network access
   • Access to other news media such as CNN, CNBC, and weather reports
2. **In 2001:**
   The 3G wireless network connectivity speed increased from 200 kilobits per second (kbps) to well over 40 megabits per second (Mbps), with data transfer rates of well over 2 Mbps occurring.

4G NETWORK ADVANCES, ABILITIES, AND NETWORK SPEEDS

1. **In March 2007:**
   The 4G LTE is introduced, and now consumers can quite easily share and transmit photos, pictures, and videos; conduct Voice over Internet Protocol (VoIP)-based streaming; and conduct push-to-talk conversations on their smartphones.
2. **In 2010:**
   The total number of 4G smartphone subscriptions increases by more than 4 times the traditional landline telephones.
   The 4G network is now enabled for multiple-application connectivity, Internet-based browsing, video streaming, and mobile linking via across all wireless devices; large data transfers can now be done, and they are backward enabled for 3G network communications as well.
   The 4G LTE network has now reached speeds that are 10 times faster than those of 3G networks.
3. **By 2019:**
   It is predicted that 90% of the world's population will have 4G network access, and among that, 65% will be on the 4G LTE network.
4. **By 2025:**
   It is predicted that there will be over 1 trillion wireless devices on the 4G network.

5. **By 2032:**
   It is predicted that each person around the world will have touched between 300 and 500 wireless devices.

5G Networks and the Internet of Things (IoT)

1. **By 2020:**
   It is heavily anticipated that 5G networks will have replaced 4G networks on a global basis.

   The 5G network will operate on a completely IP-based, centralized *supercore* model, which will unify all the services that are currently offered and will be offered into one major platform for the consumer.

   The 5G network will now completely, 100% support the IoT Infrastructure, which will have over 65,000 major connections, supporting speeds of up to and even exceeding 25 Mbps.

Technical Aspects of the Wireless Network

There are also a numerous key technical aspects of wireless networks that are important in the development of Cloud infrastructure as we know it today. This section examines this in further detail, and it can be visually represented as shown in Figure 1.1.

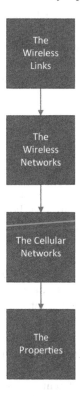

FIGURE 1.1   Technical aspects of the wireless network.

Wireless Links

First in the hierarchy are the wireless links, which are described as follows:

1. **Terrestrial Microwave:**
   Terrestrial microwave communications make use of Earth-based transmitters and receivers that essentially resemble satellite dishes. Terrestrial microwaves are in the low-gigahertz range, which restricts all communications to line of sight only. The relay stations are spaced only ≤30 miles apart from one another.

2. **Communication Satellites:**
   Satellites communicate via microwave radiowaves and are stationed in a geosynchronous orbit 22,000 miles above the equator in outer space.

3. **Cellular and PCS Systems:**
   These specific systems make use several radio communications technologies. They further divide the region covered into multiple geographic areas. Each one of them has a low-power transmitter or radio relay antenna device to relay calls from one area to the next area.

4. **Radio and Spread-Spectrum Technologies:**
   Wireless local-area networks use a high-frequency radio technology similar to digital cellular and low-frequency radio technology. Wireless LANs use spread-spectrum technology to enable communication between multiple devices in a limited area.

5. **Free-Space Optical Communication:**
   These systems make use of the visible or invisible light for communications. In most cases, line-of-sight propagation is used.

Wireless Networks

Second down in the hierarchy are wireless networks. These systems make up the wireless links, and they are described as follows:

1. **Wireless PAN:**
   Wireless personal-area networks (WPAN) are Internet-based devices that operate within a relatively small area. For example, both Bluetooth radio and invisible infrared light provide a WPAN for interconnecting a headset to a laptop.

2. **The Wireless WAN:**
   A *wireless local-area network* (WLAN) links two or more devices over a short distance using a wireless distribution method, usually providing a connection through an access point for Internet access. WLANs use of spread-spectrum or *orthogonal frequency-division multiplexing* (OFDM) technologies. They implement point-to-point links between computers or networks at two distant locations, often using dedicated microwave or modulated laser light beams over line-of-sight paths. WLANs are used primarily for connecting two entirely different network infrastructures without having to install a hardwired link.

3. **The Wireless Ad Hoc Network:**
   This is a wireless network made up of radio nodes organized in a mesh topology. Each node forwards messages on behalf of the other nodes and performs its own routing procedures. Ad hoc networks can "self-heal," meaning that they can automatically reroute themselves around a node that has lost power. Various network-layer protocols are needed to implement ad hoc mobile networks, such as the Distance Sequenced Distance Vector Routing Protocol, the Associativity-Based Routing Protocol, the Ad Hoc On-Demand Distance Vector Routing Protocol, and the Dynamic Source Routing Protocol.

4. **The Wireless MAN:**
   Wireless metropolitan-area networks (WMANs) are a type of wireless network that connects several wireless LANs in a seamless and harmonious fashion.

5. **The Wireless WAN:**
   Wireless wide-area networks (WWANs) are wireless networks that typically cover large areas. The WWAN connections between access points are usually point-to-point microwave links making use of parabolic dishes on the 2.4-GHz band. A typical WWAN contains base station gateways, access points, and wireless bridging relays. Other WWAN configurations are mesh systems where each access point acts as a relay.

Cellular Networks

A *cellular network* (also known as a *mobile network*) is essentially a radio network that is distributed over land areas called *cells*. Each cell is served by at least one fixed-location transceiver, known as a *cell site* or a *base station*. In a cellular network, each cell uses a different set of radiofrequencies from any adjacent cells to avoid any interference.

When these cells are joined together, they cover a wide geographic area. This enables numerous portable transceivers (smartphones, tablets, notebooks, etc.) to communicate with each other. These systems make up the cellular networks (and they are also third down in the hierarchy as shown in Figure 1.1), and they are as follows:

1. **The Global System for Mobile Communications (GSM):**
   The GSM network is divided into three major systems:
   • The switching system
   • The base station system
   • The operation-and-support system

   The wireless device connects to the base system station, and from there, it then connects to the operation-and-support station. At this point, it then gets connected to the switching station, where the call is transferred to where it needs to go. The GSM is the most common wireless protocol and is used for the majority of wireless devices.

2. **The Personal Communications Services (PCS):**
   The PCS is a radio band that is used by all wireless devices.
3. **The Global-Area Network (GAN):**
   The GAN is a network that is used for supporting wireless communications across an arbitrary number of local-area networks (LANs).
4. **The Space Network:**
   These are networks used for communication between spacecraft and satellites, usually in the vicinity of Earth. A prime example of this is NASA's Space Network.

The Properties

Last in the hierarchy are some of the general properties of wireless networks, and the most important ones are as follows:

1. **Performance:**
   Each wireless standard varies in geographic range, thus making one standard more ideal than the others depending on the application of the wireless network that is being used. As wireless networking has become much more commonplace, sophistication has increased through the configuration of both network hardware and software. As a result, greater capacity to send and receive larger amounts of data efficiently and quickly has been achieved.
2. **Space:**
   Space is another important property of wireless networks. For example, it offers many advantages in difficult-to-hardwire areas such as office buildings that are physically separated but operate as a single business entity. Wireless networks allow users to designate a certain space within which the specific network protocol will be able to communicate with other wireless devices from within that specific network.
3. **The Wireless Network Elements:**
   Wireless networks also consist of many interconnected wireline network elements (NEs). Reliable wireless service depends on the protection of NEs against all operational environments and applications. Of utmost importance are the NEs that are located on the cell tower to the base station. The hardware and the positioning of the antenna and associated closures and cables are required to have adequate strength, robustness, and corrosion resistance.

THE LAST EVOLUTION TO THE CLOUD: THE SMARTPHONE

As the title of this section implies, the last evolution that transpired before the full deployment and adoption of Cloud infrastructure took place was the development of the smartphone. As has been described, the smartphone (and, for that matter, actually any other form of wireless device) has now become literally the cornerstone of both the personal and the professional lives of just about everybody worldwide.

It is through our smartphones that we access most of the resources of Cloud infrastructure, whether this is the latest mobile application or the Microsoft Office 365 platform. The previous section of this chapter reviewed some of the important milestones in the development of the various wireless networks (specifically, the 1G, 2G, 3G, and 4G networks), and in this section, we will explore in more detail each one of these, and how they contributed to the evolution of the smartphone. After this section, the remainder of this chapter will be devoted to the evolution of the Cloud and its theoretical constructs.

THE 1G, 2G, 3G, AND 4G NETWORKS

The development of wireless networks is shown in Figure 1.2.

The 1G Network (Analog Cellular)

The first analog cellular system widely deployed in North America was the *advanced mobile phone system* (AMPS). The AMPS drove mass-market usage of cellular technology, but it had several security issues. For example, it was unencrypted and easily vulnerable to eavesdropping via a network sniffer. It was also susceptible to cellphone "cloning," and it used a frequency-division multiple access (FDMA) scheme that required significant amounts of wireless resources to support its overall

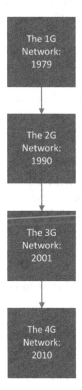

FIGURE 1.2 The evolution of wireless networks.

deployment and usage. The first US 1G network was launched by Ameritech. It cost $100 million to develop and implement.

The 2G Network (Digital Cellular)

The 2G network introduced a new variant of communication called *short-message service* (SMS) or "text messaging." The first machine-generated text message was sent in England on December 2, 1992, followed in 1993 by the first person-to-person SMS sent in Finland. The 2G network also introduced the ability to access media content on mobile phones, and as well as make mobile payments.

The mobile payment scheme first trialed in 1998 in Finland and Sweden, where a cellular phone was used to pay for various Coca-Cola vending machines and car parking. Commercial launches followed in 1999 in Norway. The first full Internet-based service for cellular phones was introduced by NTT DoCoMo (a Japanese company) in 1999.

The 3G Network (Mobile Broadband)

The main technological difference that distinguishes 3G technology from 2G technology is the use of packet switching rather than circuit switching for data transmission. By 2001, 3G technology began to be implemented using the High-Speed Downlink Packet Access Protocol (HSDPA), which is a critical component of the High-Speed Packet Access (HSPA) network protocol family.

Third-generation networks also led to creation of the "mobile web." The first such devices were known as "dongles," which plugged directly into a computer via a *universal serial bus* (USB) port. Another new class of device appeared subsequently, known as the *compact wireless router*. This made 3G Internet connectivity available to multiple computers simultaneously over a wireless fidelity (Wi-Fi) network, rather than to only a single computer via the USB plug-in.

The 4G Network (Native IP Networks)

The first two 4G networks were the WiMAX standard and the LTE standard. One of the main ways in which 4G networks differed from 3G networks was in the elimination of circuit switching. Instead, an all-IP network was utilized. This resulted in the utilization of data packet switching over LAN- and WAN-based networks, allowing for the creation of VoIP technologies.

CHRONOLOGICAL HISTORY OF KEY MILESTONES IN SMARTPHONE TECHNOLOGY

Smartphone technology evolved as follows:

1. **Mid-1995:**
   The colloquial term "smartphone" is first used. But the original smartphone appeared 3 years prior. This was the Simon Personal Communica-

tor that was created by IBM in 1992. This was the first phone to combine functionality from both a cellphone and a personal digital assistant (PDA). It had a staggering price tag of $899.00.

2. **July 1999:**
   The first wireless handheld computer, the RIM 850 by Blackberry, appears on the marketplace. The device became very popular in the business world with its ability to connect people to their corporate emails, address books, task lists, and calendars.

3. **November 2000:**
   The very first camera phone makes its debut in Japan. This is the Sharp J-SH04, but it never makes an impact in the marketplace.

4. **By late 2003:**
   The Nokia 1100 is released, and it ultimately becomes the best-selling mobile phone of all time, with over 250 million units sold worldwide. As a result, this mobile phone becomes the best-selling consumer electronics device in the world.

5. **January 2007:**
   Apple unveils the iPhone, at the Macworld Expo in San Francisco. The iPhone was officially released in the United States 5 months later in June.

6. **In July 2008:**
   The App Store is officially launched with 552 mobile applications. Most applications were priced either $1 or $10, with only 135 free applications (colloquially called "apps") available.

7. **November 2008:**
   The first-ever Android phone, the G1, makes its debut. It features the "slide-out" keyboard.

8. **April 2011:**
   Android becomes the world's most popular operating system for wireless devices. It captures most of the market share at 36.4%, while Symbian drops to second place with a 27.7% share.

9. **December 2011:**
   Windows Mobile is phased out and Windows Phone is created and launched. After finding challenges in competing with iPhone and Android, Microsoft decides to discontinue the Windows Mobile and develop a completely new operating system.

10. **December 2013:**
    Smartphone orders and shipments surpass 1 billion, covering close to one-seventh of the world's population.

11. **January 2016:**
    Samsung leads the smartphone vendor market for 16 consecutive quarters and continues to be the leading player in smartphone sales worldwide since 2012.

12. **November 2017:**
    The iPhone X is officially launched and is Apple's latest smartphone release. The "X" denotes that the iPhone has been on the market for 10

years and features strong *two-factor authentication* (2FA) with the "Face ID." This makes use of facial recognition to confirm the identity of the owner of the iPhone X.

EVOLUTION OF THE CLOUD

So far in this chapter, we have covered four major stages of technological evolution, which in part, directly or indirectly, have led to the evolution of Cloud computing infrastructure as we know it today. To recap, the following was reviewed:

- **Evolution of the Mainframe:** It was during this time period that the concept of virtualization was born, thus lending itself to the underlying principles of Cloud computing.
- **Evolution of the Personal Computer:** Within this timeframe, we witnessed the miniaturization of the massive and gargantuan mainframe computers being transformed into the first handheld computers, the prime example of which was the TRS-80 computer. This drastic miniaturization also supported the concept of a smaller but much more powerful computing processing power just as we see in Cloud infrastructure today.
- **Evolution of Wireless Networks:** In this time period, we also witnessed the first wireless connections coming to fruition, starting with the 1G networks all the way to the 5G networks that we are using it today with our wireless devices. The concept of being able to connect to a central resource (such as a server, or even an entire IT Infrastructure) at literally "lightning" speeds lay the foundation for the ability to connect to various software and hardware applications from anywhere and at any time in the world, as we use Cloud computing infrastructure today.
- **Evolution of the Smartphone:** Finally, in this time period, we not only saw the wireless connections become much more powerful but also witnessed our cellphones now rapidly becoming our PCs as well, thus playing a very central role in our lives. From these devices, we can now conduct personal and even professional matters (such as performing daily job tasks) from our smartphones. The evolution of this technology also gave birth to the concept and development of the mobile app. This process has led to the massive usage of Cloud computing infrastructure as a medium for storage and accessing of software applications.

As was mentioned previously, the remainder of this chapter is devoted to examining in close detail the components of Cloud computing infrastructure. The topics to be examined include the following:

1. Evolution of Cloud computing infrastructure
2. The basic concepts of and terminology used in Cloud computing
3. The challenges and risks of Cloud computing
4. The functions and characteristics of Cloud computing
5. Cloud computing delivery models

6. Cloud computing deployment models
7. The security threats posed to Cloud computing
8. The important mechanisms of Cloud computing
9. Cloud computing cost metrics and service quality mechanisms

However, before exploring these topics in detail, it is important, as it is for the other technological advancements, to provide a brief overview of how Cloud computing infrastructure actually evolved. It is not a concept that was conceived just a decade ago; rather, its fundamentals go all the way back to the 1940s, as will be reviewed below. This next section provides a detailed timeline of exactly how Cloud computing infrastructure became what it is today—the juggernaut of any IT environment.

EVOLUTION OF CLOUD COMPUTING INFRASTRUCTURE

The major milestones are described as follows:

1. **The 1940s:**
   In 1947, computer scientists at the University of Manchester developed the "Manchester Baby," the world's first stored program computer. It played a pivotal role in the subsequent development of the Cloud.
2. **The 1950s:**
   In 1955 there were only 250 computers in use around the world (mostly mainframes). They were rented out to other users. Thus, the concept of timesharing and allocating the users amounts of processing power gave birth to the idea of sharing resources lies at the heart of Cloud computing today.
3. **The 1960s:**
   The introduction of *data packet switching* at the National Physical Laboratory in the 1960s allowed multiple individuals to connect and use a network at the same time by breaking information down into smaller chunks, also known as *data packets*. This laid the foundations for the Cloud and the sharing of multiple resources among many users.
   Also, in 1961, a computer scientist by the name of John McCarthy made a speech at MIT suggesting that one day computing resources may be shared like any other utility. He was the first person to suggest using computer technology in this way.
4. **The 1970s and 1980s:**
   The *virtual machine* (VM) was born, which allowed users to run multiple operating systems simultaneously in one physical computer. The term *client-server* also came into use, the first technical definition of which was as follows: "Clients accessing data and applications from a central server, over a local area network." This further solidified the concept of "shared resources," which is a key feature and benefit of any Cloud computing environment today.
   The first large-scale packet-switching network, known as the *Advanced Research Project Administration* (or "ARPAnet" for short) is born, and

thus is considered to be the first Internet. For example, in 1973, servers located in Norway and the United Kingdom connected to the ARPAnet for the first time. This gave birth to the first-ever international network, which later became known as the "Internet." As we know it today, Cloud computing infrastructure is the main resource for all kinds and types of entities and individuals to store and quickly access various websites.

Also, the National Science Foundation (NSF) launched an initiative to build a national backbone network that would be based on the Transmission Control Protocol/Internet Protocol (TCIP/IP). This is the primary network connection protocol used in the Cloud today.

5. **The 1990s:**

Within this the Internet and the Cloud evolved to the point that know of them today. For example, following the ARPAnet's adoption of the TCP/IP network protocol in 1983, researchers from all over the world began to assemble the "network of networks," which thus developed into the modern Internet.

Also, computer scientist Tim Berners-Lee invented the World Wide Web (now known more loosely as the "web"). In doing so, Berners-Lee linked hypertext documents to various servers, thus making it accessible from any node on the APRAnet-based network.

In 1996, George Favaloro and Sean O'Sullivan, executives at Compaq Computer, first referred to the term "Cloud computing" in their business plan. This is the first known use of the term.

6. **In 2000:**

A major milestone in the Cloud computing era was the launch of Salesforce.com, which arrived in late 1999. This platform became a pioneer in delivering enterprise-grade applications via the Cloud, which is now known as *software as a service* (SaaS).

The multitenant applications on Salesforce.com were designed to be accessed from the Cloud, and to be used by large numbers of customers at a very low cost. This gave rise to the concept known as *scalability*, which is a prime advantage of the Cloud computing environment.

7. **In 2002:**

Shortly after the launch of Salesforce.com, Amazon launched its Cloud computing platform known as "Amazon Web Services" (AWS). The primary goal was to deliver a suite of Cloud-based computing services to customers who would pay only for what they used.

8. **In 2006:**

Amazon launched its "Elastic Compute Cloud" (EC2), which is a commercial web service allowing small companies and individuals to rent computers and run their specific applications on it. Also, it provided complete control of all computing resources for the first time ever.

9. **In 2008:**

Google launched its "Google App Engine" (GAE). It is designed to be a *platform as a service* (PaaS), enabling software developers to host web applications.

It is important to note that web-based applications hosted on the GAE platform are sandboxed and are also run across multiple servers. This allows for redundancy and the scaling of resources.

10. **In 2010:**
   Microsoft entered the Cloud computing market with the launch of "Azure." The platform was built to support the streamlined software development of both web-based and mobile-based apps over the Internet.
   Azure can also be used for the building, testing, and deploying of software applications through a global network of specialized Microsoft datacenters.

11. **In 2011:**
   IBM launched "Smart Cloud," a line of enterprise-class, Cloud computing technologies for the building of private, public, and for the first time ever, hybrid-based Cloud platforms.

12. **In 2013:**
   The "Google Compute Engine" (GCE) was officially launched as a complement to the Google Cloud platform. The offering stands as the IaaS component of the platform and thus allows users to launch virtual machines on demand.

13. **The Future:**
   The "Internet of Things" (IoT) and machine learning are expected to form the backbone for the next Cloud computing infrastructure. Also, Cloud computing is projected to be a $411 billion market by 2020.

THE BASIC CONCEPTS AND TERMINOLOGY SURROUNDING CLOUD COMPUTING

When one thinks of Cloud computing, especially the business owner, one gets very excited. Why is this so? It is the buzzword that is floating around today and will be for quite some time to come. Many business owners feel that by adopting a Cloud computing infrastructure, they will be ahead of their competitors. While this may be true to a certain extent, the chances are that the competition has already beaten them to the punch.

This is so because, in theory at least, Cloud computing can be configured and started with just a few clicks of the mouse, and at a fraction of the cost of outright owning an entire IT infrastructure. So, before we discuss the components of Cloud computing any further, exactly how is this term defined?

According to the National Institutes of Standards and Technology (NIST), *Cloud computing* can be defined as "a model for enabling ubiquitous, convenient, hands on, on demand network access to a shared pool of configurable computing resources (e.g., networks, servers, storage, applications, and services) that can be rapidly provisioned and released with minimal management effort or service provider interaction. This cloud model is composed of five essential characteristics, three service models, and four deployment models" (Erl 2013, p. 28).

This no doubt seems like a long and complicated definition; we now provide a much more distilled definition of Cloud computing: "Cloud Computing is a specialized form of distributed computing that introduces utilization models for remotely provisioning scalable and measured resources" (Erl 2013, p. 28).

Now, as we take both these definitions, we find that Cloud computing consists of a number of key components, which include the following:

1. The Cloud
2. The IT resource
3. On-premise resources
4. Scalability

See also Figure 1.3.

THE CLOUD

As we progress through these major components, the first one we look at is the Cloud itself. This component can be specifically referred to as a "distinct IT environment that is designed for the purpose of remotely provisioning scalable and measured IT resources" (Erl 2013, p. 28). As we explore this component, the Cloud is like a nebula in which various types and kinds of computing resources can be accessed.

These resources include the entire gamut of computing applications, which includes everything from the database to the individual software packages that service an entire small business, to accessing the File Transfer Protocol Server, to accessing your email server, and to even having the capability to develop and create complex software applications, to accessing content management systems for the corporate intranet, to even creating and launching an entire e-commerce platform.

FIGURE 1.3 Examining the infrastructure of the Cloud.

Two Distinctions

At this point, it is very important that two key distinctions be made. The first very important one is that these computing resources just described are not accessed from a local hard drive on an employee's workstation or laptop; nor, for that matter, are these resources even accessed from a LAN that can reside from inside a corporation. Rather, it is important to keep in mind that that these computing resources can be accessed from literally 1000 miles away, or even across the globe. The remote access is all made possible because of the Internet. With any standard web browser that is available today, any type or kind of Cloud computing resource can be accessed.

The second very important distinction to be made is that all these computing resources reside within an independent third party, which is privately owned, such as that of an Internet service provider (ISP).

The IT Resource

The second major component that we now examine is that of the of the typical IT resources that can be found from within Cloud computing infrastructure. An IT resource, or even an IT asset, can be defined "as a physical or virtual IT-related artifact that can be either software-based, such as a virtual server or a custom software program, or hardware-based such as a physical server or a network device" (Erl 2013, p. 34). According to this definition, an IT resource/IT asset is a tangible item that can be placed into the Cloud, with even some of the software applications that were previously described. However, in the world of Cloud computing, the IT resource/IT asset is typically a server, whether it is a standalone physical server or just a virtual server. As will be explored later in this chapter, a *virtual server* is also a physical server, but is partitioned so that each of the resources that it hosts appears to reside in a separate server, to the end user or small business owner.

So, as you can see, the most important IT resource, based on the preceding definition, is that of the server. After all, the software applications described above need a place to reside in, or in Cloud computing terminology, need a place to be "hosted" at. However, a key distinction must be made here. Although the virtual server can be placed into the Cloud, it also represents all of the resources that are available to the end user.

A key feature, as will be explained later in this chapter, is that Cloud computing relies heavily on shared resources in order to bring the low and predictable monthly costs to the end user and the small business owner.

On-Premise Components

The third major aspect to be examined in Cloud computing infrastructure is the "on-premise" component. Specifically, *on-premise* can be defined as "being on the premises of a controlled IT environment which is not cloud based" (Erl 2013, p. 36). A key part of this definition is the "controlled IT environment." This environment is actually that of the ISP, or, for that matter, any other private entity that has the flexibility to provide at least one or more IT assets and IT resources.

SCALABILITY

An important point needs to be made at this point is that the Cloud-based resources are not just stored in one specific computer, or even in just one particular server. Rather, all those IT assets and IT resources that it comprises are shared across hundreds, or even thousands, of servers at ISPs throughout the world.

As we are now starting to see that the Cloud consists of a controlled environment, which is that of the ISP. The ISP consists of the IT resources and the IT assets that reside on a virtual server, from which these resources and assets can be accessed by the end user or the small business owner.

This is just one example of general Cloud computing infrastructure, and there is not just one of them. There are hundreds and thousands of them worldwide, to bring to the end user and the small business owner the shared computing resources that they need and require.

As will become apparent throughout the rest of this chapter, the Cloud possesses many strong benefits, which are available to the end user and small business owner at an extremely affordable price, when compared to the other IT assets and IT resources available in the traditional models.

But apart from costs, Cloud infrastructure possesses other key benefits such as the following:

1. IT asset scaling
2. Proportional costs
3. Scalability
4. Availability and reliability

IT ASSET SCALING

In terms of the first major benefit, *IT asset scaling* merely refers to the fact that an IT asset or even IT resource can handle increased or decreased end-user demand usage. Two types of scaling are available: horizontal and vertical.

Horizontal Scaling

Horizontal scaling consists in the allocation or provisioning of valuable IT resources and IT assets that are of the exact same nature and type. The allocation of these IT assets and IT resources is known as "scaling out," and releasing or giving away IT resources to newer end users and newer small business owners is known as "scaling in."

For example, let us illustrate this with a well-known application from Microsoft, known as a *Structured Query Language* (SQL) *server.* This database software is widely available through most ISPs (also known as "Cloud providers" in some circles). The allocation of SQL Server to the existing end users of this application is known as "scaling out."

However, release of the SQL server application to new end users or the new small business owners when they first sign up for Cloud-based services is a perfect example of scaling in. This type of scenario is very typical among the ISPs who provide Cloud-based IT services.

Vertical Scaling

With regard to vertical scaling, the valuable IT assets and IT resources are merely replaced with a lower or higher version of the very exact same type or kind of IT asset or IT resource. For instance, replacing an IT resource or an IT asset with a higher version is known as "scaling up," and the opposite, which is the replacement of an IT asset or IT resource of a lower version, is known as "scaling down."

Let us illustrate again with the same SQL server example, but this time, with a known version of SQL Server 2012. The offering to the end user of a lower version of the SQL server (such as SQL Server 2000) is known as "scaling down," and the offering to an end user a later version of SQL Server 2012 is known as "scaling up." This type of scaling is less commonly offered by ISPs as opposed to horizontal scaling.

This is so because vertical scaling requires more downtime. Vertical scaling typically happens only in the Cloud environment when a later version of an IT asset or IT resource becomes available and renders the present IT asset or IT asset totally obsolete and outdated.

With respect to the second major benefit of Cloud computing, namely, reduced investments and proportional costs, it is quite true that many ISPs who offer Cloud computing services to their end users can have a revenue model based on the bulk acquirement and acquisition of the IT resources and IT assets and, in turn, offer these services to their end-user customer base at very low-price point packages.

This is what directly allows for the owners of small to medium-sized businesses to purchase a Fortune 100 enterprise-grade IT infrastructure for virtually pennies on the dollar. This is obviously of great appeal to the small business owner, who can now replace capital operational costs and expenditures (which also means the total investment and ownership in an outright, entire IT infrastructure) with a proportional cost expenditure (which means rental in Cloud-based IT infrastructure).

Because of the benefits provided by the proportional cost expenditures, this permits small to medium-sized enterprises to reinvest the saved money into other much-needed IT assets and IT resources in order to support mission-critical business functions.

However, keep in mind that ISPs are also businesses who have revenue generating models, and in order to afford such mass acquisition of IT assets and IT resources, they need to find inexpensive alternatives also. Thus, the ISP locates both types in datacenters where the two most important cost variables of network bandwidth and real estate are the cheapest possible.

PROPORTIONAL COSTS

In this second category of a major benefit, there are numerous secondary benefits of Cloud computing that are also available to end users and small business owners:

1. Access to on-demand IT resources and IT assets on a pay-as-you-go basis, and the ability to reallocate these resources to other end users who are willing to pay for them when they are no longer needed by existing end users and small business owners.

2. End users and small business owners feeling that they have unlimited use to IT assets and IT resources.
3. The ability to quickly add or subtract/delete any type of kind of IT resource/ IT asset at the most granular level (such as modifying an end user's mailbox through the email interface).
4. With Cloud computing resources, IT assets and IT resources that are not locked into any physical location, allowing the IT assets and resources to be moved around as needed.

Yet, despite these benefits, it can be quite a complex financial process for a Fortune 100 company to decide whether they wish to have their own on-premises IT infrastructure versus provisioning Cloud-based resources, as opposed to the small to medium-sized businesses, where the decision is so obvious and clear-cut.

SCALABILITY

The third benefit, *scalability*, simply refers to the ability for an IT resource or an IT asset to dynamically meet the needs of the end user or small business owner. In most types and kinds of scenarios, this dynamic nature of the IT asset or IT resource can take quite a bit of time to adjust accordingly.

However, in terms of Cloud computing infrastructure, these particular IT assets and IT resources have to adjust to the need of the end user or the small business owner in just a matter of seconds or less, once their Cloud computing infrastructure account has been configured and the desired IT assets and IT resources have been selected and paid for.

This scalability feature of the Cloud, and its dynamic nature to meet the needs of the end user and small business owner, is one of the biggest benefits of Cloud computing infrastructure, and one of its strongest selling points to small or medium-sized businesses. Imagine, if you will, a small or medium-sized business that possesses an in-house IT infrastructure.

The nature and scope of the business has grown, as has its usefulness and scope. Consequently, the cost of upgrading the entire IT infrastructure, or even just various components of it, can be very cost-prohibitive for that particular small or midsize business.

However, if they had adapted their IT assets and IT resources through Cloud-based infrastructure, they could have brought in the new services needed in just a matter of seconds and, of course, at just a fraction of the cost. Also, it is not only a matter of meeting the specific needs of the end user or the small business owner; the IT resources and the IT assets that are founded and based in Cloud computing infrastructure can also dynamically meet the needs of the processing fluctuations (of the IT assets and the IT resources) as required.

For example, an end user who requires more disk space can merely increase it in literally 2 seconds with a few clicks of the mouse. However, with traditional, in-house IT infrastructure, the entire physical hard drive would have to be replaced, thus causing the end user an extra expense.

This dynamic scalability of Cloud computing infrastructure is a direct function of a concept introduced before, known as *proportional costs*.

End users or the small business owners pay for those IT assets or IT resources that they specifically use, no more and no less. As a result, Cloud computing infrastructure has adapted the term "as a service," which will be explained later in this chapter.

AVAILABILITY AND RELIABILITY

One of the last major benefits of the Cloud to be reviewed is increased availability and reliability. Translated into the language of the small business owner, this simply means that all the IT resources and IT assets within a specific infrastructure of Cloud computing is "always going to be on."

One may ask at this point how an ISP can provide this level of availability to end users and small business owners. Well, think about the actual infrastructure that in which the ISP resides.

It is a full-blown datacenter, with dozens of redundant servers, powerlines, and even redundant power supply backups, in order to provide a continual supply of power to the datacenter, so that its IT resource and IT assets will always be available, and online to end users and small business owners on a $24 \times 7 \times 365$ basis. However, despite all these redundancies, and the best efforts that are afforded by the datacenter, downtimes do occasionally happen.

In these particular instances, remedies must be provided to the end user and the small business owner. Another beauty of Cloud computing infrastructure is that even as a particular Cloud segment grows and expands, with the addition of newer IT assets and IT resources and the deletion of older IT assets and IT resources, interruption of Cloud-based services to the end user or small business owner hardly ever happens. It is as if "business as usual is happening."

SERVICE-LEVEL AGREEMENTS

All these uptimes that are guaranteed by the ISP come to the level of the written contract known as the *service-level agreement* (SLA). In this contract, the ISP specifies what levels of uptime it can guarantee to the end users and small business owners.

Very often this uptime is defined as the "five 9s," which means that 99.999% of uptime will be made available to the end user or the small business owner. If this level is not reached, the ISP must provide remediations to its customer base.

Therefore, it is very important to the customer, whether it is an end user or a small business owner, to read this contract carefully before signing it.

THE CHALLENGES AND RISKS OF CLOUD COMPUTING

Along with these perceived benefits of the Cloud, unfortunately, come its disadvantages as well. Remember that the Cloud is still a relatively new concept, and the boundary lines that it possesses are still not clear. For example, a small business owner's Cloud computing infrastructure could be shared into another Cloud, depending on the provisioning of the various IT assets and IT resources.

Also, of course, there is also the trust factor, by placing your entire IT infrastructure into the hands of the Cloud provider (such as Amazon Web Services or Microsoft Azure), which, in this case, could be halfway around the world, to people you have never met before, let alone even heard of. Also, to make matters worse, you are even trusting your credit card information with this third party, whom, once again, you don't even know. You are even sharing your business's confidential and proprietary data and storing them into the Cloud, with other Cloud resources.

In this regard, privacy may not be ensured. Also, there is always the threat of break-ins by hackers who can steal all your mission-critical data. Yet, although large-scale thefts of confidential and proprietary information and data are rare, but it is very important that you, as the end user or the small business owner, understand these leading inherent risks, which can be classified as follows:

1. Security risks and challenges
2. Reduced operational governance
3. Limited portability
4. Compliance and legal issues

SECURITY RISKS AND CHALLENGES

In terms of the first security risk and challenge, which is about the specific security vulnerabilities, the moving of private and confidential business data ultimately becomes the responsibility of the ISP, with whom the end user's enterprise or the small business has been entrusted.

Although the contracts and the SLA agreements have been signed, it still takes quite a leap of faith for small business owners to transfer all their corporate information and data to an as-yet untrusted third party.

This is probably one of the biggest fears that the ISP must allay. Given the wide expanse of Cloud computing infrastructure, access to IT resources and IT assets cannot be granted directly to the end user or the small business owner.

Rather, these specific IT assets and IT resources must be accessed remotely [such as via the File Transfer Protocol (FTP)], which can pose even greater threats and risks, especially to a hacker who is "listening in" on the other end.

This means that all the IT resources and IT assets that reside within Cloud computing infrastructure must be reached externally, via various access points. The bottom line is that there is no foolproof, 100% way to secure those particular access points to Cloud computing infrastructure.

Another major security threat is that of access to confidential consumer data that may be stored in a particular Cloud computing infrastructure, for whatever reason (for example, a retail business owner may be using her/his Cloud infrastructure to back up customer information and data).

The relative security, safety, and reliability of this data and information rely solely on the security controls and policies implemented by the ISP.

Finally, another grave security threat or risk posed to Cloud computing infrastructure is the intersection of Cloud boundaries and the malicious Cloud consumers that it can create. For example, with shared IT resources and shared IT assets, there are much greater risks for the theft and damage of mission-critical business data stored in the Cloud.

The bottom line is that it can be very difficult for an ISP to provide strong security mechanisms when Cloud boundaries intersect one another. This Cloud computing infrastructure threat is also known as "overlapping trust boundaries," which will be discussed in further detail later in this chapter.

REDUCED OPERATIONAL GOVERNANCE

With respect to the second major security threat category, namely, reduced operational governance control, this term simply refers to the fact that end users and small business owners who use the Cloud finally have some control over the IT assets and IT resources that they own or rent.

For example, imagine end users at their place of business or organization. They once had to abide by strict IT security policies. But now, these end users have new-founded freedom to fully control the IT assets and IT assets that their business owns or rents within Cloud computing infrastructure.

Because of this feeling of unfounded power that besets the end user, this can translate into real risks for the ISP into how it should control its Cloud computing infrastructures. Now, most end users may get a short-term rush on this new control that they now possess, but these are the end users whose rush can extend into a hacker's mindset when they try to gain access to other end user's Clouds, and thus to hijack their information and data.

This disadvantage puts the ISP at graver risk, as well as the lines of communication that exist between the Cloud end users and their own individual Cloud computing infrastructures. Two distinct consequences can arise from this:

1. The guarantees as established by the service-level agreement can become null and void, thus causing the ISP significant financial loss and risk.
2. Bandwidth constraints can occur when individual Cloud computing infrastructures are located at much further geographic distances from within the platform of the ISP.

One of the best ways, and probably the only way, to avoid these kinds of risks and threats is for the ISP to keep a close and vigilant eye on all of the IT assets and IT resources that are being employed by all the Cloud users. Any suspicious activity or tampering by would-be hackers in a particular Cloud computing infrastructure must be dealt with promptly and deftly, and quickly by the ISP.

LIMITED PORTABILITY

The third major security risk with a particular Cloud computing infrastructure is the limited portability that is available among all ISPS. Essentially, what this means is that with all the ISPs around, there is no common set of standards and best practices among them, overall.

This means that each ISP can carry its own set of technologies at various version levels. While there is nothing inherently wrong with this approach, it can cause major security concerns for the end user and the small business owner, who may wish to switch to a different ISP.

For example, for end users who wish to transmit and switch over their customer database from one platform to another Cloud computing platform at the new ISP, there is no guarantee that this confidential and proprietary information and data will transfer over to the new Cloud computing platform seamlessly and easily. In fact, some of this data could even be hijacked by a third party, such as a hacker.

This problem is due largely to the fact that many Cloud computing architectures and platforms are, to a certain degree, proprietary from one ISP to another. Let us look back at our previous example once again.

Suppose that a small business owner has a customer database that is custom-made and is dependent on other various technology platforms. The new ISP may flaunt serious claims that this customer database will transfer smoothly over to their own proprietary Cloud architecture. However, in fact, what if this customer database does not transfer cleanly from the existing Cloud computing infrastructure to the new Cloud computing infrastructure?

True, the small business owner could be criticized for not doing due diligence to look at the technological compatibilities for this particular kind of database, but the real accountability will rest with the new ISP.

What lacks between these ISPs is a set of best practices and standards that allow for the ease of transfer of information and data for the end user from one Cloud computing infrastructure to another ISP.

But at least for now, the ISPs are beginning to realize this wide gap, and in lieu of it, are now offering Cloud computing technologies that are standard among the industry. Having this level of standardization is especially important for biometric templates, especially when they are stored in a Cloud computing environment.

With regard to the biometric templates, any loss of any magnitude of any type or kind from the transfer of one Cloud computing infrastructure to another one will have far-reaching and greater legal ramifications in both the courts of law and judicial processes.

COMPLIANCE AND LEGAL ISSUES

The fourth major security vulnerability posed to a particular Cloud computing infrastructure is the multiregional compliance and legal issues that can arise. What does this exactly mean? It refers to an aspect that was discussed in an earlier part of this chapter. Specifically, Cloud computing infrastructure, and any matter related to it, is distributed in different geographic regions around the world.

For example, although a small business or organization might be based in the United States, the owner of that particular business or organization can purchase a Cloud computing infrastructure from a geographic location halfway around the world, such as Germany or Russia.

The advantages of this, of course, are the very low prices that can be offered to the small business owner, as has been discussed earlier in this chapter. But in reality, to the small business owner, it makes no difference where the actual physical servers are located from within the global Cloud computing infrastructure.

Although this is seldom the case, the information and data housed in a particular Cloud computing infrastructure in a different country could very well be subject and prone to the laws of the particular country where that Cloud computing infrastructure actually resides. To this effect, these foreign governments could very well improve their own data privacy and storage policies.

Another strong security concern is the accessibility and disclosure of the information and data that reside in Cloud computing infrastructure. For example, if a small business owner in Europe owns a Cloud computing infrastructure here in the United States, her/his information and data could be prone to inspection by the United States government, due to the guises of the US Patriot Act.

THE FUNCTIONS AND CHARACTERISTICS OF CLOUD COMPUTING

So far in this chapter, we have reviewed the definition of *Cloud computing* and its major components, as well as the benefits and the major risks in terms of security that are posed to a Cloud computing infrastructure. Now, in this part of the chapter, we turn our attention to the characteristics that distinguish particular Cloud computing infrastructures from the actual IT infrastructures that exist today.

As we have alluded to throughout this chapter, the Cloud, to many people, is a very nebulous concept. *Nebulous* in this context means very murky, with no clear boundaries or any clear definitions. True, in many aspects, this is what Cloud computing infrastructure is all about. It comes from somewhere, in some part of the United States, or, for that matter, in any part of the world, even in the most remote regions imaginable.

All one needs is a computer, an Internet connection, and literally from thousands and thousands of miles away, access to an ISP. With all this, all that the end user or the small business owner, at the click of a mouse, has to do is merely select the IT assets and the IT resources that they need or desire.

In a way, this can be somewhat scary because, after all, we—as end users or small business owners—are entrusting storage of our valuable and confidential data to ISP people whom we have never even met or even heard of. However, it takes a giant leap of faith to have this kind of level and caliber of trust. But despite this degree of uncertainty, Cloud computing infrastructure does possess various quantifiable, key characteristics, which help to define and distinguish it from other IT infrastructure regimes.

These characteristics include

1. On-demand usage
2. Ubiquitous access
3. Resource pooling
4. Elasticity
5. Measured usage
6. Resilience

ON-DEMAND USAGE

The first Cloud computing characteristic, *on-demand usage*, refers to the fact that if an end user or small business owner provisions certain Cloud computing services onto her/his account, then this particular IT resource or IT asset will be made immediately available for use after it has provisioned.

With the characteristic of on-demand usage, the end user can thus request future IT assets and IT resources on literally an automatic basis, without any human intervention by the ISP whatsoever.

Also, with this characteristic of on-demand usage for Cloud computing infrastructure, end users or small business owners are literally free to turn on or off the IT resources and IT assets when they want or need them and to pay only for what they use.

UBIQUITOUS ACCESS

The second characteristic of Cloud computing infrastructure is known as *ubiquitous access*. This simply means that the IT resources and the IT assets are widely accessible from anywhere on Earth and can be reached via any mobile device via any network protocol. This can best be illustrated by a small business owner accessing her/his Cloud-based IT resources and IT assets from the other side of the world, with a mobile device, via the *Wireless Network Protocol* (WAP).

RESOURCE POOLING

The third major characteristic of an individual Cloud computing infrastructure is a feature known as *multitenancy and resource pooling*. The basic definition of *multitenancy* is "a characteristic of a software program that enables an instance of the program to serve different consumers (tenants) whereby each is isolated from the other" (Erl 2013, p. 59). Take, for example, an application that we have alluded to earlier in this chapter, namely, the Microsoft SQL server.

There may be just one instance of this server running on the physical server, but this particular instance allows the ISP to serve different and multiple end users and small business owners. This example demonstrates multitenancy and the required the principles of virtualization to make it all happen.

Although one instance of the SQL server is on the physical server and is shared with others, end users or small business owners might feel that this is their very own software through their Cloud computing infrastructure control panel.

In fact, it is this multitenancy model that allows for the Cloud-based IT resources and IT assets to be dynamically assigned repeatedly, based on the demands and the needs of the end user and the small business owner. The multitenancy model, as a result, has given rise to another concept called *resource pooling*.

Resource pooling allows for Cloud providers "to pool large scale IT resources to serve multiple cloud consumers. Different physical and virtual IT resources are dynamically assigned and reassigned according to cloud consumer demand, typically followed by execution through statistical multiplexing" (Erl 2013, p. 59).

These multitenancy and resource pooling concepts enables end users and small business owners to use the same IT assets and IT resources, while each end user and small business owner remains unaware that the same IT resources and IT assets are being used by others as well.

ELASTICITY

The third major characteristic of a Cloud computing infrastructure is elasticity. When one thinks of elasticity, very often, the image of a rubber band is conjured up. This is perfectly analogous to what a Cloud computing infrastructure should be like. It should literally be able to flow smoothly and to scale to the needs and wants of the end user or the small business owner.

For example, if an ISP expects to keep its customer base and attract newer technologies into its Cloud computing infrastructure, it must be sufficiently flexible to keep up with the changing market conditions and demands that are placed on it. An ISP that is not flexible and is rigid with respect to its technology will be sure to lose out in terms of keeping its competitive advantage.

It should be noted that ISPs with vast resources for a Cloud computing infrastructure offer the greatest flexibility and elasticity. The elasticity of a Cloud computing infrastructure can also be best measured by how quickly end users or small business owners can turn off or on their new Cloud-based services.

MEASURED USAGE

The fifth major characteristic of a Cloud computing infrastructure is *measured usage*. As this term implies, this feature simply accounts for how much usage end users or small business owners are taking from the IT assets and IT resources that they have selected to use.

According to that particular usage, the end user or small business owner is appropriately charged for the particular Cloud computing infrastructure resources utilized.

Normally, this is a flat fee calculated on a monthly basis, but if usage of the IT resources and IT assets goes beyond the expected levels, the charges will, of course, be much higher. But on other the hand, if the usage of the IT assets and the IT resources falls below the expected level, the end user or small business owner still must pay the flat monthly fee.

In this respect, a Cloud computing infrastructure possesses the "use it or lose it" feature, unless the specific services have been canceled. But the characteristic of measured usage does not necessarily mean how much to charge; rather, it also refers to the overall usage of an IT asset or an IT resource being utilized, and those not being used. In that way, future demand can be predicted, and the Cloud computing resources can be provisioned accordingly.

RESILIENCE

The sixth and final characteristic of a Cloud computing infrastructure is *resilience*. This simply means that "IT resources can be pre-configured so that if one becomes deficient, processing is automatically handed over to another redundant implementation" (Erl 2013, p. 61). In the scheme of Cloud computing infrastructure, this also means that there are redundant IT resources and IT assets available, so, in case one set fails, the end user and the small business owner will suffer 0% downtime.

In other words, smooth and seamless operations are always present in a Cloud computing infrastructure.

CLOUD COMPUTING DELIVERY MODELS

Now that we have reviewed some of the major characteristics of Cloud computing infrastructure, it is appropriate to understand how such a Cloud computing infrastructure can be brought into the hands of the end user, or the small business owner.

Although Cloud structure does involve existence in a nebulous state, the delivery method does not. There are many ways in which the Cloud can be brought to the end user or the small business owner, and there are three common types of platform:

1. Infrastructure as a service (IaaS)
2. Platform as a service (PaaS)
3. Software as a service (SaaS)

Each of these platforms has its own unique role in delivering Cloud computing infrastructure, and each will be discussed in length in this section. The first Cloud computing infrastructure deployment model, *infrastructure as a service* (IaaS), represents overall Cloud computing environment infrastructure.

In other words, IT resources and IT assets "can be accessed and managed via cloud-based interfaces and tools" (Erl 2013, p. 64).

INFRASTRUCTURE AS A SERVICE (IAAS)

As the term implies, IaaS provides the framework or the foundation from which all the IT assets and IT resources can be leveraged toward the small business owner and the end user. This infrastructure, in particular, includes the hardware, network connectivity, and all the software applications (including, e.g., all the VoIP applications, email applications, database applications, software development applications), as well as the other "raw" tools included in IaaS infrastructure.

It should be noted that most IaaS IT assets and IT resources are "virtualized" and bundled in such a package that they can be leveraged through the Cloud to the end user or the small business owner. Thus, these virtualized IT assets and IT resources can have the freedom of scalability, customization, and demand availability, which are all, of course, very crucial components of any Cloud computing infrastructure.

By possessing an IaaS Infrastructure, end users or small business owners can have total control and responsibility over their particular Cloud computing infrastructure. For example, once end users or small business owners sign up for a Cloud computing infrastructure account, they are often given access to a control panel from which they can establish the settings and the permissions, and even install and uninstall particular Cloud computing resources.

Every ISP agency gives this tool to all their customers. After all, this is the only direct way for end users or small business owners to access all their subscribed-to IT assets and IT resources. It should be noted that with the IaaS platform, end users or small business owners assume full administrative control over their Cloud-based IT assets and IT resources.

For example, when an end user or a small business owner first opens a Cloud computing infrastructure account, the IT assets and the IT resources that will be covered in the subscription are what is known as "fresh virtual instances." Let us demonstrate this with an example. Suppose that an ISP has literally hundreds of physical servers. These servers contain all the IT software–based IT resources and IT assets.

Once the end user or small business owner provisions her/his own account, the hard drive from which the software-based IT resources and IT assets will be distributed will be placed into its own partition on the physical server. Thus, this will give the end user or small business owner the look, the feel, and total control over his/her own, unique Cloud computing server.

Conversely, an end user or small business owner who needs a gargantuan account of IT assets and IT resources can lease out an entire Cloud-based server; the server in this scenario is known as a *virtual server* in the IaaS platform.

PLATFORM AS A SERVICE (PaaS)

The second deployment model for Cloud computing infrastructure is known as *platform as a service* (PaaS). Specifically, this term can be defined as "a predefined 'ready-to-use' environment typically comprised of already deployed and configured IT resources" (Erl 2013, p. 65). The primary difference between the PaaS and IaaS platforms is that the latter consists of the raw Cloud computing platform.

In other words, as was discussed previously, the IaaS contains the basic materials needed for the foundation of a Cloud computing infrastructure. Imagine, if you will, the IaaS platform that serves as the foundation for Cloud computing infrastructure. The PaaS platform fills up this foundation with the much-needed IT resources and IT assets in order to fulfill the needs of the end user or the small business owner.

As can be described, the PaaS consists of a set of prepackaged IT products and IT tools to help support the business needs of the end user or the small business owner. There are many reasons why a consumer should choose the PaaS, but the following are the most typical ones:

1. Clients have the sense of scalability.
2. Clients can use the literally ready-to use-environment, and specifically modify it to their own needs and desires.
3. End users or small business owners who feel sufficiently confident can even offer their own services, using PaaS, to other Cloud consumers.

The PaaS permanently relieves the end user or small business owner of the need to fill up the foundation of Cloud computing infrastructure and the overall responsibility for administering the IaaS. Rather, the ISP must provide this option to its consumer base. So, as you can see, it is the PaaS that contains all the needed IT resources and IT assets that the end user or small business owner can choose from.

So, to summarize thus far, the IaaS is a service that provides the foundation for a Cloud computing infrastructure, and the PaaS makes the IT assets and IT resources available to the end user or the small business owner either as a deployed Cloud package or a single service. This latter platform is known as *software as a service*, which is discussed next.

SOFTWARE AS A SERVICE (SAAS)

The next Cloud computing infrastructure to be discussed here is *software as a service* (SaaS), as alluded to before. As we discussed earlier in this section, the IaaS platform provides the foundation for Cloud computing infrastructure, the PaaS platform fills up this foundation, with all the IT assets and IT resources that would fulfill the needs of all types and kinds of end users and small business owners.

Now, these end users and small business owners will not need to use all the IT resources and IT assets that are available in the PaaS; this is where the SaaS platform comes into play.

Specifically, the SaaS model in Cloud computing infrastructure can be defined as "a software program positioned as a shared cloud service and made available as a 'product' or general utility which represents the typical profile of a SaaS offering" (Erl 2013, p. 66).

So, as you can see from the definition, the SaaS component of Cloud computing infrastructure can be viewed much as a "marketplace" in which end users or small business owners can literally cherry-pick the IT assets and the IT resources they need or desire.

At the SaaS level, small business owners and end users can select all the software packages or bundles that they require in order to keep their businesses running smoothly, and to maintain a competitive advantage. For example, one such SaaS offering that popular feature is the hosted e-commerce store. With this, a small business owner can attract many customers. Yet, despite all these advantages of SaaS, it does have serious limitations.

End users and small business owners have very little control over the IT resources and IT assets that they have selected from the SaaS platform. This control is administrative only, after the IT assets and the IT resources have been selected and paid for. Very little can be done in the way of administration of those IT assets and IT resources that reside in the SaaS.

SUMMARY

In summary, we have looked at three major Cloud delivery models:

1. **Infrastructure as a Service (IaaS):** This platform lays the foundation, or the nuts and bolts, of Cloud computing infrastructure.
2. **Platform as a Service (PaaS):** This model provides all the IT resources and IT assets that an ISP can provide to its consumers. All these resources

and assets include everything from the virtual server to the hard-drive partitions that provide end users and small business owners with the look and feel of their own Cloud-based server, as well as the necessary software applications, which range from content management systems to e-commerce platforms.

3. **Software as a Service (SaaS):** As reviewed, this model provides the software applications (also known as the *IT assets* or *IT resources*) via an à la carte method to the end user or the small business owner. Under this regime, the customer can pick and choose the software applications that are needed or desired, and within seconds, it can be provisioned at the click of the mouse after it has been paid for.

CLOUD COMPUTING DEPLOYMENT MODELS

Now that we have reviewed how a particular Cloud computing infrastructure can fit into a certain platform, we will see how Cloud computing infrastructure can be handed over to the small business owner or the end user.

In other words, Cloud computing infrastructure in the present context can be defined via three different infrastructure models, but now, it has to reach the power of end users and small business owners via the network to their desktop computers, laptops, notebooks, tablets, or even smartphones. Cloud computing infrastructure is brought to the end user or small business owner via four different kinds of deployment models:

1. The public Cloud
2. The community Cloud
3. The private Cloud

THE PUBLIC CLOUD

We will now discuss each of these Cloud computing infrastructure deployment models in much greater detail. In terms of Cloud computing infrastructure, the public Cloud can be specifically defined as "a publicly accessible cloud environment owned by a third-party cloud provider" (Erl 2013, p. 73).

As the term implies, this type of Cloud computing infrastructure is available via any type or kind of ISP. The IT assets and resources as described throughout this chapter can be provisioned among all three delivery models just described (IaaS, PaaS, SaaS), and are also available to end users and small business owners at almost very low cost or price, and the IT assets and resources are very often "commercialized" via other methods such as advertisements on the Internet, or in print, such as in magazines and newspapers.

With the public Cloud deployment model, the ISP has the primary responsibility for this kind of deployment, the acquisition and procurement of the IT assets and resources that belong in the PaaS platform, and its ongoing maintenance (such as licensing fees and any other necessary types or kinds of software and hardware upgrades).

It should be noted that almost all (~98% of) Cloud computing infrastructure provisions are offered to small business owners and end users via this type of deployment model, so that all types and kinds of IT resources and assets can be made available plentifully and at low cost to all entities involved.

THE COMMUNITY CLOUD

The second type of deployment, the community Cloud, is also closely related to that of the public Cloud. Access to this particular type of Cloud computing infrastructure is strictly limited to a specific grouping of end users and small business owners.

It should be noted that at this point the community Cloud could be jointly owned by the members of the Cloud community, or even an ISP could own this community Cloud.

Members of the community Cloud typically share the responsibility for defining the rights and responsibilities of the community Cloud. However, it should be noted also that membership in the Cloud community is not a status, and that membership within it does guarantee access to the IT resources and the IT assets that reside in Cloud computing infrastructure.

THE PRIVATE CLOUD

The third type of Cloud computing deployment model is the private Cloud. Private Cloud computing infrastructure is literally owned by a single entity. This type of Cloud computing infrastructure deployment model allows for a small business owner or any other kind of organization total control over the IT assets and IT resources from within the different locations and departments at the place of business or organization.

Typically, under a private Cloud computing infrastructure deployment model, its administration can take place internally, thus giving the private Cloud owner even more sense of ownership and control. From within the private Cloud computing infrastructure deployment model, it is typically either the place of business or organization that is both the consumer and the Cloud owner.

To help the place of business define and differentiate these roles between consumer and Cloud owner, the following guidelines have been established:

1. A separate department from within the place of business or organization assumes the Cloud provisioning duties to be performed. These groups of people become the private Cloud owners.
2. All the departments at the place of business requiring access to the IT resources and IT assets from within private Cloud computing infrastructure become Cloud consumers.

THE HYBRID CLOUD

The Cloud computing infrastructure deployment model that we examine next is the known as the *hybrid Cloud*. As this term implies, this model consists of a combination of the various Cloud deployment models just discussed, namely, the public, community, and private types.

The hybrid Cloud does not have to consist of all three of these Cloud types, but it must contain at least a combination of two of them, and from that, any other Cloud deployment model can work just as well, with the different deployments of IT assets and IT resources.

For example, a small business owner can choose to protect her/his confidential and private data (financial information, customer data, etc.) from within private Cloud infrastructure. Now, if this small business grows in size over time to a multi-national corporation, the business owners can then develop the private Cloud computing infrastructure into a hybrid one and put it into a community Cloud and create more if necessary.

So, as you can see, trying to implement a hybrid Cloud deployment model can become very complex and much more of a challenge to administer and maintain because of the different Cloud environments that are presently available. For this reason, an alternative exists to the hybrid Cloud; this is called the *virtual private Cloud*.

Under this Cloud regime, end users or small business owners are given a self-contained Cloud environment that is dedicated solely to their use, and also are given full administrative rights to do what they wish to do once they're in their own, particular virtual private Cloud environment.

SECURITY THREATS POSED TO CLOUD COMPUTING

Now that we have covered in some detail and depth the characteristics and properties of Cloud computing delivery and deployment models, we will focus on the security weaknesses (see Figure 1.4) that are posed to the Cloud. Specific examples are presented in greater detail in Chapter 3 of this book.

More specifically, these can be categorized as "threat agents." But before we dig deeper into what a threat agent specifically is for a Cloud computing infrastructure, we must first review some very basic terms and concepts as they relate to Cloud computing threat agents, as discussed below.

TERMS AND CONCEPTS RELATED TO CLOUD SECURITY

The following concepts and properties are considered in this section:

1. Confidentiality
2. Integrity
3. Authenticity
4. Availability
5. Vulnerability
6. Security risk
7. Security controls
8. Security mechanisms
9. Security policies

FIGURE 1.4   Addressing the challenges of Cloud security.

These concepts and definitions form the basis for understanding the specific significance and function of threat agents within a Cloud computing infrastructure. The definitions and concepts presented and discussed above will be reviewed and examined in more detail in Chapter 3, but at this point, it is also equally important to review the risks that threat agents pose to an overall Cloud computing infrastructure. There are four basic types of threat agent:

1. Anonymous attackers
2. Malicious service agents
3. Trusted service attackers
4. Malicious insiders

Apart from these four Cloud computing threat agents, there are also more specific security threats to a Cloud computing infrastructure, as follows:

1. Traffic eavesdropping
2. Malicious intermediary
3. Denial of service
4. Insufficient authorization
5. Virtualization attack
6. Overlapping threat boundaries

Confidentiality

In simple terms, the IT assets and IT resources are made available only to autho-rized users. In this case, it means that paying subscribers such as the end users and small business owners have access only to those IT assets and IT resources that they have paid for, especially when those resources and assets are in transit across the network medium, and that after access remains very strict when it comes to remote logins.

Integrity

Integrity in this context means that the IT assets and IT resources that reside at the ISP are not altered or changed in any way or form. But more importantly, it is the end user's and the small business owner's data and information that is being processed at the virtual servers located at the ISP that need strong assur-ance that this confidential and private information is not altered in any way, or in any malicious form. In other words, "integrity can extend to how data is stored, processed, and retrieved by cloud services and cloud-based IT resources" (Erl 2013, p. 119).

Authenticity

Authenticity in this context means that all IT resources and assets are legitimate, and that all the information and data processed at the virtual server at the ISP and all the output that comes from it is genuine, and that all this has been provided to the end user or small business owner from a legitimate Cloud computing infrastructure provider.

Availability

In the context here, *availability* means that all the IT assets and IT resources will always be accessible and be rendered usable whenever and wherever the end user or small business owner needs to access them at a second's notice. This uptime is very often spelled out in the service-level agreement that the end user or small business owner must subscribe to.

With regard to threats, it is a threat agent of sorts that can fatally challenge the defenses afforded to Cloud computing infrastructure. It should be noted that the threat just defined, if carried out with a malicious intent, is known as a "cyber attack."

Vulnerability

In terms of the next important security foundation, *vulnerability* is a weakness in Cloud computing infrastructure that can be easily overcome by a cyber attack, as described previously. A vulnerability in Cloud computing infrastructure can be caused by a whole host of reasons, which can include both software and hardware miscon-figurations, very weak security policies, administrative or user errors, hardware and software deficiencies, and an overall poor security architecture for Cloud computing infrastructure.

Security Risk

In terms of the discussion here, *security risk* to Cloud computing infrastructure represents the statistical probability of a loss occurring to that infrastructure. Cloud computing risk is typically measured according to the specific threat level, or in general when compared to the total number of possible or known threat agents. Two known metrics are used to determine the statistical probability of risk:

1. The statistical probability of a threat occurring to exploit the IT assets and resources in Cloud computing infrastructure.
2. The chances of the expectations of a magnitude of a loss occurring from the IT resource or the IT asset within the Cloud computing infrastructure.

Security Controls

With regard to *security controls*, certain countermeasures are employed to protect Cloud computing infrastructure and the IT assets and resources that reside within it. Details on how to implement and use such security controls from within a Cloud computing infrastructure are often specified in the security policy.

Security Mechanisms

In terms of *security mechanisms*, certain countermeasures and protective mechanisms are used to provide the general framework that protects the IT assets and resources that reside in Cloud computing infrastructure.

Security Policies

Finally, the *security policies* associated with Cloud computing infrastructure are the security rules and regulations that govern its safety. It is the Cloud computing security policies that determine which types and kinds of rules and regulations are needed to provide maximum security to Cloud computing infrastructure.

THE THREAT AGENTS AND ENTITIES

Having looked at some of the very important terms and concepts that underpin a Cloud computing infrastructure, as alluded to before, we now consider the points of vulnerability. These are those specific entities or agents who can carry out malicious activity against a Cloud computing infrastructure and bring great harm to the end user or the small business owner.

The first type of threat agent or entity are generally known as "threat agents or entities." As the term implies, these agents or entities can carry out a direct attack against Cloud computing infrastructure. What is even more dangerous about this type of attacker is that the agent or entity can originate either internally within the place of business or organization, or externally, outside it.

This part of the section outlines the major threat agents that are posed to any type of Cloud computing infrastructure.

The Anonymous Attacker

The first formal type of threat agent or entity is known as the *anonymous attacker*, which is a malicious third party without any specific Cloud resource-based permissions. This type of attacker exists as a software program and can launch specific attacks on virtual servers via the public network. Anonymous attackers have limited information or knowledge about the security defenses of the ISP, so the easiest way that they can get into a Cloud computing infrastructure is by hacking into and stealing user accounts.

The Malicious Service Agent

The second formal type of threat agent is known as the *malicious service agent*. This type of entity typically resides within a particular Cloud computing infrastructure and is capable of intercepting and forwarding network traffic. Again, this type of threat agent usually exists as a software program.

The Trusted Service Attacker

The third formal type of threat agent is specifically known as the *trusted attacker*. As the term implies, the trusted attacker is already a consumer of a particular Cloud computing infrastructure and, therefore, has advanced knowledge (to some degree) of its inner workings.

Trusted service attackers usually launch attacks from within a Cloud computing infrastructure, very often using their own login information from within that infrastructure, as well as their own access credentials.

The main threat of trusted attackers is that, given their knowledge of a particular Cloud computing infrastructure, they can attack just about every type of virtual server from within the Cloud computing environment.

The Malicious Insider

The final formal type of threat agent is known as the *malicious insider*. Typically, malicious insiders are contracted employees or former employees for whom login and access information into the particular Cloud computing infrastructure have not yet been deleted. Given this short window or timeframe until their access information is totally deleted, malicious insiders can still log into their former Cloud computing infrastructures and cause great harm and damage.

THE MAJOR THREATS

This part of the section outlines the major security threats and cyber attacks that are posed to any Cloud computing environment. The text that follows is intended only as a brief introduction to the terms and concepts; as mentioned earlier, they will be examined in much further detail in Chapter 3 of this book.

Traffic Eavesdropping

The first type of threat, known as *traffic eavesdropping*, occurs when the end user's or small business owner's information and data, which is still being transferred to the particular Cloud computing infrastructure, is covertly intercepted by a third party (such as a malicious hacker) for the illegal purposes of misusing and abusing that particular information and data.

The purpose of this kind of attack is to breach the relationship between the end user or small business owner and the ISP. The traffic eavesdropping security threat very often goes unnoticed for very long periods of time.

The Malicious Intermediary

The second type of threat to a Cloud computing infrastructure is known as a *malicious intermediary*. In this type of attack scenario, the end user's or the small business owner's information and data is intercepted by a malicious third party, and is intentionally altered, thereby compromising the integrity of that particular information and data, resulting in total spoofing of the consumer.

Denial of Service

The third type of threat to a Cloud computing infrastructure is *denial of service*. The primary objective of this sort of attack is to constantly overload and bombard both the physical and virtual servers up to the point where they can no longer operate and are forced to literally shut down, thus depriving the end user or small business owner of her/his IT assets and IT resources.

Here is how a denial-of-service attack could conceivably work:

1. The physical servers and the virtual servers are totally bombarded with malformed data packets.
2. Subsequently, the network traffic is greatly reduced and responsiveness between the ISP and the end user or small business owner is totally choked off, as is connectivity to her/his IT assets and IT resources.
3. Next, the memories of both the physical and the virtual servers are totally bogged down by processing the malformed data packets to the point where they are forced to shut down, thus cutting off all forms of access.

Insufficient Authorization

The fourth type of attack to a Cloud computing infrastructure is *insufficient authorization*. In this scenario, an attacker is granted access by a simple mistake made by the ISP, thereby giving the attacker complete access to all the physical and virtual servers, and IT assets and IT resources. Another type of attack of this kind is known as *weak authentication*. This occurs when there is very low entropy, or when weak passwords are being used by end users and small business owners to access their specific IT assets and IT resources.

Virtualization Attack

The fifth type of attack to a Cloud computing infrastructure is *virtualization attack*. Because of the nature of Cloud computing Infrastructure, the end user or small business owner has, to a certain degree, full administrative privileges. Because of this inherent risk, end users and small business owners can become a Cloud computing infrastructure threat in of themselves.

More specifically, the virtualization attack takes pure, 100% advantage of the weaknesses of the confidentiality, integrity, and availability platforms of the virtual servers that reside within the Cloud computing infrastructure.

Overlapping Threat Boundaries

The sixth formal type of attack to a Cloud computing infrastructure is a phenomenon known as *overlapping trust boundaries*. One must remember that with a Cloud computing infrastructure, all the IT assets and resources are shared among one another, even though the end user or small business owner feels that it is her/his very own.

So, given this shared resource nature, a small business owner or end user who has an extensive IT background and a very strong malicious intent can easily take advantage of the vulnerability of shared resources, launch an attack, and totally corrupt the information and data, and even bring down the virtual servers of other end users and small business owners.

In other words, the goal here is to literally target the overlapping trust boundaries between the various Cloud computing infrastructures that exist at the ISP.

THE IMPORTANT MECHANISMS OF CLOUD COMPUTING

The Cloud itself has inner workings of its own that enable it to function the way it does. These components of Cloud computing infrastructure can be referred to as *specialized Cloud mechanisms*. In this part of the chapter, we review seven major mechanisms (there are, of course, many others, but these are the most important) ones:

1. The load balancer
2. The pay-per-use monitor
3. The audit monitor
4. The failover system
5. Hypervisor
6. Resource clustering
7. The server cluster

The Load Balancer

With the *load balancer* mechanisms of Cloud computing infrastructure, workload strain is placed on two or more IT assets or resources, rather than just one, to help increase the performance and capacity. Load balancers can perform the following workload distributions:

1. **Asymmetric Distribution:** The larger workloads are given to those IT assets and IT resources that have more sophisticated processing power capabilities.

2. **Workload Prioritization:** The Cloud computing infrastructure workloads are scheduled and distributed according to the priority level.
3. **Content-Aware Distribution:** The requests set forth by the end user or small business owner are sent over to the various IT asset and IT resources in the particular Cloud computing infrastructure.

It should be noted that the load balancer is preconfigured with performance rules for the optimization of the client-based IT assets and IT resources, and to avoid overload in the particular Cloud computing infrastructure. These rules can exist as follows:

1. A multilayered switch
2. A dedicated hardware appliance
3. Dedicated software
4. A service agent

It should be noted that the load balancer is usually located in the end user or small business owner's IT resources and IT assets that are generating the workload and performing that actual workload.

The Pay-per-Use Monitor

The second mechanism, the *pay-per-use monitor*, "is a mechanism which measures cloud-based IT resource usage in accordance with predefined pricing parameters and generates usage logs for free calculations and billing purposes" (Erl 2013, p. 184). This mechanism can monitor variables such as (1) the data volume and (2) the bandwidth consumption.

It should be noted that the pay-per-use mechanism is monitored by the billing department by the ISP, in order to transmit the proper fees to the end user or the small business owner.

The Audit Monitor

The third type of mechanism, the *audit monitor*, collects and analyzes various types and kinds of data and network traffic and activity within Cloud computing infrastructure, which are dictated primarily by the regulations set forth in the SLA agreement.

The Failover System

The fourth kind of Cloud computing infrastructure mechanism is the Cloud-based *failover system*. This type of mechanism is used to increase the availability of the IT resources and IT assets that are made available to the end user and the small business owner.

The basic premise is to provide large amounts of redundancy in case of a failover, so that all of the IT assets and IT resources will always be available on a $24 \times 7 \times 365$ basis.

The failover system is designed simply to roll over to another IT asset or IT resource in case one fails. In other words, the failover system provides redundancy so that all Cloud-based assets and resources will always be available to the end user or small business owner.

It should be noted that failover systems are used primarily in mission-critical programs and applications. A redundant Cloud computing infrastructure mechanism can span thousands of miles across many countries, and in many divisions of the ISP in order to provide the $24 \times 7 \times 365$ redundancy for the IT assets and IT resources.

The failover or redundancy systems for IT assets and IT resources are provided in two basic types and configurations: active–active and active–passive.

With an *active–active* failover or redundant system, many instances of the same IT asset and IT resources act together synchronously (in sync). Then one type of failover occurs with one or more of the IT assets or resources fail, then those failed IT assets and resources are removed by a mechanism known as a *load balancer scheduler*.

After the failed IT resources and IT assets are removed, the remaining IT assets and resources still continue in the operational mode.

With the *active–passive* failover or redundant system, only a portion of the IT assets and IT resources remain active. So, in this type of configuration, the inactive IT assets become available or active when any of the other IT resources and IT assets fail, and the processing workload is redirected to those IT assets and IT resources that become active and functionable.

It should be noted that in both types of failover or redundant systems, switching over to a new IT asset or IT resource is not done until at least a new IT asset or IT resource thoroughly dies out. However, certain Cloud computing Infrastructure failover or redundant systems can detect failover conditions before total failure occurs, and can literally shut down that IT asset or IT resource before it fails.

The Hypervisor

The fifth very important type of Cloud computing infrastructure mechanism is the *hypervisor*. This is a very important tool in Cloud computing, as it is utilized to create or generate virtual servers as offset instances of the physical server system.

The Server Cluster

With the *server cluster* scheme, the physical and virtual servers are all clustered together in one large-scale effort to boost IT resource and IT asset performance and availability. In terms of database clustering in Cloud computing infrastructure, this is designed and created to help improve the data availability that is owned by the end user or the small business owner.

The database cluster consists of a synchronization feature that helps ensure the consistency of the data and information that can be stored at various different storage devices that are contained in the database cluster.

With a large dataset cluster, the data partitioning and distribution are set forth so that the end user's and small business owner's datasets can be efficiently partitioned without compromising the structure or integrity of the datasets.

There are two basic types of resource cluster: the load-balanced cluster and the high-availability (HA) cluster. In the event of a multiple failure at the ISP, the load-balanced cluster possesses redundant implementations of all the clustered IT assets and resources. With the HA system, a failure system mechanism is quite often used, and this monitors failure conditions and will automatically redirect any Cloud computing infrastructure workload from the failed IT assets and failed IT resources.

CLOUD COMPUTING COST METRICS AND SERVICE QUALITY MECHANISMS

Now that we have looked into what makes a Cloud computing infrastructure work from the inside as well as the outside, we will study another very important aspect of Cloud computing Infrastructure: the metrics that are associated with them (see Figure 1.5).

Why are metrics so important? Well, it is to give a sense of protection to both end users and small business owners, assuring them that there is something that they can gauge, or compare with other ISPs who are also offering the levels of IT assets and IT resources.

In other words, end users and small business owners, given these metrics, can now quantitatively benchmark to see what will work best for them. In this section, we will look at both cost metrics and service quality metrics. But first, we look at cost metrics in much greater detail, including the following factors:

1. Network usage
2. Server usage
3. Cloud storage device usage
4. Service availability

FIGURE 1.5   Cloud computing–based metrics.

5. Service performance
6. Service scalability
7. Service resilience

NETWORK USAGE

Network usage is defined as the "amount of data transferred over a network connection, network usage is typically calculated using separately measured inbound network usage traffic and outbound network usage traffic metrics in relation to cloud services or other IT resources" (Erl 2013, p. 387).

As described in the preceding definition, network usage consists of the following:

1. **Inbound Network Usage Metric:**
   a. This metric measures the amount of inbound network traffic.
   b. This metric is measured in bytes.
2. **Outbound Network Usage Metric:**
   a. This metric measures the amount of outbound network traffic.
   b. This metric is measured in bytes.
3. **Intra-Cloud WAN Usage Metric:**
   a. This metric measures the amount of network traffic of the various IT assets and IT resources that are located in diverse geographic segments.
   b. This metric is measured in bytes.

It should be noted that network usage metrics are ascertained by the following components:

1. Assigned IP address usage
2. Network load balancing
3. The virtual firewall

SERVER USAGE

The *server usage* metric is defined as "measuring using common pay per use metrics in IaaS and PaaS environments that are quantified by the number of virtual servers and ready-made environments" (Erl 2013, p. 389).

As defined, the server usage metric is subdivided into the following metrics:

1. The on-demand virtual machine instance allocation metric
2. The reserved virtual machine instance allocation metric

The first metric measures the usage fees in the short term, whereas in the latter, the usage is measured can calculated over the long term:

1. **The On-Demand Virtual Machine Instance Allocation Metric:**
   a. This metric measures the availability of the virtual server instance.
   b. The measurement component is the time interval between the virtual start date and virtual server stop date.

2. **The Reserved Virtual Machine Instance Allocation Metric:**
   a. This metric measures the cost of securing a virtual server.
   b. The measurement component is the time interval between the reservation start date and the expiration date.

CLOUD STORAGE DEVICE USAGE

Cloud storage device usage can be defined as follows:

> The amount of space allocated within a predefined period, as measured by the on-demand storage allocation metric. Similar to IaaS based-cost metrics, on-demand storage allocation fees are usually based upon short-term increments. Another common cost metric for cloud storage is the I/O data transferred, which measures the amount of transferred input and output data.

> *(Erl 2013, p. 390)*

1. **The On-Demand Storage Space Allocation Metric:**
   a. This metric measures the time length as well as the dimensions of the on-demand storage space.
   b. The measurement component is the time length between the date of storage release and the date of storage reallocation.
2. **The I/O Data Transferred Metric:**
   a. This metric measures the amount of data being transferred between Cloud computing infrastructures.
   b. The measurement component is in given in bytes.

Along with these usage metrics, there are also other cost management considerations that need to be described, as follows:

1. **Cloud Service Design/Development:** This is when the pricing models and the cost templates are defined by the ISP.
2. **Cloud Services Deployment:** This is when the usage measurement is ascertained and put into place in a particular Cloud computing infrastructure.
3. **Cloud Service Contracting:** At this stage, the ISP determines the actual usage cost metrics.
4. **Cloud Service Offerings:** This is when the ISP formally publishes the actual costs for usage of the IT assets and the IT resources.
5. **Cloud Service Provisioning:** This is when the Cloud service thresholds are established.
6. **Cloud Service Operations:** This is when the active usage of Cloud computing infrastructure results in actual cost usage metric data.
7. **Cloud Service Provisioning:** This is when a Cloud computing infrastructure is decommissioned, and the cost data are archived and stored.

Now that we have looked at some very important costing metrics, at this point in the chapter, we turn our attention to the quality metrics that define a Cloud computing infrastructure. These quality metrics consist of the following components:

1. **Availability:** This refers to the service duration of a Cloud computing infrastructure.
2. **Reliability:** This refers to the minimum time between failures.
3. **Performance:** This refers to the response time, and capacity of a particular Cloud computing infrastructure.
4. **Scalability:** This refers to the fluctuations in demand on part of the end user or the small business owner.
5. **Resilience:** This refers to how quickly a Cloud computing infrastructure can be backed up and recovered in a time of disaster.
6. **Quantifiability:** This variable must be clearly established and absolute.
7. **Repeatability:** This variable is the ability to receive identical results.
8. **Comparability:** The units of measure (such as the number of bytes) need to be standardized and made the same for all levels of comparison within a Cloud computing infrastructure.
9. **Attainability:** This should be a common basic form of measurement that can be most importantly used and understood by end users and small business owners.

Cloud computing infrastructure quality metrics are as follows:

1. Service availability metrics
2. Service reliability metrics
3. Service performance metrics
4. Service scalability metrics
5. Service resilience metrics

SERVICE AVAILABILITY

The *service availability* metric is composed of two submetrics:

1. **The Availability Rate Metric:** This refers to the fact that an IT asset or IT resource can be expressed as a percentage of total uptime of an entire Cloud computing infrastructure.
   a. This metric is measured as a total percentage of service uptime.
   b. The measurement component is expressed in total uptime.
2. **The Outage Duration Metric:** This metric measures both maximum and average continuous outage service-level targets.
   a. This metric is measured in terms of the duration of a single outage.
   b. The measurement component is the interval between the date/time when the outage started and the date/time when it ended.

The *service reliability* metrics can be defined as "the reliability that an IT resource can perform its intended function under pre-defined conditions without experiencing failure. Reliability focuses on how often the service performs as expected, which requires the service to remain in an operational and available state" (Erl 2013, p. 407).

As can be seen from this definition, the service reliability metric consists of two submetrics:

1. **The Mean Time between Failures:**
   a. This metric measures the expected time between failures.
   b. This metric is measured in terms of ISP operating times and the total number of failures.
2. **The Reliability Rate Metric:** This metric can be defined as "the reliability rate that represents the percentage of successful service outcomes. This metric measures the effects of non-fatal errors and failures that occur during uptime periods" (Erl 2013, p. 407).
   a. This metric measures the actual percentage of the successful outcomes under certain conditions.
   b. The measurement component is the total number of successful responses per the total number of requests.

SERVICE PERFORMANCE

The *service performance* metric "refers to the ability on an IT resource to carry out its functions within expected parameters. This quality is measured using service capacity metrics, each of which focuses on a related measurable characteristic of IT resource capacity" (Erl 2013, p. 407). This overall metric consists of the following specific metrics:

1. **The Network Capacity Metric:**
   a. The measurement component is the amount of total network capacity.
   b. This metric is measured in terms of throughput (bits per second).
2. **The Storage Device Component Metric:**
   a. This metric is measured in terms of storage device capacity.
   b. This metric is measured in gigabytes.
3. **The Server Capacity Metric:**
   a. The measurement component is the server capacity.
   b. This metric is measured in terms of CPU frequency in gigahertz and RAM storage size in gigabytes.
4. **The Web Application Capacity Metric:**
   a. The measurement component is the web application capacity.
   b. This metric is measured in terms of the rate of requests issued per minute.
5. **The Instance Starting-Time Metric:**
   a. The measurement component is the time required to start a new instance.

b. This metric is measured in terms of the interval between the date/time of instance startup and the date/time of the start request.

6. **The Response-Time Metric:**
   a. This measurement component is the time required to perform synchronous operations.
   b. This metric is measured in terms of the total number of responses divided by the total number of requests.

7. **The Completion-Time Metric:**
   a. The measurement component is the time required to start and finish an asynchronous task.
   b. This metric is measured by the date of requests and responses divided by the total number of requests.

(Erl 2013, p. 407)

Service Scalability

Service scalability metrics can be defined as "metrics which are related to IT resource elasticity capacity, which is related to the maximum capacity that an IT resource can achieve, as well as measurements of its ability to adapt to workload fluctuations" (Erl 2013, p. 409). As can be inferred from this definition, the service scalability metric contains the following submetrics:

1. **The Storage Scalability Metric:**
   a. The measurement components are the required changes to higher and more demanding workloads.
   b. This metric is measured in gigabytes.

2. **The Server Scalability (Horizontal) Metric:**
   a. The measurement components are the server's capacity changes in the face of increased workloads.
   b. This metric is measured in terms of the number of virtual servers that are available.

3. **The Server Scalability (Vertical) Metric:**
   a. The measurement components are the virtual server spikes.
   b. This metric is measured in gigabytes.

Service Resilience

The service resilience metric can be described as follows:

The ability of an IT resource to recover from operational disturbances is often measured using service resiliency metrics. When resiliency is described within or in relation to SLA resiliency guarantees, it is often based on redundant implementations and resource replication over different physical locations, as well as various disaster recovery systems.

(Erl 2013, p. 411)

This type of metric can occur at all phases of Cloud computing infrastructure:

1. **The Design Phase:** In this phase one can determine how well prepared a particular Cloud computing infrastructure is to cope with challenges and disasters.
2. **The Operational Phase:** In this phase one can measure the different levels of service agreements during and after a serious downtime or even a service outage.
3. **The Recovery Phase:** In this phase one can determine the rate at which the IT assets and IT resources can recover from downtime.

As can be seen from the above definitions, there are two types of primary metrics here:

1. **The Mean Time to Switch over Metric:**
   a. The measurement component is the expected time to complete a virtual server switchover from a failure to another virtual server that is located in a totally different geographic region.
   b. It is measured in terms of switchover completion divided by the total number of failures.
2. **The Mean Time System Recovery Metric:**
   a. The measurement component is the expected time to perform a complete recovery from a disaster.
   b. It is measured in terms of time of recovery divided by the total number of failures.

This chapter has reviewed the evolution that has led to the current Cloud computing environment and its theoretical concepts, and the various models have been thoroughly examined as well. Chapter 2 discusses the practical application of a Cloud-based infrastructure, namely, Amazon Web Services. This is by far the largest Cloud environment that is available today, even surpassing that of Microsoft Azure. We will examine both the technical and security aspects of Amazon Web Services.

SOURCES

1. https://arstechnica.com/information-technology/2014/04/50-years-ago-ibm-created-mainframe-that-helped-bring-men-to-the-moon/
2. http://ceet.unimelb.edu.au/publications/ceet-white-paper-wireless-cloud.pdf
3. Erl, T. *Cloud Computing: Concepts, Technology & Architecture*. Arcitura Education, 2013.
4. http://www.pcm.com/n/mkt-3150
5. https://en.wikipedia.org/wiki/History_of_personal_computers
6. https://en.wikipedia.org/wiki/History_of_personal_computers
7. http://www.opengardensblog.futuretext.com/archives/2014/12/infographic-the-evolution-of-wireless-networks.html
8. https://en.wikipedia.org/wiki/Wireless_network
9. http://www.opengardensblog.futuretext.com/archives/2014/12/infographic-the-evolution-of-wireless-networks.html
10. https://en.wikipedia.org/wiki/Wireless_network

11. https://www.flowfinity.com/blog/the-evolution-of-smartphones-12-key-highlights. aspx.
12. https://thehub.smsglobal.com/smartphone-evolution-infographic
13. https://en.wikipedia.org/wiki/History_of_mobile_phones
14. http://www.synextra.co.uk/evolution-cloud-computing/
15. https://www.computerworlduk.com/galleries/cloud-computing/history-of-cloud-computing-3672729/
16. https://searchcloudcomputing.techtarget.com/feature/Cloud-computing-timeline-illustrates-clouds-past-predicts-its-future
17. https://www.business2community.com/infographics/interactive-history-cloud-computing-01304429

2 Amazon Web Services

INTRODUCTION—CHAPTER OVERVIEW

The first chapter of this book provided an overview of the events in the history of information technology that led to development of the Cloud computing environment as we know it today. An introduction to the theoretical concepts was also provided, focusing on the different aspects that it offers. In summary, Chapter 1 covered the following topics:

- Evolution to the Cloud: the mainframe
- Evolution to the Cloud: the personal computer
- Evolution to the Cloud: the wireless network
- The last evolution to the Cloud: the smartphone

The concepts of the Cloud computing environment included the following:

- Evolution of Cloud computing infrastructure
- Basic concepts and terminology surrounding Cloud computing:
  - The Cloud
  - The IT resource
  - On-premise
  - Scalability
  - IT asset scaling (horizontal and vertical)
  - Proportional costs
  - Availability and reliability
  - Service-level agreements (SLAs)
- Challenges and risks of Cloud computing:
  - Security risks and challenges
  - Reduced operational governance
  - Limited portability
  - Compliance and legal issues
- Functions and characteristics of Cloud computing:
  - On-demand usage
  - Ubiquitous access
  - Resource pooling
  - Elasticity
  - Measured usage
  - Resilience
- Cloud computing delivery models:
  - Infrastructure as a service
  - Platform as a service
  - Software as a service

 DOI: 10.1201/9781003459569-2

- Cloud computing deployment models:
  - The public Cloud
  - The community Cloud
  - The private Cloud
  - The hybrid Cloud
- Security threats posed to Cloud computing:
  - Confidentiality
  - Integrity
  - Authenticity
  - Availability
  - Vulnerability
  - Security risk
  - Security controls
  - Security mechanisms
  - Security policies
  - Anonymous attacker
  - Malicious service agent
  - Trusted service attacker
  - Malicious insider
  - Traffic eavesdropping
  - Malicious intermediary
  - Denial of service
  - Insufficient authorization
  - Virtualization attack
  - Overlapping threat boundaries
- Important mechanisms of Cloud computing:
  - The load balancer
  - Pay-per-use monitor
  - The audit monitor
  - The hypervisor
  - Resource clustering
  - The server cluster
- Cloud computing cost metrics and service quality mechanisms:
  - Network usage
  - Server usage
  - Cloud storage device usage
  - Service availability
  - Service performance
  - Service scalability
  - Service resilience

The following chapter is devoted to Amazon Web Services, focusing on the following topics:

1. An overview of the evolution of Amazon Web Services (AWS)
2. A review of the major components of Amazon Web Services

3. A review of Amazon Elastic Cloud Compute (EC2)
4. A review of Amazon Simple Storage Service (S3)
5. A review of AWS security services

AN OVERVIEW OF THE EVOLUTION OF AMAZON WEB SERVICES

Amazon Web Services (which from here will be referred to as "AWS") is today the leading powerhouse of Cloud computing services. It is used widely by software developers, individuals, businesses, corporations, nonprofit agencies, the federal government, and others. Just consider some of these key statistics:

- In the first quarter of 2016, the revenue was $2.57 billion with a net income at $604 million. This represents a 64% increase over the first quarter of 2015.
- Also in the first quarter of 2016, Amazon experienced a 42% rise in stock value as a result of increased earnings, to which AWS contributed 56%.
- AWS had $17.46 billion in annual revenue in the fiscal year 2017.

Amazon Web Services did not become the powerhouse that it is today over a short of period of time; rather, it has evolved over the last 20 years as the following timeline illustrates:

1. **In 2002:**
   AWS was initially formally launched as a free service that allowed businesses and corporations to incorporate Amazon.com features on their own sites. This was targeted primarily toward software developers to build applications that would allow them to incorporate many of the unique features of Amazon.com into their websites that they create.
2. **In 2006:**
   AWS formally launched with its first Cloud-based products, enabling businesses and corporations to build their own applications using Amazon's infrastructure. The first was Simple Storage Service (S3), followed by Elastic Compute Cloud (EC2), its server rental and hosting service.
3. **In 2009:**
   The Virtual Private Cloud was launched as a private, self-contained partition of the AWS datacenter.
4. **In 2012:**
   The first major AWS developer conference was held in Las Vegas in 2012, highlighting its growing user community.
5. **In 2013:**
   AWS built a dedicated infrastructure for the US Central Intelligence Agency (CIA) worth $600 million. CIA's choice of AWS was symbolic of a shift in power and boosted AWS' credentials as an enterprise-grade Cloud supplier.

Also, the data warehousing as a service platform "Redshift" was launched as part of the ongoing process of building out the data processing capabilities of AWS.

6. **In 2015:**
AWS achieves revenues of $4.6 billion and has a growth rate of 49% to $6.2 billion in 2015.

7. **In 2016:**
AWS releases "Snowball," a 50-TB appliance allowing large-enterprise customers to transfer large volumes of data into the AWS Cloud by shipping the appliance between their offices and AWS datacenters.

AWS also reveals "Snowmobile," an 18-wheel truck filled with hard drives that can store up to 100 PB of data and that supports data transfer at a rate of 1 Tbps across multiple 40-Gbps connections.

Also, AWS launches its first UK datacenter.

8. **In 2017:**
AWS registers $12.2 billion of revenue in 2016, with $3.1 billion in operating income profit.

9. **In 2018:**
AWS now offers nearly 100 Cloud services to customers for compute, storage, database, analytics, networking, mobile, developer tools, management tools, IoT (Internet of Things), security, and enterprise applications.

Amazon Rekognition, a text-to-voice service (also called "Amazon Polly," discussed in the section titled "AWS Artificial Intelligence") is also launched.

FIGURE 2.1 Exploring Amazon Web Services.

MAJOR COMPONENTS OF AMAZON WEB SERVICE

As described previously, AWS is a gargantuan Cloud computing environment, with many components (see Figure 2.1). Not too many people are aware of all of them; therefore, it is important to provide an overview of each of them. In the next section, a much more detailed review will particularly examine Amazon Elastic Cloud Compute, also known as EC2. This is perhaps considered to be one of the most crucial aspects of AWS.

Here is a breakdown of the major facets that make up AWS:

1. **AWS Management Console:**
   It is from this specific portal that one can access and manage Amazon Web Services. It is designed to be a simple and intuitive user interface to support the rapid development and deployment of all kinds of software development projects.
2. **AWS Command-Line Interface:**
   This is the same as the AWS management console, but rather than having a graphical user interface (GUI), you can access and launch your portal via the command-line approach. It is designed to be a unified tool to manage your AWS-based services. With just one tool to download and configure, you can control multiple AWS services from the command line and automate them through various scripting languages.

AWS COMPUTE SERVICES

1. **Amazon Elastic Compute Cloud (also known as the Amazon EC2):**
   As described, this is deemed to be one of the most critical aspects of the AWS. It is a web service that provides secure and scalable computing capacity in the Cloud. It is designed to make web-scale computing more efficient and robust for software developers.
2. **Amazon EC2 Container Service (ECS):**
   The ECS is a highly scalable, high-performance container management service that supports Docker containers. It allows you to easily run applications on a managed cluster of Amazon EC2 instances. With custom-created API calls, you can launch and stop Docker-enabled applications, query the complete state of your cluster, and access many familiar features of the security groups from within AWS.
3. **Amazon EC2 Container Registry (ECR):**
   The ECR is a fully managed Docker container registry that makes it easy for developers to store, manage, and deploy Docker container images. It hosts your images in a highly available and scalable architecture, allowing you to reliably deploy containers for your applications. It also integrates with the AWS Identity and Access Management (IAM) and thus provides resource-level control of each repository.
4. **Amazon Lightsail:**
   This is a virtual server, which consists of a solid-state drive (SSD)-based storage, data transfer, Domain Name System (DNS) management, and a static IP address.

5. **AWS Batch:**
   This enables software developers to easily and efficiently run hundreds of thousands of batch computing jobs on AWS. It allows you to plan, schedule, and execute your batch computing workloads across the full range of AWS compute services, such as the Amazon EC2 and Spot Instances.

6. **AWS Elastic Beanstalk:**
   This enables software developers to quickly and easily deploy web applications and services developed with Java, .NET, PHP, Node.js, Python, Ruby, Go, and Docker on web-based servers such as Apache, Nginx, Passenger, and Internet Information Services (IIS).

7. **AWS Lambda:**
   With Lambda, you can run the source code for any type of application or backend service. The source code can be set up to automatically trigger from other AWS services, or you can call it directly from any web or mobile app.

8. **AWS Auto Scaling:**
   The Auto Scaling component helps you maintain application availability. As a result, you can scale your Amazon EC2 capacity up or down automatically according to the requirements of the software development project.

Amazon Simple Storage Service (Amazon S3)

Amazon S3 is an object storage with a simple web service interface to store and retrieve any amount of data from anywhere on the web. It is used primarily for the following purposes:

- As a means of primary storage for Cloud-native applications
- As the primary means of bulk data repository
- For backup and recovery and disaster recovery
- For serverless computing

1. **Amazon Elastic Block Store (EBS):**
   Amazon EBS provides persistent block storage volumes for use with Amazon EC2 instances in AWS Cloud. Each Amazon EBS volume is automatically replicated from within its availability zone to protect software developers from component failure.

2. **Amazon Elastic File System (EFS):**
   Amazon EFS provides simple, scalable file storage for use with Amazon EC2-based instances in AWS Cloud. Also, multiple EC2 instances can access an Amazon EFS file system at the same time. As a result, this enables Amazon EFS to provide a common data source for multiple workloads and applications.

3. **Amazon Glacier:**
   Amazon Glacier is a service for data archiving and long-term software development backup purposes.

4. **AWS Storage Gateway:**
This functionality allows for transpiration of storage between on-premises storage environments and AWS Cloud.

AWS DATABASE

1. **Amazon Aurora:**
Amazon Aurora is a MySQL- and PostgreSQL-compatible relational database engine that is used heavily by software developers worldwide.

2. **Amazon Relational Database Service (Amazon RDS):**
Amazon RDS makes it easy to set up, operate, and scale a relational database in the Cloud. It has six database engines to choose from, which are as follows:
- Amazon Aurora
- PostgreSQL
- MySQL
- MariaDB
- Oracle
- Microsoft SQL Server

3. **Amazon DynamoDB:**
This is a NoSQL database service for all kinds of applications and is used to create document and keyvalue data models.

4. **Amazon ElastiCache:**
This is a web service that makes it easy to create, deploy, and scale an in-memory cache in the Cloud. It supports two open-source in-memory caching engines:
- *Redis:* This is an open-source, in-memory data store and cache. Both single-node and up to 15 shared clusters are available, enabling scalability to ≤3.55 TB of in-memory data.
- *Memcached:* This is a memory object caching system.

AWS MIGRATION

1. **AWS Database Migration Service:**
This service helps the software development team migrate databases to AWS easily and securely. It also supports homogenous migrations such as Oracle to Oracle, as well as heterogeneous migrations between different database platforms, such as Oracle to Amazon Aurora or Microsoft SQL Server to MySQL. AWS Database Migration Service can also be used for continuous data replication as needs and requirements dictate.

2. **AWS Application Discovery Service:**
This helps systems integrators quickly and reliably plan application migration projects. AWS Application Discovery Service automatically collects configuration and usage data from servers, storage, and networking equipment to develop a list of applications, including their performance and interdependence.

3. **AWS Server Migration Service:**
   This allows you to automate, schedule, and track incremental replications of live server volumes as they are transferred to AWS.

4. **AWS Snowball:**
   AWS Snowball is a petabyte-scale data transport solution that uses secure appliances to transfer large amounts of data into and out of AWS.

5. **AWS Snowball Edge:**
   This is a 100-TB data transfer device with onboard storage and compute capabilities. Snowball Edge devices can be clustered together to form a local storage tier and process your data on premises.

6. **AWS Snowmobile:**
   This is an exabyte-scale data transfer service used to move extremely large amounts of data to the AWS platform. You can transfer up to 100 PB per Snowmobile. After your data is loaded, the Snowmobile is driven back to AWS where your data is imported into Amazon S3 or Amazon Glacier.

AWS NETWORKING AND CONTENT DELIVERY

1. **Amazon VPC:**
   Amazon VPC allows you to provision a logically isolated section of the AWS Cloud where you can launch AWS resources in a virtual network that is already predefined. You have control over your own IP address range, subnets, and configuration of routing tables, and network gateways.

2. **Amazon CloudFront:**
   Amazon CloudFront can be used to deliver an entire website project, including dynamic, static, streaming, and interactive content using a global network of edge locations. It also works with any non-AWS-origin server that stores the original, definitive versions of the web project files.

3. **Amazon Route 53:**
   This is a Cloud-based Domain Name System (DNS) web service. It is designed to give software developers and businesses an avenue to route end users to Internet applications by translating domain names, such as www. bn-inc.net, into the numeric IP addresses, such as 192.0.2.1. Amazon Route 53 is fully compliant with IPv6. Amazon Route 53 can also be used to configure DNS health checks to route traffic to healthy endpoints or to independently monitor the health of the software development application and its endpoints.

4. **AWS Direct Connect:**
   You can use this app to establish a dedicated network connection from your on-premise servers to AWS-based servers. AWS Direct Connect also lets you establish a dedicated network connection between your software development network and one of the AWS Direct Connect locations.

5. **Elastic Load Balancing:**
   This allows you to automatically distribute incoming application traffic across multiple EC2 instances. There two specific types of load balancer:

- *Classic Load Balancer:* This routes traffic based on either application or network level information.
- *Application Load Balancer:* This routes traffic based on advanced application-level information that includes the content of the request.

AWS MANAGEMENT TOOLS

1. **Amazon CloudWatch:**
   This is a monitoring service for the AWS Cloud resources and the applications that you run on it. CloudWatch can also collect and track metrics and/or log files, set alarms, and automatically react to changes in AWS resources that have been established.

2. **Amazon EC2 Systems Manager:**
   This is a service that automatically collects software inventory, deploys operating system (OS) patches, and creates system images. It also configures Windows and Linux operating systems. This package comes with numerous auxiliary tools as well, which are as follows:
   - *Run Command:* This provides a simple way of automating common administrative tasks such as remotely executing shell scripts or PowerShell commands, installing software updates, and so on.
   - *State Manager:* This enables the software development team to define and maintain consistent OS configurations such as firewall settings and antimalware definitions to comply with the policies that have been already preestablished.
   - *Inventory:* This allows you to gather details about the instances such as installed applications, Dynamic Host Configuration Protocol (DHCP) settings, agent detail, and custom items.
   - *Maintenance Window:* This permits the software development team to define a recurring window of time to run administrative and maintenance tasks across the various instances.
   - *Patch Manager:* This allows the software development team to select and deploy operating system and software patches automatically across large sets of instances.
   - *Automation:* This simplifies common software development maintenance and deployment tasks, such as updating Amazon machine images (AMIs).
   - *Parameter Store:* This allows the software development team to store important administrative information such as passwords and database strings in an encrypted fashion.

3. **The AWS CloudFormation:**
   This tool gives software developers and network systems administrators an easy way to create and manage a collection of related AWS resources, in effect, creating a version control tool of various sorts.

4. **The AWS CloudTrail:**
   This is a web-based service that records AWS API calls for your account and delivers log files to you. It collects the following kinds of information:
   - Identity of the API caller

- Time of the API call
- Source IP address of the API caller
- Request parameters
- Response elements returned by the AWS service

5. **AWS Config:**
   This is a fully managed service that provides the software development team with an AWS resource inventory, configuration history, and configuration change notifications.

6. **AWS OpsWorks:**
   AWS OpsWorks uses Chef (which is an automation platform that treats server configurations as software development code) to automate how servers are configured, deployed, and managed across your EC2 instances.

7. **AWS Service Catalog:**
   This allows for businesses and corporations to create and manage catalogs of IT services that are approved for use on the AWS platform.

8. **AWS Trusted Advisor:**
   This is an online resource to help the software development team reduce cost, increase performance, and improve the levels of security by optimizing the overall AWS environment.

9. **AWS Personal Health Dashboard:**
   The Health Dashboard provides alerts and remediation guidance when AWS is experiencing events that might affect the overall software development project at hand.

10. **AWS Managed Services:**
    AWS Managed Services automates common activities such as the following:
    - Change requests
    - Monitoring and patch management
    - Security and backup services
    - Full-lifecycle services to provision, run, and support the entire software development infrastructure

AWS Software Development Tools

1. **AWS CodeCommit:**
   This a fully managed source control service that helps software development teams host secure and highly scalable private Git repositories.

2. **AWS CodeBuild:**
   This package is a fully managed build service that compiles source code, runs tests, and produces software packages that are ready to deploy.

3. **AWS CodeDeploy:**
   This is a tool that automates code deployments to any software development instance, including EC2 instances and instances running on premises.

4. **AWS CodePipeline:**
   CodePipeline builds, tests, and deploys your code every time there is a code change, based on the release process models that the software development team defines. It also allows for integration and continuous delivery service for fast and reliable application and infrastructure updates.

5. **AWS X-Ray:**
   This helps developers analyze and debug distributed software applications in production or under development, such as those built using a microservices architecture. With X-Ray, software developers can understand how applications and their underlying services are performing so that the team can identify and troubleshoot the root cause of performance issues and errors. X-Ray can be used to analyze applications in both development and in production, from simple three-tier applications to complex microservice applications consisting of thousands of services.

AWS Security, Identity, and Compliance

1. **Amazon Cloud Directory:**
   This tool enables the software development team to build flexible, Cloud-native directories for organizing hierarchies of data along multiple dimensions. With Cloud Directory, you have the flexibility to create directories with hierarchies that span multiple dimensions. The directory automatically scales to hundreds of millions of objects and provides an extensible schema that can be shared with multiple applications. For example, you can quickly and easily define the schema, create a directory, and then populate your directory by making calls to the Cloud Directory API.

2. **AWS Identity and Access Management:**
   This enables you to securely control access to AWS services and resources for the software development team. It consists of the following features:
   - *Manage IAM Users/Access:* You can create users in IAM, assign them individual security credentials, such as access keys, passwords, and multifactor authentication devices [also known as *two-factor authentication* (2FA)], or request temporary security credentials, and even manage various permissions so that users access only what they need, and nothing more.
   - *Manage IAM Roles/Permissions:* The software development team can create roles in the IAM and manage permissions to control which operations can be performed; and also define which end user is allowed to assume these various roles.
   - *Manage Federated Users/Permissions:* This allows for identity federation to enable existing identities (users, groups, and roles) in the business to access the AWS Management Console, call AWS APIs, and utilize other kinds of access resources.

3. **Amazon Inspector:**
   This an automated security assessment service that helps improve the security and compliance of applications deployed on the AWS platform. It even provides a detailed list of the security vulnerabilities that have been discovered and is prioritized by the specific degree of severity.

4. **AWS Certificate Manager:**
   This is a service that enables the software development team to easily provision, manage, and deploy Secure Sockets Layer/Transport Layer Security (SSL/TLS) certificates for use with AWS Platform. The SSL/TLS

certificates are used to secure network communications and to establish the identity of websites over the Internet. An added benefit is that AWS Certificate Manager removes the time-consuming manual process of purchasing, uploading, and renewing SSL/TLS certificates.

5. **AWS CloudHSM:**

   The AWS CloudHSM service allows the software development team to protect the encryption keys within HSMs that have been designed and validated to government standards for secure key management. As a result, one can securely generate, store, and manage the cryptographic keys that are used for data encryption in such a manner that they are accessible only to you and other members of the software development team. CloudHSM instances are provisioned inside the VPC with an IP address that only you can specify.

6. **AWS Directory Service:**

   This is also known as the "AWS Microsoft AD" and thus enables your directory-aware workloads and AWS resources to use a managed active directory that is based in AWS Cloud. The AWS Microsoft AD service is built on an actual Microsoft active directory and can use standard active directory administration tools such as Group Policy, trusts, and single sign-on.

7. **AWS Key Management Service:**

   This is a managed service that helps the software development create and control the encryption keys used to encrypt the relevant information and data. This service uses HSMs to protect the security of the relevant keys.

8. **AWS Organizations:**

   This allows you to create groups of AWS accounts that members of the software development team can use to more easily manage security and automation settings in the project.

9. **AWS Shield:**

   This is a fully managed Distributed Denial of Service (DDoS) protection service that safeguards web applications that the software development team creates while running the AWS platform. It is available in two types:

   - *AWS Shield Standard:* This defends against the most common, frequently occurring network and transport-layer DDoS attacks that target the websites and/or applications that the software development team creates and implements.
   - *AWS Shield Advanced:* This detects and mitigates against a large and sophisticated scale. It also is supplied in with a web application firewall.

10. **AWS Web Application Firewall:**

    This is a web application firewall (WAF) that helps protect web applications from common web exploits that could affect application availability, compromise security, or consume excessive resources. You can also use AWS WAF to create custom rules that block common attack patterns, such as SQL injection or cross-site scripting.

AWS ANALYTICS

1. **Amazon Athena:**
   This is an interactive query service that makes it easy to analyze data in Amazon S3 using standard SQL.
2. **Amazon EMR:**
   This tool provides a managed Hadoop framework that allows the software development team to process vast amounts of data across dynamically scalable EC2 instances. It also handles a broad set of big data use cases, including log analysis, web indexing, data transformations (ETL), machine learning, financial analysis, scientific simulation, and bioinformatics.
3. **Amazon CloudSearch:**
   This is a managed service in AWS Cloud that allows the software development team to set up, manage, and scale a search solution for website or application project.
4. **Amazon Elasticsearch Service:**
   This is a package that specifically deploys APIs and real-time capabilities that are required by production workloads.
5. **Amazon Kinesis:**
   This a platform for the streaming of data on AWS Platform, offering powerful services to facilitate loading and analysis of streaming data, and also providing the ability for you to build custom streaming data applications for specialized software development needs.
6. **Amazon Kinesis Firehose:**
   This tool enables the software development team to load streaming data into AWS Platform. It can also batch, compress, and encrypt the data before loading it, thus minimizing the amount of storage used at the destination point and at the same time increasing security.
7. **Amazon Kinesis Analytics:**
   This tool allows for the processing of streaming data in real time with standard SQL statements.
8. **Amazon Kinesis Streams:**
   This tool allows the software development team to build custom applications that process or analyze streaming data for specialized needs. It can continuously capture and store terabytes of data per hour from hundreds of thousands of sources such as website clickstreams, financial transactions, social media feeds, IT logs, and location-tracking events that are all related to the development project at hand.
9. **Amazon Redshift:**
   This is a petabyte-scale data warehouse that makes it simple and cost-effective to analyze all the data as it relates to the software development project at hand. It uses columnar storage, data compression, and zone maps to reduce the amount of I/O needed to perform queries. It also possesses a massively parallel processing (MPP) data warehouse architecture.

10. **Amazon QuickSight:**
    This is a Cloud-powered analytics service that makes it easy to build visualizations, perform ad-hoc analysis, and quickly gain insight into the software application data.

11. **AWS Data Pipeline:**
    This is a web-based service that helps the software development team process and move data between different AWS compute and storage services. It can also create complex data-processing workloads that are fault-tolerant, repeatable, and highly available.

12. **AWS Glue:**
    This is a fully managed ETL service that allows the software development team to move data between data stores. It automatically crawls the data sources, identifies data formats, and then suggests various other kinds of schemas and transformations.

AWS MOBILE SERVICES

1. **AWS Mobile Hub:**
   This is an integrate console that can create and configure powerful mobile app backend features and integrate them into the software application mobile app. It is supplied with the following features:
   - App analytics
   - App content delivery
   - Cloud logic
   - NoSQL database
   - Push notifications
   - User data storage
   - User sign-in
   - Connectors
   - Conversational bots
   - User engagement

2. **Amazon Cognito:**
   With this tool, you easily add user sign-up and sign-in to both the mobile and web apps. It also provides the option to authenticate users through social identity providers such as Facebook, Twitter, or Amazon, and even Security Assertion Markup Language (SAML) identity-based solutions.

3. **Amazon Pinpoint:**
   This package allows you to create targeted campaigns to drive user engagement in mobile apps. Amazon Pinpoint helps you understand user behavior, define which users to target, determine which messages to send, schedule the best time to deliver the messages, and then track the results of the specific campaign.

4. **AWS Device Farm:**
   This is an app testing service that lets you test and interact with your Android, iOS, and web apps on many devices all at the same time. It also reproduces issues on a device in real time.

5. **AWS Mobile SDK:**
   AWS Mobile SDK includes libraries, code samples, and documentation for iOS, Android, Fire OS, and Unity so that apps can be built to deliver great experiences across devices and platforms.
6. **Amazon Mobile Analytics:**
   This can measure app usage and app revenue. Key charts can also be viewed in the Mobile Analytics console. You can also automatically export your app event data to Amazon S3 and Amazon Redshift to run various types of custom analyses.

AWS APPLICATION SERVICE

1. **AWS Step Functions:**
   This tool makes it easy to coordinate the components of distributed applications and microservices using visual workflows. The Step Functions tool provides a graphical console to the software development team and arranges and/or visualizes the components of the application as a series of steps. It also automatically triggers and tracks each step, and retries them when there are errors, so that the development project executes in order and as expected, and it logs the state of each step.
2. **Amazon API Gateway:**
   This is a fully managed service that makes it easy for software developers to create, publish, maintain, monitor, and secure APIs at any scale. Amazon API Gateway handles all the tasks involved in accepting and processing up to hundreds of thousands of concurrent API calls, including traffic management, authorization and access control, monitoring, and API version management.
3. **Amazon Elastic Transcoder:**
   This tool converts media files from their source format into versions that will play back on devices such as smartphones, tablets, and PCs.
4. **Amazon SWF:**
   This package helps software developers build, run, and scale background jobs that have parallel or sequential steps, that take more than 500 milliseconds (ms) to complete.

AWS INTERNET OF THINGS (IoT)

1. **AWS IoT Platform:**
   The AWS IoT can support billions of devices and trillions of messages. It can also process and route those messages to various AWS endpoints and to other devices reliably and securely.
2. **AWS Greengrass:**
   This is a software package that enables the software development team to run local compute, messaging, and data caching for connected devices in a secure way. It connects devices that can run AWS Lambda functions, keep device data in full synchronization, and communicate with other

devices securely, even when not connected to the Internet. It also seamlessly extends AWS Platform to devices so that they can act locally on the data that they generate, while still using the Cloud for management, analytics, and durable storage. AWS Greengrass authenticates and encrypts device data at all points of connection using the AWS IoT security and access management capabilities.

3. **AWS IoT Button:**
This is a programmable button that is based on Amazon Dash Button hardware. The button's logic can be coded in the Cloud to configure button clicks to count or track items, call or alert someone, start or stop something, order services, or even provide feedback. It can also integrate with third-party APIs like Twitter, Facebook, Twilio, and Slack.

AWS ARTIFICIAL INTELLIGENCE

1. **Amazon Lex:**
This is a service for building conversational interfaces into any software development application using voice and text. Amazon Lex provides the advanced deep-learning functionalities of automatic speech recognition (ASR) for converting speech to text, and natural language understanding (NLU) to recognize the intent of the text. As a result, this enables the software development team to build web-based applications with highly engaging user experiences and lifelike conversational interactions.

2. **Amazon Polly:**
This is a package that turns text into lifelike speech. Amazon Polly lets you create web-based applications that talk, enabling the software development team to build entirely new categories of speech-enabled products. This is an Amazon artificial intelligence (AI) service that uses advanced deep-learning technologies to synthesize speech that sounds like a human voice.

3. **Amazon Rekognition:**
This makes it easy to add image analysis to web-based applications. With Amazon Rekognition, you can detect objects, scenes, and faces in images. You can also search and compare faces. The API enables software developers to quickly add sophisticated deep-learning-based visual search and image classification into web-based applications. It also uses deep neural network models to detect and label thousands of objects and scenes in your images that are prevalent in the software development project.

4. **Amazon Machine Learning:**
This is a service that helps software developers use machine-learning technology in web-based applications. It provides visualization tools and wizards that guide the software developer through the process of creating machine-learning (ML) models without having to learn complex ML algorithms. It is highly scalable and can generate billions of predictions daily and apply those predictions to the software development project in real time and at high throughput.

AWS MESSAGING

1. **Amazon SQS:**
   This is a fast, reliable, scalable, fully managed message queuing service. It can be used to transmit any volume of data, without losing messages that are relevant to the software development project. It also includes standard queues with high throughput and first-in, first-out (FIFO) queues that provide FIFO delivery and exactly-once processing.

2. **The Amazon SNS:**
   This package is a fully managed push notification service that lets you send individual messages or to fan out messages to large numbers of recipients who are associated with the software development project. One can even send notifications to Apple, Google, Fire OS, and Windows devices, as well as to Android devices.

3. **Amazon SES:**
   This is a cost-effective email service built on the reliable and scalable infrastructure that Amazon.com developed to serve its own customer base. One can even send transactional email, marketing messages, or any other type of high-quality-content people who are associated with the software development project at hand.

AWS BUSINESS PRODUCTIVITY

1. **Amazon WorkDocs:**
   This package is a fully managed, secure enterprise storage and sharing service. Software developers can comment on files, send them to others for feedback, and even upload new versions of the source code files.

2. **Amazon WorkMail:**
   This tool is a secure, managed business email and calendar service with support for existing desktop and mobile email client applications. It enables software developers to seamlessly access their email, contacts, and calendars using the client application of their choice, including Microsoft Outlook, native iOS, and Android email applications, as well as any client application supporting the Internet Message Access Protocol (IMAP).

3. **Amazon Chime:**
   This is a communication service that transforms online meetings with a secure, easy-to-use application that software developers can trust.

AWS DESKTOP & APP STREAMING

1. **Amazon WorkSpaces:**
   This tool is a fully managed, secure desktop computing service that runs on AWS Cloud. It allows software developers to easily provision Cloud-based virtual desktops and provide other people who are associated with the software development project with access to the documents, applications, and resources that they need. These can be accessed by any supported device,

including Windows and Mac computers, Chromebooks, iPads, Fire tablets, Android tablets, and Chrome and Firefox web browsers.

2. **Amazon AppStream 2.0:**
   This package is a fully managed, secure application streaming service that allows you to stream desktop applications from AWS to any device running a web browser. With Amazon AppStream 2.0, software developers can easily import existing desktop applications to AWS Platform and instantly start streaming them to an HTML5-compatible browser. Software development applications run on AWS compute resources, and data is never stored on individual devices, thus offering high levels of security.

AWS GAME DEVELOPMENT

1. **Amazon GameLift:**
   This is a managed service for deploying, operating, and scaling dedicated game servers for session-based multiplayer games. It helps software developers manage server infrastructure, scale capacity to lower latency and cost, match players into available game sessions, and defend them from Distributed Denial-of-Service (DDoS) attacks.
2. **Amazon Lumberyard:**
   This is a three-dimensional (3D) game engine for software developers to create the highest-quality games, connect games to the vast compute and storage of AWS Cloud, and engage fans on Twitch.

Figure 2.2 provides an overview of the major AWS components.

A REVIEW OF THE AMAZON ELASTIC CLOUD COMPUTE (EC2)

Our last section provided an extensive overview of the major facets of AWS Platform. When people hear about it, they often think of the AWS as just one huge Cloud infrastructure, of which it really is; but there is so much more to it than just hosting. As one can see, AWS Platform is a service that is heavily used by software developers as well in order to create many kinds of complex software as well as web-based applications.

In this aspect, one of the most crucial components of AWS Platform is a feature known as the "Amazon Elastic Cloud Compute," also known as the "EC2" for short. This is also known more technically as an *infrastructure as a service* (IaaS)-based "compute as a service." This simply means that all the resources and assets that are available in the EC2 are offered as a service, which, in turn, means that it is available on demand and is a service that is completely scalable to the software application development needs.

This section is divided into the following segments:

1. An overview of the Amazon EC2
2. How to access the EC2 via the AWS console
3. Setting up the environment variables
4. Setting up the security environment
5. Setting up the region
6. Computing resources

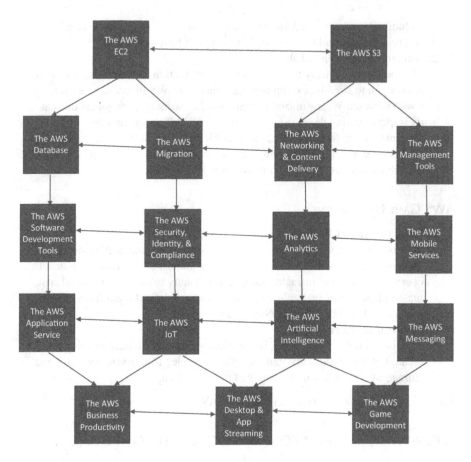

FIGURE 2.2   Major components of Amazon Web Services.

7. Software on the EC2
8. Regions and availability zones
9. Load balancing and scaling
10. EC2 storage resources
11. S3-backed instances versus EBS-backed instances
12. EC2 networking resources
13. Instance addresses
14. Elastic TCP/IP addresses
15. Route 53
16. Security groups
17. The virtual private Cloud
18. How to set up a web server

An Overview of Amazon EC2

EC2 allows for businesses and corporations to define what their brand of a virtual server is all about. The key components of EC2 are virtual storage and virtual networking. Of course, the exact computational and processing resources will vary from organization to organization. For example, some software development applications might be heavily compute-intensive, and other projects may be less so and thus require much less storage space.

Also, certain applications may need differing development requirements and needs, and others may need what is known as "computational clustering" in order to run effectively and efficiently. As alluded to earlier, networking is a critical aspect here as well, and because of the diversity of the EC2 with regard to compute hardware, automatic maintenance, and the strong ability for scalability, it can meet these needs as well.

How to Access EC2 via AWS Console

EC2 can actually be accessed via AWS Web Services Console, which is found at the following link:

http://aws.amazon.com/console

This console can enable a software developer to create a specific instance (also known as a "compute resource"); check the status of the of these various instances in real time, or even end a session (which will actually discard the project). Of course, it can also be used to create as many instances that are necessary by the software development project.

When you are in AWS Console, first click on the "Launch Instance" button. This will take you to the location where the set of supported operating system images [these are also technically known as *Amazon machine images* (AMIs)]. From here, you can then select the various image(s) that your application will further require.

Once a certain image is chosen, the EC2 instance wizard will appear, and this will allow you to set up further options to choose from, such as the following:

- The specific OS kernel version that needs to be used
- Enabling software development monitoring

In order to proceed to the next step, you need to generate at least one cryptographic keypair value that will be used to establish a secure and robust connection to the instances that you create. Follow the online instructions to create this specific keypair, and save it into the following file syntax:

My_keypair.pem

It is important to note that this same keypair value can be reused as many times as necessary throughout the software development lifecycle.

Once the keypair has been established and defined, the next step is to create the security groups that are necessary in order to ensure that the network ports are either open or blocked, depending on the requirements. An example of this is choosing the "Web Server" option, which will enable you to establish a connection at Port 40 (which is the standard HTTP port). You can even set up much more advanced firewall-based rules as well.

Once the newly created instance has been launched, it is assigned a public DNS name so that you can log into it remotely and use it in such a manner that it can even be accessed through a client on your own computer. An example of this would be is to use a client that is already established on the Linux operating system; you would issue the following command line:

Ssh -1 my_keypair.pem ec2-67-202-62-112.compute-1.
amazonsws.com

This will give you root access to the instance(s) that you have previously created. In terms of the Windows environment, you will need to open the following file type:

My_keypair.pem

From here you would use the "Get Windows Password" button that is located on your customized AWS Instance page. This will now return the administrative password that can be used to connect to your newly created instance using the Remote Desktop Protocol (RDP), which can be selected as follows:

- Select "Start."
- Select "All Programs."
- Select "Accessories."
- Select "Remote Desktop Connection."

This same logic can also be applied to the EC2 command-line interface. In this regard, the EC3 makes use of a specialized API in order to initiate and launch any form of specialized operations at hand. This API consists of the command-line tools that can be downloaded very easily, from the "Amazon EC2 API Tools." It will be made available to you as a zipped (compressed) file. These tools are written in Java, and thus, they can run in a Linux, UNIX, or even a Windows-based environment in the appropriate Java Runtime Environment.

After these tools have been unpacked from the zipped file, the next step is to establish the environment variables, which is the discussed in the next section.

SETTING UP THE ENVIRONMENT VARIABLES

The first command that is executed specifies the directory in which the Java Runtime Environment will be placed. It is important to note that PATHNAME should be the full and complete pathname of the directory structure in which the "java.exe" file can be located.

The second command then further specifies the location of the directory in which the EC2 tools reside. TOOLS_PATHNAME must be used in order to establish the full and complete pathname of the directory, which is found by the following code:

Sc2-api-tools-A, B -nnn

The third command will now execute and establish the path where the EC2 command utilities are located. This is illustrated as follows:

For a Linux environment:

```
$export JAVA_HOME = PATHNAME
$export EC2_TOOLS = TOOLS_PATHNAME
$export PATH = $PATH : SEC2_HOME/bin
```

For a Windows environment:

```
C:\SET JAVA_HOME = PATHNAME
C:\SET EC2_TOOLS = TOOLS_PATHNAME
C:\>SET PATH = %PATH%, %EC2_HOME%\bin
```

SETTING UP THE SECURITY ENVIRONMENT

Obviously, this is one of the most crucial aspects in any AWS environment that you create and implement. In other words, you want to have the EC2 command-line utilities to securely authenticate to your AWS instances at each point in time that you access them. In order to do this, you need to download an X.509 digital certificate as well as a private key, which will, in turn, authenticate the various HTTP requests that are sent to the AWS servers.

The X.509 digital certificate can be automatically generated by clicking on the "Account" link. From there, click on "Security Credentials." From here, there should be specific stepwise directions on getting your new certificate. The X.509 digital certificate files should also be downloaded onto an ".ec2" directory in a Linux/UNIX-based environment; and in a Windows-based environment, it should be set as follows:

```
C:\ec2
```

In order to launch the actual security environment, issue any of the following commands, depending on the environment in which you are currently working:

For a Linux environment:

```
$export EC2 – CERT = -/ .ec2/f1 .pem
```

For a Windows environment:

```
C:\ set EC2-CERT = -/ .ec2 / f1 .pem
```

SETTING UP THE REGION

The next step in this process is to set up the various regions that the EC2 command line tools will be working with. In fact, this is the exact location where the virtual machines will be created and established. In terms of the virtual sense, each region represents an actual AWS datacenter. Use the following command to test the EC2 command at this point:

Ec2 – describe – regions

Keep in mind that the default geographic location used in AWS Platform is the eastern region of the United States, and is specified by the following command:

Us-east-1

The service URL for this region is as follows:

http://ec2us-east-1.amazonaws.com

Any specific region can be set, and the following commands need to be issued, depending on the environment that you are working in:

For a Linux environment:

$export EC2-URL = https: //ENDPPOINT_URL>

For a Windows environment:

C:\>set EC2 – URL = https://<ENDPPOINT_URL>

The next subsection provides an overview of the computing resources that are available on EC2.

COMPUTING RESOURCES

The computing resources that are available on EC2 are often referred to as "EC2 instances." These consist of a combination of computing power resources, coupled with other types of resources; computer memory is the prime example. In AWS Platform, the computing power of an EC2 instance is measured by a metric known as "EC2 Compute Units," also known as "CU" for short. This concept is analogous to the way the term *bytes* is used to refer computing storage levels.

It is important to note that one level of an EC2 CU actually provides the same amount of computing power as a 1.2-GHz Opteron or Xeon processor. So, for example, a software developer who requests a resource at 1 EC2 CU (assuming that this is allocated specifically on a 2.4-GHz processor), will then obtain 50% of the CPU processing power.

This convention as described above allows software developers to request a standard amount of CPU processing power regardless of kind of hardware that is being used. However, the number of EC2 instances that a software development team may require for most projects can be seen in Table 2.1.

Other relevant instances that are available on the Amazon AWS Platform include the following:

- The High Memory Instance family (suitable primarily for databases)
- The High CPU Instance family (suitable primarily for compute-intensive based applications)
- The Cluster Compute Instance family (suitable primarily for High Performance Compute–based resources)
- The Cluster CPU Instance family [suitable primarily for graphics-intensive applications, measured by *graphic processing units* (GPUs)]

SOFTWARE ON EC2

AWS Platform has access to various combinations of operating systems and application software application packages. These are known specifically as *Amazon machine images* (AMIs). But this package should be requested when the EC2 instances are issued. The AMI package that is running on the EC2 package is also known as "Root AMI."

The operating systems that are available on the AMIs include the following:

- The various and kinds of Linux [which include the Red Hat Enterprise and SuSE (Software und System-Entwicklung) editions]
- Windows Server
- Solaris

The database packages that are supplied with the AMI include the following:

- IBM DB2
- Oracle
- Microsoft SQL Server

TABLE 2.1
EC2 Standard Instance Types

Instance Type	Compute Capacity	Memory (GB)	Local Storage (GB)	Platform
Small	1 virtual core of 1 CU	1.7	160	32-bit
Large	2 virtual cores, 2CU each	7.5	850	64-bit
Extra large	4 virtual cores, 2CU each	15	1690	64-bit

Source: Rountree and Castrillo, 2014

Other software packages that are supplied with the AMI include the following:

- Hadoop
- Apache
- Ruby on Rails

But these are not the only software packages that are available on the AMIs, and there are two ways in which to obtain what you require for the software development project. For example, you can just request a standard AMI package and then install those various software applications that you need. Or, you could import a specific VMWare image as an AMI by executing the following two commands in succession:

Ec2-import-instance-

Ec2-import-disk-image

REGIONS AND AVAILABILITY ZONES

As reviewed earlier, EC2 also has various geographic regions. With a specific region, there are multiple time zones that can be selected. A specific time zone that is selected is automatically linked to a virtual datacenter that is isolated. The primary advantage of having multiple instances created is that a business or corporation could possess a very powerful configuration that is fault-tolerant in case of a failure in one specific region.

LOAD BALANCING AND SCALING

EC2 is also available with a tool known as the "Elastic Load Balancer." This is a sophisticated service available on AWS Platform that balances the various loads across the multiple serves that are being used. There is a default load-balancing policy, and that is to treat and regard all load-balancing tools as being independent from one another.

However, the software development team can also have timer-based and application-controlled sessions, as well. For example, successive requests can be routed to the same AWS server, based on the time and applications variables and constraints. The load balancer can also either scale up or scale down the number of servers, depending on how light or heavy the load is.

EC2 can be utilized as a failover policy as well, because if there a server failure, it is also detected by the load balancer. An example of this would be is if the load balancer detects that the load on a particular server is way too high, then it will create and initiate a new server instance.

EC2 STORAGE RESOURCES

The computing resources that are available in AWS Platform can also be utilized in conjunction with the various storage and network resources that are available. An example of this would be to use the S3 files to access an HTTP server. It is important to keep in mind that any software development project will perform multiple disk inputs and outputs (also known technically as "Ios").

So, in order to optimize the level of performance, the software development team also needs to have firm control over the storage configuration. The resources can be configured to resemble the physical disks that reside on the EC2 Server. These are also known as "Block Storage Resources." There are two types:

- The Elastic Block Service (EBS)
- The Instance Storage

Elastic Block Service

To utilize Elastic Block Storage Service for EC2, the software development team can request a specific Elastic Block Service volume of a certain size. This can then be attached to a volume of multiple EC2 instances, making specific use of the instance ID when the volume was created. It should be noted that Elastic Block Service has an existence that is totally separate from any other kind of EC2 instance.

Instance Storage

It should be noted that every instance of an EC2 also has a local storage pool that can be configured as well, and this is specifically known as "Instance Storage." Table 2.2 depicts the default portioning of the instances that are associated with each EC2 instance.

One should remember that the Instance Storage that is created and executed will exist for only as long the specific EC2 instance is in existence as well. Also, this Instance Storage cannot be attached to any other type or kind of other EC2 instance. Additionally, if the EC2 instance is terminated for some reason, then the Instance Storage is also terminated at the same time.

This can be a serious limitation in a large-scale and complex software development project, and thus, a software developer can use either Elastic Block Service or

TABLE 2.2

Partitioning of Local Storage in Standard EC2 Instance Types

OS	Small	Large	Extra Large
Linux	/dev/sda1: root file system	dev/sda1: root the system	/dev/sda1: root the system
	/dev/sda2 /mnt	/dev/sdb: /mnt	/dev/sdb: /mnt
	/dev/sda3: /swap	dev/sdc	dev/sdc
		/dev/sdd	/dev/sdd
		/dev/sde	/dev/sde
		/dev/sda1: C:	/dev/sda1: C:
Windows	/dev/sda1: C:	/dev/sda1: C:	/dev/sda1: C:
		Xvdb	Xvdb
		Xvdc	Xvdc
		Xvdd	Xvdd
		xvde	xvde

Source: Rountree and Castrillo, 2014

TABLE 2.3

Key Comparisons between Instance Storage and Elastic Block Storage

Feature	Instance Storage	Elastic Block Storage
S3 Snapshot	Can be snapshotted to S3	Can be snapshotted to S3
Creation	Created by default when an EC2 instance is created	Created independently of EC2 instances
Sharing	Can be attached only to the EC2 instance from which it has been created	Can be shared between EC2 instances
Attachment	Attached by default to an S3-backed instance; can be attached to EBS-backed instances	Not attached by default to any particular instance
Persistence	Not persistent; it vanishes if the EC2 instance is terminated	Persistent even if the EC2 instance is terminated

Source: Rountree and Castrillo, 2014

S3 for repetitive storage and sharing. Also, Elastic Block Storage can be attached to an instance, as needed.

Table 2.3 illustrates some very important differences between Instance Storage and Elastic Block Storage.

S3-Backed versus EBS-Backed Instances

As can be seen from Table 2.3, EC2 compute- and storage-based resources behave in slightly different formats. This is dependent on whether the root AMI for a specific EC2 instance is stored in either the Amazon-based S3 or in Amazon Elastic Block Service. It should be noted that that these specific instances are also known as "S3-backed instances" and "EBS-backed instances."

For example, in the case of an S3-backed instance, the root AMI is literally stored in S3. As a result, it must be copied to the root device in any EC2 instance before it can be executed and launched. However, because this level of Instance Storage is not in a persistent state, any form of alteration made to the AMI of an S3-backed instance will not remain in any persistent state for more than the lifetime of that specific instance.

EC2 Networking Resources

In this regard, EC2 also offers a software development team both public and private TCP/IP addresses. It even has DNS-based services for management of DNS names that are associated with those exact TCP/IP addresses. Any access to these addresses is set up and controlled by various policies that have been established. The virtual private Cloud that is supplied in EC2 can make it possible to provide a secure line of communication between a corporate intranet and the EC2 network that it is currently utilizing.

Also, the software development team can create and implement a total, logical subnetwork and expose it to a public one based on its own set of firewall rules. EC2 also offers Elastic TCP/IP Addresses, which are independent of any other instance. Thus, it can be used to support fault tolerance and server failures.

INSTANCE ADDRESSES

Each instance of an EC2 has at least two TCP/IP addresses that are associated with it, namely, the public TCP/IP address and the private TCP/IP address. The latter can be resolved (as well as its DNS name) only from within EC2 Cloud. For any form of communication to transpire between the various EC2 instances, the internal TCP/IP address is the most effective one to make use of, since and data packets can flow through the entire AWS-based network.

It should be noted that the public TCP/IP address and its associated DNS name can be used outside the realm of the Amazon Cloud.

ELASTIC TCP/IP ADDRESSES

These types of TCP/IP addresses are totally independent of any instance, and thus, they can be assigned in a dynamic, real-time fashion to any instance that is involved in the software development project at hand. For this reason, they are very effective for deploying any failover techniques. For example, if one EC2 instance has failed, the Elastic IP address can then be assigned in a dynamic fashion to another EC2 instance. But it is important to note that other Elastic TCP/IP addresses cannot be assigned automatically; rather, they must be created when they are needed and from there, manually assigned.

ROUTE 53

Suppose that a business or corporation wants to make use of a *uniform resource locator* (URL). Since the EC2 by default resides within the domain of www.amazon.com, a URL cannot be thus assigned from an external environment. This is where Route 53 comes in. It is a DNS-based server that can be used to associate an Elastic TCP/IP address or even a public TCP/IP address with any domain (or URL) that is created and implemented by the software development team.

SECURITY GROUPS

In order to create a strong level of security, it is very common for a software development team to set forth and establish various network security policies that restrict certain ports. This can restrict the virtual machines that can be accessed, or which TCP/IP address can access which server. This same concept can also be applied to the EC2 instances.

For our purposes here, a *security group* is defined as a cumulative collection of the network security policies that have been created and implemented. Different security groups should be created for different server types. The default security group allows the EC2 instance to connect to any publicly available TCP/IP address, but it will forbid and disallow for any incoming network connections to occur.

VIRTUAL PRIVATE CLOUD

This is a type of Cloud infrastructure that gives the business or corporation that would like to have more control over their network configuration. This is where the virtual private Cloud (VPC) comes into play. Following are examples of the advanced networking feature that is offered by a VPC:

- The ability to allocate and distribute both public and private TCP/IP addresses to any other instance from any TCP/IP range
- The ability to divide the TCP/IP addresses into both subnets and allow for control between subnets to occur
- The ability to connect an EC2 network with a corporate intranet using a virtual private network (VPN) tunnel

How to Set Up a Web Server

In this section, we take all the concepts just described and review step by step how a software development can build a Web-based server (see Figure 2.3). In this case, it is assumed that a Web server will be created in an EBS-backed instance. The Web server is created and launched in these four major steps:

1. Select the AMI for the instance that will be used.
2. Create the EC2 instance and from there, install the server.
3. Attaching a separate EBS volume for the data (this would include such items as the HTML files).
4. Establish and implement the various networking and access rules (this is also known as "allowing external access to the web server").

In this project, two more assumptions are made:

- All the relevant data points, such as the HTM files, scripts, and .exe files, have already been uploaded onto EC2.
- The required Web server has also been uploaded to EC2.

FIGURE 2.3   Building an Amazon Web Service server.

Selecting the AMI

In order to select the right AMI for your software development project, you can use the drop-down menu to select "Amazon Images" and "Amazon Linux." This will populate with many images that are available on the Linux platform, which are, in turn, available on the AWS. On the screen that appears, there will be some key parameters for you to examine, which include the following:

- **Root Device Column:** This indicates whether the root device for the selected image(s) is for the Elastic Block Storage.
- **Description Tag:** Since it is the Linux platform that is primarily being used, this field will populate with a 64-bit Amazon Linux image with the root device set to /dev/sda1 in the Elastic Block Storage.
- **Block Devices Field:** Here, you will find the "DeleteUponTerminate" flag. This will indicate whether the device is persistent. In our model, we assume that it is persistent; therefore, this will completely disappear if this instance of the EC2 also vanishes.
- **Launch Button:** This will bring up the launch wizard and will go through a series of iterations before the EC2 instance is executed.

Creating the EC2 Instance

This will be done using a command-line approach. The following two steps must transpire here:

- Creating the keypair that provides access to the EC2 servers that are created
- Creating a security group that will be associated with that instance, and specifying the networking rules and policies that will be set forth

The keypair can be created from the EC2 console, by clicking on the "Key Pair" link. You then create a script to set up an environment label, which is known as "EC2-PRIVATE-KEY."

Script for the Linux Platform:

```
$export EC2-PRIVATE-KEY = ~/ .ec2/f2.pem
$ec2addgrp "Web Server" -d "Security Group For Web Servers"
$ec2run ami – 74f006 – b dev/ sda1 = :: false -k f2.pem -g "Web Server"
```

Script for the Windows Platform:

```
C:\> set EC2-PRIVATE-KEY = C:\.ec2\f2.pem
C:\> ec2addgrp "Web Server" – d "Security Group for Web Servers"
C:\> ec2run ami – 74f0061d -b "xvda=::false" -k f2.pem -g "Web Server"
```

Here is what the various commands mean:

- **ec2addgrp:** A new security group called "Web Server" is thus created, and it disallows all external access to it.
- **ec2run:** This is used to execute a persistent instance an EBS root volume.
- **False:** This indicates that the "DeleteUponTerminate" flag in this volume is actually set to false. This means that the volume instance will not be deleted even if the EC2 instance is terminated, for whatever reason.
- **-k -g:** This specifies the keypair that can be used to communicate with this particular instance and the security groups that are associated with them.
- **-instance -count:** This specifies the number of specific instances that can be launched.

At this stage, it is important to note that the DNS name for the newly created EC2 instance can come directly from the AWS console itself. You can also use the following command for this very same purpose:

Ec2-describe-instances

Once this has been accomplished, you can then use tools like SSH, PuTTY, or even the Remote Desktop Connection Protocol to log into the newly created EC2 instance and download the needed software packages. Once these have been downloaded, the AMI image can then be saved using the Elastic Block Storage, by executing this following command:

Ec2-create-instance

From here, the variable parameter known as "instanceId" then becomes the instance ID of the relevant EC2 instance that was just created. The newly created AMI ID is then established. These steps are further illustrated by the following scripts:

Script for the Linux Platform:

```
$ec2din
$ssh -1 f2.pem instance-id
$ec2-create-instance -n "Web Server AMI instanceId
```

Script for the Windows Platform:

```
C:\>ec2-describe-instances
C:\>putty
C:\>ec2-create-instance -n "Web Server AMI" instanceId
```

Attaching an EBC Volume

Because the HTML pages must be in a persistent state, you need to create another Elastic Block Storage volume to just hold these pages. These pages will then be served by the newly created Web server. To do this, from the EC2 Console, click on the "Volumes" link.

This will then bring up all the relevant Elastic Storage Block volumes that are currently owned and being used by the software development team. The "Create Volume" option will then bring up a screen where the size of this needed Elastic Storage Block volume (to hold the HTML files) can be specified.

The device name can then be specified as follows:

For a Linux Environment:

/dev/sdf **to** /dev/sdp

For a Windows Environment:

Xvdf **to** xvdp

Once this has been specified, click on the "Attach" button to attach the newly created Elastic Storage Block volume to the selected instance. Now, here is what has happened cumulatively thus far:

- The EC2 instance has been created.
- The Web Server has been installed.
- A separate, persistent store on the Elastic Block Storage has been created and attached.

Allowing External Access to the Web Server

Now that the Web Server has been created and launched, external access to it can be made possible. To do this, click on the "Security Groups" link located at the left side of the EC2 Console. This will bring up a listing of all the available security groups.

From here, click on the "Inbound Tab" to input rules that will specify the type of network traffic that will be allowed to reach to it. For example, you can allow this kind of traffic on Port 80 from all the relevant TCP/IP addresses. If you need to add in just a specific TCP/IP address, then click on the "Add Rule" button.

Once all the rules have been applied, click on the "Apply Rule Changes" button. This will implement and activate the newly created rules. Once external access to Web Server is allowed, it essentially becomes its own demilitarized zone (DMZ). This is a specific region in an AWS platform where external access can also be granted. If you disable the external access from other servers, then they become totally inaccessible from the DMZ.

A REVIEW OF THE AMAZON SIMPLE STORAGE SERVICE (S3)

Amazon Simple Storage Service (also known as S3") has become literally the de facto standard for software developers worldwide in terms of infrastructure as a structure (IaaS). This section reviews AWS S3 in more detail, by focusing on the following issues (see also Figure 2.4):

FIGURE 2.4   Focusing on Amazon Simple Storage Service.

1. Accessing S3
2. Getting started with S3
3. Organizing data in the S3: buckets, objects, and keys
4. S3 administration
5. Regions

ACCESSING S3

S3 can be accessed in three different ways:

- Via AWS Console
- Via the GUI to AWS
- Via a REST-ful API with HTTP functionalities such as GET, PUT, DELETE, and HEAD

It is important to note that since S3 is a specific storage service, there are numerous S3 browsers in existence in order to fully explore the account by the software development team. Also, various file systems are available that allow the software development team to treat their respective S3 accounts just like another local directory structure on their workstation.

GETTING STARTED WITH S3

Here is the typical scenario as to how a software development team would get started with S3:

1. One can sign up for at the following URL:

   http://aws.amazin.com/s3

   Once you sign up for an account, you then receive what is known as a "AWS Access Key" and a "AWS Secret Key." These are similar to the user ID–password combination that is used to grant authorization for all the transactions that transpire from within AWS Plaform.

2. From here, you can access S3 from AWS Management Console at this link:

   https://console.aws.amazon.com/s3/home

3. Next, create a bucket by giving it a name that is specific and unique to your software development project. All S3 files are called "objects," and these are all stored in the bucket. This bucket then represents a collection of the related objects that are at hand.

4. Next, click on the "Upload" button and from there, follow the instructions to upload your respective files.

5. All your files should now be uploaded, and they are also automatically backed up to the S3. Further, these files can now be shared provided the appropriate permissions have been granted.

ORGANIZING DATA IN S3: BUCKETS, OBJECTS, AND KEYS

The software development files in the S3 are called "objects." From here, objects are then referred to as "keys." A key is essentially an extra directory pathname that is followed by the name of the object at hand. It is important to note that the objects in the S3 are duplicated (or replicated) across many geographic locations. The purpose of this is to establish a multilayer failover system in case of any outages in these specific geographic areas.

If any further object versioning is required, recovery is thus possible from any accidental deletions or modifications. The fully versioned S3 object can be up to 5 TB in size, and there are no limits whatsoever on the total number of objects that can be stored onto a specific bucket. Further, a software development team can have up to 100 buckets per account, and an unlimited number of objects can be stored into any kind of bucket.

Also, each object has an associated key, and this can be utilized as the direct path to the resources in the URL. For instance, if a bucket is named RAVIDAS, and the key to it has an object called "technical document," then the URL becomes the following:

http://s3.amazonaws.com/RAVIDAS/technical document.doc

or

http://s3.amazonaws.com/tehnical document.doc

For ease of notation, slash-separated keys are used heavily in order to create and establish a directory-like naming convention so that standard browsing can take place in S3 Explorer. It should be noted that S3 is not a hierarchical filenaming system. This is because the bucket namespace is shared, and thus, it is not at all possible to create and establish a bucket with a specific name that already has been used by another S3 user.

Also, entering preceding-level URLs into a web browser will not work. This is so because certain values are purely test data and are thus fictional in nature. Even if real-world values were to be selected and used, the software development team would receive the following error message:

HTTP 403 Forbidden

The primary reason for this is that the URL lacks any form of authentication parameters. Also, the S3 objects are private by default, and further, any requests should carry the authentication parameters only to prove that the person requesting them has the needed rights to access that object (unless the object has any form of public permissions attached to it).

Also, the client library, or the SDK, will typically make use of the AWS Access Key as well as the AWS Secret Key in order to calculate a specific signature that completely identifies the requester. This should then be attached to the signature of the S3 request.

So, for example, a file by the name of "TECHNICAL DOCMENT XYZ" will be stored in the "awsdocs" bucket at the following URL:

S3/latest/s3-gsg.pdf

The associated key will remain anonymous in nature and will have read permissions that are attached to it. Thus, this document will then become available to the entire software development team at the following URL:

http://s3amazonaws.com/awsdocs/s3/latest/s3-gdg.pdf

S3 ADMINISTRATION

In any business or corporation, any kind of dataset is always conjoined to various rules in order to determine its location, availability, and those members of the software development team who do or don't have access to them. For this reason, one should possess the ability to audit and log all sorts of information and data. Also, this person should also be able to correct any accidental end-user actions. S3 possesses all these functions, which are described in further detail in the next subsections.

Security

Security is provided in two different aspects.

Access Control

The S3 function offers a feature known as *access control*, which consists in storing the objects in the S3 buckets. From this, the end user can thus establish and implement permissions that allow others access to their objects. This can be achieved via AWS Management Console. Establishment of the permissions can be initiated by a right click of the mouse on an object. In turn, this will bring up the "Object Actions Menu," from which the granting of rights such as read access will make objects readable to everybody on the software development team. This can be established by making use of the "Make Public" option on the object menu.

One can also restrict (or narrow down) the various read/write permissions by making use of the "Properties" tab. From here, another menu appears that allows the members of the software development team to enter their respective email addresses to be considered for granting of read/write permissions.

Also, members of the software development team can allocate objects into a bucket in a very similar fashion. A typical example of this is for documentation to be uploaded that has to revised, edited, or altered in any manner that is deemed necessary. These documents can then be stored in a different bucket, where the customers of the software development project can then have permissions created in order have these revised documents delivered directly to them.

The Collection of Audit Logs

These displayed logs allow the members of the software development team to turn on the "Logging Functionality" for a bucket. These logs contain the following information:

- Which AWS account has been accessed for the objects.
- The time of the access.
- The TCP/IP address from which the various accesses took place.
- The specific operations that were performed.

The logging functionality can be enabled from AWS Management Console, or it can be initiated at the time the bucket has been created and launched.

Data Protection

The S3 has two features that prevent any loss of information and data.

The Default Setting

The S3 automatically replicates data across the multiple storage devices, and by design, it has been customized to have the ability survive two replica failures.

Reduced Redundancy Storage (RRS)

This feature is used for information and data that are deemed noncritical in nature. With this functionality, the datasets in RSS are designed to be replicated twice and to have the ability to survive at least one replica failure. It should be noted that AWS Platform does not offer any sort of consistency guarantee among all the replicas that have been created. In other words, versioning is not guaranteed by default; this is discussed next.

Versioning

It is important to note that versioning must be enabled onto a bucket. Once this functionality is enabled, S3 will automatically store the full history of all the objects in that certain bucket from the specific period of time when it was first established and onward. Also, the object can be restored to a previous (or prior) version, and even undo any type of accidental deletes. This provides assurances to the software development team that the datasets will never be lost or just simply "disappear."

Regions

For many reasons, especially from an optimization, resource allocation, and performance standpoint, it could very well be necessary to have the S3 data located and running in separate geographic regions. This task can be accomplished at the level of the bucket by selecting that region in which the bucket is stored when it is first created by the software development team.

It is important to note that in the present context a *region* refers to a very large geographic area, such as Europe, Canada, the United States, India, or China.

Large Objects and Multipart Uploads

The size limit for any object created on the S3 is 5 TB. But if, for some reason, this is not estimated to be enough, the object can be broken down, separated, and stored into smaller chunks. The recomposition of the data in this regard is managed by the application itself. The software development team needs to keep in mind that uploading large S3 objects can take a generous amount of time to accomplish.

If an entire upload fails, then it needs to be reuploaded multiple times until there is success. But if this is the case, then it is highly recommended that you take the approach of a multiple-upload process, where chunks of data are uploaded separately and then reconstituted once again in the S3 bucket. In fact, S3 also provides specialized APIs just for this and has functionality for the software development team to write customized scripts to facilitate a multiple-transfer process based upon the needs of their project.

It is important to note that multiple-transfer uploads can also be done in parallel with one another, in order to maximize both speed and network utilization. An advantage of uploading by this method is that if one upload fails, then only that specific upload needs to be attempted again. At the present time, S3 can support up to 10,000 parts per object.

Amazon Simple DB

This unique package provides a rudimentary data storage pool interface that is in the form of a key-value store. The purpose of the SDB is to allow for the storage and retrieval of a set of attributes based on the values and the attributes that the key possesses. This process is a well-chosen alternative to the relational databases that make use of SQL-based command lines.

Data Organization and Access to Amazon Simple DB

The datasets that reside in Amazon SDB are organized and divided up into various domain structures. Each dataset can have up to 256 attributes, which become name-value pairs. As it is associated with the relational model, in each row there is a primary key that translates the attribute name-value pairs. Unlike a *relationship database management system* (RDBMS), the attributes in Amazon SDB can also have multiple values with them. Finally, SDB has a query language that is very similar to that of SQL, but unlike it, SDB can also automatically index all the attributes in real time.

SDB Availability and Administration

It should be noted that SDB possesses various features that maximize its efficiency and effectiveness. For instance, the data stored in an SDB is automatically replicated across different geographic locations to increase the level of availability. It will also add various compute resources that are in proportion to the request rate and will also index all the datasets automatically that correspond to these specific requests. There is no built-in schema in an SDB, which means that fields can be added to the various datasets on an as-needed basis.

The Amazon Relational Database Service

This specific package is a MySQL instance, which is based in the Cloud. From here, an RDS instance can be created by using the RDS tab In AWS Management Console. In this regard, AWS also performs many of the administrative tasks that are associated with relational database management. For example, it is regularly backed up, and can be as frequent as 5 minutes. The backup is then retained for whatever time period is deemed necessary and can be as long as 8 days. AWS also provides the ability to create separate snapshots of the database. Once again, all of this can be done via AWS Console, or likewise, the software development team can also create and implement a customized tool that can conduct these tasks the RDS APIs, as discussed earlier.

A REVIEW OF AWS SECURITY SERVICES

As we all know, the cyber security threat of today is changing on a constant and daily basis. It seems that once one cyber attack is launched, the next comes in just after a few minutes, like the salvo of an artillery barrage. For this reason, it has become sort of like a "cat and mouse" game, where the cat is the cyber attacker and the and the "mouse" is the victim.

Trying to combat these cyber attacks can be a very daunting task, as it can take a very long time for a business or corporation to not only recover from a Cyber attack but also to investigate what exactly happened, and how it all transpired can take even longer. Unfortunately, during this time period, an entire barrage of new cyber attacks could transpire.

Yet, it is important to keep in mind that most cyber attacks are not entirely new ones; rather, they are variants from preexisting ones. However, they have become more sophisticated and powerful, and in a way this can be compared to the old adage of "building a better mouse trap." A perfect example of this is the "phishing" cyber attack. Many new variants have come from this, which include "business email compromise" and "spear phishing."

In the end, of the most sought-after attacks for cyber attacks is actual Cloud infrastructure itself. There are numerous reasons for this; one of them is that many businesses and corporations are now moving their IT infrastructure from on premises ("on prem") to the Cloud. This transition brings in a lot of valuable information and data that a cyber attacker can go after, especially those of customer data (credit card information, Social Security numbers, etc.) and confidential company assets as well, such as intellectual property.

In this regard, even AWS Platform is significantly prone to a large cyber attack. As has been demonstrated throughout this entire chapter, AWS Platform is the largest of its kind in the world, hosting hundreds on hundreds of software development projects. As a result, AWS has become a "target-rich environment" for the cyber attacker.

Therefore, securing AWS Platform is of prime importance. In fact, the remaining chapters of this book discuss in great detail how Cloud infrastructure can be fortified and protected, for example, the specific strategies that can be used to mitigate the risk of cyber attacks to Cloud Infrastructure, and how to create the appropriate backup and recovery procedures.

But for the purposes of this chapter, we focus primarily on AWS Platform, and focus on two key areas in which the software development team can beef up their levels of protection:

- How to establish AWS security credentials
- How to conduct a security audit

THE ESTABLISHMENT OF AWS SECURITY CREDENTIALS

Whenever you first get started with AWS Platform, you must first set up the AWS credentials in order to confirm who you are and also to determine whether you access the specific resources that you need. In this regard security credentials are thus used for authentication and authorization in order to give you the access that you need to your software development project.

It is important to note that that all the accounts in AWS Platform are established at the root level. This will give you full access to the resources that are in your account. Thus, they should be kept in a safe and secure place, such as AWS Identity and Access Management (IAM). With the use of this tool, you can easily control how AWS Platform resources as well as the related services are accessed by members of the software development team.

Unique credentials can be created for all members of the software development team; therefore, credentials will not have to be shared.

Types of Security Credentials

The software development team should make use of the different types of security credentials according to their specific needs as dictated by the application development project. For instance, at AWS Management Console, you will have to create a basic username and password. Or, if you need to make source-based calls to the various APIs, then the access keys should be used. Following are examples of the types of security credentials that can be established from within AWS Platform:

1 **Email and the Password:**
   When the software development team signs up for an AWS account, an initial email and password have to be created. These credentials can then be used to sign into the secure web pages such as AWS Discussion Forums, AWS Management Console, and AWS Support Center. Keep in mind that these credentials that are established will have root access that are associated with them.

2 **IAM Password and Username:**
   When multiple applications and individual members of the software development team need access to the root AWS Platform account, the Identity and Access Management (IAM) tool should be utilized. With this method, unique IDs can thus be created for all members of the software development team, by using their own username and password combinations.

3 **Multifactor Authentication (MFA):**
   This provides extra layers of authentication that can also be applied to AWS Platform. Along with your username and password, you will be provided an authentication code, which makes up the two levels of security. Of course, more permissions can be created and applied at a granular level or at deeper levels of the software development project. This MFA can also be applied to the various IAM users and the root account.

4 **Access Keys:**
   These are composed of an Access Key ID and a Secret Access Key. This type of credential is used for making requests to access or make alterations to the source code. AWS Software Development Kits (SDKs) will also make use of the access keys that you create so they can automatically sign the request that you are making. But if you do not have an SDK, then these requests can also be made manually, on a case-by-case basis.

   The access keys can also be used at the Command-Line Interface (CLI). If you ever use the CLI in development of the source code, any commands that you issue and execute will be automatically signed by the access keys as well. Temporary access keys can also be created as well, and these are more commonly referred to as "temporary security credentials." These also have a security token that must be submitted to AWS Platform. These keys have a limited lifespan, and once they expire, they can no longer be reissued. These kinds of keys are typically given out to contractors or other temporary employees on your software development team.

5 **Keypairs:**
   These comprise both public and private keys. The former is used to confirm the validation of a digital signature, and the latter is used for the sole purpose of creating an actual digital signature. These keypairs are used only in AWS CloudFront and Amazon EC2. With regard to the latter, the keypairs

should be used only for accessing EC2 instances such as making use of SSH for logging into an instance of Linux.

How to Obtain Security Credentials

Once you have lost or forgotten any of your security credentials, they are lost for good. This has been set up by design as a security feature in AWS Platform. For example, AWS Platform will not allow for the retrieval of passwords or secret keys, nor will it allow for the storage of private keys. But new sets of credentials can always be created, and once this is done, the old credentials are then disabled or deleted.

The following is the stepwise process in which to create new access for the root user:

1. At AWS Management Console, go to the page titled "Security Credentials."
2. From there, select "Continue to Security Credentials."
3. Select "Access Keys (Access Key ID and Secret Access Key."
4. Select "Create New Access Key."
5. Select "Show Access Key or Download Key File."

AWS Account Identifiers

In AWS Platform, each account is assigned two IDs:

- An AWS account ID
- A canonical user ID

The *account ID* for AWS Platform has 12 digits, and this is required for creation of the Amazon Resource Names. Once you begin to refer to the resources such as Amazon Glacier or an IAM user, the account ID will differentiate your resources from those of other AWS accounts that are involved in the scope of the software development project.

The *canonical user ID* can be used in Amazon S3 bucket policy for the sole purpose of cross-account access, which simply means that one AWS account can access the resources of another AWS account. For example, when you need to grant another member of your software development team access to your bucket, you can do this by specifying the canonical user ID for your account in the access policy that you have formulated in your own bucket.

It is also important to note that an access key is made up of an access key ID and a secret key.

Removing Root Account Access

When anybody has an access key for the root account, this usually means that s/he has unrestricted access to the entire AWS Platform account, even including the confidential billing information. Permissions cannot be restricted at the root level.

Thus, to protect your AWS Platform account, you should not have an access key for the root account. (This is one of the most practical approaches.) Alternatively, one or more IAM users can be created instead, and granting them the necessary permissions, and from there, you should make sure that they use those credentials to interact with AWS Platform on a daily basis.

However, if you have created an access key for the AWS Platform account, check those parts of the software development project where you are using that access key. From there, then replace the root access key with an IAM user access key instead. Only the designated head of the software development team should have the ability to disable and remove the root access key.

Rotating Access Keys for IAM Users

It is important to note that access keys can be changed and rotated out on a regular basis; the sole purpose of this strategy is that this is a way to implement superb security practices for your AWS Platform. A primary advantage is that this kind of practice will reduce the lifespan in which access will remain active, thus reducing any downtime not only to a business or a corporation.

In order to rotate out an access key, the following steps must be adhered to:

1. Create a new access key; this will replace the existing one that you are currently using.
2. Update all the applications that you have in your AWS Platform so that the new access key can be used on them.
3. After creating the new access key, change the previous key to an inactive state.
4. Validate and confirm whether the applications in the software development project are working with the new access key.
5. Once the old access key has been deactivated, it is very crucial that you deactivate it.

Typically, it is the AWS Command Line Interface (CLI) that is used to create the new access key and rotate it. It will use various APIs from the IAM, so you can always use the AWS Software Development Kit for this approach as well. Alternatively, you can also use the GUI to create new access keys in IAM Management Console, which will be described further in the next subsection.

Here are the steps in creating a new access key and rotating it in, using the Command-Line Interface:

1. Install the CLI with the following command:
   Aws iam list-access-keys –user-name USER X
   After you execute this command, you will then get an output that looks like:

```
{
    "AccessKeyMetaata:[
        {
            "Username":  "USERX",
            "Status":  "Active",
            "CreateDate":  "2018-07-12T18:30:11Z"
```

```
    "AccessKeyId" : "AKIAI44QH8DHBEFORPROJECT"
  }
]
{
```

2. To create the access key, with this command:
   Aws iam create-access-key –user-name USERX
   After you execute this command, you will then get an output that looks like:

```
{
    "AccessKeyMetadata" : [
    {
      "Username" :   "USERX",
      "Status" : "Active",
      "CreateDate" :   "2018-07-12T18:30:11Z"
      "AccessKeyId" : "AKIAI44QH8DHBEFORPROJECT"
    },
    {
      "Username" :   "USERY",
      "Status" : "Active",
      "CreateDate" :   "2018-07-12T18:30:11Z"
      "AccessKeyId" : "AKIAI44QH8DHBEFORPROJECT"
    }
  ]
{
```

3. Now, distribute the access keys to the instances of the applications of the software development project that will make use of it. As a check, make sure that each instance is able to function with the new access key according to the requirements set forth.
4. Now, change the previous access key to an inactive state, by executing the following command:
   Aws iam update-access-key –access-key-id AKIAI44QH8DHBEFOR PROJECT –status Inactive –user-name USER X
5. After executing step 4, confirm that the key has been disabled by executing the following command:
   Aws iam list-access-keys –user-name USER X
   After you execute this command, you will then get an output that looks like:

```
{
    "AccessKeyMetaata : [
      {
        "Username" :   "USERX",
        "Status" : "Inactive",
        "CreateDate" :   "2018-07-12T18:30:11Z"
        "AccessKeyId" : "AKIAI44QH8DHBEFORPROJECT"
      },
      {
        "Username" :   "USERY",
```

```
              "Status": "Active",
              "CreateDate":  "2018-07-12T18:30:11Z"
              "AccessKeyId": "AKIAI44QH8DHBEFORPROJECT"
          }
   ]
   {
```

Important note: Now that the key is an inactive status, it cannot be used anymore to further authenticate AWS API calls. It is at this point that you need to make sure that the applications in the software development project are functioning at an acceptable level with the new access key. If, for some reason, something is not working properly, you can always reactivate the old access key by executing the following command:

Aws iam update-access-key

6. Once everything has been confirmed in the last step, you can now delete the previous access key by issuing the following command:

Aws iam list-access-keys –user-name USER X

```
  {
        "AccessKeyMetaata: [
          {
              "Username":   "USERX",
              "Status": "Active",
              "CreateDate":  "2018-07-12T18:30:11Z"
              "AccessKeyId": "AKIAI44QH8DHBEFORPROJECT"
          }
      ]
      {
```

Important note: Once the old key has been deleted, it is irreversible, and the process cannot be undone. The old access key for USERX will not be listed, as demonstrated in the output above. Also, if you use EC2 instances to create the access keys, then continue to use that same method, as the old access keys and new access keys will be rotated in and out automatically, respectively. But otherwise, it is always a good security practice to manually create new access keys and rotate the old ones out.

How to Create, Disable, and Delete Access Keys by Using AWS Management Console

The process presented above can also be done from a GUI perspective, at AWS Management Console, by following these steps:

1. Log into AWS Management Console with your login credentials, with either the username/password combination or the IAM user-based credentials.
2. After logging in, click on "Security Credentials."
3. On this page, expand out the section entitled "Access Keys (Access Key ID and Secret Access Key)."
4. Click on "Create New Access Key."

5. Click on "Download Key File," and from there, the access key ID and the secret key to the .csv file locally on your computer.
6. When you are ready to disable the old access key, click on "Make Inactive." If, for some reason, this needs to be enabled, click on the "Make Active" option.
7. To delete the old access key, click on "Delete."

How to Conduct a Security Audit

For any AWS Platform that is created and used, it is always a good security practice to audit the various configurations for your own system so that not only will it be in line with the fundamental goals of your software development project but also you will be proactive in keeping your AWS environment in a safe and secure environment.

By conducting a security audit, the administrator of AWS Platform will also be available to remove and delete any unauthorized IAM-based roles, users, groups, and policies.

Also, you will be ensuring that all the applications that are created in the development project and that all associated members on the software development team will have only the absolute minimum of permissions and access rights that they need to access AWS Platform.

However, given how large-scale software development projects are in an AWS Platform, is not necessary to conduct a security audit on a daily basis. It should be done only under the following conditions:

1. At periodic but regular intervals.
2. Whenever there are any changes in the business or corporation, such as with personnel changes on the software development team.
3. In case the software development team is not using one or more of the AWS services. In this case, it is always a good idea to remove and permanently delete the permissions of the users who are no longer on the software development team.
4. Any removal or addition of software packages from the Amazon EC2 instances, the AWS Cloud-Formation templates, and the AWS OpsWorks stacks, and so on.
5. In the case you suspect that an unauthorized user is accessing resources on your AWS Platform.

General Auditing Guidelines

Whenever you are reviewing the security configurations for your AWS Platform, follow these specific guidelines:

1. *Be complete and thorough.* This means that you should check on all the aspects of your security configuration, even the ones that you might not use regularly.

2. *Avoid making assumptions.* Do not merely assume something that you don't know with the security aspects of your AWS Platform. If you are unsure about something, always consult a cyber security specialist.

3. *Make things simple.* It is important to keep the security audit as simple and easy as possible, for the purposes of efficiency and effectiveness. In order to help with this, make sure that the software development group is making use of consistent naming schemes, IAM group naming conventions, and so on.

Reviewing AWS Account Credentials

Here are some general guidelines for auditing AWS account credentials:

1. If you are not making regular use of the root access keys, then just remove them. You should not use your AWS root credentials for daily usage. Rather, IAM-based permissions and access rights should be created and used on a daily basis.

2. If you need to keep your account's access keys, just rotate them out on a regular basis, as discussed in detail in the previous section.

Reviewing IAM Users

The following procedures are required in order to carry out a full audit of the IAM user credentials that have been established on your AWS Platform:

1. It is very important to delete any users who are not actively engaged and/or participating in the software development project.

2. Identify those groups in which those software developers do not absolutely have to belong, and delete them from the directory.

3. On a prescribed basis, always critically review the security policies governing those specific groups to which the software developers and other end users have been assigned and/or attached.

4. Also on a prescribed basis, identify the security credentials that could have been potentially exposed to the outside world, or the ones that are no longer needed. In these particular cases, just delete the password in its entirety. Also, from within AWS Platform, it is possible to generate a specific report that shows all the IAM users who are active or inactive in the AWS Platform and their corresponding security credentials. This report will also display how the established credentials have been used. If any of these credentials have not been used lately, then simply remove from AWS Platform.

5. Also, on an established timetable, keep rotating the security credentials of the members of the software development team; the use of a Password Manager software package will help in this process.

Reviewing the IAM Groups

The following procedures are required in order to carry out a full audit of the IAM groups that have been established on your AWS Platform:

1. Always delete any unused groups.
2. Remove those software developers and/or other users who do not belong or are actively participating in any groups.
3. On a prescribed basis, always review the security policies that have been created and implemented for each group on the AWS Platform.

Reviewing IAM Roles

The following procedures are required in order to carry out a full audit of the IAM roles that have been established on your AWS Platform:

1. Confirm and identify any roles from within AWS Platform that are not being used, and immediately delete them.
2. On a regular basis, also review the trust policies that have been established for each particular role.
3. On a prescribed basis, also review the access policies so that the correct permissions can be established going forward on the progress of the software development project.

Reviewing the IAM OpenID Connect and SAML

In those particular instances where an IAM identity has been created and established with an OIDC identity provider or even an SAML, it is important to follow these procedures:

1. Immediately delete any of the unused providers.
2. Make sure to download and review AWS Metadata from the SAML provider, and then confirm and also ensure that these documents are reflective of the current needs of the software development project and the AWS Platform on which it resides.

Reviewing the Mobile Apps

In the event that one or more mobile apps have been created in order to forward particular requests to AWS Platform, observe these steps:

1. Be sure that the mobile app has no embedded access keys attached to it, even if they have been kept in an encrypted storage pool.
2. Always obtain the temporary credentials for the mobile app(s) by making use of the APIs that have been created for this very specific purpose. One tool that can be used for this is the Amazon Cognito. This is a service that allows the members of the software development team to authenticate their login credentials by using Google, Amazon, Facebook, Twitter, LinkedIn, and so on. This service can also be used for the purpose of managing those credentials for which the mobile app(s) will use for making requests to the AWS Platform.

Reviewing the Amazon EC2 Security Configuration

The following procedures are required in order to carry out a full audit of the regions roles that have been established on your AWS Platform:

1. Always delete the Amazon EC2 keypairs that are not in use or those that might have been exposed to unauthorized users.
2. On a regular basis, also review the security groups for Amazon EC2. This can be done by identifying those security groups that do not meet the needs of the software development project, and then removing those rules. Make sure to take note of the network protocols, port numbers, and the TCP/IP address range that have been allowed and established for these groups.
3. Identify and confirm those instances that are not meeting the needs of the software development project. At this stage, it is important to note that once an instance has been created and started in a role, with the applications that are running on that instance, it will be in a position to access the resources that have been granted to that particular role.
4. Cancel the Spot Instance Requests that are not serving the needs of the software development project.

Monitoring the AWS Platform Activities

1. In every account that has been created, turn on AWS CloudTrail, and then make full use of it in each of its supported regions.
2. It is important to examine and critically review CloudTrail log files on a pre-established basis.
3. Enable the logging feature in the Amazon S3 bucket, as this will allow you to monitor requests as they are made on each bucket that has been created.
4. If there has been any unauthorized use on AWS Platform, disable all credentials (even the temporary ones that have been assigned) and create new login credentials.
5. Allow for the billing alerts to be enabled for each account, and then set up a cost threshold that will let you know if any charges are exceeding normal usage levels.

SOURCES

1. https://www.computerworlduk.com/galleries/cloud-computing/aws-12-defining-moments-for-the-cloud-giant-3636947/
2. https://docs.aws.amazon.com/aws-technical-content/latest/aws-overview/aws-overview.pdf?icmpid=link_from_whitepapers_page
3. Rountree, D., and I. Castrillo. *The Basics of Cloud Computing: Understanding the Fundamentals of Cloud Computing in Theory and Practice.* Elsevier, 2014.
4. Sammons, G. *The Introduction to AWS Beginner's Guide Book: Learning the basics of AWS in an Easy and Fast Way.* Desktop published document, 2016.

3 Threats and Risks to Cloud Infrastructure and Risk Mitigation Strategies

INTRODUCTION

Chapter 2 provided an extensive review of Amazon Web Services. This platform is deemed the world's largest Cloud computing infrastructure, even far surpassing that of Microsoft Azure, its next closest competitor. In summary, Chapter 2 specifically reviewed the following:

- An overview of the evolution of Amazon Web Services
- A review of the major components of Amazon Web Services:
  - AWS Management Console
  - AWS Command-Line Interface
  - AWS Compute Services
  - Amazon Simple Storage Service (Amazon S3)
  - AWS Database
  - AWS Migration
  - AWS Networking and Content Delivery
  - AWS Management Tools
  - AWS Software Development Tools
  - AWS Security, Identity, and Compliance
  - AWS Analytics
  - AWS Mobile Services
  - AWS Application Service
  - AWS Internet of Things (IoT)
  - AWS Artificial Intelligence
  - AWS Messaging
  - AWS Business Productivity
  - AWS Desktop & App Streaming
  - AWS Game Development

Of course, each of these major components has its many subcomponents as well, which were also examined in Chapter 2.

Other major three topics were reviewed in detail as well:

- Amazon Elastic Cloud Compute (EC2)
- Amazon Simple Storage Service (S3)
- AWS Security Services

DOI: 10.1201/9781003459569-3

These three components were examined in greater detail. For example, with regard to EC2, an example of how to build and launch a web server was provided. In terms of AWS Security Services, the entire credentialing process was reviewed, as well as the specific steps that are needed to conduct a complete security audit on AWS Platform.

As we transition over to the present chapter, we will focus on the security threats and risks to Cloud computing infrastructure. Given the extensive popularity and usage of all Cloud-related products and services, especially those that are available in AWS, this environment has become a prime target for cyber attackers to launch large-scale attacks.

There are many of these targets, and unfortunately, the list continues to grow on an almost daily basis because of the constantly changing and developing cyber threat landscape. In fact, it would take an entire series of books to describe them in detail. However, for the purposes of this chapter, we will provide detail only on some of the major and more recent risks and threats to the Cloud.

Therefore, the first third of this chapter will focus on these risks and threats, and the remainder of the chapter will focus on the risk and threat mitigation strategies that a business or corporation can undertake in order to protect their digital assets. We start with cyber threats and after that we will discuss Cloud risks.

CYBER THREATS TO THE CLOUD

In the world of Cloud Computing, there is often confusion between what a threat is and what a risk is. The primary reason for this is that the two are very often used synonymously with each other, although they both have their subtle differences.

Therefore, the specific definition of a Cyber threat (see also Figure 3.1) is as follows:

> The possibility of a malicious attempt to damage or disrupt a computer network or system in the Cloud ... the threat is more closely identified with the actor or adversary attempting to gain access to a system. Or a threat might be identified by the damage being done, what is being stolen or the Tactics, Techniques and Procedures (TTP) being used [1].

In this chapter, we provide a technical overview of the following Cloud threats:

1. Ransomware
2. Risk mitigation strategies for ransomware
3. Malware, spyware, and adware
4. Spear phishing
5. An incident response playbook for a phishing attack
6. Malware injection attacks
7. The malicious insider
8. Online cyber theft
9. Real-world examples of cyber threats to a Cloud infrastructure

FIGURE 3.1   Cyber security team examining Cloud threat dashboard.

RANSOMWARE

There is currently a new trend in Cloud infrastructure security threats: namely, cyber attackers want to hold your computer hostage until you literally pay a ransom payment. This kind of attack is known as *ransomware*, and it can be further elaborated on as follows:

> "It is a type of malware that prevents or limits a user's access to their computer system, either by locking the system's screen or by locking the user's files unless a ransom is paid" [2].

So, as you can see from the definition, ransomware is literally virtual kidnapping. You cannot access anything on your computer unless you pay the ransom that is demanded by the cyber attacker. But the caveat here is that the cyber attacker does not want to be paid in the normal currency; rather, s/he wants to be paid in terms of a virtual currency, known as the *bitcoin*.

HOW RANSOMWARE IS DEPLOYED

There are two primary ways for your Cloud infrastructure to be infected by ransomware:

1. **Via MalSpam:**
   This is essentially a spam email that comes into your inbox, but it contains a malware-based .EXE code that will launch itself once the attachment is downloaded and opened. These types of attachment are typically .DOC, .PPT, and

.XLS files. You can also get ransomware by clicking on a phony link in the content of the email message.

The techniques of social engineering are often used in this regard in order to make the email appear to be authentic and coming from either a trusted, legitimate organization or personal contact.

2. **Via Malvertising:**

This is when a cyber attacker uses online advertising in order to capture the unwitting attention of end users and ensnare them into clicking on a genuine-looking hyperlink. If this does happen, then the servers that are used by the cyber attacker will collect details about the soon to be victim's computer, and even where it is geographically located.

Once this has been accomplished, the ransomware attack is subsequently launched. Malvertising very often makes use of what is known as an infected "iframe." This is actually an invisible webpage element and will redirect the end user to an authentic-looking landing page. From there, the malicious code is then deployed onto the end user's computer.

TYPES OF RANSOMWARE ATTACKS

There are three types of ransomware that can attack Cloud computing infrastructure:

1. **Scareware:**

As the term implies, this kind of attack is designed merely to scare the victim. Scareware attacks primarily make use of annoying pop-up messages. One of the most famous of these is the pop-up claiming that some sort of malware has been detected on your computer, and in order to get rid of it, you have to pay a small ransom fee. You will know that you have been hit by a scareware attack if these pop-ups appear repeatedly. The only way to get rid of it is to install antimalware software, such as the ones available from Norton and Kaspersky.

2. **Screen Lockers:**

This is the next step up in terms of the severity level of ransomware attacks. With this type of attack, your computer screen locks up, and as a result, you are completely frozen from accessing your files and folders. To make matters even worse, the message that appears will typically have an FBI, Secret Service, or Department of Justice official seal, to make it look authentic and to fool you into believing that you have been caught doing some sort of illicit activity online.

In order to unfreeze your screen, there will also be a message that you have pay a rather hefty fine. But keep in mind that legitimate government agencies would never ask you to pay up front. Probably the best way to get your screen unlocked is to take it to a local Best Buy store and have Geek Squad employees clean your computer of the ransomware. If this doesn't work, you may have to buy a new computer all together.

3. **Encrypting Ransomware:**

These are considered to be the worst kind of attack. In encrypting ransomware attacks, the cyber attacker will steal your files and encrypt them with a very complex mathematical algorithm, which will be very difficult to crack. To get your files back, the cyber attacker will demand a large sum of money, to be paid by bitcoin.

Once they receive this money, they claim that they will send you the decryption key in order to not only retrieve your files but also unscramble them into a decipherable state (in other words, to return them to their original state before they were hijacked). But this rarely happens because once you pay up, the cyber attacker often disappears.

Since you have paid with a virtual currency, there is no way to track them down, either (unlike paper currency, where you can use marked bills for these purposes).

RISK MITIGATION STRATEGIES FOR RANSOMWARE

Detailed below are some top risk mitigation strategies:

1. **Always back up your data.**
   This should be a no-brainer, and in fact it is one of the oldest mantras in the word of cyber security. There are various methods for backing up your data. For instance, you can have both an on-premises solution and an off-premises solution. In fact, depending on the size of your data and files, it is recommended that you have both. With the former, it is highly recommended that you keep this backup in a different physical location, and with the latter, using the Cloud is the prime choice. Equally important is to make sure that you back up all your mission-critical files on at least a daily basis, if not more. So, if you ever do become a victim of a ransomware attack, all you have to do is procure another computing device(s) and restore your files from backup.

2. **Do not open any unfamiliar or suspicious-looking links or attachments in your email.**
   Believe it or not, sending out a phishing email is still one of the most favored techniques of the cyber attacker. Therefore, as mentioned above, do not click on any suspicious links or open any kind or type of email attachment that you do not expect to receive. Be especially careful of those file extensions that end with .DOC, .PPT, and .XLS.

   In this regard, it is also important to keep in mind that a cyber attacker will often use the name and email address of an individual in your electronic address book, in an attempt to make the fake email look legitimate.

   If you receive an email like this (in other words, not expecting it), always contact the sender to confirm whether s/he has actually sent the email. If not, *delete it immediately*!!! This warning also applies for those pop-up messages that appear in your web browser.

   They often make use of scare tactics so that you will be tempted to click onto the link that is imbedded in them. Very often, these links contain the ransomware .EXE files that will very quickly find their way into your computer if clicked on.

3. **Always keep your computer updated.**
   It is always important to keep your servers, computers, and even your wireless devices up to date with the latest software patches and upgrades. True, it may be inconvenient sometimes to do this (especially if you have Windows 10), but doing so will pay huge dividends in the end. Apart from this, there are also other preventive measures that you can take, which include the following:
   - Always keep your Adobe Flash Player, and other Java-based web browsers, up to date as well. This will help prevent any kind of "exploit kit" ransomware attacks from occurring.
   - Disable the VSSADMIN.exe file. This is an obscure file in Windows designed to administer what is known as the "Volume Shadow Copy Service." This is used to keep a version history of files in your computer that are not used very often, or that are deemed arbitrary in nature. Since very few people use this tool, it has become a favored avenue of the cyber attacker.
   - Disable the other automated services in Windows 10 operating systems. These include the following:
     - Script Host
     - Power Shell
     - Auto Play
     - Remote Services

4. **Shut down your entire computer system(s).**
   If you think you might be in the beginning stages of a ransomware attack, immediately unplug your computer. This action will help mitigate the actual .EXE file from entering your computer. However, if your IT infrastructure is large, shutting down the entire system is still your best bet.
   True, this will cause some downtime, inconvenience, and lost revenue, *but this cost is minimal* when compared to the scenario if your business or corporation were to be become an actual victim of a ransomware attack.

5. **Never, ever pay the cyber attacker.**
   If in the unfortunate case that you do become a victim, *never pay the cyber attacker under any circumstances*. There are two primary reasons for this:
   - Even if you do pay the ransom, there is no guarantee that you will get the decryption key with which to unlock your computer and files.
   - Paying the cyber attacker will only fuel their motivation and greed to launch more ransomware attacks.

Malware, Spyware, and Adware

In this section, we review the key differences between malware, spyware, and adware.

Malware

Malware is an abbreviated form of the term *malicious software*. It is defined as follows:

This is a software that is specifically designed to gain access or damage a computer without knowledge of the of the owner. There are various types of malware including key loggers, viruses, worms, etc. [3].

In a way, malware can be considered as a step up from adware. The goal is not to merely deploy a Trojan Horse virus to cause as much damage as possible to your Cloud environment, or even your smartphone. As noted in the definition, even a worm can be considered as a form of Malware.

In this regard, unlike adware, *malware can actually spread itself from one computer to another, in just a matter of a few minutes.* Some of the common objectives of the cyber attacker when deploying malware include the following:

- Gain covert, remote control to an unsuspecting machine.
- Send unwanted spam messages from an infected machine to other unsuspecting targets (this is also known as a "Botnet" attack, where the malware that resides on the infected device can be used to target thousands of other computers).
- Investigate in more granular detail the kind and type of network that the infected computer is using and steal any relevant information and data.

Spyware

As the term implies, spyware is designed to literally "spy" on you. It does not mean that you are being tracked down in a physical sense; but rather, your every move is being watched virtually. A formal definition of spyware is as follows: "It is any software that installs itself on your computer and starts covertly monitoring your online behavior without your knowledge or permission" [4].

Spyware is actually a subset of malware. But the main difference between the two is that the *former will collect your personal information and data.* The latter is just meant to cause widespread turmoil by spreading itself to hundreds if not thousands of computers.

Spyware literally uses up most of your network bandwidth and collects such items about you as your name, home address, web browsing habits, website preferences, and even what you download. This is mostly done with what is known as a "keylogger."

So, if you notice a drastic slowdown in your network connectivity for long periods of time, there is a good chance that your computer has been infected with some sort of spyware. Other telltale signs include that of unexpected "behaviors" on your computer, such as new icons appearing, a different toolbar in your web browser, system crashes, and even failure to boot your computer up properly.

Worse yet, if your computer is indeed infected with spyware, it can also serve as an invisible beacon alerting other cyber attackers that it has a weak spot and can thus be easily penetrated. So, in the end, you may not be dealing with just one cyber attacker; you could be dealing with many at the same time.

Adware

According to the security experts, adware can be specifically defined as "the name given to programs that are designed to display advertisements, and your redirect your search requests to advertising websites and collect marketing data about you" [5].

Adware used to appear merely as annoying pop-up messages in your web browser that you could just exit out of. But now, they have become much more covert and malicious in nature. For example, they can now deploy the Trojan Horse virus. These days, adware cannot even be seen; and there are two ways that your computer can get them:

1. **Via Free Software Packages or Other Shareware that You Might Download:** These are often used by the open-source software community as a way of funding their projects. But very often, cyber attackers can take advantage of this, and often create spoofed ads that look like the real thing. If ever in doubt, always contact the organization in question to confirm the legitimacy of their ads.
2. **Visiting an Infected Website:** Web browsers these days will warn you about a malicious website before you visit it; therefore, it is important that you pay attention to it. Any adware that is deployed from such a site is known specifically as "browser hijacking."

SPEAR PHISHING

As we know it today, phishing has become one of the most commonly used tactics by the cyber attacker in order to garner personal information and data from a Cloud infrastructure. This primarily involves our physical (street) addresses, email addresses, credit card numbers, banking and other financial information, Social Security numbers, and so on.

Phishing involves sending an email with either a malicious file (such as those .DOC and .XLS) or link. Once the victim has downloaded the files or clicked on the link (or perhaps even both), the malware (most likely a Trojan Horse) then spreads itself onto the victim's computer or wireless device.

Generally, phishing attacks involve sending mass emails out; in other words, there is not one targeted individual or organization. Whatever contact information the cyber attacker can get his/her hands on is used. But lately, there appears to be a new trend developing: a tactic known as "spear phishing," which can be defined specifically as follows:

> It is a phishing method that targets specific individuals or groups within an organization. It is a potent variant of phishing, a malicious tactic which uses emails, social media, instant messaging, and other platforms to get users to divulge personal information or perform actions that cause network compromise, data loss, or financial loss [6].

Thus, in these instances, the cyber attacker has already done some research ahead of time and knows who or what to specifically target. In a way, this is similar to that of a *business email compromise* (BEC) attack, in which the C-level executive is primarily targeted to transfer funds.

Trends in Spear Phishing

Just consider some of these alarming statistics of the magnitude that a spear phishing attack can have on a Cloud computing environment:

- At least 77% of the spear phishing attacks are laser-focused, targeting only 10 email inboxes, and only 33% of them are focused on just one email inbox.
- At least 47% of spear phishing attacks lasted less than 24 hours. All other types of phishing schemes lasted at least 30 days.
- Another tactic that the cyber attacker uses is what is known as the "drip campaign." For example, 35% of the spear phishing attacks lasted at least 12 months.
- The cyber attacker has become even stealthier in terms of bypassing the email spam filters. In these instances, 20% of spear phishing–based emails were able to get around these filters and make their way into the inbox.
- At least 42% of IT security professionals consider spear phishing to be one of the top three cyber attack concerns.
- At least 30% of the spear phishing campaigns are deemed successful.
- Compared to a general phishing campaign, spear phishing campaigns cost the victim 20 times more, and the return is 40 times greater.
- Cyber attackers will spend an enormous amount of time also trying to find a hidden "crack" or "hole" in the organization as a stepping stone to collect the relevant information or data on their victim.

What the Spear Phisher Is After

So how is that cyber attackers are so successful when launching these kinds of campaigns against your Cloud computing infrastructure? For starters, they are consistently honing their skills in conducting the research needed in order to launch a laser-focused attack. Moreover, they do not rely on fancy technology in order to execute a spear phishing campaign. Rather, they rely on the old-fashioned techniques of social engineering in which to thrust their attacks forward.

Cyber attackers demonstrate a considerable amount of patience. For instance, they spend an enormous amount of time researching their primary target. They are in no rush to get this task accomplished. The more accurate the information that they have, the greater the statistical probability that their well-crafted email will make it through the spam filters.

They often rely on social media sites that the individual or even the organization uses. They try to glean as much contact information as possible. An Internet-based background search is a commonly used tool as well. So, what is the cyber attacker exactly looking for when launching a spear phishing campaign? There are three main items of interest:

1. **Money, Money, Money, and Lots of It:**
   While other phishing-based campaigns focus on getting any kind of personal information and data, the cyber attacker, in this case, wants just one thing: your cash. As a result, they tend to target the following:
   - Credit card companies
   - Insurance organizations
   - Credit unions

- PayPal
- Amazon

In their spear phishing emails, cyber attackers do not traditionally attach a .DOC or .XLS file. Rather, they will instead attach an .HTML file, or include the relevant HTML data in the body of the message.

Victims will either download this attachment or click on the link and will then be taken to a very authentic-looking but spoofed website in which they enter their passwords. From this point, the cyber attacker then hijacks it, and logs into whatever online financial account they know that the victim possesses and steals as much money as possible.

According to the FBI, over 7000 financial related institutions have been targeted since 2015, which has resulted in a loss of well over $612 million.

2. **Waiting for Specific Times of the Year:**
   It is important to note that spear phishing attacks do not just occur randomly at any time of the year. Rather, they occur at specific points in time, where there is a lot of activity happening, especially between the financial organization and the individual or organization during tax season. A typical example of this is the tax season.

   To launch their spear phishing campaigns, a cyber attacker will covertly pose as some sort of tax-related entity (primarily that of the IRS) requesting the tax preparer to send over sensitive information of the victim (primarily that person's Social Security number). This request will often come in the form of an email message, with a typical mailing address such as one of the following:
   - assupport@gov.com
   - support@link2.gov

   These types of email messages often contain a Visual Basic for Applications (VBA) script that is malicious in nature, and worse yet, it will automatically execute itself once opened. Another example of when a spear phishing attack will typically occur is during a catastrophic event, such as a natural disaster. For example, in such scenarios, the cyber attacker will send out a phony email from the Red Cross asking for donations or other kinds of financial assistance.

   Very often, after clicking on that link, the victim will be taken once again to a very authentic-looking but spoofed website. But rather than being asked to log in to a website so that their login information can be captured, the victim is asked to donate money. From there, the money is deposited into a fake bank account that is set up by the cyber attacker.

3. **Stealing Corporate Data:**
   Another prime interest of the cyber attacker in this regard is stealing sensitive data. This typically includes contact information of their customers, such as names, phone numbers, and email addresses.

   Once this information is collected, cyber attackers then have enough information at hand to conduct further and deeper research into their intended victims. Also at stake here is the information that is pertinent to the IT infrastructure of the business or corporation, so that a ransomware attack can be launched, targeting the organization's workstations, servers, and wireless devices.

AN INCIDENT RESPONSE PLAYBOOK FOR A PHISHING ATTACK

Here are some top risk mitigation techniques that can be implemented in order to protect your Cloud computing infrastructure:

1. **Identification:**
   This is the first step in responding to a phishing attack. At this stage, an alert is "sounded" of an impending phishing attack, and it must be further investigated. It is important to collect as much information and data about the phishing email as possible, and the following items should be captured:
   - The email address of the sender
   - The intended recipient of the email
   - The subject line of the email

   Carefully examine the email message, and if there is an attachment with it, make sure that you use the appropriate protocols to download it safely, that you store it in a separate folder (or even a zipped file), and that it is also password-protected so that only the appropriate IT personnel can access it.

   If there is a suspicious link as well, which takes the recipient to a potentially spoofed website, this will also have to be investigated. However, for these purposes, it is important to use a dedicated computer solely for just these purposes. Do not use any other server, workstation, or wireless device for this, as the potentially spoofed website could contain malware that could download itself rapidly.

2. **Triage:**
   If the investigation described above reveals that an actual phishing attack is underway, certain steps must be taken. First, determine what kind of phishing email it is. For example, is it
   - A BEC (business email compromise)?
   - Spear phishing (where one or more individuals are targeted)?
   - Clone phishing (where an original email message has been transformed into a malicious one)?
   - Whaling (this is similar to BEC, but primarily C-level executives are specifically targeted)?
   - Link manipulation (this where a spoofed website is involved)?
   - Website forgery (this is where JavaScript code is used to maliciously alter the URL bar)?
   - Covert redirect (this occurs when a website address looks genuine and authentic, but the victim is taken to a spoofed website)?
   - Social engineering (this occurs typically in a business environment where lower ranking employees [such as administrative assistants] are targeted and conned to give out corporate secrets)?
   - SMS (in these instances, wireless devices, primarily smartphones, are targeted, and malicious text messages are sent instead)?

   Once the above has been determined, then determine the priority level [this will be on a scale that you have determined, such as low priority to medium priority to high priority (this would be considered as a "severe" type of ranking]). From there, notify the IT staff, primarily those involved with the Security aspects of the organization, that an attack is underway, if they are not aware of the situation already.

3. **Investigation:**

At this phase, the actual email message and its contents need to be examined carefully, and the degree of damage needs to be ascertained. In terms of the former, the following must be investigated:

- Analysis of the email header:
  - *The "From" field:* This will contain the name of the sender.
  - *X-Authenticated User:* This will contain the email address of the sender (such as johndoe@anywhere.com).
  - *The Mail Server IP Address:* This will contain the actual TCP/IP address of the email server from where the phishing email was sent. It is important to keep in mind as well that the physical location of the email server does not necessarily imply that the cyber attacker is located in that geographic area as well. Often, the attacker will be in a location separate from that of the email server.
- Analysis of the email message:
  - At this phase, the actual contents of the email message need to be examined carefully, as there are many telltale signs that can be difficult to spot at first glance.
- Analysis of the domain link:
  - If the phishing email contains a suspicious link, as stated before, carefully examine the spoofed website, and determine where the data on the website is actually posted (such as in determining the TCP/IP address of the web server that hosts the spoofed website).

With regard to the latter point in this part, the level and/or severity of the damage needs to be ascertained and ultimately determined. Examples of this include the following:

- The total number of impacted employees.
- What actions were carried out by the employees with regard to the phishing email, for instance:
  - Did they download an attachment?
  - Or, did they go to a spoofed website and unknowingly submit their personal information, or even sensitive business login information?
- What was impacted:
  - Servers
  - Workstations
  - Wireless devices
  - Network infrastructure
  - Other aspects of IT infrastructure

4. **Remediation:**

This is deemed to be one of the most critical phases, as this is where the damage of the phishing attack will be contained. This will involve the following:

- After determining who the impacted employees are, immediately change their usernames and passwords.
- After determining the impacted points in IT Infrastructure, also immediately change login credentials of the people who have access to those particular resources.
- If the impacted points include smartphones, immediately execute the "Remote Wipe" command to those affected phones, so that any sort of sensitive information or data residing on them will be deleted and cannot be accessed. In these instances, have your employees return the affected smartphones back, and issue new ones with new usernames and passwords.
- Continue to monitor all systems within your IT infrastructure and all user accounts for any misuse, or for any unusual anomalies that may be occurring. If any of these are happening, you may want to consider shutting down those systems to conduct a more detailed investigation as to what is happening. But this should be done with careful planning, as this could cause downtime in normal business operations.

5. **Risk Avoidance:**

Once the damage has been contained and all impacted points within the business or the corporation have been remedied, the final stage is to determine how to avoid this kind of cyber attack (or, for that matter, any other kind of attack) from happening again. Some areas that should be considered are as follows:

- Consider hiring an outside cyber security firm to assist you in conducting an in-depth analysis of what really transpired. They can offer solutions that are specific to your situation, and even conduct various penetration testing techniques to determine whether there are other unknown security vulnerabilities in your organization.
- Always make sure that you are on a regular schedule of deploying software upgrades/patches on all your servers, workstations, and wireless devices. This includes ensuring that the web browsers across all workstations, wireless devices, and servers are up to date as well as making sure that you are making use of the latest antispyware/antiphishing/antimalware software packages available.
- In a phishing attack, in the end, it is always individuals who are impacted first, then the IT Infrastructure after the login data has been hijacked by the cyber attacker. Therefore, the greatest emphasis must be placed on this area, which is employee awareness. In this respect, consider the following:
- Conduct training programs at regular intervals (at minimum at least once a quarter) with your employees. Teach them the following:
  - What the signs of a phishing email look like, paying careful attention to fake-looking sender names, sender domains, and in particular, any misspellings in either the subject line or the content of the email message.

- How to determine whether a link is malicious, by explaining how to hover over the link in question to see if the domain on it matches up to what is displayed. If they do not match up, then the link is a malicious one.
- If they receive an email or an attachment that they were not expecting but it comes from somebody they know, to contact that particular sender first to determine whether s/he really sent it. If not, they should be instructed to forward that email message to the IT security staff, and then it should be deleted from the inbox.
- Always instruct them to trust their instincts, and if anything looks suspicious, to report it, and again, delete the message from the inbox.
- Instruct them how to verify the authenticity of any website that they may using, paying extra attention to the "HTTPS" in the URL bar.
- Also instruct them to never click on any type or kind of pop-up messages that they may receive on their work-related devices.
- At random intervals, have the IT staff launch phony, phishing emails to see if they are picking up what you are teaching them. If they open that email message, then they should be immediately notified that they fell prey to a phishing email and will require further training.
- Have your IT staff, especially your network administrator, stay on top of the latest phishing techniques.
- Install Ani Phishing toolbars on all servers, workstations, and wireless devices. These packages run checks on the websites that your employees are using against various databases of known phishing websites.
- Make sure that your network infrastructure is up to date as well, by routinely testing your firewalls, network intrusion devices, and routers. Once again, a cyber security firm can help you establish the appropriate protocols in conducting these tasks.
- Determine what controls have failed and take the necessary steps to either rectify them or implement new ones instead.
- Implement a special hotline where employees can get into direct contact with the appropriate IT staff in case they see or witness anything suspicious that is associated with a phishing attack (of course, they should also be able to report any other security issues as well).

MALWARE INJECTION ATTACKS

Cloud computing Infrastructure is also susceptible to malware injection attacks. In these instances, the cyber attacker creates a malicious application and injects it into the SaaS, PaaS, and IaaS, respectively. Once the injection is completed, the malicious module is executed as one of the valid instances running in Cloud Infrastructure. From this point, the cyber attacker can then launch any sort of attack, such as covert eavesdropping, data manipulation, and data theft.

It is important to note that among all the malware injection attacks, the SQL injection attack and the cross-site scripting attacks are the two most common forms that can be launched against a Cloud computing infrastructure, and are further reviewed in the next two subsections.

SQL Injection Attack

Structured Query Language injections target SQL servers in Cloud Infrastructure that run vulnerable database applications. Thus, the cyber attacker exploits the vulnerabilities of the web servers, and from there, injects a malicious code in order to circumvent the login credentials and gain unauthorized access to the backend databases.

If this is successful, the cyber attacker can then further manipulate the contents of the SQL server databases, retrieve confidential data, remotely execute system commands, or even take control of the web server for further criminal activities. The SQL injection attacks can also be launched by a botnet.

For example, the Asprox botnet used a thousand bots that were equipped with an SQL injection kit to fire an SQL injection attack [7]. The bots first sent encoded SQL queries containing the exploit payload to Google for searching web servers that ran the ASP.net framework.

Then, the bots started executing a SQL injection attack against the websites returned from those queries. In the end, over 6 million URLs belonging to 153,000 different websites that were hosted on various Cloud Infrastructures were impacted the Asprox botnet.

Cross-Site Scripting (XSS)

With this, the cyber attacker injects malicious scripts, such as JavaScript, VBScript, ActiveX, HTML, and Flash, into a vulnerable dynamic webpage in order to execute these various scripts on the victim's web browser. Afterward, the cyber attacker could then steal the session cookie used for authorization for the purposes of accessing the victim's account or tricking the victim into clicking on a malicious link.

For example, cyber researchers in Germany have successfully demonstrated an XSS attack against Amazon AWS Cloud Computing Platform. The vulnerability in the Amazon store allowed the team to hijack an AWS session and gain successful access to all of the customer data (this included authentication data, tokens, and plaintext passwords) [8].

Wrapping Attack

Wrapping attacks make use of the XML signature wrapping (or XML rewriting) to exploit a weakness when web servers validate signed requests. This type of cyber attack is accomplished during the translation of SOAP messages between a legitimate user and the web server.

The cyber attacker embeds a bogus element (the wrapper) into the message structure, moves the original message body under the wrapper, and replaces the content of the message with malicious code. From here, it is then sent to the server hosted on Cloud computing infrastructure.

Since the original message body is still valid, the server will be tricked into authorizing the message that has been altered. As a result, the cyber attacker is then able to gain unauthorized access to protected resources. From here, the illegal operations can then proceed.

Since Cloud users normally request services from Cloud computing service providers through a web browser, wrapping attacks can cause damage to Cloud systems as well. Amazon's EC2 was discovered to be vulnerable to wrapping attacks in 2008 [9].

Research showed that EC2 had a weakness in the SOAP message security validation mechanism. A signed SOAP request of a legitimate user could be intercepted and modified. As a result, the cyber attacker could then take unprivileged actions on victim's accounts in the Cloud environment.

By using the XML signature wrapping technique, cyber researchers also demonstrated an account hijacking attack that exploited a vulnerability in AWS [10]. By altering authorized digitally signed SOAP messages, cyber researchers were then able to obtain unauthorized access to a customer's account. They could also delete and create new images on the customer's EC2 instance and perform other administrative tasks.

THE MALICIOUS INSIDER

Cyber security threats to Cloud Infrastructure can transpire from both within and outside of businesses, corporations, and organizations. In fact, according to the 2011 CyberSecurity Watch Survey conducted on over 600 businesses, government agencies, security professionals, and consultants, 21% of cyber attacks were caused by insiders. Other findings of this survey were as follows:

- About 33% of the respondents believed that insider attacks were more costly and damaging to business entities.
- Approximately 63% of the respondents claimed that the most common inside attacks were unauthorized access to and use of corporate information and data.
- About 57% of the respondents believed that the unintentional exposure of private or sensitive data continues to exist.
- About 37% of the respondents felt that viruses, worms, or other malicious codes were launched by inside attacks.
- About 32% of the respondents also felt that the most dangerous insider attack threat was that of the theft of intellectual property.
- The majority of the respondents firmly believed that the vulnerabilities to a Cloud computing infrastructure to a malicious insider attack are as follows [11]:
  - Unclear roles and responsibilities
  - Poor enforcement of role definitions
  - Need-to-know principles and methodologies not effectively applied
  - AAA vulnerabilities
  - Server, IT systems, and/or OS vulnerabilities
  - Inadequate physical security procedures
  - The impossibility of processing data in encrypted form

- Software application vulnerabilities and/or poor patch and software upgrade management techniques

There are three types of Cloud Infrastructure-related insider threats:

1. **Rogue Network Administrators:**
   They have the privilege to steal unprotected files, launch brute-force attacks over passwords, and download sensitive customer information and data from the victim's business, corporation, or organization.
2. **Malicious Insiders:**
   They can exploit the vulnerabilities of a Cloud computing infrastructure in an attempt to gain unauthorized access to confidential data in an organization and either selling this sensitive data or using the information for their own future business transactions.

Malicious insiders who use Cloud computing infrastructure to conduct nefarious activities carry out attacks against their own employer's IT infrastructure. Since these kinds of insiders are familiar with the IT operations of their own companies, the attacks are generally difficult to trace using forensic analysis [12].

ONLINE CYBER THREATS

Cloud computing services provide users and business entities with very powerful processing capabilities and massive amounts of storage space. For example, Netflix leases computing space from Amazon Web Services (AWS) to provide subscription service for watching television-based programs and movies. Dropbox offers Cloud storage service to customers and businesses alike for storing terabytes of data.

However, in the meantime, the sensitive information and data stored on a Cloud computing infrastructure thus become an attractive target for online cyber theft. In fact, according to the analysis of data breaches of 209 global companies in 2011, 37% of information/data breaches cases involved malicious attacks. The average cost per compromised record is $222 [13].

The covert stealing of information and data stored on a Cloud computing infrastructure also occurs on social networking sites, such as Twitter, Facebook, and LinkedIn. According to a recent *USA Today* survey, 35% of adult Internet users have a profile on at least one social networking site [14].

However, the private data that is stored on these social media sites can be hacked by online cyber thieves, provided they find access to the Cloud computing infrastructure on which these social media sites are hosted. For example, LinkedIn, the world's largest professional networking website that has well over 175 million subscribers, reported that their password database was compromised in a security breach [15].

Online cyber attackers could also use stolen passwords to launch malicious attacks against the subscriber base of these social media sites. For example, Dropbox confirmed that its users were victims of a spam attack. Usernames and passwords stolen from social media sites were used to sign in covertly to Dropbox accounts [16].

Online cyber attackers could also take the advantage of the computing power offered by Cloud computing service providers to launch massive cyber attacks. For example, AWS EC2 Cloud Service was used by hackers to compromise private information and data about its user base. By signing up Amazon's EC2 service with phony information, the cyber attackers then rented a virtual server and launched an attack to steal confidential information and data from Sony's PlayStation Network [17].

REAL-WORLD EXAMPLES OF CYBER THREATS TO A CLOUD INFRASTRUCTURE

In this section, we provide some illustrations of some real threats that have been experienced:

1. **Using IaaS to Host Crimeware:**
   In its most basic offering, a Cloud computing infrastructure rents out storage space, processing cycles, and network components to consumers and businesses entities. But IaaS was used as a platform to control a malicious botnet derived from the crimeware Zeus.

   The Zeus crimeware toolkit is well established in the "Dark Web" as being an easy to use and powerful tool for stealing personal information and data from remote systems. Specifically, this crimeware allows entry-level hackers to create their own versions of botnets.

   As in the case of any botnet, there is a need to be able to communicate and command all the computers infected with it. In 2009, security experts uncovered a variant of Zeus using Amazon's EC2 IaaS to command and control their botnets [18].

   Even though making use of an Internet service provider (ISP) has the potential to offer better anonymity, making use of a Cloud computing infrastructure can provide what is known specifically as "traffic camouflaging." This is the instance where it is much harder to detect and blacklist harmful activity that is hiding in traffic disguised as a valid Cloud computing service.

2. **Blue Pill Rootkit:**
   Strong compartmentalization should be utilized to ensure that individual customers do not impact the operations of other tenants running on the same Cloud Infrastructure provider. However, back in 2006 Joanna Rutkowska, a security researcher for IT security firm COSEINC, claimed to have developed a program that can trick a software application into thinking that it is running on a certain system, where in reality it is running on a virtual version of this system [19].

   This rootkit, which is termed the "Blue Pill," creates a fake reality for an entire operating system and all of the software applications that are running on it, including antimalware sensors. The risk of such an executable program is that it could easily intercept all hardware requests from any software application that is also running on the same system.

   The creators of the "Blue Pill Rootkit" claim it to be completely undetectable, although some other cyber security researchers have disputed this claim [10]. Whether it is detectable or not, this clearly demonstrates how exploits can be developed based on virtualization technologies that reside on a Cloud Computing Infrastructure.

3. **Cloud Computing Outage and Data Loss:**
   Various leading Cloud computing service providers have experienced and, in multiple instances, from data loss or suspension of service. The following are just a few examples of such threats:
   - In 2009, Salesforce.com suffered an outage that locked more than 900,000 subscribers out of crucial credit card applications and data needed to transact business with customers. Such an outage has even greater impact on those businesses and corporations with a bulk of their operations conducted from within a Cloud computing infrastructure [20].
   - Also in September 2009, an estimated 800,000 users of a smartphone known as "Sidekick" temporarily lost access to personal information and data. This outage lasted almost 2 weeks. The data at the time was stored on servers owned by Microsoft, and accessed as a Cloud service. At the time, this was described as the biggest disaster in the history of Cloud computing [21].
   - Rackspace was forced to pay out between $2.5 million and $3.5 million in service credits to customers in the wake of a power outage that hit its Dallas datacenter in late June 2009.

Cyber Risks to the Cloud

A cyber risk model is shown in Figure 3.2.

FIGURE 3.2 Penetration testers examining a Cloud risk model.

A FORMAL DEFINITION OF RISK

It is very important to note that the term is risk comprises four independent variables:

1. *Threats:* These are defined and illustrated in the last section of this chapter.
2. *Vulnerability:* This can be defined as "a software application, hardware, or procedural weakness that may provide an attacker the open door to enter a computer or network and have unauthorized access to resources within the environment" [22].
3. *Impact:* This can be defined as a "measure of the tangible and intangible effects (consequences) of one thing's or entity's action or influence upon another" [23].
4. *Likelihood:* The probability of an event or situation taking place. It is typically used to refer to events that have a reasonable probability of occurring but are not definite or may be influenced by factors not yet observed or measured [24].

Thus the formal of definition of risk, as it relates to the Cloud computing environment, is as follows: "[It] is the likelihood of a threat agent taking advantage of vulnerability and the corresponding business impact. It ties the vulnerability, threat, and likelihood of exploitation to the resulting business impact" [25].

The mathematical representation of risk is as follows:

$$\text{Vulnerability} \times \text{Threat} \times \text{Impact} \times \text{Likelihood}$$

In the remainder of this section, we examine the specific risks that are posed to a Cloud computing infrastructure.

CLOUD COMPUTING INFRASTRUCTURE RISKS

1. **Supply Chain Failure:**
   A Cloud provider could potentially outsource certain aspects of its "production chain" to outside third parties, or even make use of another Cloud provider as the "backend." In such a situation, the level of security of the Cloud service depends on the level of security of each one of the links.

   Any interruption or corruption in the chain between all the parties involved can lead to one or more of the following:
   • Unavailability of services
   • Loss of data confidentiality, integrity, and availability (CIA)
   • Economic and reputational losses due to failure to meet customer demand
   • Violation of service-level agreement (SLA)
   • Cascading service failure
2. **Isolation Failure:**
   In hosted environments, such as that of a Cloud computing infrastructure, one customer has to another customer's or data. In the case of a cyber attack, the hacker can gain access to the resources, informa-

tion, and data of one customer, or even all of them. This class of risks includes the following:

- So-called guest-hopping attacks
- SQL injection attacks exposing multiple customers' data stored in the same table
- Side channel attacks
- IP addresses being blocked
- Spamming and port scanning

3. **Malicious Insiders:**
   The malicious activities of an insider could potentially impact the following:
   - Confidentiality, integrity, and availability (CIA) of all kinds of stored datasets
   - TCP/IP protocols
   - The level of customer trust
   - Negative experiences faced by employees of the Cloud provider

   It is important to note that the threat of malicious insiders can be considered especially important in the case of Cloud computing. This is so because Cloud architectures require certain roles that are extremely high-risk.

4. **Control Panel Interface Compromise:**
   The control panels that are offered by public Cloud providers are Internet-accessible and thus require access to larger sets of resources. This poses an increased risk, especially when combined when remote access is used and any associated web browser vulnerabilities.

5. **Interception of Information and Data in Transit:**
   Cloud computing, which is a distributed architecture, involves the traversal of more information and data will be traversing across various network mediums. For example, information/data must be transferred in order to synchronize multiple distributed machine images as well as images distributed across multiple physical machines. As a result, sniffing, spoofing, person-in–the-middle attacks, and side channel and replay attacks have to be considered as possible threat sources.

6. **The Insecure or Ineffective Deletion of Data:**
   Whenever a Cloud provider is changed, the resources are scaled down, physical hardware is reallocated, and so on. As a result, the information and data will not be made available beyond the lifetime specified in the service-level agreement (SLA).

7. **Distributed Denial-of-Service (DDoS) Attacks:**
   DDoS-style attacks overload the resources of a Cloud Computing Infrastructure by flooding it with many requests for services from a wide array of geographic locations or even network-based topological regions. As a result, legitimate users are unable to use Cloud computing resources as they were originally intended to.

8. **Economic Denial of Service (EDoS):**
   There are several different scenarios in which Cloud computing resources can be impacted in this regard:

- With regard to identity theft, a cyber attacker covertly hijacks an account and uses the customer's resources from that account in order to damage the customer economically.
- The Cloud Provider has not established effective limits on the use of paid resources. As a result, unexpected loads are experienced on these resources with long periods of downtime.
- A cyber attacker establishes a public channel to exhaust the Cloud provider's metered resources.

It is important to note that an EDoS destroys the entire economic resources of a Cloud provider.

9. **Compromise of the Service Engine:**
Each Cloud-based architecture makes use of a highly specialized platform, known as the "service engine." This resides up above the physical hardware resources and manages the customer resources at different levels. In most instances, the service engine is the hypervisor. A cyber attacker can compromise the service engine by hacking it from inside a virtual machine (via an IaaS platform), through a runtime environment (via a PaaS platform), or through an application pool (via an SaaS platform), or even through the means of an API.

10. **Loss or Misuse of Cryptographic Keys:**
This includes the following:
- Disclosure of secret keys (private keys)
- Accidental disclosure of passwords to malicious parties
- Loss or corruption of public/private key combinations
- Unauthorized use of digital signatures for authentication and nonrepudiation purposes

11. **Loss of Backups:**
The backups of a Cloud provider can get lost or be damaged, or the physical and/or digital media on which the backups reside can be covertly stolen or even hijacked by a cyber attacker.

12. **Data Protection Risks:**
Examples of this include the following:
- It can be very difficult for the customer to effectively check the data processing that the Cloud provider executes. Thus, the ability to make sure that the information or data are handled in a safe and secure fashion is not available. The only guarantees that a customer has are the provisions that are detailed in the SLA.
- There could be instances where information or data security breaches occur and the customer is not made aware of this.
- The Cloud customer (CC) may lose control of the data processed by the Cloud provider (CP). This issue is increased in the case of multiple transfers of data (e.g., between federated CPs).
- The customer could potentially lose control of the information/datasets (of which s/he owns) that are processed by the Cloud provider. This issue is increased in the instances of multiple transfers of these datasets between federated Cloud providers.

13. **Loss of Governance:**

On making using of a Cloud infrastructure, the customer totally loses control to the Cloud provider on a number of key issues that will affect security. Also, the SLAs may not even offer a commitment to provide security-based services on the part of the Cloud provider. As a result, this leaves a disparaging gap in security defenses.

This also includes compliance risks, because Cloud providers are not mandated by federal legislation to acquire security or quality assurance certification.

14. **Risk from Changes in Geographic Jurisdictions:**

When information and datasets are stored or processed in datacenters located in a foreign country (in other words, if the Cloud provider has no physical premises at these particular geographic locations), changes in legal jurisdiction can also have a huge impact on the levels of security that is associated with those information/datasets.

So far, this chapter has examined the specific threats and risks that are posed to a Cloud computing infrastructure. The remainder of this chapter discusses in detail the risk management Strategies that you can utilize to protect your business or corporation from those risks and threats.

THREAT AND RISK MANAGEMENT STRATEGIES FOR A CLOUD COMPUTING INFRASTRUCTURE

For the most part, it would be fair to say that many of the threat and risk management strategies one may have to undertake for Cloud computing infrastructure will have close parallels to what mature, well-regulated businesses have had to undertake within their own on-premises computing environments.

SHARED SECURITY RESPONSIBILITY

For resources within a public Cloud environment to be kept secure and operate under a minimum risk profile, the business must understand its security responsibilities.

To assist their customers, AWS provides a variety of security guidelines, but the most pertinent is their *Shared Responsibility Model*, which outlines the demarcation of responsibilities between an AWS customer and AWS themselves. A redrawing of this model is shown in Figure 3.3.[1]

The AWS Shared Responsibility Model establishes a clear line between areas for which AWS customers must maintain security, and areas where AWS themselves are responsible—defined effectively as responsibility for security *in*, and *of* the Cloud, respectively.

The AWS Shared Responsibility Model establishes not only the demarcation point between what the customer and what AWS is responsible for in terms of security,

---

1 The AWS Shared Responsibility Model is published online at https://aws.amazon.com/compliance/shared-responsibility-model/

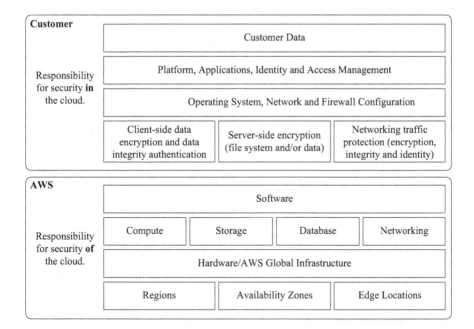

Customer

Responsibility for security **in** the cloud.

Customer Data

Platform, Applications, Identity and Access Management

Operating System, Network and Firewall Configuration

Client-side data encryption and data integrity authentication	Server-side encryption (file system and/or data)	Networking traffic protection (encryption, integrity and identity)

AWS

Responsibility for security **of** the cloud.

Software

Compute	Storage	Database	Networking

Hardware/AWS Global Infrastructure

Regions	Availability Zones	Edge Locations

FIGURE 3.3   AWS Shared Responsibility Model.

but effectively also provides a line in the sand on what customers should *trust* when moving into the public Cloud. For instance, AWS states that the security of its hardware, and more generally, AWS global infrastructure, is its responsibility. Thus, AWS clearly establishes that it is its responsibility to ensure that hardware platforms, network switching, and so on are secure, and that, in order for a business to make use of the public Cloud, the business has to trust in the fundamental security of that Cloud. This reflects the decision that any company has to make when determining the level of security activities that it undertakes. For instance, a business running a traditional datacenter will have to trust that core hardware platforms [the actual server hardware deployed, storage-area network (SAN) and network-attached storage (NAS) devices, network switching, etc.] is appropriately secure. This does not remove the requirement to apply appropriate security controls *on top* of those functions, and, indeed, in an on-premises environment, the business will be responsible for applying patching not only to operating systems and applications but also to low-level infrastructure: server BIOS updates, SAN and NAS operating systems, and the operating systems for network switches themselves. Once in the public Cloud, security of such lower-level infrastructure is not a Cloud customer function.

Infrastructure security is not taken lightly, as it has the greatest potential to cause a major security breach; indeed, failure of security, systems, or access to core infrastructure can be the difference between an incident affecting a single customer or tens of thousands of customers.

To date, perhaps the most serious allegation of infrastructure security issues has come from Bloomberg's October 4, 2018 article, "The Big Hack," wherein it was alleged that Chinese intelligence had leaned on IT manufacturing companies to have additional components added to servers so that they could be used to hack systems within highly secured networks and potentially exfiltrate data from selected targets. Such allegations strike at the core of infrastructure security; they suggest the risk that the underlying hardware might be compromised in an unrecoverable way:

> "Hardware hacks are more difficult to pull off and potentially more devastating, promising the kind of long-term, stealth access that spy agencies are willing to invest millions of dollars and many years to get."
>
> *Robertson, J., and M. Riley, "The Big Hack: How China Used a Tiny Chip to Infiltrate U.S. Companies," Bloomberg Businessweek, October 4, 2018, https://www.bloomberg.com/news/features/2018-10-04/ the-big-hack-how-china-used-a-tiny-chip-to-infiltrate-america-s-top-companies*

At the time of writing, the accuracy of the Bloomberg article was still being hotly debated, and Bloomberg seems increasingly isolated in its stance as to the reliability of the claims in the article. Companies named as directly affected in the article expressly denied the allegations, and even the US government issued a strong denial of its accuracy. Security researchers and IT experts have questioned the plausibility of some of the suggested aspects of the hardware hack, or even the efficacy of the hack to result in exfiltration given the high level of network monitoring that takes place within service providers. One of the named sources in a *Risky Business* podcast stated:

> "But what really struck me is that like all the details that were even remotely technical, seemed like they had been lifted from from [sic] the conversations I had about theoretically how hardware implants work and how the devices I was making to show off at Black Hat two years ago worked."
>
> *Transcription from John Gruber, Daring Fireball: https://daringfireball.net/ linked/2018/10/09/big-hack-doubts*
> *Patrick Gray, Risky Business podcast: https://risky.biz/RB517_feature/*

Business Insider quotes the secretary of the US Department of Homeland security:

> "With respect to the article, we at DHS do not have any evidence that supports the article," Kirstjen Nielsen said … "We have no reason to doubt what the companies have said."
>
> *Leswing, K., "Security Community Increasingly Thinks a Bombshell Bloomberg Report on Chinese Chip Hacking Could be Bogus," Business Insider, October 14, 2018, https://www.businessinsider.com.au/security-community-voicing-increasing-doubts-about-bombshell-bloomberg-chinese-chip-hacking-2018-10*

Regardless of whether the Bloomberg allegations are either verified or proven inaccurate, the reaction to such allegations rippled across the IT industry rapidly.

Vendors not even named in the article but who were known to have either a current or former relationship with hardware suppliers named found themselves being questioned by customers over the security of their products, and some businesses even started to isolate equipment that they felt might have come from the named hardware supplier.

The nation-state threat alleged in the Bloomberg article may not have occurred this time, but security experts generally agree such injection at the time of manufacturing represents at least *some* risk, which does reinforce the need for security to be a multilayered approach. It is not sufficient to assume that hardware is safe; instead, robust security principles will see monitoring of network traffic for unexpected or suspicious behavior, blocking Internet access for systems that do not need it, keeping detailed logging to enable forensic analysis at any point, traffic encryption, firewalls, and so on.

Consideration of "How much can we trust our environment?" is not a new issue. In fact, it goes back almost to the genesis of the Internet. In 1984, accepting the Association for Computing Machinery (ACM) Turing Award, Ken Thompson made a remarkable speech titled "Reflections on Trusting Trust."[2] In his speech, he described a security hack that effectively resided in binary copies of programs only: a C compiler that would detect when it was compiling the UNIX "login" program used to access systems, and inject additional code into the "login" program. This code would allow any user account on the system to be logged into using both the recorded user's password *and* a specific, hardcoded password known to Thompson.[3] Thompson noted that such a hack would be immediately obvious to anyone who inspected the source code to the C compiler, so it was not kept in the source code to the C compiler; instead, when a C-compiler binary code compiled with the original hack detected that it was compiling its own source code, it would inject the hack generation into the binary, thus keeping the hack entirely within the binary code once originally injected.

Thompson's point was profoundly important; it does not suffice to say that a system can be trusted because you can see its source code; there are still ways that trust and security can be circumvented by someone with sufficient skills and access. The tagline to his speech was an effective summary of his lesson:

"To what extent should one trust a statement that a program is free of Trojan horses? Perhaps it is more important to trust the people who wrote the software."

Thompson, K., "Reflections on Trusting Trust," ACM Turing Award Speech, 1984.

---

2 "Reflections on Trusting Trust," ACM Digital Library (available at https://dl.acm.org/citation.cfm?id=358210)

3 Since all UNIX systems include *at least* a "root" user, this effectively meant that Thompson could log onto any UNIX system with administrative privileges on which the modified login binary was installed.

Any form of virtualization creates the trust conundrum; a malicious hypervisor could potentially inject code into the operating system of a guest virtual machine,[4] at a layer that might make detection or blocking difficult. Regardless of whether we are talking about the core hardware infrastructure or the virtualized infrastructure, operating in the public Cloud requires an alteration to how we approach security and trust.

Moving into the public Cloud does not eliminate security considerations; it just makes the security a shared responsibility. To quote the New Zealand Government Information Security and Privacy policy:

> "Note: it is important to understand that although agencies can outsource responsibility to a service provider for implementing, managing and maintaining security controls they cannot outsource their accountability for ensuring their data is appropriately protected."

> *Cloud Computing–Information Security and Privacy Considerations, New Zealand Department of Internal Affairs, April 2014. https://www.digital. govt.nz/dmsdocument/1-cloud-computing-information-security-and- privacy-considerations/html*

Legal and Regulatory

Before a business even considers moving workloads into the public Cloud, it should first understand the legal and regulatory requirements that it may face in relation to data ownership and placement. Such considerations, if they exist, can place stringent limitations on how or even *if* the business can make use of the public Cloud.

For instance, Amazon's AWS provides not only a public Cloud experience but also a *US GovCloud* platform, allowing US government agencies and other eligible entities the option to make use of a public Cloud environment while still tightly controlling risk and security in a way that conforms to government requirements. AWS's page for GovCloud describes it as follows:

> "AWS GovCloud (US) is an isolated AWS region, subject to FedRAMP High and Moderate baselines, and it allows customers to host sensitive Controlled Unclassified Information (CUI) and all types of regulated workloads."

> *"Introduction to the AWS GovCloud (US) Region," https://aws.amazon.com/ govcloud-us/*

In addition to having compliance with a wide variety of protocols [e.g., International Traffic in Arms Regulations (ITAR), FIPS 140-2], AWS describes access to the isolated specialized Cloud environment as follows:

---

4 Indeed, something security researchers fear is the chance of a *guest* being able to inject code into its hypervisor, which, if successfully executed, might involve a guest system taking over other guest systems running on the same hypervisor. Indeed, the runC vulnerability outlined in CVE-2019-5736 demonstrated the ability for hackers to escape Linux container environments to gain root access to host servers. (This triggered the requirement for urgent remediation in affected hosts.)

"The region is operated by employees who are U.S. citizens on U.S. soil. The region is only accessible to vetted U.S. entities and root account holders, who must confirm they are U.S. Persons to gain access to this region."

Ibid.

Without such specialized public Cloud environments, US government agencies and affiliates would either have to build their own certified *community* Cloud or restrict services to on-premises environments, through either traditionally designed infrastructure or a private Cloud experience.

Such restrictions do not apply only to the United States, however. Other countries have similar legal requirements over who can handle government data, requiring similar approaches, which can often lead to the rise of government-sponsored Cloud services. For instance, New Zealand established options with several in-country service providers and advertise the availability of these certified options:

"We have negotiated commercial agreements with cloud providers to enable agencies to access their services with a single price book and standard terms and conditions."

Cloud Services, NZ Department of Internal Affairs, https://www.digital.govt.nz/ standards-and-guidance/technology-and-architecture/cloud-services/.

New Zealand also defines quite clearly what types of government data can be placed in the public Cloud, regardless of whether it is a standard public Cloud provider or a contracted service provider. Its "Cloud first" policy states that agencies are to

"[O]nly store data classified as RESTRICTED or below in a cloud service, whether it is hosted onshore or offshore."

Ibid.

Likewise, the Australian federal government states of government agencies:

"The Privacy Act 1988…does not prohibit the use of cloud computing and an agency, having conducted appropriate due diligence, may contract for cloud computing services and comply with its Privacy Act obligations, as with current ICT contractual practice.

"Agencies are advised to conduct a risk-based analysis of their information, including a Privacy Impact Assessment, to determine the most appropriate ICT environment to deploy to support the classification of their information and business requirements.

"Where an agency cannot adequately address their privacy obligations it will not be appropriate to transfer that information into a public cloud environment."

Privacy and Cloud Computing for Australian Government Agencies, Version 1.1, February 2013, https://www.finance.gov.au/files/2013/02/ privacy-and-cloud-computing-for-australian-government-agencies-v1.1.pdf

Of course, legal restrictions on what can and can't be placed in the public Cloud may not just apply to government agencies. Companies operating in the financial sectors are quite often placed under high levels of governance for IT. The Australian Prudential Regulation Authority (APRA) monitors banking, insurance, and superannuation institutions operating within Australia, and has issued guidance multiple times for APRA-regulated companies as Cloud computing has evolved. Its September 2018 guidance paper states:

> "APRA recognises that the risks associated with the use of cloud computing services will depend on the nature of the usage, and for the purposes of this paper APRA has classified these risks into three broad categories: low, heightened and extreme.
>
> - For arrangements with low inherent risk not involving offshoring, APRA would not expect an APRA-regulated entity to consult with APRA prior to entering into the arrangement.
> - For arrangements with heightened risk, APRA would expect to be consulted after the APRA-regulated entity's internal governance process is completed.
> - For arrangements involving extreme inherent risk, APRA encourages earlier engagement as these arrangements will be subjected to a higher level of scrutiny.
>
> APRA expects all risks to be managed appropriately commensurate with their inherent risk. However, for extreme inherent risk, APRA expects an entity will be able to demonstrate to APRA's satisfaction, prior to entering into the arrangement, that the entity understands the risks associated with the arrangement, and that its risk management and risk mitigation techniques are sufficiently strong."
>
> *APRA Information Paper, "Outsourcing Involving Cloud Computing Services," September 24, 2018, https://www.apra.gov.au/sites/default/files/information_ paper_-_outsourcing_involving_cloud_computing_services.pdf*

A broad variety of other industry verticals, almost invariably regardless of their country of operation, need to consider the legal ramifications of using Cloud services. Industries commonly affected include the following:

- Financial sector
- Government
- Healthcare
- Essential services (e.g., power generation, water and sewerage services)

Additionally, even industries that have few regulations placed on them in general relating to Cloud computing may find themselves having to step cautiously for working in the public Cloud with particular types of data, such as the following:

- Credit card and other financial data
- Personally identifiable information (PII)
- Sensitive personal information

A common challenge in evaluating legal implications of moving workloads into the public Cloud is the tendency for "shadow IT" to explore services without the direct involvement of the IT department.

To address such considerations, businesses should ensure that guidance is published and regularly updated outlining key obligations and considerations.

While some businesses may have a "Cloud first" policy (or a more recent variant, "Cloud fit"), the fundamental legal operational requirements that a business operates under cannot be ignored, and have to remain a core consideration of public Cloud security.

DATA SOVEREIGNTY

Data sovereignty quite simply is the premise that data can be subject to the laws and regulatory frameworks of specific countries or jurisdictions; this can refer to *where* the data was gathered, from *whom* it was gathered [for example, consider the rise of general data protection regulation (GDPR) considerations for EU citizens], or *where* it is stored.

While data sovereignty shares obvious overlap with our previous "legal and regulatory" topic, its influence is arguably broader. While the legal and regulatory topic explores situations where there might be legal restrictions on where you can place your data (which can become a sovereignty consideration), sovereignty also covers considerations of data placement that may not have a direct legal requirement, but still represent a threat or a risk to public Cloud operation.

In a discussion paper in 2012, the Swedish National Board of Trade wrote:

> "The issue of the sovereignty of national data, data sovereignty, is central for states. This term is broader than confidentiality, for example, since it relates to the actual ownership rights to the information."
>
> *How Borderless is the Cloud? Swedish National Board of Trade, September 2012,*
> *978-91-86575-45-8.*

The board further noted:

> "At the World Economic Forum in 2011, the strong requirement for the creation of an international framework for cloud services was expressed from several directions, but the central issue concerning the management of data sovereignty appears to be difficult to resolve."
>
> *Ibid.*

Arguably, one might suggest that only minor *collective* progress has been made on the issue of data sovereignty since 2011. Instead, individual jurisdictions are increasingly asserting via legislation how and where companies can store data relating to their citizens.

In July 2018 it was reported that

> "Apple's Chinese iCloud partner, Guizhou-Cloud Big Data (GCBD), has cut a deal with the state-run China Telecom to move user data to the latter's servers, according to

a public-facing WeChat post from China Telecom. Though the iCloud data is end-to-end encrypted, the encryption keys are also stored in China, raising the possibility the Chinese government could gain access to it."

Statt, N., "Apple's iCloud partner in China will store user data on servers of state-run telecom" The Verge, July 18 2018, https://www.theverge.com/2018/7/18/17587304/ apple-icloud-china-user-data-state-run-telecom-privacy-security

While Apple iCloud data for China had previously been hosted outside of the country, the movement of data for Chinese iCloud users firmly into mainland China clearly changes the sovereignty under which the data operates, and by extension, creates at least a risk, if not an outright threat, to those who had relied on the prior physical data locality. Data sovereignty of course has greater considerations than consumer public Cloud systems that act as a service enabler for smartphones. It can come up regularly in academic circles for instance – in Australia data sovereignty is routinely flagged as a requirement for accepting research grants. The University of New South Wales, when rolling out Office 365 to its students, staff and academics, posted:

"Data sovereignty is a major concern for many academics, as some research grants will require all research data to stay in Australia. Storing research in "the cloud" can make this difficult, as it's often hard to tell where exactly the servers that make up a cloud offering are based, and many providers will mirror your data across multiple servers in multiple countries.

Well, the good news is all data stored in Office 365 and OneDrive accounts linked to a UNSW account will be stored right here, in Australia. Late last year, Microsoft moved all data from UNSW customers from servers in Singapore to servers here in Australia, ahead of the university wide roll out of Office 365."

Office 365 at UNSW—Your Data Stays in Australia, University of New South Wales, February 1, 2017, http://blogs.unsw.edu.au/unsw-it/blog/2017/02/ office-365-at-unsw-your-data-stays-in-australia/

Data sovereignty is not always fully explored by companies moving into the public Cloud, which can result in either costly reversals or terminations of workload migration, or costly legal reviews. One might *infer,* for instance, from the University of New South Wales that Office 365 data was initially placed in the Singapore O365 datacenter, potentially creating a sovereignty issue. Prior to the deployment of an Australian datacenter, other companies in Australia halted and even reversed Office 365 programs when they realized their data was leaving the country.

Sovereignty remains a vexing legal issue that continues to create concerns relating to privacy and security in public Cloud environments. In January 2018 it was reported:

"Australian privacy advocates are concerned about a case that could see data held by American companies seized anywhere in the world.

"Microsoft has been in a five-year legal standoff with the US Justice Department over whether a warrant issued in the United States as part of a drug trafficking case can be used to access an email held on its servers in Dublin, Ireland."

> *Bogle, A., "Could US warrants access Australian data? Microsoft*
> *case worries privacy advocates" ABC News Australia, January*
> *19, 2018, http://www.abc.net.au/news/science/2018-01-19/*
> *us-warrants-able-to-access-australian-data-microsoft/9338866*

The Microsoft/FBI case that started in 2013 was part of the rationale behind the US CLOUD Act (Clarifying Lawful Overseas Use of Data) of 2018. In an opinion piece in April 2018, Tom Daemen (Director of Corporate, External and Legal Affairs at Microsoft Australia) wrote that prior to the passage of the CLOUD Act:

"By serving a CSP with a warrant, a government could potentially gain access to personal data without an end user ever knowing. Although we at Microsoft have both the interest and resources to support our customers by pushing back and even litigating when appropriate, this approach is fraught with legal complexity and uncertainty."

> *Daemen, T., "What new US CLOUD laws mean for*
> *Australian businesses" Australian Financial Review, April*
> *16, 2018, https://www.afr.com/technology/cloud-computing/*
> *what-new-us-cloud-laws-mean-for-australian-businesses-20180413-h0ypuu*

Daemen noted that the CLOUD Act addresses some of the sovereignty concerns that had been plaguing countries, stating:

"One of the ways it does this is by recognising and entrenching a vital right to challenge search warrants if we see a conflict between different countries' laws. This is fundamental in a digital age where those holding data are subject to cross-border legal expectations.

"The CLOUD Act also empowers CSPs with added legal rights to inform foreign governments when their citizens are impacted by a US warrant."

> *Ibid.*

Data sovereignty will continue to gain traction as more countries enact legislation enforcing more stringent attention to the storage of data relating to its citizens:

"Indonesia, Vietnam and China are among the Asian countries tightening requirements to store citizen and consumer data locally for the purpose of data protection. Many government agencies and other data collectors store confidential information at data centers within their own countries out of hacking or leakage concerns."

> *Tani, M., "Data center competition heats up in Southeast Asia", Nikkei Asian*
> *Review, October 19, 2018, https://asia.nikkei.com/Business/Business-Trends/*
> *Data-center-competition-heats-up-in-Southeast-Asia*

What should be clear by now is that data sovereignty is a critical consideration for any business that is evaluating whether a workload should be moved into the public

Cloud. For some businesses, this may be readily answered—financial, medical, and government institutions are perhaps most likely to have a clear definition in their home country of data sovereignty practices that must be followed; for other industry verticals, and other countries, research may be required to qualify workload suitability for the public Cloud to avoid creating a thorny legal, privacy, or security issue. Such a review may require involvement from multiple groups within the business: IT, legal, and individual business units, to ensure that data is classified correctly, public Cloud location options are identified, and the appropriate decision is made. Even in situations where the rules are clear, those rules may require extensive work between organizations and regulatory bodies (e.g., consider the APRA guidance mentioned earlier) to qualify workload types that have not been previously evaluated.

COST PLANNING

Although not a security threat as such, a particular risk that should be considered within the public Cloud is the simple one surrounding cost. While the public Cloud can be consumed with very little startup cost (as opposed to having to, say, purchase and deploy a new fleet of servers and storage platforms for a datacenter), the public Cloud is not free. As such, moving workloads into public Cloud should also include a cost analysis phase to avoid placing the business at financial risk.

Such an analysis, in its simplest form, should cover the following issues:

- What is the expected monthly run cost of the workload? This should account for both expected average monthly run costs and potential peak run costs if the workload has seasonal peak activity periods.
- What is the expected growth in the run cost of the workload?
- What is the life expectancy of the workload?
- What is the expected total cost to the business over the lifespan of the workload for running in public Cloud?

Businesses conducting a comprehensive review may then compare that modeling against costing for running the workload on premises. Even if the workload is cheaper to run on premises, it may be that financially the short-term reduction in spending outweighs the long-term increased spending. (It may also spark conversations with on-premises vendors for utility consumption models. This is particularly likely in situations where data will grow for an extended period of time.)

Cost planning is an "eyes wide open" aspect of the public Cloud, particularly when workloads are being moved without any refactorization for public Cloud efficiency, which has led to situations where a year's IT budget was consumed in just a few months after an inadequately planned *lift-and-shift* move into the public Cloud.

The flexibility of the public Cloud can result in higher costs as well if appropriate system management processes are not put in place:

> "Bauer Media was not expecting its infrastructure costs to triple after it migrated to Amazon Web Services."

...

"Eighteen months ago, in the excitement of deploying changes to its properties a lot more quickly, costs were overlooked, and when the company received a massive bill from its infrastructure provider AWS, it hit hard."

"The newly-implemented continuous delivery approach meant developers were spinning up servers constantly for testing and leaving them running when they weren't in use."

"This posed a problem, because while Bauer wanted to offer its developers the freedom to spin up servers as needed, it wasn't too keen on a repeat of its big bill."

> *Coyne, A., "How Bauer Media dealt with public cloud bill shock", IT News, June 2, 2016, https://www.itnews.com.au/news/ how-bauer-media-dealt-with-public-cloud-bill-shock-420319*

Understanding the cost profile doesn't just let us properly plan out the financial models around the public Cloud, but it can also provide some degree of oversight from a security perspective in the same way that any environmental monitoring (which we will cover in more detail later) addresses: namely, if your monthly bill suddenly doubles, it's not an expected variation, and the overall workload profiles have not changed, it might highlight the need for a security review.

ADJUSTING SECURITY MODELS

In the early days of the Internet, before security became a major consideration, it was not unusual for many servers within an organization to have direct Internet access, and, indeed, for the Internet to have direct access to the servers. Eventually, a basic security model grew up around the notion of a demilitarized zone (DMZ) that sat between the Internet and the infrastructure. This is schematically represented in Figure 3.4.

Over time, security practices have become more robust, which can lead to the implementation of additional security zones within the core internal network of an organization, effectively hardening access to systems hosting mission critical data. This is shown at a high level in Figure 3.5.

In such network security models, those servers holding sensitive data are kept even more tightly controlled; they may be kept entirely inaccessible (bidirectionally) from the Internet, requiring manual patch copying processes, and only very specific systems will be able to access them.

Network security frequently focuses on two different topologies; north–south and east–west. This is effectively modeled on racks of systems within a datacenter. *North–south security* refers to incoming connections, outside the datacenter, to systems within the datacenter (i.e., coming in from top of rack or above), or similarly, outgoing connections from systems within the racks. Earlier security practices focused almost entirely on north–south security models: determining what external systems and users could gain access to systems and data housed within the datacenter. However, this was built on the premise of highly trusted internal networks, and effectively meant that security was a *perimeter* activity. In this, consider perimeter security to be similar to a castle with defensive walls and a moat; there are rings of security, as shown in Figure 3.6. The moat represents the external DMZ firewall,

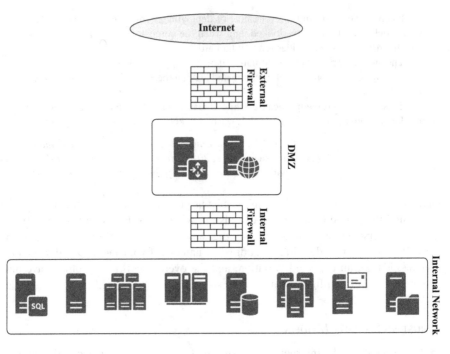

FIGURE 3.4 Classic datacenter security model.

the castle walls represent the internal DMZ firewall, and once you're into the castle courtyard, it's assumed not only that you're perfectly safe, but that you're also reasonably trustworthy.

East–west traffic within a datacenter refers to the ability of individual servers and systems within a particular zone to communicate with one another. Unchecked east–west communication (i.e., a lack of east–west security) is premised around the somewhat flawed assumption these days that if something is connected to the internal network, it is trusted.

East–west security refers to having more stringent controls of traffic flow between elements within the corporate network. Just because someone is on the corporate network [e.g., via a retail point-of-sale (POS) terminal] does not mean that they should have network connectivity to the finance database. Note that here we are differentiating between *network access* and *login access*. (In other words, perimeter security is not about giving the keys to every room in the castle to someone as soon as s/he has passed over the moat and through the gate walls, but it does assume that it's OK for them to knock on any door in the castle.)

Businesses following a more mature security model are likely to implement east–west security controls, limiting the amount of network interaction permitted between elements in the datacenter. While users who have access to the file server may also have a desktop application allowing them to access the timesheet application, why should the file server itself need to have access to the timesheet database?

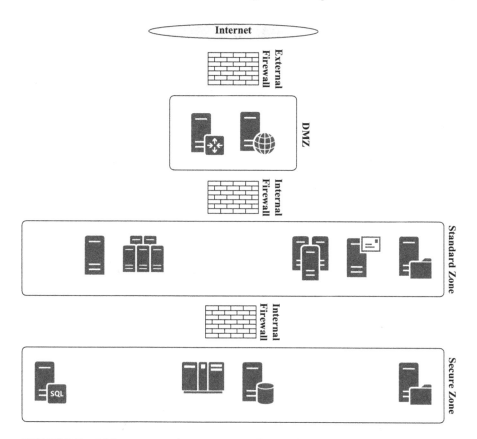

FIGURE 3.5   Adding a secure zone to an internal network.

In essence, east–west security is about (wherever possible) automatically denying access between systems, unless there is a specific call for them to have access.

The challenge that many businesses face with east–west security models is that unless they've been implemented from the beginning, they are difficult and time consuming, either procedurally or technically, to get working: *technically* because a large number of interdependencies may build up between systems over time in a classic perimeter security model, and *procedurally*, because decision makers within the business may be reluctant to agree to access being cut off between systems just in case it causes a problem further down the track.

The creation of a security zone within an internal network not only provides additional north–south protection but also starts to establish some east–west isolation, but within on-premises environments, many businesses may not progress very much further past this point. Within the datacenter, network virtualization is starting to address this, allowing *microsegmentation* to be adopted, effectively establishing stringent east–west security controls over workloads *in addition* to the north–south security models that we would expect. In its simplest interpretation, this is

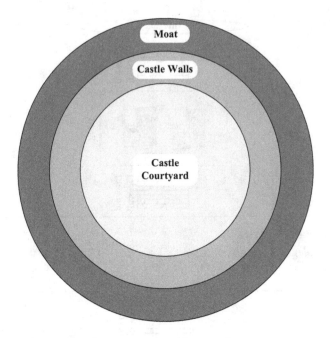

FIGURE 3.6   Perimeter security as represented by a castle.

the equivalent of being able to deploy a virtual firewall around every host or service within the network. This is represented conceptually in Figure 3.7.

We've discussed this within an on-premises context to provide the background to how we work with security when we move into a public Cloud environment.

Security within the public Cloud is closely designed around enabling east–west security practices. In this, many businesses will see a move into the public Cloud as enabling them to revisit existing security processes and improve on them. Consider, for instance, the AWS Virtual Private Cloud (VPC) function. To quote Amazon:

> "Amazon Virtual Private Cloud (Amazon VPC) enables you to launch AWS resources into a virtual network that you've defined. This virtual network closely resembles a traditional network that you'd operate in your own data center, with the benefits of using the scalable infrastructure of AWS."

> *What is Amazon VPC? https://docs.aws.amazon.com/vpc/latest/userguide/what-is-amazon-vpc.html*

Businesses desiring tighter security controls when moving into the public Cloud will consider options such as VPC, but logically isolating specific workloads into their own VPC and achieving higher levels of security than would necessarily be achieved by running all public Cloud resources within a single security zone. VPCs may be entirely isolated, connected to the Internet, connected to a datacenter, and so forth, depending on the specific access requirements to and from that VPC. A logical view of two VPCs is shown in Figure 3.8.

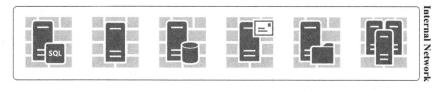

FIGURE 3.7 Network virtualization allowing for tighter east-west network security controls.

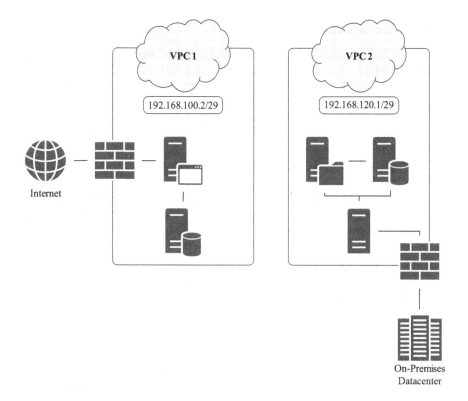

FIGURE 3.8 Conceptual view of virtual private Clouds (VPCs).

In our VPC example, we have two distinct workloads. VPC 1 is presumably some form of web application wherein there is an application server and database server operating within the VPC, and the application server has access to the public internet. VPC 2 is not connected to the Internet but *does* have a connection back to the business datacenter, and presumably is used for some form of analysis or data crunching activity comprising files and database information.

As you might expect, VPCs also allow elements of the overall public Cloud subscription to be isolated from broader access within the business; each VPC can be segregated for access permissions in addition to perimeter controls.

Strategies such as virtual private Clouds within public Cloud environments allow a Cloud user to establish strong isolation policies between workloads, effectively establishing a *deny-access-unless-exception* model. In addition to standard security processes, following such models can substantially reduce security risks within a public Cloud environment. Even where options such as VPCs are not used, it is imperative in a public Cloud environment to limit connectivity in between systems to only the connectivity required; this then becomes a natural defense to "cross-contamination" in the event of an individual system's security being compromised.

STANDARD SECURITY PRACTICES

Let us briefly reconsider the AWS Shared Responsibility Model outlined in Figure 3.3, where an Amazon outline shows that subscribers are responsible for security *in* the public Cloud. Some of the security responsibilities for subscribers include the following:

- Customer data
- Platform, applications, identity, and access management
- Operating systems, network and firewall configurations

In this sense, it is worthwhile emphasizing the importance of public Cloud subscribers continuing to follow security best practices, regardless of whether they are operating within their own datacenter or within the public Cloud.

Patching

Of primary concern within IaaS, a base consideration for standard security practices is to ensure that systems remain patched. This means that the overall environment as deployed must be designed to support systems being rebooted when required for systems maintenance functions.

In 2017 it was reported that

> "MongoDB databases are being decimated in soaring ransomware attacks that have seen the number of compromised systems more than double to 27,000 in a day.
>
> Criminals are accessing, copying and deleting data from unpatched or badly-configured databases."
>
> *Pauli, D., "MongoDB ransom attacks soar, body count hits 27,000 in hours", The Register, January 9, 2017, https://www.theregister.co.uk/2017/01/09/mongodb/*

While a significant number of the hacks were undoubtedly related to minimum security controls being enabled as the default for MongoDB installations, it is quite common to see system hacks originating from tools exploiting known, repaired vulnerabilities, and no doubt this was a factor in the MongoDB example as well.

While trained infrastructure and application administrators usually understand the importance of keeping systems well patched, a challenge within the public

Cloud, of course, is that there is no guarantee that trained infrastructure or application administrators will be deploying the systems in the first place. For some organizations, this may be done by "shadow IT"—people within the business who may not have an IT background but nevertheless are able to use easy-to-consume Cloud services to deploy an application or function. In other organizations (usually smaller ones, or startups), there may be no formal IT people at all; in either case, essential infrastructure/application operations such as covered in this section may fall through the cracks. It is imperative, therefore, that a business moving workloads into the public Cloud ensure that there is appropriate planning and rigor around patching.

Access Control

It's rarely, if ever, good security practice to have an open slather policy for access to systems being deployed, regardless of whether they are deployed within the public Cloud or an on-premises environment.

Access control will cover all the following:

- *Who* can access the system
- *How* they are authenticated
- *What* can they do once they are authenticated

The level of granularity, of course, will depend on what functionality is available, either in the public Cloud provider of choice, or at a higher level, what system is being deployed or used within the public Cloud environment.

The way in which access is authenticated (and, consequently, their mapping to specific things that they can do) is critically important. An ad hoc/lazy approach might be to use basic access authentication (e.g., the equivalent to local accounts on Windows or Linux) for each system deployed, but this quickly becomes a management nightmare. Enterprises with more rigorous control systems will typically seek to tie in, wherever possible, on-premises authentication system with public Cloud access, ensuring that the level of access to any system can be controlled by a single point, and this practice will undoubtedly continue. (Alternately, they may seek to use multi-function single sign-on systems that integrate traditional on-premises authentication systems and next generation services.)

In some cases, access control is even deployed to act as a means of ensuring that the IT team is made aware of shadow IT activities. For instance, an organization may force the use of a single-sign-on (SSO) system, under the full control of the IT department, in order to access any internal systems. Thus, if a group within the business develops some service around a Cloud-based application, the application either will have to act in isolation, or, if it is to be connected to any business-owned data, will require SSO integration, thereby allowing control, maintenance, and life-cycle of the workload to be formalized.

Access control applies not just in IaaS situations but in any situation where an account must be configured to provide functionality. Let us consider, for instance, backup and recovery solutions for SaaS-based products, such as Office 365 and Salesforce. In order for a backup service to connect into the SaaS environment to retrieve content, or write content back in, it will require particular permissions. For instance, for Office 365 mail, it might need permissions such as:

- List users
- Impersonate user
- Read email for user
- Write email for user
- Create email folder

In such situations, the account or API permissions that are granted to the SaaS backup and recovery product should be limited to an exact list of the documented, required permissions. Depending on the maturity of the business, this will either come naturally or may be counter to normal techniques; in some businesses it is not uncommon to see access permissions for services "solved" by simply granting full administrative privileges to the service and trusting that the service is trustworthy. Yet, when we *reflect on trusting trust*, if a service documents the exact permissions required, it's foolish and hazardous to provide additional permissions simply because it's easier to perform.

Hardening

Just as an armadillo protects itself by rolling up into a ball covered by its hard, leathery shell, security hardening is about reducing the number of ways in which an attacker can breach or cause damage to a system. For example, consider a virtual storage appliance deployable from a public Cloud marketplace that is supplied with the following services for accessing its console and command interface:

- Standard HTML service (http)
- Secure HTML service (https)
- Secure shell (SSH)
- Telnet
- Representational state transfer (REST) API

From a hardening perspective, there are several things that a security team might require for such an appliance. These include, but are unlikely to be limited to, the following:

1. **Disable insecure protocols:**
    a. Both **http** and **telnet** are inherently insecure; while they may be acceptable for use in lab environments, or on systems which are physically isolated from external networks, they are usually disabled in hardening processes.
2. **Replace self-signed certificates** with official, validated certificates:
    a. Protocols such as **https** are secured through the use of a certificate. Most systems make use of certificates, which an accessing client can import, and compare on subsequent visits to confirm that the host it is accessing is authentic. While self-signed certificates may be deemed acceptable in low-security environments, security-conscious organizations will

use authorized, third-party certificate suppliers to generate appropriately trustworthy certificates that can be used.

3. **Require key-based access for ssh:**
   a. Rather than necessarily using a password, use shared keys that have been securely exchanged. Unlocking the key on the client system can require a password, but it is the key rather than a password which is sent over the network.

4. **Limit access to specific hosts:**
   a. Particular systems may have access locked down so that regardless of whether a user has valid credentials, the user may only access the system from particular hosts within the environment. (For example, protocols such as ssh can be configured to require both key based access, and limit access to specific hosts, reducing the access risk profile further.)

5. **Require automatic timeout of sessions:**
   a. Just as we expect a laptop, desktop, tablet, or smartphone to automatically lock itself after we haven't used it for a few minutes, security-hardening processes will force the logout of accessing users if they have been idle for a certain period of time. This might be either hardcoded or configurable by a security administrator.

6. **Require appropriate password protocols.** This might include such options as:
   a. Maximum number of days before a user password must be changed.
   b. Minimum number of days before a user password can be changed.
   c. Automatic disabling of a user account after a certain number of unsuccessful logins.
   d. Increasing delays on login reattempts after a failed login (e.g., after the first failed attempt, the system may wait 5 seconds before allowing the next attempt; after the second, 30 seconds; and after the third, 5 minutes).
   e. *Password history*—preventing users from reusing passwords that have been used recently. This may also prevent users from using password that are *too similar* to previous passwords, stopping common lazy techniques such as incrementing a number at the end of a password each month. (E.g., 'B0$$access1', 'B0$$access2', 'B0$$access3', and so on.)
   f. *Password complexity*—preventing users from using as a password such as their own username, simplistic strings such as "abc123" and "password"; passwords that are too short, or passwords that do not include a variety of letters, digits, and special characters.
   g. Integration into a third-party enterprise password management system. In some cases, the business will require passwords to be stored in an appropriately secured database, with users being able to "check out" passwords only when they need to access a system, but in a way that they do not get to see the password themselves.

7. **Integrate into SSO:**
   a. Where single sign-on is used within an organization, hardening practices will usually require its use to prevent mismanagement of local accounts on individual systems.
   b. Disable, wherever possible, default accounts after SSO has been enabled.

8. **Differentiate between security and system administrators:**
   a. This may mean that an authorized administrator on a system (particularly a virtual appliance) cannot erase data without approval provided by a security administrator and cannot change the security settings for users (including themselves).
   b. Likewise, the security administrator may have no control whatsoever over any other aspect of the system configuration *other* than security.

Hardening is at once simple in the goal but potentially complex in the implementation, but for each step taken in the hardening process, tangible risks can be eliminated from the environment.

Basic security principles such as hardening's enforcement password controls, even for temporary data or systems, is often something that businesses fail to fully achieve in a public Cloud environment, leading to a seemingly never-ending stream of breaches. For example:

> Veeam has blamed "human error" for the exposure of a marketing database containing millions of names and email addresses.
>
> "The unencrypted MongoDB resource was left open for anyone to view after a migration between different AWS systems, Peter McKay, co-CEO and president at Veeam, told The Register. The resource – which wasn't password-protected – was left open for 13 days between 28 August and 10 September."

> Leyden, J., "Veeam holds its hands up, admits database leak was plain 'complacency'" The Register, September 14, 2018, https://www.theregister. co.uk/2018/09/14/veeam_leak_follow_up/

Data leaks are quite common when it comes to object storage; not because object storage is inherently secure, but because best-practice security approaches, such as appropriate hardening, is all too frequently missed:

> "A company that sells surveillance software to parents and employers left "terabytes of data" including photos, audio recordings, text messages and web history, exposed in a poorly-protected Amazon S3 bucket."

> Franceschi-Bicchierai, L., "Spyware Company Leaves 'Terabytes' of Selfies, Text Messages, and Location Data Exposed OnlineMotherboard," August 23 2018, https://motherboard.vice.com/en_us/article/9kmj4v/ spyware-company-spyfone-terabytes-data-exposed-online-leak.

Accept That Bad Things Can Happen

It is imperative that the business accept that undesirable events can take place: that a breach, or a data loss situation might occur.

This isn't about being fatalistic, but about ensuring that appropriate recovery processes are developed and acted upon, such as the following:

- **A breach might occur:** If the business has a legislative requirement to report a breach, it should have processes in place to clearly articulate the required details of the breach to the mandated parties. One might also suggest that regardless of legislation, businesses should consider themselves *ethically obliged* to report breaches to affected customers or users of their services.

- **A data loss situation might occur:** In this we are not referring to exfiltration of data (that's covered by a breach), but instead, data may be erased or corrupted. This requires appropriate consideration of how data can be recovered in such situations and is a topic that we will explore extensively in the following chapter.

In General

We might say that more broadly, making use of the public Cloud does not give you a get-out-of-jail card when it comes to leveraging best practices approaches to security. It matters naught whether you use a database, deploy a server or subscribe to a service on premises, or in the public Cloud; you still have to follow appropriate security protocols to reduce the risk of a data breach, corruption, or loss.

Situational Awareness

If you own your own datacenter, you'll likely have 24×7 security in some form or another. It might be a permanent presence of security staff, or it might be staffed during the day with motion sensors and proximity alarms at off hours that can notify contracted security staff. Regardless, if someone physically breaks into your datacenter, there's a good chance you'll know about it in some form or another.

In a similar fashion, if the datacenter floods, there's a fire, a power outage, or some other major event, you'd expect that the appropriate people within your business would be aware of the situation. Depending on how they are impacted, your customers or partners, too, might become aware of the situation. This knowledge can be considered to be *situational awareness.*

Cloud service providers, of course, are expected to provide high degrees of physical security, and they do. One does not expect to hear a story of a Cloud service provider's datacenter left unguarded with the doors unlocked. The question you must ask yourself, though, is: When moving into the public Cloud, how will your situational environment awareness change?

Disclosure laws can evolve in any jurisdictions, but as one loses control of the infrastructure, there is an implicit trust relationship that has to be established. If you don't trust the fundamental security of the environment, don't use the environment. (This is effectively the Shared Responsibility model that AWS documents; you are encouraged to trust that they look after the security of their public Cloud, while you look after security **in** your environment within their public Cloud.)

Trust should never be *blind* trust, however. A person who invests her/his retirement savings with a particular fund is usually advised to track and monitor how that fund is going; rather than just believing that the fund should achieve an optimum return on investment and not do anything wrong, the fund investor should stay appraised of the fund's performance, and remain alert to any publicized cases of incorrect behavior by the fund manager that could have a flow-on effect.

Likewise, moving workloads into the public Cloud means you need to remain *alert* to issues that occur. This might range from the largest sorts of incidents (e.g., terrorists attacking a Cloud provider datacenter) through to very platform or workload specific incidents (e.g., a database you have deployed from the marketplace having a security vulnerability alert issued).

Another aspect of situational awareness relates to monitoring: understanding normal system and access behaviors, which can be critical in detecting hacking attempts, cyber espionage, data exfiltration in progress, ransomware attacks, and a myriad of other security issues.

For example, consider the following scenarios:

- *System load:* Capacity monitoring may establish that the environment runs at 50% resource loading on any normal day of the month, but for 2 days prior to and 1 day after end of month, resource loading may be as high as 80%. If continuous monitoring shows that 10 days into the month the system load is sitting at a consistent 90%, the system could be investigated to determine if (a) there is some issue with an element of the environment or (b) there is some form of cyber attack underway.
- *Bandwidth consumption:* On a normal basis, the business might see 1 TB per day of data flowing out of the public Cloud environment, and 5 TB per day flowing into the public environment, but by 8 a.m. 10 TB of data has flowed out of the public Cloud environment, and the normal amount has flowed in, and it is not an expected "seasonal variant."
- *Cyber espionage:* Do users at the Broken Hill retail outlet normally log onto the corporate file server at 2 a.m.? Is it common for someone in to VPN into the corporate network from Bugtussle, Kentucky, and then log onto a server in Cork, Ireland, before connecting to an IP address in the Ukraine?
- *Data exfiltration:* System access matching may reveal that on an average day, a salesperson accesses 1% of the corporate customer database. It would perhaps warrant investigation, then, if, within a 2-hour period, a salesperson accesses 35% of the corporate customer database. (Especially if the person then starts sending large emails to an external email address.)
- *Ransomware:* Your average twice-daily snapshot of a file server residing in a VPC represents a 3% change rate. If the most recent snapshot represents a 17% change, perhaps there's just a lot of activity (e.g., end of month), but perhaps there's some form of ransomware attack currently underway.

This sort of monitoring is not only a point-in-time view but an understanding from a capacity management and trending point of view, otherwise the monitoring required for this analysis has too much risk of raising false positives. Such monitoring also needs to understand seasonal spikes, such as:

- Does traffic double over holiday seasons?
- Do supplier databases see twice the number of updates on a quarterly basis?
- Do the number of new user accounts increase by 50 times over a 2-day period at the start of each semester?

As you may observe from the above, seasonal spikes or variations may include some scenarios that happen regardless of the industry that the business operates in, and some may be very specific to the industry the business operates in.

Understanding growth (or declination) patterns is also important: what may be seen as aberrant behavior within the public Cloud environment today may be perfectly normal in a year's time after fully expected 10% annual growth.

Situational environment awareness might best be summed up with a quote from fictional character, "Alastor Moody" from Harry Potter: *"Constant vigilance!"*[5]

We might sum up our review of threat and risk mitigation within the public Cloud by a few simple rules:

1. In the public Cloud, security may be a shared responsibility, but your business will undoubtedly remain accountable for security of your data and workloads, regardless of who, individually, is responsible for any specific aspect of security.
2. Data sovereignty requires careful analysis and understanding of the content of data and the nature of the workloads that you are placing in the public Cloud, and this will need regular review in order to ensure changes to sovereignty requirements, either within your own country or in the country in which your data resides with a Cloud service provider; this is essential.
3. The more sensitive your industry (finance, government, medical, etc.), the more likelihood there is that there will be legislative requirements within your jurisdiction on what types of data and workloads you can put in public Cloud (or where you must keep copies). It is imperative, therefore, that workloads moving into the public cloud do so under careful scrutiny to avoid placing your data at risk, and your organization at legal risk.
4. Even if your organization has been focused within the datacenter on perimeter-based security, you must be prepared to move to a comprehensive east–west approach analysis to ensure that your data and systems remain secure.
5. Normal security practices don't go away; practices such as appropriate patching, hardening, and careful access control remain critical.
6. You must plan for bad things happening; there's no point wondering how you might recover data after it is lost because of a security incident; you need to have planned in advance for that recovery scenario and enacted the appropriate protection policies in advance.
7. Situational environment awareness is important. This lets you continuously monitor your environment while maintaining a clear view of your risk or threat profile at any point in time on the basis of internal or external factors.

SOURCES

1. https://www.secureworks.com/blog/cyber-threat-basics
2. https://www.trendmicro.com/vinfo/us/security/definition/ransomware
3. www.us.norton.com

---

5 It seems appropriate to revisit *trusting trust*, given the fictional Alastor Moody was actually being impersonated by someone else who was exclaiming "Constant vigilance!".

4. www.veracode.com

5. www.usa.kaspersky.com

6. https://www.trendmicro.com/vinfo/us/security/definition/spear-phishing

7. Provos, N., Rajab, M. A., and Mavrommatis, P. "Cybercrime 2.0: When the Cloud Turns Dark," *ACM Communications* 52(4), 42–47 (2009).

8. *Researchers Demo Cloud Security Issue with Amazon AWS Attack*, October 2011 (available online at http://www.pcworld.idg.com.au/article/405419/researchers_demo_cloud_security_issue_amazon_aws_attack/).

9. Gruschka. N., and L. L. Iacono, "Vulnerable Cloud: SOAP Message Security Validation Revisited," *IEEE International Conference on Web Services*, Los Angeles, 2009.

10. *Researchers Demo Cloud Security Issue with Amazon AWS Attack*, October 2011 (available online at http://www.pcworld.idg.com.au/article/405419/researchers_demo_cloud_security_issue_amazon_aws_attack/).

11. Catteddu, D., and G. Hogben, *Cloud Computing Benefits, Risks and Recommendations for Information Security*, The European Network and Information Security Agency (ENISA), November 2009.

12. *Insider Threats Related to Cloud Computing*, CERT, July 2012 (available online at http://www.cert.org/).

13. *Data Breach Trends & Stats*, Symantec, 2012 (available online at http://www.indefenseofdata.com/data-breach-trends-stats/).

14. "A Few Wrinkles Are Etching Facebook, Other Social Sites," *USA Today*, 2011 (available online at http://www.usatoday.com/printedition/life/20090115/socialnetworking15_st.art.htm).

15. "An Update on LinkedIn Member Passwords Compromised," *LinkedIn Blog*, June 2012 (available online at http://blog.linkedin.com/2012/06/06/linkedin-member-passwords-compromised/).

16. "Dropbox: Yes, We Were Hacked," August 2012 (available online at http://gigaom.com/cloud/dropbox-yes-we-were-hacked/).

17. "Amazon.com Server Said to Have Been Used in Sony Attack," May 2011 (available online at http://www.bloomberg.com/news/2011-05-13/sony-network-said-to-have-been-invaded-by-hackers-using-amazon-com-server.html).

18. *Zeus Crimeware Using Amazon's EC2 as Command and Control Server* (DOI = http://www.zdnet.com/blog/security/zeus-crimeare-using-amazons-ec2-as-command-and-control-server/5110).

19. *The Blue Pill* (DOI = http://theinvisiblethings.blogspot.com/2008/07/0wning-xen-invegas.html).

20. *Salesforce.com Outage Hits Thousands of Businesses* (DOI = http://news.cnet.com/8301-1001_3-10136540-92.html).

21. BBC, *The Sidekick Cloud Disaster* (DOI = http://www.bbc.co.uk/blogs/technology/2009/10/the_sidekick_cloud_disaster.html).

22. Dahbur, K., M. Bassil, and A. B. Tarakji, *A Survey of Risks, Threats, and Vulnerabilities in Cloud Computing*, School of Engineering and Computing Sciences, the New York Institute of Technology.

23. http://www.businessdictionary.com/definition/impact.html

24. http://www.businessdictionary.com/definition/likelihood.html

25. The European Network and Information Security Agency (ENISA), *Cloud Computing: Benefits, Risks and Recommendations for Information Security,*" Rev. B, December 2012.
26. Chou, Te-Shun. "Security Threats on Cloud Computing Vulnerabilities," *The International Journal of Computer Science and Information Technology (IJCSIT)*, 5(3):79–88.
27. Dahbur, K., Mohammad, B., and Tarakji, A. B. 2011. ACM
28. ENISA.

4 Cloud Data Protection

INTRODUCTION—THE LEGEND OF DAEDALUS AND ICARUS

One of the most enduring and frequently told stories in Greek mythology is that of Daedalus and Icarus. According to the legend, having fashioned for the King of Crete a labyrinth from which escape was impossible without very specific knowledge, Daedalus fell afoul of his sponsor, perhaps as much as anything else because as the builder of the labyrinth, Daedalus knew how to escape it.

The King of Crete therefore imprisoned Daedalus, and his son Icarus, in a tower, on an island from which escape by land or sea was impossible. Daedalus was, however, a da Vinci–like genius—an inventor of prodigious expertise. Daedalus noticed that while escape from sea or land was impossible, there was an endless number of seabirds who flew to from the island with ease, and so the escape plan was hatched. Using wax from candles to hold together dropped feathers from the seabirds, Daedalus constructed wings for his son, and himself, so that they might escape to freedom.

Smart enough to understand the risks involved, Daedalus warned his son that they had to fly sensibly if they were to successfully escape: too low, and they might fall into the Aegean Sea to drown; too high, and their wings made from wax would be exposed to the heat of the sun. But Icarus, young and eager, became lost in the moment, enjoying the sensation of flight too much. One of the more eloquent retellings of the myth comes from Josephine Preston Peabody, in "Old Greek Folk Stories Told Anew" (1897) [1], where she wrote:

> At first there was a terror in the joy. The wide vacancy of the air dazed them, —a glance downward made their brains reel. But when a great wind filled their wings, and Icarus felt himself sustained, like a halcyon-bird in the hollow of a wave, like a child uplifted by his mother, he forgot everything in the world but joy. He forgot Crete and the other islands that he had passed over: he saw but vaguely that winged thing in the distance before him that was his father Daedalus. He longed for one draught of flight to quench the thirst of his captivity: he stretched out his arms to the sky and made towards the highest heavens.
>
> Alas for him! Warmer and warmer grew the air. Those arms, that had seemed to uphold him, relaxed. His wings wavered, drooped. He fluttered his young hands vainly, — he was falling, —and in that terror he remembered. The heat of the sun had melted the wax from his wings; the feathers were falling, one by one, like snowflakes; and there was none to help.
>
> He fell like a leaf tossed down the wind, down, down, with one cry that overtook Daedalus far away. When he returned, and sought high and low for the poor boy, he saw nothing but the bird-like feathers afloat on the water, and he knew that Icarus was drowned.

In some respects, the story of the public Cloud is the story of Daedalus and Icarus. A business, feeling trapped by the confines of IT, may escape by using the public Cloud; this is not, by itself, undesirable. Yet, if the business rises too high, too

DOI: 10.1201/9781003459569-4

fast—if it gives into the giddy sensation of a multitude of services available at the simplest access, without considering the consequences and the safety requirements therein—it may find itself figuratively flying too close to the sun and lose everything.

ALL CARE, NO RESPONSIBILITY

The phrase "all care, no responsibility" is used primarily as a basic description of many service contracts or legal obligations. In short, it means "we take all care to avoid X, but take no responsibility if X happens." Such disclaimers are used everywhere: by governments large and small, by publicly traded entities, by owner/operator tradespeople, and even by teachers taking children on a school excursion. *We promise to do our best but aren't legally responsible if something goes wrong.* It is with this phrase in mind that we should consider what obligations Cloud service providers have on keeping your data safe.

Perhaps the most fundamental mistake that a business or individuals can make when moving data or services into a public Cloud environment is to *assume* that the public Cloud vendor will protect their data. This is simply, drastically, false.

There is no doubt that public Cloud providers such as AWS, Azure, and Google all have a degree of responsibility for the services that they sell to businesses, large or small. This involves a base level of infrastructure protection, which is similar to the protection applied to infrastructure within a datacenter. This entails "the basics," so to speak, such as:

- Protecting provisioned compute instances from the failure of a hypervisor
- Protecting provisioned storage from the failure of a single disk
- Protecting provisioned databases from the failure of an underlying disk

However, this is effectively where the responsibility of public Cloud providers ends when it comes to protecting your data when it resides in their datacenters. It is worth considering some of the terms and conditions of common public Cloud service providers to understand the importance of this key fact. A sufficiently common problem in the digital age is that almost everything we use has a lengthy service agreement attached to it; users quickly become apathetic toward such agreements and quickly scroll through to click "Accept" without reviewing. This might be consequence-free when one is setting up a new smartphone, or installing software to edit Nanna's 80th birthday video, but it has more dire consequences when signing up to a service that will run mission-critical systems or store sensitive customer data.

Microsoft Office 365 Service Agreement [2], which was published on March 1, 2018 and became effective on May 1, 2018, states under Item 6, "Service Availability," item 6.b.:

> We strive to keep the Services up and running; however, all online services suffer occasional disruptions and outages and Microsoft is not liable for any disruption or loss you may suffer as a result. In the event of an outage, you may not be able to retrieve

Your Content or Data that you've stored. We recommend that you regularly backup Your Content and Data that you store on the Services or store using Third-Party Apps and Services.

The AWS Customer Agreement [3], as of its May 14, 2018 update, states under the section, "Your Responsibilities," item 4.3:

Your Security and Backup. You are responsible for properly configuring and using the Service Offerings and otherwise taking appropriate action to secure, protect and backup your accounts and Your Content in a manner that will provide appropriate security and protection, which might include use of encryption to protect Your Content from unauthorized access and routinely archiving Your Content.

By and large, the core *Google Cloud Service Terms* document simply doesn't mention data backup responsibilities, although the liability statements specifically eschew responsibility for data loss situations. Google's *Cloud Platform Documentation* [4], specifically when comparing the Google Compute Engine to AWS EBS, does, however, explicitly state:

Each service provides redundancy within a single zone for increased durability. While this feature provides some protection against hardware failure, it does not protect against data corruption or accidental deletions due to user or application error. To protect important data, users should perform regular data backups and disk snapshots.

Meanwhile, NVIDIA-specific sections of the Google Cloud Service Terms [5] (release date August 25, 2016) explicitly state:

In addition, you agree that you are solely responsible for maintaining appropriate data backups and system restore points for your Enterprise systems, and that NVIDIA will have no responsibility for any damage or loss to such systems (including loss of data or access) arising from or relating to (a) any changes to the configuration, application settings, environment variables, registry, drivers, BIOS, or other attributes of the systems (or any part of such systems) initiated through the Software; or (b) installation of any Software or third party software patches initiated through the Software.

While the Microsoft Azure Cloud platform does offer a very limited service for backup and recovery, this is not enabled by default as it a paid subscription. Furthermore, the Microsoft Azure Agreement [6] (January 2014) states under Section 2, "Security, privacy, and data protection":

Security. We maintain appropriate technical and organizational measures, internal controls, and data security routines intended to protect Customer Data against accidental loss or change, unauthorized disclosure or access, or unlawful destruction. Current information about our security practices can be found within the Trust Center. You are wholly responsible for configuring your Customer Solution to ensure adequate security, protection, and backup of Customer Data.

The Cloud provider, DigitalOcean, has perhaps some of the most direct language for its terms and conditions [7] (May 8, 2018), stating unequivocally:

9. Backup

9.1 Subscriber is solely responsible for the preservation of Subscriber's data which Subscriber saves onto its virtual server (the "Data"). EVEN WITH RESPECT TO DATA AS TO WHICH SUBSCRIBER CONTRACTS FOR BACKUP SERVICES PROVIDED BY DIGITALOCEAN, TO THE EXTENT PERMITTED BY APPLICABLE LAW, DIGITALOCEAN SHALL HAVE NO RESPONSIBILITY TO PRESERVE DATA. DIGITALOCEAN SHALL HAVE NO LIABILITY FOR ANY DATA THAT MAY BE LOST, OR UNRECOVERABLE, BY REASON OF SUBSCRIBER'S FAILURE TO BACKUP ITS DATA OR FOR ANY OTHER REASON.

It is pertinent to note that DigitalOcean even advises subscribers that they are still responsible for having a backup of their data *even if they are using backup services provided by DigitalOcean*. If that weren't enough, DigitalOcean have a "lay view" or a summarized version of their terms and conditions, which interprets the above to mean:

In other words,

We trust that you'll be responsible and back up your own data. Things happen!

Similar guidance that protection of data stored within a Cloud service is the sole responsibility of the account holder can be found for most, if not all, Cloud platforms. (To the extent that if a Cloud service provider does not mention data backup responsibilities in its terms and conditions, it would be a remarkably brave subscriber who assumed this meant they were fully covered.)

Yet, it is not just whether your data is protected from accidental or malicious deletion/corruption, or systems failure in public Cloud that you must consider when deploying workloads in that space. While there remains heated debate in many Cloud circles as to whether you should think of your Cloud as "another datacentre," there is a parallel to traditional colocation/rental datacenters that you need to think; specifically, what happens if the datacenter closes down?

Traditional datacenter relocations or closures are *usually* orderly affairs. It is quite reasonable for a datacenter provider to give at least a year's notice to its customers that they will need to vacate the premises and find a new datacenter. As IT infrastructure has become more complex, with greater interdependencies, it is increasingly rare to see any other than small companies, occupying maybe only a rack or two, migrate between datacenters by performing a physical "lift and shift"; instead, new equipment will be procured and workloads migrated with minimal disruption to the customers and employees. A complete shift of workloads from one location to another is complex and will remain so for some time to come.

The same may not be said of public Cloud services. Even with adequate warning of impending closure of a Cloud datacenter, businesses may suddenly find themselves facing substantial fees for data egress, even *if* the timeframe allowed is practical. For instance, Mark Dargin on March 16 wrote in article titled "What to do if your cloud provider stops offering its services" (*Network World*) [8]:

> In 2013, Nirvanix stopped offering it Cloud services and gave customers only two weeks' notice to move their data off of their platform.

For any customer that had significantly invested in workloads within such a Cloud, a 2-week exit time might have been a worst-nightmare scenario. Yet, 2 weeks could seem luxurious. Consider "A CIO's worst nightmare: When your cloud provider goes bankrupt" by Derek du Preez, January 6, 2015 for *diginomica* [9]:

> Paul Golland, CIO of the north-east London borough of Waltham Forest, in early 2013 faced a crisis that I'm sure all CIOs would never wish to go through–being told that your sole cloud provider is going into administration and that you have 24 to 48 hours to get your business' data and systems out and into a new environment.

If there's one thing that should come out of these stories, it's that when it comes to your data in public Cloud, there should be an appreciation that if *you* don't take the time to protect your data, no-one else will.

There is another consideration of course beyond the extreme situation of a service provider closing up shop, and that's data or service *availability*. Throughout the rest of the chapter, we will discuss various techniques for backing up and recovering your data as it relates to the public Cloud, but all the protection in the world doesn't matter if the data (or more correctly, the service that uses the data) can't be accessed at the *right time*.

Let's consider, for example, how we normally would look at provisioning for an on-premises primary and failover datacenter arrangement. For a start, we need to ensure that the two datacenters are sufficiently physically separate such that a major physical incident at one datacenter should not have an effect on the other. For instance, in cities they should not be on the same power grid block, and, as we have seen in tragic terrorist incidents, should be far enough apart that an event that causes the physical destruction of one is unlikely to cause the physical destruction of the other. This could also cover the potential for natural disaster situations. There's always a limit to what can be planned, of course,[1] and part of any normal risk mitigation planning for the business will establish likely scenarios—and potentially outline possible scenarios that the business cannot budget to mitigate.

Disregarding the IT services inside each datacenter, for *each* datacenter, we would aim to have:

- Dual incoming power supplies, preferably from alternate power suppliers.
- Dual incoming/outgoing network links, preferably from alternate suppliers who do not share the same backbone (this would cover interdatacenter links as well as internet links in a modern environment).
- The abovementioned dual power and network links should be serviced from geographically separate connection points to the datacenter (e.g., it should not

---

1 There also always reaches a point where once a particular scale of disaster happens; the last thing your employees are going to be worried about is whether your customers can access your services.

be possible to sever all network connections to the datacenter from the same location).

- Local power generation services for mission-critical systems (e.g., diesel generators, extended battery reserves).
- Uninterruptable power supplies (where possible, redundant).

Within the datacenters, service resilience starts with the basics: dual power supplies fed from different core power services for every rack, and every item of equipment, dual network connections to redundant switches (IP and fiber), hardware fault tolerance, and so on.

The objective of such configurations is not to *gold-plate* the IT environment, but a simple, humble recognition that, in order to protect the business from service failure, there's a plethora of activities that need to be considered relating to data and service availability long before you get to the point of planning adequate backup and recovery services: bad things can go wrong, and sometimes we can't be in control of those processes (e.g., someone with digging equipment a hundred metres away from the business tearing through fiberoptic data lines).

When you move to the public Cloud, *none of the above considerations disappear,* either. Public Cloud providers do not run an environment that guarantees your data is always *available.* They provide regions of access, and within those regions, different availability or reliability zones. It is not their responsibility to ensure your service fails over from one location to the other *unless you include that in the services you engage.* Even then, it is highly possible that the management of that failover is likely to be your responsibility, not theirs.

Also bear in mind that it is possible for the Cloud service provider to accidentally engender a situation that makes your data unavailable. In June 2018, for instance, the Google virtual machine public Cloud compute environment encountered an error whereby some virtual machines became unavailable because they were allocated a duplicate external IP address [11]. Although Google resolved the situation, it also advised affected customers they might still need to recreate their virtual machine:

The issue with Google Compute Engine VM instances being allocated duplicate external IP addresses has been resolved for all affected projects as of Saturday, 2018-06-16 12:59 US/Pacific. Customers with VMs having duplicate internal IP addresses should follow the workaround described earlier, which is to delete (without deleting the boot disk), and recreate the affected VM instances. We will conduct an internal investigation of this issue and make appropriate improvements to our systems to help prevent or minimize future recurrence.

*Google Compute Engine Incident #18005 https://status.cloud.
google.com/incident/compute/18005#18005007*

Without taking this into consideration, moving your workloads into the public Cloud is no guarantee of data availability, and ultimately, if your data is unavailable at a critical point in time, it may as well have been deleted.

YOUR BUSINESS IS NOT UNIQUE

It is a common enough refrain in IT: "Our business has unique needs."

Perhaps, if you exclusively sell insurance to 7-feet-tall redheads with brown eyes for the sole purpose of providing compensation if they are abducted by aliens and forcibly examined, you might be able to say that your business *is*, indeed, unique.

For the most part, though, your business is not unique. This is, in fact, how pubic Cloud providers are able to offer a consumable service in the first place; they rely on being able to produce services that can be consumed en masse in a reliable, repeatable way. Sure, each business might spin up a different combination of resources, but the underlying resources are likely to be the same: IaaS, PaaS, and SaaS. The combination of services that you provide, the capabilities of your employees, and the systems that you use to provide those services *may* be unique, but your needs are not.

With this in mind, it is worth understanding that there are relatively few reasons why data *doesn't* need to be protected, and they're usually fairly predictable. Here are a few examples:

1. **The data is irrelevant:** Sometimes, you need a *volume* of data that fills particular characteristics, but you don't care what the content of the data is. This is usually for some type of performance testing. For instance, there's a fair chance that if your developers need 100 GB of random, moderately uncompressible data for testing, there will be little need to wrap that data up into comprehensive protection policies (unless those tests need to be iteratively repeated with the same data, of course).

2. **The data is transient:** A good example of transient data is streaming video from a service such as Netflix. While Netflix certainly needs to ensure that their data is protected, you, as the consumer, retrieving that data temporarily, do not need to protect it. Likewise, if data is being generated at point A in your organisation, passing through point B and being stored at point C, there's a good chance you only need to protect it in *one* location, not all three. (Unless, of course, there is processing taking place at each step and the amount of time taken to process exceeds the time it might take to recover the data.)

3. **The data is a copy:** Businesses can usually be more granular about whether to protect development and test data that is sourced from production systems. Rather than automatically protecting such data, data that can be readily copied back out of production (or restored from a data protection copy *of* the production data) may not need to be protected. (Businesses may refer to original data as "master" or "gold" data.)

4. **The data can be reliably reproduced:** Some data can be algorithmically reproduced. For example, given source data, and a set of calculations or algorithms, specific data will be generated. If the cost of reproducing the generated data is less than the cost of protecting the generated data, there may be no justifiable reason to protect the generated data.

There will be other examples, of course, but for the most part those examples will fall into one of the above categories (e.g., example 1 might even be considered to be a subset of example 4 in the list above).

When workloads (and usually, their data) are moved into or created in the public Cloud, the data almost invariably will need protection. There's the chance that it won't, but the likely scenario is that a requirement will be found if appropriately evaluated.

In fact, even if the data for the workload fall into one of the above categories, there may *still* be a need to consider protecting them; consider, for instance, item 3 above, where the data is a copy. If there is a copy of the data held on-premises, but the working copy in the public Cloud is lost, it's important as part of planning for that workload to understand how long it will take to repopulate the in-Cloud copy from the on-premises copy. If the workload is important but the data copy between on-premises systems and in-Cloud systems will be considerably longer than recovering from an in-Cloud backup or snapshot, there is still a good argument for providing data protection. (In short: the service restoration requirements may necessitate data protection even if the data is not an original copy.)

In such cases, there is a clear requirement of the business, the data owner and the data manager to agree on what data protection should be enacted on that data. While the public Cloud might change some of the *details* of that data protection compared to an on-premises workload, there's a fair to strong chance that it will not *eliminate* those requirements.

Before we begin to understand those data protection requirements, it's worthwhile to step back a little and take time to consider the following question: What is data protection?

A DATA PROTECTION PRIMER

WHAT IS DATA PROTECTION?

Like so much of IT and computing, the term *data protection* may seem innocuous, but has hidden complexity, and multiple meanings.

There are, in fact, three core interpretations to *data protection*: security, privacy, and storage. When we talk about data protection in a security context, it's typically a reference to ensuring only that those people who are authorized to access data or information can, in fact, do so. This is so regardless of whether we mean viewing, copying, deleting, or changing. In business IT in particular, this will often encompass activities including, but not limited to:

- Identity management
- Access control
- Firewalls
- Authentication and passwords
- Access monitoring
- Virus scanning

Such functions remain relevant regardless of where data might be placed—that is, the traditional data security considerations for a business exist regardless of whether the data resides in the datacenter or in someone else's. That being said, as soon as data moves outside the physical confines of a business, or as soon as someone with minimum IT security understanding can start deploying systems that gather data, the surface vector for data security concerns increase potentially by orders of magnitude.

There are various examples of situations where data protection from a security context has been lax and caused issues in public Cloud environments. One of the more depressingly common examples, for instance, is the simple scenario of developers leaving sensitive passwords for Amazon account access within source code that they upload to online code-sharing repositories such as GitHub or SourceForge. Equivalent to locking your house but leaving the keys in the front door (on the outside), such is the banality of this error that would-be attackers can 'break' the security simply by running basic scripts that download code and search for sensitive keys. For example, these private keys:

> are easily discoverable via a simple GitHub search and, according to Ty Miller, founder of penetration testing firm Threat Intelligence, almost 10,000 of them can currently be found on the popular hosting service for software projects.
>
> *Zorz, Z., "10,000 GitHub Users Inadvertently Reveal*
> *Their Secret AWS Keys," HelpNetSecurity, March 24 2014 [12].*

A similar recurring problem in Cloud-based security is the notion of the publicly accessible S3 bucket. Cloud object storage systems such as Amazon S3 offer highly desirable storage options (ease of access, low cost, and scalability, to name just a few), but leaving them publicly accessible rather than appropriately secured behind an application or API has resulted in some appalling security breaches over time. Given the amount of data that the public Cloud allows easy storage for, the magnitude of such breaches can be extreme. For instance, in 2017, the company Deep Root Analytics was found to have stored 198 million records relating to American voters in publicly accessible S3 storage, which included considerable personally sensitive information, including documents where:

> Each record lists a voter's name, date of birth, home address, phone number, and voter registration details, such as which political party a person is registered with. The data also includes "profiling" information, voter ethnicities and religions, and various other kinds of information pertinent to a voter's political persuasions and preferences, as modeled [sic] by the firms' data scientists, in order to better target political advertising.
>
> *Whittaker, Z., "198 million Americans hit by 'largest ever' voter*
> *records leak", Zack Whittaker, ZDNet, June 19, 2017 [13].*

While security by obfuscation is traditionally not considered to be *sufficient* protection for data, it has always at least *contributed* to data protection. One such way this has been achieved is that complex, difficult-to-deploy systems (e.g., traditional databases) have been largely unapproachable to non-IT elements within a business. The Cloud has changed this—the relative ease with which Cloud services allow nontechnical users to deploy systems typically the purview of IT has resulted in lax consideration of security, usually by simply working with whatever the default security model of an in-Cloud application is. In addition to data leakage described above, this has led to data destruction events as well, such as:

> MongoDB databases are being decimated in soaring ransomware attacks that have seen the number of compromised systems more than double to 27,000 in a day.
>
> Criminals ARE accessing, copying and deleting data from unpatched or badly-configured databases.
>
> ...
>
> MongoDB security is a known problem: up until recently, the software's default configuration is insecure. Shodan founder John Matherly warned in 2015 that some 30,000 exposed MongoDB instances were open to the internet without access controls.
>
> *Pauli, D.,* "MongoDB ransom attacks soar, body count hits 27,000 in hours," The Register, *January 9, 2017 [14].*

Perhaps the oldest definition of data protection as it applies in IT relates to data storage, that the process of ensuring that data can be stored reliably in such a way that it can be retrieved without corruption, or recovered from a secondary copy in the event of a serious issue. While this may sound simple, it is a multidisciplinary function that involves a large number of disparate functions within most IT departments—understandable, given data is essential to successful business operations.

In a perfect world, this form of data protection would not be needed. In a perfect world, storage systems would never fail, users would never delete data, no one would create viruses, and cyber espionage would not exist. Until such time as it *is* a perfect world, this form of data protection will be an essential part of business and IT processes, regardless of whether or where data is stored—in the Cloud or otherwise. It is *this* form of data protection that we will consider in this chapter.

The use of data protection as a *privacy* function is perhaps more recent, and has been driven by legislative changes, most recently from the European Union, around granting individuals the right to demand disclosure from a business about what data is held on them, and, should they so wish, having that data deleted—the right to be forgotten, so to speak. The General Data Protection Regulation (GDPR), which became active in the European Union on May 25, 2018, even set about defining the notion of a *data protection officer* (DPO) for a business, a role that defines the central authority for a business in terms of establishing compliant privacy policies and ensuring that they are followed. While this definition of data protection might initially seem at odds to other definitions, they all indeed fall under a cooperative umbrella. After all, if a business cannot secure its data, it cannot protect the privacy of the people for whom it holds data for, or about. Equally, if a business cannot adequately protect data once it is stored, it has little hope of accurately cataloguing data, classifying it, and understanding whether it is meeting privacy objectives for the data and the person or people to whom that data pertain.

Ultimately, all forms of data protection are worthy of consideration for data when these data reside in, or pass through, the public Cloud.

REPLICATION

One of the simpler forms of data protection is *replication*, which refers to copying data as it is generated. This is typically used to generate a physically separate yet identical copy of selected data so that should the original volume or storage system hosting the data fail, there is another copy that is either exactly up to date, or nearly up to date.

Whether the copy is exactly the same as the original depends on whether replication has been deployed as *synchronous* or *asynchronous*. A view of the way writes are handled in synchronous replication is shown in Figure 4.1.Figure 4.1   Steps involved in synchronous replication.

Synchronous replication requires the acknowledgment of the write instruction at both the primary copy and the secondary (replica) copy. Assuming that replication is being handled at a LUN[2] level between two storage arrays, this works as follows:

1. The host performs a write to its local storage.
2. The data is written to the local storage LUN.
3. The write instruction is sent to the remote storage LUN.
4. The remote storage LUN writes the data.
5. The remote storage system acknowledges that the write has been completed back to the primary storage system.
6. The primary storage system acknowledges that the write has been performed to the host.

Synchronous replication is effectively considered to be guaranteed consistency. Asynchronous replication on the other hand offers *eventual* consistency, and the sequence in which data is written resembles that shown in Figure 4.2.

Assuming, again, that replication is being performed at the LUN level between two storage arrays, the order of operations is as follows:

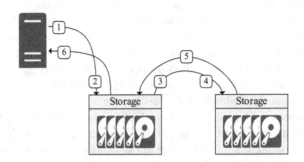

FIGURE 4.1   Steps involved in synchronous replication.

---

2 Logical unit number

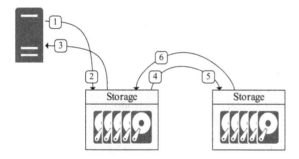

FIGURE 4.2   Steps involved in asynchronous replication.

1. The host instructs the local or "primary" copy to write data.
2. The primary storage array writes the data to its LUN.
3. The primary storage array informs the server that the write has been completed.
4. The primary storage array instructs the secondary storage array to write the data.
5. The secondary storage array writes the data.
6. The secondary storage array informs the primary storage array that it has written the data.

Typically, replication will need to be performed between two systems with similar performance characteristics (particularly necessary when using synchronous replication) to ensure that workload performance requirements are met.

Since replication between the two locations is asynchronous, there will need to be a replication buffer; should this buffer become overrun, replication may cease until manual intervention occurs. In a worst-case scenario, this may corrupt the destination replica, resulting in the need to "reseed" the target. As a result, careful consideration must also be given in designing asynchronous replication to ensure that the I/O profile of the workload being protected has been adequately catered for.

The single most important governing factor in choosing between synchronous and asynchronous replication is the bandwidth and latency between the two storage platforms. While bandwidth is not limitless, we usually have some level of control over it within financial considerations. A business, for instance, might deploy very high bandwidth links between its two primary datacentres, but much employ much lower bandwidth links from the datacenters to remote offices, on the basis of the amount of data that need to be sent at any one time. However, latency can be affected by the quality of components, the type of link (e.g., satellite links tend to have high latency), and the *distance* that data must travel. For instance, the Australian cities of Melbourne and Perth are separated by approximately 2700 km (1677 miles); since the fastest links are still limited by the speed of light, the *absolute shortest* period of time that data could be transmitted from one city to the other would be 0.009 second, which means that the *minimum achievable latency* is 9 milliseconds between the two state capitals. This would also assume that a direct, single-hop fiberoptic link can be established over that distance, with the cable running in a direct line; in reality, signal boosters are typically implemented at particular intervals on the basis of the technology used to retransmit the data, which will also add a measurable impact on the latency. For instance, Australia's primary communications carrier, Telstra, claims 10-millisecond (ms) latency for Melbourne to Sydney [16] (a distance of approximately 713 km, or 443 miles), and *50-ms* latency for Sydney to Perth, a distance of 3290 km (2044 miles).

The net result of this is that while synchronous replication will typically be used within the same datacenter, campus, or metropolitan region, going beyond this distance will either make bandwidth requirements too expensive for all except the most profitable of enterprises, and risk making the latency too high to accommodate the performance profiles required of the storage system. So long as sufficient buffering is available, asynchronous replication can be deployed over considerably larger distances to provide remote disaster recoverability. Businesses requiring both fast local disaster recovery and protection against potential regional issues may therefore even deploy *both* synchronous and asynchronous replication, at least for mission critical data. Such a configuration sees the local copies kept synchronously replicated, with a tertiary, asynchronous copy hundreds or perhaps thousands of miles away. This type of configuration is shown in Figure 4.3.

Replication is an excellent way of ensuring that there is more than one physical copy of the data, although it should be noted that:

1. Except when storage virtualisation is used, the replication source and target usually must be the same (or certified compatible) technology.
2. Replication copies all writes, including instructions to delete or alter data. Therefore, replication by itself provides no protection against malware that encrypts, corrupts, or deletes, or against users that do the same.

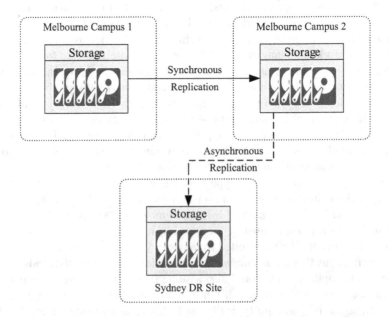

FIGURE 4.3   Synchronous and asynchronous replication for multisite recoverability.

The inability for replication to protect against all forms of failure or recovery scenarios will be a limitation that we see play out across all forms of data protection; this is why you will see data protection being treated as a *holistic strategy* combining multiple techniques in order to meet all operational and compliance requirements.

A higher-level form of replication is continuous storage availability; this is effectively created by mirroring volumes presented by two or more entire storage arrays to present virtual volumes. This allows the failure of an entire storage array, or depending on physical locations, an entire site, while still preserving data availability. In traditional replication, a system might be configured to only write to the primary copy, until such time as it is instructed to work with the replica copy (via a *failover*). With continuous storage availability, the underlying volumes/arrays are effectively virtualized away, with a single logical volume or storage array presented to the accessing host(s). As useful as this can be for fault tolerance, however, it remains susceptible to the same challenges as described in standard replication—data deletion or data corruption will still be just as effectively copied, should it take place.

CONTINUOUS DATA PROTECTION

Continuous data protection (CDP) might be considered as a form of replication, but with the option to *rewind*. CDP is often compared to the functionality provided by a digital videorecorder (DVR), which provides a streaming buffer as you are watching your movie or TV show; if at any point you miss what someone said, you simply rewind to before the event on screen, and watch it again.

As a data protection function, CDP works via journaling; as writes occur to the primary copy, they are also written to a journal. The journal can be used to provide local recoverability, or its content may be copied to a similar journal at a remote location to provide remote recoverability (in fact, it is not unusual to see both options available in a configuration). In fact, the normal approach for deploying CDP is to work with input/ output (I/O) splitters; these allow writes to be intercepted inline, as they are being made, with one copy sent to the local storage, and one sent to the journal.

A key aspect to the journaling system is that it keeps track of writes in the order in which they were made; it is this write ordering that allows the copy to be *rewound* to any particular point in time; this is essential when the data being that is protected has the same content constantly or regularly updated. CDP works similarly to the system shown in Figure 4.4.

In order to minimize the impact of CDP on the primary copy, it is imperative that

- The I/O splitter operate as close as possible to the operating system kernel.
- The journal reside on storage as close to the performance profile as the primary copy as possible.

While not always the case, CDP is more likely to support different storage platforms at the source and destination—or perhaps more accurately, is more likely to be *storage agnostic* compared to standard replication.

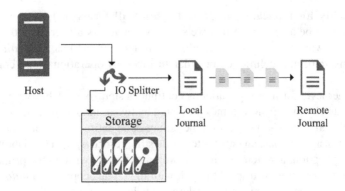

Host   IO Splitter   Local Journal   Remote Journal

Storage

FIGURE 4.4   Conceptual view of continuous data protection.

It is the ability to "rewind" that offers the most differentiating feature between CDP and replication. While replication will serve excellently to protect against physical failure (e.g., site loss, or storage array lost), it can do nothing to protect against *logical* failure—data corruption, accidental deletion, and so on. It is there that the operational recovery advantage of CDP comes into the fore. Consider, for instance, CDP deployed against a key business database. If a DBA comes back from lunch at 13:05 and accidentally issues a SQL command that drops a key table, a conventional *replication*-based copy will be similarly affected. With CDP, the DBA or storage administrator (depending on where the CDP controls are accessible from) can instead "rewind" the protected copy to, say, 13:04, and instantiate a copy of the database (or even recover back over the affected database) prior to when the accidental delete occurred by "undoing" the writes that took place between 13:04 and 13:05. This may pull back a crash-consistent copy of the database, or alternately the CDP environment might be configured to take application-consistent "bookmarks" at periodic intervals (e.g., every 15 minutes), allowing instead an application-consistent recovery of the database back to 13:00.

Usually, the limiting factor on CDP is the required size of the journals involved. Consider, for instance, an environment protected by CDP that has 10 TB of data change within a 24-hour period. If the business requests CDP-based recoverability for a 14-day period, this requires a minimum of 140 TB of journal space *at each journal location* (e.g., local and remote). In practice, journals are typically sized using a metric higher than an average daily change rate to account for unexpected spikes in I/O workloads.

For this reason, while CDP offers excellent recovery granularity, it is unusual to see it used to provide recoverability past several days, or else the storage requirements of the journal will become cost prohibitive. (Equally, cyber-attacks such as malware that encrypts all content it finds *can* overwhelm the journals of CDP systems if too many changes are made.)

SNAPSHOTS

A "snapshot" is an *on-platform* data protection technique that is optimized for storage efficiency and speed of execution. Particularly when we consider on-premises storage systems, this typically comes at the expense of being physically tied to the original copy/storage; this is why it is referred to as *on-platform*.

On traditional storage systems, when a snapshot is taken, no data is initially copied. Instead, the snapshot is empty. There are two common ways a snapshot may run from this point in time:

1. Copy-on-write
2. Redirected write

A *copy-on-write* snapshot works by taking a copy of data that is written to the original storage, before it is altered or deleted, and copying it into the snapshot area so it is preserved. Consider the initial snapshot, which is "blank," other than being a series of pointers in the snapshot back to the original blocks of data. This may resemble that shown in Figure 4.5.

If a host needs to read from the snapshot in this state, the process is straightforward; an attempt to read from an unpopulated snapshot block will instead see the read redirected to the currently unaltered block residing in the original volume. This is shown in Figure 4.6.

In the example shown in Figure 4.6, the process is as follows:

1. The accessing host attempts to read from a block in the snapshot that points back to an unaltered block from the original volume.

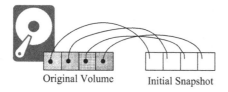

Original Volume   Initial Snapshot

FIGURE 4.5 Freshly Initialised Copy-on-Write Snapshot.

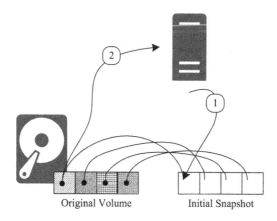

Original Volume   Initial Snapshot

FIGURE 4.6 Reading from unaltered data in a copy-on-write snapshot.

2. The unaltered block from the original volume is read, and the data is sent back to the host as if it were from the snapshot.

The goal of a copy-on-write snapshot is to allow rapid snapshot creation while keeping the original volume in a read/write state. Therefore, a specific data preservation process must be used whenever an attempt is made to write to the original volume, which is where the *copy-on-write* comes in. The copy-on-write process is outlined in Figures 4.7 and 4.8.

Per the sequence numbers in the two figures, the write works as follows:

1. The host attempts to write new data to a block on the original volume that still has a snapshot block pointing to it.
2. The data already residing on the original volume, that will be overwritten, is copied to the matching block in the snapshot volume. This removes the pointer back to the original volume's block.

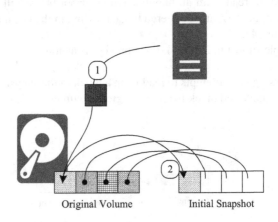

Original Volume   Initial Snapshot

FIGURE 4.7   Writing to a volume with a copy-on-write snapshot, part 1.

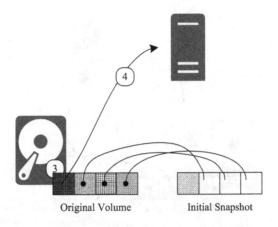

Original Volume   Initial Snapshot

FIGURE 4.8   Writing to a volume with a copy-on-write snapshot, part 2.

3. The new data is now written to the original volume, updating it.
4. The write is acknowledged back to the host.

At the end of the write process, the snapshot is still preserved as a point-in-time copy of the volume as of the time when the snapshot was taken, but the original volume has been successfully changed. (Further updates to the same block on the original volume do not change the snapshot, else the data it represents would become corrupt.)

An alternate form of snapshot is typically referred to as *redirect-on-write*. Unlike the copy-on-write snapshot process, redirect-on-write works by effectively making the original system "read only" while the snapshot is active. Writes are performed on snapshot or journal areas instead, preserving the original copy. This allows a snapshot to be released either as a rollback to the original (which results in deleting the writes performed to the snapshot/journal area), or merged by copying the writes from the snapshot into the source data, merging original and snapshot data. These snapshot processes are used for a variety of systems, such as the VMware Hypervisor. While redirect-on-write allows the snapshot to be deleted and updates thrown away with minimum effort, merging the snapshot back in can be a very write intensive process, particularly if there was a high change rate while the snapshot was active.

While some snapshot processes in traditional, on-premises storage infrastructure can be used to create a wholly independent replica copy of the data being protected, it is more usual to see it used in the space-efficient manner that we have described so far. Snapshots taken with an intent to create a complete replica copy will usually see a background copy process initiated and advance, to the front of the copy queue, any data that is read from the original volume while the snapshot/replica is being taken. (Such a process is typically referred to as "copy on first access," since data is copied as it is accessed.)

While snapshots (particularly traditional, on-premises storage-based snapshots) provide an excellent means for allowing rapid recoverability in a storage efficient format, they are rarely cost-effective against longer-term retention requirements (e.g., into months or years), and may not offer the same level of recovery granularity as traditional backup systems. Thus, like replication, snapshots are best considered as part of a holistic data protection strategy as opposed to offering a complete solution in themselves.

BACKUP AND RECOVERY

One of the oldest forms of data storage protection is *backup and recovery*, which fundamentally centers around taking a copy of data and placing it on storage that is physically separate and optimally even a different platform to the original copy.

While many other forms of data protection are referred to as *on-platform* protection, the key point of a backup is to create a copy that is logically and physically isolated from the original copy, so that if the original system holding that copy fails, there is a safe version of the data elsewhere that can be used to restore from.

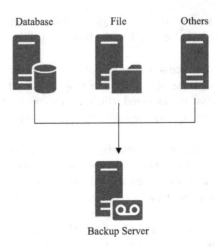

FIGURE 4.9   Simple backup server topology.

One of the earliest forms of backup and recovery would see a tape drive attached to most, if not all, servers deployed in a datacenter. Over time, as the number of servers and the amount of data increased, this model proved impractical to scale, and the backup server was born. In its simplest sense, this model is shown in Figure 4.9.

While backups might be manually started where there was a tape drive attached to each host, the introduction of a backup server allowed a more coordinated scheduling approach; one of the earliest truisms in data protection was that if users are left to run their own backups, the backups will not run.

Over time this model introduced scale first by supporting multiple backup devices on a backup server, and then moving to a three-tier architecture where servers would send their data to storage nodes, or media servers under the control of the primary backup server. This allowed the alleviation of server and network bottlenecks, but still resulted in complete copies of data being regularly sent across a network to the backup environment.

Unlike traditional storage systems using snapshot and replication, backup environments are designed to store a secondary, point-in-time copy of data on an independent platform to that of the original copy. Whereas replication can be effectively instantaneous, with continuous data protection measured in seconds or minutes, and snapshots performed frequently throughout a day, backup processes are usually executed once a day, providing longer recovery points than on-platform systems, but more cost-effective recovery over time, highly efficient granularity, and off-platform storage.

Traditional backup environments, before virtualization became a core feature of the modern datacenter, a backup agent would be deployed. At the time a backup is executed by the server, the backup agent will traverse the file system, reading data that need to be backed up. Backups typically are run as either full, incremental, or differential, although the nomenclature for incremental and differential can be confusing at times. A full backup will read all data encountered (except any data that an administrator has excluded from backup); incremental backups read all data that has changed since the last backup that was performed. Differential backups, meanwhile, seek to "roll up" multiple days of change into a new backup; for instance, if a full backup were performed on Friday night, with incremental backups performed Saturday and Sunday, a differential backup executed on Monday would capture all data changed since the full, regardless of whether that data was captured by the Saturday or Sunday incremental, or had been modified between the Sunday incremental and the Monday backup. Differential backups are less required in modern environments as their primary utility was to reduce the number of physical tapes that might be required to perform a recovery, particularly if full backups were performed only monthly. (For instance, consider a scenario where a full backup is performed on the first Saturday of the month, differentials are performed on all other Saturdays, and incremental backups are performed all other days of the week. This means that at most, any complete recovery would require the full backup, the most recent differential backup, and any incremental backups done since that time.)

Initially, databases were backed up via a process referred to as "dump and sweep," where, at a scheduled time, the database server would generate an export of the database to either a binary or a plaintext file, and this would be scheduled so that it would complete before the file system backup started. The "dump" was the database export, and the "sweep" was the backup agent walking the file system and encountering a new file that needed backing up.

Such processes scale poorly. For any number of reasons (e.g., manually started jobs, or jobs delayed due to batch processing activities), a database dump might not complete on time, and not be complete by the time the file system backup commenced. This would result in capturing a file that could not be used to meaningfully restore the database. Over time, as database size and complexity grew, simple exports could no longer guaranteeably enforce referential integrity, particularly for relational databases, so database vendors had to develop better processes and enable true hot backup options. (The notion of "cold" backups, wherein the database is entirely stopped for the duration of the backup, has largely died in the Internet age, where customers and users might access services requiring the database at any time of the day or night.)

By allowing hot backups, database vendors also opened the door to full agent-based integration in backup services. Thus the concept of a database or application plugin was born. In such environments, the backup agent has additional functionality deployed or enabled to allow it to integrate into the database backup process as well. While usually these backups would still be run separately (allowing greater control over system resources, and higher predictability over runtime), it would allow the backup software to place the database in a state that allowed for hot backup, copy the database files, and then perform any final steps to complete the backup process. (Contrary to popular misconception, this does not typically redirect writes to the database to log files during the backup process, but establishes markers on when the backup starts and allows access to the database files, so that recovery becomes a two-step process: (1) the retrieval of the raw (and likely inconsistent) database files from the backup medium and (2) the playback of logs generated during the backup process which enable the database to return to a consistent point in time.)

While dump and sweep may still be used in some environments, this will be because of either (1) a database that supports no other protection option (a serious development flaw, particularly common in emerging database formats) or (2) intransigence on behalf of the database administrators that the business allows to flourish.

A key focus of backup systems is to provide recoverability of data over what we typically refer to as the operational retention window. For most businesses, this is typically somewhere in the order of 4–6 weeks (although it can go as low as 2 weeks for some, and as high as 3 months for others). With a typical execution frequency of daily, backups will meet somewhere in the order of a 24-hour recovery point objective over an extended period of time. The operational retention period will be governed by a variety of factors, including service-level agreements (SLAs) with the business, likelihood of data loss based on when it was created or modified, and how frequently compliance-focused, or long-term retention backups are executed. (We will cover such backups in a later section.) If backups are executed daily, with an operational retention window of 4 weeks, this means that there should be a daily copy of protected systems to off-platform storage and kept for a minimum of 28 days. (In fact, where backups use full and incremental or differential backups, higher-quality systems will use dependence tracking between the full and other backups, so that backups expire in groups only when all dependent backups are older than their retention time. This ensures that a complete system can be recovered for the entire specified retention period, not just individual files.)

While most backups are executed on a daily basis, there are, of course, exceptions to the rule. Returning to database backups briefly, it is not unusual to see database backups executed more frequently than daily, particularly for mission critical databases. In some cases, for instance, a full backup might be executed daily, but transaction log backups are performed every 15 minutes, allowing the backup environment to deliver a much lower recovery point objective. While such recovery point objectives could be met with via high availability database configurations (e.g., active/passive clustered servers providing standby copies of the databases), the licensing costs associated with such configurations are often prohibitively expensive for many businesses, often forcing the backup environment to fill the gap.

The proliferation of data and complexity of systems has seen tape displaced in modern backup environments, first with plain disk storage systems, and then deduplication.

The simplest operational and cost aspect of any backup environment is the amount of data that must be transferred, and stored during a backup operation; this is the core issue that deduplication addresses. Within the evolving datacenter, it has not been uncommon to see core networking bandwidth upgrades (e.g., from Fast Ethernet to Gigabit Ethernet, or from Gigabit Ethernet to 10 Gigabit Ethernet, and so on) driven not so much by the production throughput requirements, but the backup throughput requirements. After all, if an environment has 100 TB of data but less than 5 TB is actively accessed and changed on a daily basis by business operations, even a gigabit network will have no problem supporting the business workload. However, come Friday night when a full backup is performed and 100 TB needs to be transferred, the network bandwidth requirements are substantially different.

In its simplest form, deduplication might be described as *global compression*, since it has the same basic goal as compression: eliminating repeated or redundant data to reduce content down to the smallest footprint required, while still being able to reconstruct, or rehydrate the data when required. To understand the differences between compression and deduplication, though, it's first worthwhile revisiting how compression has typically been used within backup environments.

In backup, compression has been primarily stream-based; that is, as a data stream is received, it is compressed before being written to the storage medium. This usually achieves storage savings in the order of 2–3:1, although very sparse data, or preallocated data that has not been changed, may yield higher compression ratios. However, data is only compressed against the stream being received. A tape drive, for instance, might feature built-in compression, wherein as it receives "buffers" of, say, 1 MB of data at a time, applies compression, and writes the compressed data to the physical medium.

The simplest form of deduplication is nothing more than *single-instance storage*. Single-instance storage is popular with email and file archive systems, recognizing that multiple copies of the same data may be stored. For instance, if the CEO emails an update including the annual general report to 10,000 employees, 10,000 copies of the data are created as user mail clients download a copy of the email, and the attachment. The email itself may contain only 5 kB of text and inline graphics, but the annual general report may be a 20-MB attachment. Stored across 10,000 laptops/ desktops, almost 200 GB of data will be generated. Email archive software will automatically deduplicate as these emails are archived for long-term compliance by saving only a single instance of the email and the attachment; as each copy is archived, pointers are established to single copy stored, limiting the amount of data stored. So instead of storing 200 GB when the CEO's email and report is archived, a maximum of 30 MB of storage might be consumed—a single copy of the email, a single copy of the attachment, and the metadata/pointers associated with references to the copy.

Single instancing has its place in storage efficiency, but well-implemented deduplication will offer considerably better efficiency. If we return to our original description of stream-based compression, we can consider deduplication to be single instancing applied to all those compressed containers generated as an incoming stream is received.

In order to achieve this level of efficiency, deduplication works by analyzing data that is received and then assembling fingerprints to represent the data. If a deduplication system had to reread all data stored each time a backup was performed to determine whether incoming data were new, it would become progressively slow and untenable; instead, deduplication is done in segments, or blocks, of either varying or fixed size. Each segment stored on the deduplication platform will have its own signature, or fingerprint, that uniquely identifies it. As data is evaluated for storage on the deduplication platform, it is segmented and fingerprinted; if the fingerprint generated is *unique*, that is, if it does not match any data already stored on the system, the fingerprint is stored, and the data is compressed and stored. If, on the other hand, the calculated fingerprint matches a fingerprint of data already stored on the system, a pointer is stored on the system to that existing data, and the nonunique data discarded, thus adding to the storage efficiency.

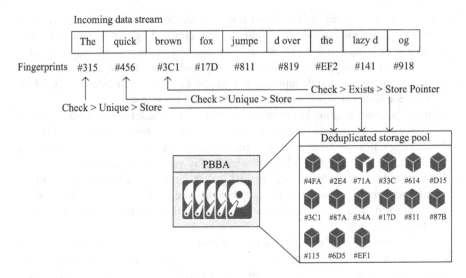

FIGURE 4.10   Conceptual overview of deduplication process.

Such is the complexity of deduplication that storage platforms expressly designed to provide this service into a backup environment are often referred to as *purpose-built backup appliances* (PBBAs).

A high-level view of the deduplication process is shown in Figure 4.10.

Reviewing the deduplication conceptual diagram, we can see that as the incoming data stream is received, it is broken into segments, and those segments are fingerprinted. As fingerprints are generated, the deduplication system compares those fingerprints against fingerprints already known to the system, effectively checking to see if the data received is unique to the storage system. In our example, the first two fingerprints (#315 and #456) do not exist in the deduplication storage pool, and therefore those data segments will be compressed and stored, with the fingerprints added to the system database. The third data segment received, though, matches a known fingerprint, so the segment is not stored again; instead, a pointer is stored to the previously written matching segment.

In this sense, backups are not stored linearly on a deduplication system. Instead, each backup or data stream received is stored as a sequence of pointers to data segments on the system. When data is deleted by the backup software, this does not result in an immediate delete from the deduplication system; instead, the number of pointers referencing stored segments is decremented as the backup references are cleared from the system database. At some point, the deduplication storage will then run a file system cleaning operation (sometimes known as a "garbage collection" process). It is only during this periodic maintenance operation that space is reclaimed—when the system encounters a stored data segment that has *no* pointers referring to it, it knows that the data is no longer required and can delete it.

There are three other aspects to deduplication that need to be understood: *what* is deduplicated, *when* the deduplication happens, and *where* the deduplication happens:

1. First, we consider *what* is deduplicated. The example diagram shows the sentence, "The quick brown fox jumped over the lazy dog" being deduplicated. In reality, deduplication typically works on larger blocks of data than just a word or two, as there is a trade-off between the size of the segment, the metadata associated with each segment, and the storage savings that can be achieved. In practice, deduplication segments averaging 8 KB yield high deduplication ratios without unduly increasing the amount of metadata that is stored; deduplication segments in the order of 64 or 128 KB might make for less metadata, but comes at the cost of storing a lot of duplicate data, since a single byte change within a 64- or 128-KB segment would create an entirely *new* segment for storage. Also associated with segment size is whether segmentation is *fixed* or *variable*. Again, this comes down to *ease* or *efficiency*. Programmatically, it may be easy to use a rule "every time 128 KB is received, a new segment will be created for evaluation," but this results in a hideously inefficient deduplication process, particularly for data that is subject to updates rather than simply being appended to. Variable segmentation deduplication is programmatically more challenging to achieve but renders significantly better storage efficiency, by segmenting data variably, but consistently, a minimum amount of data must be detected and stored for data updates or inserts. Consider, for instance, having previously backed up "The quick brown fox over the lazy dog"; this might have generated two segments, "The quick brown fox" and "over the lazy dog." Now consider a new backup, this time of "The quick brown fox *jumped* over the lazy dog." Variable segmentation hopes to store this more efficiently by just storing "jumped" and retaining the other two segments as preexisting data, that is, by detecting the new data within a chunk of data, and avoiding, as much as possible, copying data that has already been copied. Fixed segmentation on the other hand is more likely to see entirely new segments of data, "The quick brown fox jum" and "ped over the lazy dog," resulting in more data stored than necessary. (While the data sizes evaluated will be larger than our example, the principle remains the same.)

2. Next, let us consider *when* the deduplication occurs. In backup environments, the *when* is defined as either inline or postprocess deduplication. In the examples we have discussed so far, we have effectively explained *inline* deduplication. That is, as the incoming data stream is read, data is segmented, fingerprinted, and analyzed, with only unique data written to the deduplication platform. This is the most storage-efficient option and also renders the fastest processing—the fingerprint databases will be held mostly in memory, so the process is primarily a CPU- and memory-based operation. Postprocessing, on the other hand, writes all incoming data in its originally received format to a staging area on the storage system. After the system is no longer busy receiving the data stream, a deduplication process will be executed to reread the data from local staging storage, do segmenting and fingerprint analysis, then update the deduplication storage pool with unique data, before deleting the content of the staging area. This is a highly inefficient process that renders the deduplication process I/O-bound

and requires excessive additional storage to accomplish what should simply be performed in memory/CPU to begin with. Incorporating flash storage into the environment achieves little here; although it reduces the I/O bottleneck of postprocessing, it introduces extra cost for the staging area, and the staging area will always act as a hard bottleneck on the amount of data that the deduplication storage can receive at any point in time.

3. *What* is deduplicated directly effects the storage efficiency of our deduplication pool. By itself, *when* deduplication is performed directly affects the overall size of the storage allocated to the deduplication appliance. Finally, we consider *where* deduplication is performed, which has considerable impact on the network bandwidth requirements of the backup process. Assuming that we commit to inline deduplication, we can perform deduplication at either the *source* or the *target* of the data stream. The programmatically simpler of the two, target deduplication, sees the entire content of the backup sent (over the network) to the deduplication storage system for evaluation and storage. While simple, this means that the network capacity becomes a limiting factor in the backup process, and the backup process will become a governing factor in network bandwidth increases as data sizes grow. In short: it's simple, but grossly inefficient and costly from a network utilization perspective.

By comparison, source-based deduplication sees a deduplication-integrated backup agent deployed on the individual clients being protected and creates a *distributed deduplication* process. As data is read on the client, the deduplication libraries segment the data and fingerprint them. Fingerprints may be compared initially against a local cache of previously observed fingerprints on the same system for additional efficiency, but we will see required fingerprints transmitted to the deduplication appliance so that it can determine whether it needs to receive the actual data. This is considerably more efficient than transmitting the original data for evaluation; a 20-byte fingerprint may be more than sufficient to represent our previously mentioned optimal 8-KB segment size. Even when unique data that must be stored is detected, we can optimize the amount of data to be sent by compressing the segment first. As the amount of data stored on the deduplication appliance increases, the chances of matching fingerprints also typically increases; this can mean that after the first full backup has been completed, subsequent full backups might see a reduction in network bandwidth requirements of ≥95%.

Thus, deduplication will work most efficiently in a backup environment when it uses variable segmentation, aiming for smaller segment sizes, and distributes an inline deduplication process out to the individual hosts being protected. In addition to storage efficiency and network bandwidth savings, this has an added benefit: simplifying the flattening the backup topology. Recall our earlier discussion about backup evolution; the ongoing growth of data and speed at which backups needed to be completed saw the introduction of a secondary tier of servers—storage nodes, or media servers, that were required to funnel data from the hosts being protected to the protection storage. Such servers typically must be high-performance systems to keep data flowing rapidly. Inline, source-based deduplication eschews this

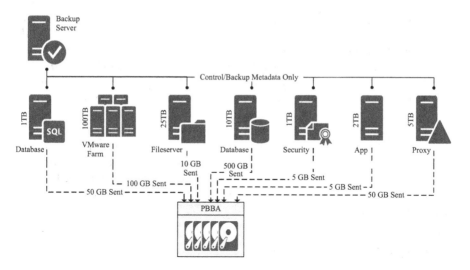

FIGURE 4.11 Impact of source-side, inline deduplication on backup systemstopology.

secondary tier of backup services, allowing data to flow directly from the individual clients to the storage. This effectively lifts the backup server to a "director" role only; it exists to coordinate backup and recovery operations, and hold indices for granular recoverability, but does not need to handle the data flow itself. This is represented in Figure 4.11.

In the diagram, we see that the backup server is removed from the data path, with data flowing directly from the hosts being protected to the protection storage. Deduplication takes place as the data is being read, with fingerprint analysis of segmented data as a shared task between the clients and the deduplication appliance. Thus, the 1-TB SQL database server sends only 100 GB to the storage platform, the 25-TB file server only sends 10 GB of data, the 100-TB VMware farm sends only 100 GB, and so on.

This combined network and storage efficiency solves many of the headaches posed by conventional tape-based backup systems, while avoiding a scenario where disk-based backup systems consume orders of magnitude more storage than the systems that they are protecting.

Particularly in the situation where backups were done to tape, there was a strong perception that they existed only as an "insurance policy" and represented little more than lost budget. With the move toward efficient, disk-based backup storage, a growing trend is the enablement of secondary use cases for backup data. At its simplest, this might be generating a new copy of a test database by recovering the production database backup—less intrusive than, say, copying the production database while it is in use. Additional use cases can include automated compliance testing, seeding data lakes, and live access to read/write snapshots of backup data—for example, starting the read/write snapshot of a virtual machine backup for testing or emergency access, and even copying the data across into the virtual machine farm while it is being accessed.

Our final piece of the backup jigsaw puzzle before moving on to other forms of data protection is to dwell briefly on the concept of *single source of failure*. While a backup of a database or file should represent an off-platform copy protected from the sorts of failures that can strike the primary copy, it shouldn't be a *singular* off-platform copy. Therefore, when we deal with backup and recovery solutions, following the best practical approaches will be to see a copy made of all backups performed, with the copy stored elsewhere than the original (if not all backups, then at least all backups of production systems). Taking this approach prevents the backup environment from being a single source of failure within the overall environment. It should be noted that even here, deduplication can play a factor in improving the overall process; by generating a copy, or clone, of the data in its deduplicated format, the amount of time it takes to send a copy off site, or to another location, can be drastically reduced.

LONG-TERM RETENTION

While backup and recovery solutions are the primary means of providing long-term retention for most businesses, it's worthwhile to consider requirements around long-term retention separately from those for what we normally refer to as *operational recovery*.

Operational recovery covers the shorter-term data recovery activities essential to business continuity and dealing with day-to-day data loss. This includes rapid recovery via snapshots, replication, or CDP, and recovery from backup for data worked on over a relatively short period of time, such as the past month. As protected data ages, however, the recovery requirements usually shift away from operational recovery and to *compliance* recovery.

The two recovery rationales engender different service-level agreements (SLAs) and user expectations. Recovery of a database corrupted overnight needs to be rapid, whereas a user or group of users will likely be more patient waiting for retrieval of a copy of a spreadsheet that was backed up 3 years ago.

While a simplistic approach will see short-term/operational retention, and compliance retention maintained on the same tier of backup storage, in reality this is an option that will only suit organizations that have little data, or little long-term retention compliance requirements. To understand why, let us consider a business that has 100 TB of data, with a 4-week operational retention window, and with monthly backups retained for 7 years (84 months). Consider a full backup run once per week, with incremental backups daily, and a daily change rate of 5%. This tells us that our operational backup cycle will be:

- 4 full × 100 TB = 400 TB
- 24 incremental × (5% of 100 TB) = 120 TB

So, without any deduplication to drive storage efficiency, the *operational* backup cycle will be 520 TB. Without even bothering to factor in annual growth, our 84 monthly backups will be 8400 TB, or just over 94% of the total storage requirements. If we apply 10% annual growth (a relatively modest rate), amortized monthly (1.007974× increase per month), then at the end of the 7-year period the data to be protected will be 193.33 TB, yielding an operational retention backup size of 1005.32 TB, and a long-term retention size of 11,897.42 TB. While this increases the operational retention component of total storage requirements to 7.79%, the long-term retention requirements clearly continue to make up the lion's share of the overall storage requirements.

It is for this reason that there has been considerable attention to achieving optimum storage efficiency for long-term retention backups, in terms of both occupied space and cost per gigabyte stored.

One might consider tape to be the most storage-efficient format for long-term retention data, but continuing to consider our prior example, we might assume that the 11,897 TB of long-term retention data would require approximately 5948 TB of tape storage at a 2:1 compression ratio. Yet, it's worthwhile keeping in mind that a typical tape protection strategy will remove tapes from their drives, or tape libraries after backups have been completed, regardless of whether they are full.[17]

If we consider Linear Tape-Open LTO-7 tape, which stores 6 TB native data per tape, and adhere to our 2:1 compression ratio, then 9 tapes are used for each copy at the start of the 84-month period, and 17 tapes are used for each copy at the end of the 84-month period, assuming, somehow, that the same tape format is used for the entire 7-year period.[18] Indeed, using the same monthly growth rates, this would consume 1034 LTO-7 tapes by the end of year 7 for long term retention. Since, of course, tapes can fail, and long-term retention data should be protected from physical media failure, it's likely that there would end up being two tape copies each month, bringing us up to 2068 tapes after 7 years.

On the other hand, consider the storage requirements for long-term retention. If we assume an extremely modest, 10:1 deduplication ratio for the entire dataset in operational retention, then the previously stated operational retention storage requirements of 520 TB might come down to as low as 52 TB occupied. For long-term retention, deduplication will see some drift, however, and with a trend downward—as the number of copies increases, we would normally see an increase in deduplication ratios, but as the age of the individual copies spreads out further, there will be more differences between individual copies taken, thus reducing the overall deduplication efficiency. A 10:1 operational deduplication ratio might amortize out to a 7:1 deduplication ratio, for instance, over an 84-month timeframe. The long-term retention data requirement of 11,897.42 TB would require 1699.63 TB of physical storage, or 3399.26 TB if we store two copies.

While this may seem like a large amount of storage, there are additional costs that need to be factored for a true cost comparison between the two types of storage. Storage systems will require maintenance, power, and cooling, of course, but consider tapes that would require cost consideration of the following:

---

17 This allows us to ensure that the backup copy does not remain on site with the original data, creating a single point of risk.

18 The number of tapes used per month would always be rounded up, since the tapes are removed from the end of the environment after the backup has been completed.

- Maintenance.
- Power.
- Cooling.
- Migration to new formats.
- Periodic testing to ensure recoverability has not been compromised by physical degradation.
  - Generation of new copies from the second tape copy for content that has been compromised by physical degradation.
  - Recall and testing of tapes purchased at similar times to confirm that no additional physical degradation has taken place.
- Auditing requirements: recall, validation, and so on.

The other consideration, of course, is that as data value increases to a business, having the data offline becomes a negative factor. Tape is accessible only when it has been loaded into a tape drive; long-term retention data is the "history" of the company and can be mined by analytics systems to provide additional business insights into the long-term trends that the company faces, but this can be done only if the data is accessible. Thus, keeping it online in an accessible format (while appropriately protecting it from damage or deletion, such as via invulnerability architectures and compliance-based locking) provides a secondary business benefit of the ability to mine the data at any time.

For this reason, the simple consignment of long-term retention data to tape is losing its appeal to the modern enterprise; one might even argue that more than anything, *tape* is the driving factor behind businesses seeing data protection, particularly backup and recovery, as a "sunk cost" that yields little tangible return.

CYBER RECOVERY

In earlier days of IT security, traditional forms of threat included concerns about data theft or exfiltration and viruses that might disrupt systems operations.

As computer systems and networks increase in complexity, rogue elements of society have been able to increase the sophistication of their cyberattacks on businesses, governments, and individuals. Two increasingly common forms of attack are categorized as ransomware and hacktivism.

Ransomware is the classification of particular forms of viruses or trojans that, once activated on a computer, will seek to encrypt as much data as possible. A ransom notice is then displayed to users, advising them that they must contact the ransomware writers and pay a particular amount (typically via bitcoin or one of its variants, as this is often deemed as being untraceable) in order to receive a decryption key.

Given the networked nature of computer systems, ransomware can do far more than just scrambling Jim's Microsoft Word document, or Mary's work in progress on the company finance spreadsheet. With network-accessible shares, shared Cloud sync folders (e.g., OneDrive or Dropbox), a ransomware strike on even a single computer within a business may result in many terabytes of data being compromised. While much of the ransomware market is random, some ransomware will be deliberately targeted at sensitive businesses that are considered more likely to be willing to pay the ransom quickly, such as healthcare providers. On February 16,

2016, Anita Balakrishnan, writing for CNBC, reported in "The hospital held hostage by hackers" [19]:

> For more than a week, hackers have shut down the internal computer system at a Hollywood-area hospital for a ransom of 9,000 bitcoin, or almost $3.7 million, according to NBC 4 Los Angeles. The hospital says patient care has not been compromised, though the cyberattack has forced the facility, Hollywood Presbyterian Medical Center, to revert to paper registrations and medical records and send 911 patients to other area hospitals.

Such attacks are becoming increasingly common; in 2017 the UK health system was the target of significant ransomware attempts, and it took less than 10 days before the occurrence of the first reported attack against a hospital in 2018. According to Patrick Howell O'Neill, writing for Cyberscoop on January 15, 2018, in an article titled "Indiana hospital shuts down systems after ransomware attack" [20]:

> The infection began on Thursday Jan. 10 with ransomware malware known as SamSam. One day later, the hospital paid the full bitcoin ransom of four bitcoins to the attackers. On the day the ransom was paid, four bitcoins was [sic] worth approximately $45,000.
>
> Hospital administrators received the private keys from the hackers on Friday and, by Monday, all hospital systems were restored, according to a hospital spokesperson.

While there has been a growth in *cyber insurance* of late (whereby companies can claim against an insurance policy after a ransomware attack, among other things), it goes without saying that recovery from ransomware should be a critical foundation in the data protection functionality of modern businesses. Cyber insurance *might* (and that's a *might*) pay the ransom in such cases but does little to protect against the reputational losses that businesses suffer in these instances. Even if the ransom is paid, there is no guarantee that the criminals will send the decryption keys (if they exist at all), or not strike again. (In addition to reputational loss, an insurance payout will not recreate the lost data, so the business will still be facing lost time, effort, business insight and possibly even intellectual property.)

Hacktivism can represent a larger threat to modern business IT systems than even a particularly successful ransomware attack—and, indeed, ransomware may even be leveraged as part of a hacktivism attack. *Hacktivism* in itself is a portmanteau term that combines *hacking* and *activism*, and defines a more sophisticated attack conducted by an individual (or, more usually, a group) against a business or government agency. A supermarket chain might find itself the target of hacktivism because it sells products with palm oil; an energy company that promotes the use of a coal-fired power station might similarly find itself the target of such an attack, or a media company might draw attention to itself by marketing a film that a particular group finds offensive. It should also be noted that the activities typically undertaken in *hacktivism* can also be representative of outright complex cyberattack from nation states or organized crime.

In hacktivism, the goal is not a swift attack, but a destructive attack designed to maximize damage, which may be weeks or months in the planning. The purpose might be to cause significant harm to the business, extreme cyber espionage, or even to leave the business in a state where it has no option but to close. Particularly sophisticated attacks see intruders (or even agents employed by the company) gain access to data protection systems as well as primary business systems. When the attack is started, it happens by first deleting backups and other secondary copies of the data before or simultaneously with deletion of primary copies. The purpose of such attacks is not to exfiltrate data (although that might happen in some circumstances), or to encrypt data, but typically to delete so much data that the company being attacked is unable to function any longer—permanently.

In Norway, the Svalbard Global Seed Vault exists to securely store seed samples of a diverse number and type of plants from around the world; these could be used to repopulate crops after an environmental disaster, conflict, or catastrophic event, or even simple loss of a particular genetic sample through mismanagement or a more pedestrian accident. In much the same way, cyber recovery systems are designed to preserve the "kernel" of a business even in the event of the most catastrophic attacks.

Cyber recovery solutions (which may also be referred to as *isolated recovery sites*) will be a mix of heavily automated hardware and software that captures the core data from a company in a secure way, and holds the data isolated from the rest of the environment. Key aspects of cyber recovery processes include the following:

1. The primary data protection systems within the organization (e.g., the enterprise backup and recovery software) are unaware of the cyber-recovery software. This obfuscates it from view and removes it from traditional administrative access and also prevents a compromised primary backup and recovery service from being an access point into the cyber-recovery environment.
2. The copy is "airgapped"; this may be either a physical or a virtual airgap, with replication access opened periodically only to allow a new copy of the protection data to be received.
   a. A physical airgap will literally be a complete lack of connectivity. This will require either a manual transport of a data copy between the primary and the cyber recovery solution or periodic temporary manual connection of a network port.
   b. Virtual airgaps allow for more automation and will have a controlling system *within* the cyber recovery environment that can turn on and off network ports that allow connections from the primary network.
3. The storage system to which the cyber recovery data is written will have the following:
   a. Versioning control (e.g., via snapshot copying).
   b. Electronically enforced retention periods (e.g., no copies can be deleted until they are at least 45 days old).
   c. Compliance or governance security restrictions—deletes or other activities that would change the behavior of the system require the authorization of two different officers, such as an IT administrator and a security officer.
4. Data validation/verification services should be supplied. These functions may be as simple as performing automated recoveries of the data that was

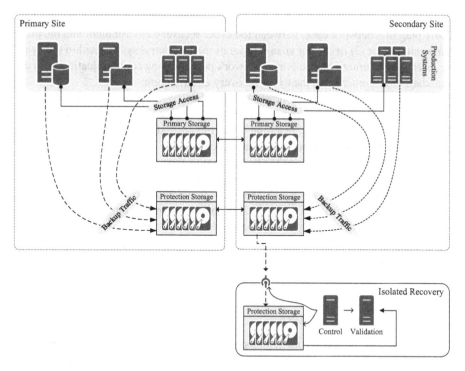

FIGURE 4.12   Conceptual diagram of cyber recovery solution.

replicated to confirm the copy was successful, or it may be a more complicated verification process. This could consist in checking that data within a
database still "make sense" or that certain rules on changes between copies
are not violated (e.g., an alert is raised if more than 10% of the data transferred on any given day differs from the data transferred on the previous day).

A brief high-level view of a cyber recovery solution can be seen in Figure 4.12.

As shown in Figure 4.12, a primary site and a secondary site are still used for normal operations and normal recoverability functionality. Systems will attach to their
primary storage for standard data functions and will have traditional data protection
functions such as backup and recovery services applied to them.

In addition to the primary and secondary sites, however, there will be an isolated or cyber recovery site. This may be either a physically distinct third site or an
additionally secured area within one of the other two sites (e.g., a locked cage area
within one of the other datacentres, that administrators cannot gain access to without
an appropriate work order and direct escort from a security officer). The protection storage system for one of the primary backup services might be configured to
replicate a specific subset of data to a protection storage system within the cyber
recovery environment. However, the cyber recovery environment is detached from
the network either physically or through the use of switch-port controls within the
cyber recovery environment. At a designated time each day, one of two things will

happen: (1) in case of *physical* separation, an authorized staff member will physically plug in a network cable between the cyber recovery environment and the main environment, or (2) in case of *virtual* separation, the control system within the cyber recovery environment will activate a network port allowing communication from the standard environment into the cyber recovery environment.

In either case, networking controls will have been established to prevent all traffic other than simple replication traffic between the two protection storage arrays, which prevents anything else from "reaching in" to the normally isolated environment. At a designated time, the connection will be severed.

Data validation services can then be run against the newly received data to ensure it is recoverable and logically useful, to alert if corruption is detected.

This isolated cyber recovery environment is not intended for use for standard, day-to-day recovery processes; instead, it would be recovered only from in the event of a cyber attack that leaves the business otherwise crippled. Even the restoration process, of course, will be handled carefully, either to prevent exfiltration of data being physically carried out of the isolated recovery environment or to prevent a cyber-attack from extending into the isolated recovery environment.

FUNDAMENTAL FAULT TOLERANCE

Each of the data protection methodologies we've discussed so far are perhaps best described as operational processes, regardless of whether they are grounded in infrastructure configuration. Underlying almost all forms of data protection, however, is fundamental storage fault tolerance—protecting against data loss from, say, individual hard or solid-state drive failures. While there is a continuum of data protection options, in practice there are usually only a couple of key options when in terms of providing the underlying fault tolerance that so many data protection mechanisms overlie. These are RAID and erasure coding, and we'll provide a brief overview of them here.

Redundant Array of Inexpensive Disks

The redundant array of inexpensive disks (RAID) technique was introduced in 1986 as a means of protecting against the failure of an individual hard drive in a system, and has been a fundamental consideration in providing a basic level of fault tolerance for data storage. RAID became a gold standard for servers in the datacenter, even as the letter "I" in the acronym RAID became subject to alternative interpretations: *independent* versus *inexpensive*, particularly recognizing the cost of early hard drives.

It is important to note, in fact, that RAID is not, in the truest sense of the word, data protection, since it does not create either a logical or physical second copy of data but rather provides fault tolerance against component failure.

A RAID storage volume may be created either at a hardware or software level. *Software RAID* is defined as such when the operating system, or a special volume management application running on a server handles the work associated with RAID. *Hardware RAID* is instead controlled by a controller card within a server or by a storage array that presents volumes to connected servers.

We will limit our technical review of RAID to a subset of RAID formats: RAID1, RAID5, and RAID6. While we will mention other formats, and still more exist, this will suffice for the purposes of understanding RAID's role in the overall protection of environments.

RAID1, or *mirroring*, is the concept of two hard drives kept 100% in sync with one another. What is written to one is written to the other, and therefore the system can handle the loss of a single drive from the pair. This essentially creates a virtual disk by ensuring that two physical disks have an exact copy of each other's data. Logically, this works similarly to the schema shown in Figure 4.13.

Conceptually, RAID1 is quite similar to synchronous replication; that when a write is performed, either the RAID hardware or the RAID software will not acknowledge that the write has been completed until such time as the write has been performed to both underlying physical devices. (RAID controllers using a battery backup cache may include the option to acknowledge the write sooner. This is usually considered more risky in actual controller cards rather than full storage arrays, since controller cards will have less fault tolerance themselves and will have a limited battery backup time.)

Both RAID5 and RAID6 are referred to as *parity RAID*. They provide protection by striping data across multiple drives, with parity data written to other drives (one drive for RAID5, two drives for RAID6). This provides more storage capacity than RAID1; combining two 4-TB drives in RAID1 will result in a 4-TB logical volume. Combining three 4-TB drives in RAID-5 will create an 8-TB volume, and likewise, combining four 4-TB drives in RAID6 will also create an 8-TB volume. A high-level view of RAID5 is shown in Figure 4.14.

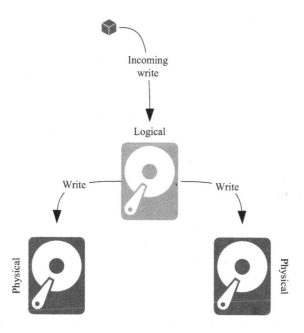

FIGURE 4.13   RAID1 conceptual view: logical versus physical volumes.

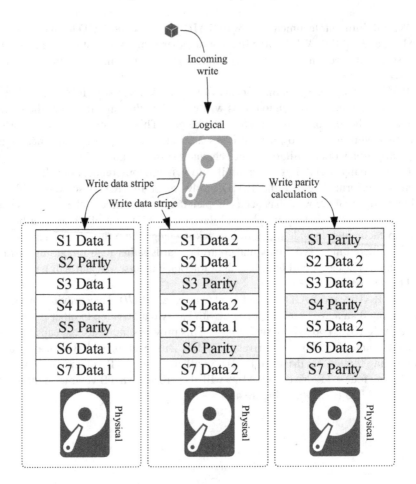

FIGURE 4.14 Conceptual view of RAID5.

Parity RAID systems provide fault tolerance by striping data and parity across the drives in the RAID set. Parity, in this sense, is a calculated value based on the actual content of the other data elements in the stripe. In a RAID5 configuration, the capacity of a single drive is consumed by parity, but this is spread evenly across all the drives in the logical volume. In a RAID6 configuration, the capacity of two drives is consumed by parity, with two different types of parity calculations performed. In this, RAID5 has a minimum of three drives and can lose a single drive, and RAID6 has a minimum of four drives, and can lose up to two drives, while still being able to access the data. In the event of a drive loss, data is either read in its entirety off the remaining drives (e.g., the drive with parity for the required data has failed) or by calculating the missing data by the parity data and remaining data segments.

For the most part, other types of RAID are a derivation or combination of RAID1, RAID5, and/or RAID6. RAID4, for instance, is functionally similar to RAID5, expect parity is dedicated to a single drive. RAID0, although still RAID, does not offer fault tolerance, with data striped across all drives, but no parity calculation,

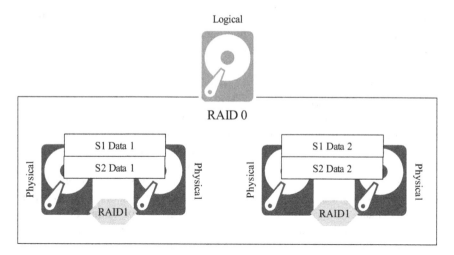

FIGURE 4.15   Conceptual view of RAID(0+10).

meaning the loss of a single disk will corrupt the data. You may also encounter "nested" RAID combinations, where either greater levels of fault tolerance and/or performance is generated by applying one form of RAID to a series of volumes that have been created with another form of RAID. For example, RAID(0+1) is a stripe of two mirrors, with a high-level overview shown in Figure 4.15.

Such a configuration allows for at least four drives to participate in read operations, offering higher performance than a traditional RAID1 configuration. (In theory, multiple drive losses can be survived, but in practice, only if they are in the form of one drive per RAID1 set—if, for instance, connectivity is lost to an entire RAID1 pair, the entire volume becomes inaccessible, corrupt, or both.)

The final type of RAID that merits mentioning is subdrive RAID. Up until this point, our discussion about RAID has focused entirely on whole drives. RAID1 uses two drives, RAID5 uses a minimum of three, and so on. These configurations require all drives to be of the same size, or else the RAID volume will be sized on the basis of the lowest-capacity drive. Another approach to RAID, used in both high-end all-flash arrays, and consumer-level RAID equipment, is best referred to as *subdrive RAID*.

In consumer-level RAID equipment, subdrive RAID is typically oriented toward providing maximum capacity when drive sizes may differ. This might, for instance, allow two 6-TB drives and one 4-TB drive to be combined in such a way that 4 TB of each of the 6-TB drives is combined with the other 4-TB drive to create an 8-TB RAID5, while the remaining 2 TB of each of the 6-TB drives is combined to create a RAID1 volume. (This *might* be literally executed in that fashion, or it may instead be logically combined into a single storage volume for the end user.)

Particularly in all-flash arrays, subdrive RAID is not about mirroring between individual drives, but ensuring that the same block of data (regardless of block size) is written to at least two drives in the array. This allows for reasonably distributed performance, and maximizes speed during recovery. Since data is distributed across a large number of drives in the storage system, rather than a rebuild focusing a large number of IO operations on a small number of drives, the rebuild instead distributes the IO operations across a much larger number of drives, bringing the rebuild time down from potentially hours or days to minutes or hours.

Erasure Coding

As drive capacities increase, the amount of time taken for RAID rebuilds increases as well, as does the risk of a secondary failure during a rebuild operation.

While the concept of erasure coding has been around for quite some time, it has seen significant growth in popularity for providing object-based storage, initially by archival systems, but popularized by cheap Cloud storage.

Erasure coding is typically premised around providing protection for each of the atomic elements that are being accessed by the user, or the application. Whereas RAID, for instance, is typically oriented around block storage (either direct block via a SAN or DAS or the underlying block storage for a NAS server), erasure coding can be regarded as providing a similar type of fault tolerance, but at the object or file level, not the underlying disk storage.

If we revisit RAID5 for a moment, consider that a block of data written will be split up, and striped across multiple disks, with an additional block of data written to another disk (the *parity* data). In this environment, the loss of a single disk can be tolerated—either the entire data is still readable from the surviving disks, *or* the missing data can be calculated against the surviving data *and* the parity data.

While the algorithms may be different, erasure coding provides similar protection, albeit with a little more work. A data object will be split into m fragments; the data will then be recoded into n fragments, where $n > m$. However, the original data can be reconstructed at any point merely by reading any m of the n coded/written fragments. Logically, this also means that up to $(n - m)$ failures can be accommodated while still preserving the data accessibility. Logically, this process resembles that shown in Figure 4.16.

When coupled with appropriate fault detection mechanisms (e.g., some sort of hashed verification that written segments have not become corrupted), erasure coding storage can readily scale to the petabyte or exabyte capacity. (While RAID enabled systems can provide high storage capacities, the time taken to rebuild RAID volumes in the event of a failure increase as the individual drive sizes increase. This results in a need to use more drives in smaller RAID sets to mitigate long rebuild times.)

RAID and Erasure coding should not be considered competing formats or methods of achieving fault tolerance; each has its own place. Erasure coding is arguably the heart of object storage in Cloud environments (e.g., Amazon S3 or Azure Blob), yet for high transactional workloads, particularly with smaller I/O block sizes, RAID remains the preferred option.

Erasure coding will typically see data spread across a potentially large number of hard drives in a distributed pool of storage; in our example diagram, for instance, the resulting $(n = 6)$-coded segments will each be written to a different hard drive, of course. However, further resilience might be provided by locality rules. An object storage system will typically consist of a series of nodes that provide sufficient compute and connectivity, and a collection of disk drives. If each node is 4RU and

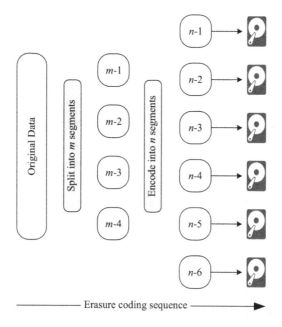

FIGURE 4.16 Conceptual view of erasure coding process.

contains 60 disks, we might see those $n = 6$ segments written to six different 4RU nodes, so that data remain accessible in the event of not only an individual disk failure but also an individual *node* failure. In larger environments, locality rules might also include protection against rack or even site failure (typically referred to as *geodistribution*). However, just as network bandwidth and latency come into play with replication, so, too, do they affect geodistributed erasure coding; this will usually see erasure coding configured for *eventual consistency*. In such a configuration, all the segments might initially be written in one location, but over time sufficient segment copies are written to other locations throughout the object storage system (with appropriate storage reclaimed from the original site).

By using appropriate levels of segmenting for higher levels of redundancy, and geodistribution (either literally, or simply multi-campus), erasure coding can allow the eschewing of traditional storage replication techniques; replication, after all, is designed to ensure there is a secondary copy of the data accessible *elsewhere* from the original site. An erasure coding storage platform with three different sites in geodistribution that can survive an individual site failure achieves the same level of protection while circumventing the need to add replication on top of the storage process (although clearly at a cost of additional storage).

COPIES, COPIES, EVERYWHERE (OR, WHAT'S ALL THIS GOT TO DO WITH PUBLIC CLOUD?)

A simple rule of thumb is to consider that for every instance of production data, you may have 30 or more copies of the data. In addition to literal copies (e.g., copying a database to do testing against it), this also includes the following:

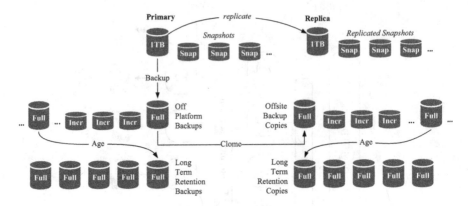

FIGURE 4.17   Understanding copies generated for data.

- Replicas
- Snapshots
- Replicas of snapshots
- Multiple backups for operational recovery
- Multiple backups for long term retention

A brief view of this is shown in Figure 4.17, but you may note that this is in no way exhaustive regarding the amount of storage potentially used—remember, after all, that some form of storage fault tolerance, such as RAID, will likely be applied to most, if not all, of the copies (or perhaps, erasure coding for object storage, which is becoming increasingly popular for long-term retention data).

Since public Cloud charges not only by gigabytes or terabytes consumed in public Cloud but also for the resources involved in that data creation (e.g., RAM, CPU, and—depending on the type— networking), this means having appropriate copy control, and data efficiency is imperative.[21]

When a business decides to move, say, 1 TB of data into the public Cloud, how that 1 TB of data is handled is important, of course, but the often unforeseen cost and challenge of the public Cloud will come in handling all those extra copies that need to be generated as part of best-practices data protection. It's not only entirely conceivable but also quite normal to see that the majority of data that resides within in a business relates to protection copies.

In this section, we've provided a *quick* primer relating to data protection concepts. It's easy to *assume* that data protection is a simple, singular activity; in addition to giving a broad overview, the primer should help to demonstrate that it is anything but. The level of protection that can be offered for a single chunk of data within an enterprise can be singular or multiple and can range from basic backup and minimal fault tolerance through to continuous availability with maximised fault tolerance. In

---

21 We should note that public Cloud providers typically charge by usable, allocated storage, not by raw storage; hence, customers are not explicitly charged for any underlying RAID that the public Cloud provider user, although no doubt this factors into the calculation of fees by the public Cloud provider.

fact, it is the exception, rather than the rule, to see only a single form or layer of data protection provided for on-premises infrastructure.

So, in summary, all this has everything to do with moving data to the public Cloud, because none of these considerations go away just because your data now resides on someone else's servers.

UNDERSTANDING THE NEW WORLD

SHIFTING CONTROL

When your data resides in your own datacenter, you are effectively in complete control of them. Your company has control over everything from the network, storage, servers, virtualization, operating system, application, and other facilities, all the way up to the data presented to users via the various applications that are used.

However, as you move into the public Cloud, and "up" the service chain from infrastructure as a Service (IaaS), Platform as a Service (PaaS) and finally, Software as a Service (SaaS), the degree of specificity of the atomic service offering increases, while the level of flexibility for control and access types decreases. In this sense, traditional on-premises infrastructure versus the public Cloud is invariably a choice between the level of control you have over the total environment and the amount of effort that you have to expend to obtain the service that you want. This is shown conceptually in Figure 4.18.

Within IaaS, you still manage everything from the operating system up (OS, applications, data, etc.). With PaaS, you'll still manage the data and applications; with SaaS, your management as such might simply be limited to creating accounts to access the service within your tenancy.

For instance, if you wish to deploy Microsoft Exchange on-premises, you will need to supply effectively everything: networking, servers, storage, operating systems, and so on. You can deploy these in a myriad of ways, and to a degree, the equipment that you deploy can be used for a myriad of other functions, as well, but you will also have to expend the most effort to get a running service ("Microsoft email").

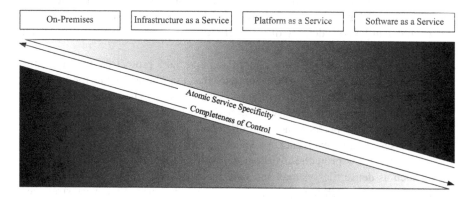

FIGURE 4.18 The choice of control versus atomic service specificity in on-premises versus Cloud models.

Conversely, if you wish to provide the service "Microsoft email" to the business quickly, SaaS (i.e., Office 365) will let you get there quickly, with minimum effort—but at the cost of control. You'll be an administrator over your email service, of course, but you will not have any control over the underlying infrastructure whatsoever. Your control effectively starts and ends with users and the data.

Although this may not seem particularly important on initial deployment and can allow the business to refocus IT staff on more direct customer-facing service delivery, it *does* present new challenges to the business in relation to data protection.

When Microsoft Exchange is deployed on site, a continuum of data protection can be deployed to offer a variety of service levels: Exchange servers can be clustered to provide protection against host failure, storage array snapshots and replication can provide fast disaster recoverability, and backup systems such as Dell EMC NetWorker can provide highly granular operational and long-term recovery, not only of the complete email environment, but down to the individual user message level.

Each of these levels of protection is achieved by the business integrating its processes and controls to different levels of infrastructure. Snapshot and replication are provided by controlling functions in the storage subsystem; clustering is provided by controlling failover options between the operating systems deployed, and backup is provided by installation of agent, or plugin software on the application servers providing the email service.

In a SaaS environment such as Office 365, however, you do not have access to the storage services, so you cannot control snapshot and replication functionality. You do not have access to the operating systems running the service, so you cannot control the clustering. For this reason as well, you cannot install your own plugins or agents into the application providing the service.

It's a story akin to that of transport: running Microsoft Exchange on-premises is like getting into your own car and going for a drive, you choose the destination and the time it takes you to get there. Subscribing to a business mail service is like riding the bus; you can hop on and hop off whenever you want, but you don't get to choose where the bus goes, or how it gets there.

Thus, the type of data protection that will be available in public Cloud situations will be directly proportional to the level of access that is available to the underlying infrastructure. What the business might normally do to protect data within its own datacentres can be considerably different from the options available for protecting data in the public Cloud.

The level of access doesn't just affect PaaS and SaaS protection options; it also considerably impacts the protection options that may be available for IaaS data protection. On-premises infrastructure has become heavily virtualized over the past decade, and backup and recovery solutions have leveraged that virtualization to achieve many of the performance and efficiency improvements currently enjoyed by businesses. Image-level backups (backing up the virtual machine container files) not only allow protection without deploying agents but also eliminate fussy issues such as dense file systems and bare metal recovery. More recently, image-level backups have been incorporated into reuse and alternate recovery strategies. Rather than even recovering a virtual machine, some products allow you to perform "instant access": presenting a read/write snapshot of a backup image residing on protection storage up into the hypervisor layer for access without recovery, and even allowing the copy to be dynamically copied back into the hypervisor environment while it is running.

Like our reduced access with PaaS and SaaS, it is extremely common to lose access this these advanced functions when moving backup into the public Cloud: simply put, when you subscribe to IaaS resources from companies such as AWS, Azure, and Google, you do not get access to the hypervisor. Multitenancy is a function of the hypervisor, and thus you can't have the administrative control of the hypervisor that is required to perform image-level backup and recovery with changed block tracking, and so on. Except in emerging situations (e.g., VMware on AWS), you must rethink your backup strategy *back* to a 1990s style solution: agents on every host that you wish to protect, with traditional filesystem backups, and plugins for any on-system databases that require application consistent protection. For this reason, some companies will completely eschew traditional backup and recovery services in IaaS situations; in practice, it speaks to a more careful planning process to determine where you need options beyond native, in-Cloud protection mechanisms. [We will cover this issue in greater detail in the section titled "Traditional Backup and Recovery in the Public Cloud," below (the next main section following Figure 4.23).]

WHAT DO YOU PROTECT?

It may seem an odd question to consider at this point, but what do you actually protect? Your business has a series of functions that allow it to operate: those functions will effectively be graded in terms of how essential they are, and whether they directly contribute to the operational, tactical, and strategic goals for the business. These goals will differ, of course, depending on the overall mission of the business; nonprofit organizations are unlikely to be focused on increasing shareholder wealth, whereas traditional financial organizations might see that as an absolute core requirement of essential business functions.

The business functions are sustained by workloads, which we can consider to be specific outcomes that we expect from applications, and the applications invariably depend on data in order to operate as required.

Since data is the fundamental component that we operate within IT, we *focus* on data protection, but by itself, data protection is only a means to an end. Ultimately our goal is *workload protection*. Workload protection almost invariably requires the protection of the underlying data, but there can be more to it than just that; when the applications that maintain and deliver a workload have complex interdependencies, those interdependencies must be accounted for in planning the workload protection. For example, it's not uncommon to encounter workloads provided by multiple systems working in tandem; document collaboration systems may feature application, database, and file servers all working together. You can theoretically back up each system one after the other, but at that point you're thinking only about the data, not the workload. The interdependencies of the application functions that go into a workload may create more complex protection requirements, such as ensuring that they have shared consistency checkpoints at the start of a data protection operation to ensure useful recoverability.

Data is almost never moved by itself into the public Cloud—there is always a workload of some type of another. Even if you're just moving files from a fileserver that have not been updated by end users in the past 3 years, you're still effectively moving a workload (in this case, effectively an archival or tiering workload); the workload may be only informally defined, but it's still a workload.

As we consider data protection in the public Cloud, always keep in mind that while your chosen protection operations will be applied to *data*, the root requirement from the perspective of the business is *workload* protection.

MAKING USE OF CLOUD-NATIVE DATA PROTECTION

The term *Cloud-native data protection* is used to describe data protection options that are inherently provided by a Cloud service provider and that can be called on to provide some level of protection without additional service subscription.

In situations where the public Cloud provider includes some form of user-accessible data protection within their service, it is quite important to not assume that this will have the same (or more) functionality as a traditional data protection product. For instance, Microsoft Azure has a basic backup service included that has a low cost for the software subscription but is inefficient with storage, simply compressing individual backups as they execute, and can result in higher-cost storage requirements over time. Beyond simple cost considerations, consider the automated backups provided by AWS for their Relational Database Service (RDS) [22]:

> Amazon RDS creates and saves automated backups of your DB instance … Amazon RDS creates automated backups of your DB instance during the backup window of your DB instance.

Such automated backup processes are undoubtedly useful, but consider guidance given a little later in the same document:

> All automated backups are deleted when you delete a DB instance. After you delete a DB instance, the automated backups can't be recovered. If you choose to have Amazon RDS create a final DB snapshot before it deletes your DB instance, you can use that to recover your DB instance.

A backup service that also automatically deletes the backups (or renders them unusable) when the original protected system is deleted has limited practicality against a full gamut of typical recovery scenario requirements; appropriate care and attention toward data protection will undoubtedly see businesses using protection other than just the automated backups in such scenarios (e.g., also performing the manual snapshots), but one can imagine all too easily that this limitation will be missed when assumptions are made linking on-premises terminology with in-Cloud functions.

For most public Cloud users, this will fall into the category of snapshots, the most pervasive type of Cloud-native data protection offered by the public Cloud providers.

While there are numerous similarities between traditional snapshot systems and those available from public Cloud providers such as AWS and Azure, there are some differences that should be taken into consideration, and may impact how and where you choose to use Cloud native snapshots.

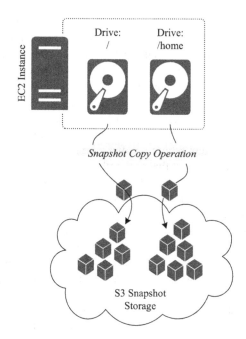

FIGURE 4.19   Conceptual view of AWS initial snapshot.

If we consider AWS specifically as our example, the first item of note is that your first snapshot of an EBS volume is quite literally a full copy. When the snapshot is initiated, the contents of the volume are copied into S3 storage (although it should be noted that this isn't accessible as an S3 bucket, as such).

Conceptually, this might be as shown in Figure 4.19.

This approach differs from most of the on-premises snapshot options that we've mentioned and does effectively create a physically independent copy of the data compared to the original. Whereas a standard "copy on write" snapshot will only populate content in the snapshot region with copied data from the original before it is altered, a first/full snapshot in AWS will copy the entire content of an EBS volume from block, to object storage.

Typical options you would expect to see from Cloud-native snapshot functionality include the following:

- Image-level protection.
- Image-level recovery (individual virtual disks).
- Database recovery (e.g., AWS supports snapshots of databases maintained in RDS; these are manual snapshots, not related to the automated backups mentioned earlier).

The levels of functionality, such as file-level recovery from the snapshot, will be dependent on the individual functions of the Cloud service provider and/or any third-party services used. (For instance, file-level recovery may not be explicitly supported, but recovery of an image to another virtual disk, with quick search and retrieval of that virtual disk for the required files, may be supported.)

Unless a specific level of additional functionality is injected into the process (e.g., AWS has options to support VSS Enabled snapshots with Microsoft Windows virtual machines), snapshots are 'crash consistent' (AWS documentation explicitly advises you to ensure that all I/Os are flushed prior to taking a snapshot). This is, in effect, a limitation similar to those of snapshots on conventional storage arrays; unless there is an integration point with the operating system, the system being restored from that snapshot will mimic a system rebooting after a crash.

AWS goes so far as to suggest that optimally the root or boot volume for a virtual machine (e.g., the C: drive for a Windows virtual machine, or the / file system for a Linux virtual machine) should be "locked" while the snapshot is created, where "locked" effectively means *dismounted*. As this isn't possible in a running virtual machine, the implication is obvious; to guarantee recoverability from a snapshot of the boot drive, the virtual machine should be shut down prior to taking the snapshot. Since shutting down virtual machines is typically inimical to production operation, for the most part snapshots will be taken *hot* with the obvious risks accepted as a necessity.

As such, the snapshot that is taken is a point-in-time view of the volume as of the time the snapshot was initiated; any writes performed to the volume *after* the time the snapshot was started are not copied in and would be dealt with on subsequent snapshot activities.

After this first snapshot has been taken, subsequent snapshots are incremental against the prior. A conceptual view of this process is shown in Figure 4.20.

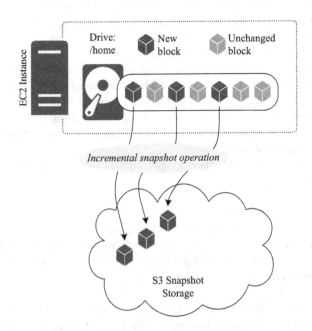

FIGURE 4.20 Conceptual view of AWS incremental snapshot.

In theory, this process makes snapshots *reasonably* space-efficient while still ensuring that the entire volume can be reconstructed from snapshot without reference to the original (an issue we mentioned as being a challenge in many on-premises snapshot processes).

In practice, while individual snapshots may not consume much storage, the number of systems receiving snapshots, and the number of snapshots taken, can result in *snapshot sprawl*, particularly if they are not managed.

To understand this, consider an environment that has 10,000 AWS virtual machines. We might assume on average that each of these has two EBS volumes: one for boot and another one for application/data. Some might only have a single EBS volume, while others might have three or four, but across the entire collection, we'll assume an average of two EBS volumes. Consider a situation where the business tries to run with the following snapshot policies:

- Daily snapshots retained for 32 days
- Monthly snapshots retained for 12 months

Since snapshots are performed at the volume level, a single day's snapshot activities would create 20,000 snapshots. Over the course of the 32 days that makes up the short-term retention, a total of 640,000 snapshots are generated, and when we add monthly snapshots into that equation, we get to 880,000 snapshots under management each year.

However, "under management" is perhaps an overenthusiastic description of the process, which we will cover soon.

If we work under the assumption that each instance averages 60 GB, and our incremental snapshots comprise approximately 2% daily change, snapshot storage requirements quickly become a tangible billing factor. For example, 10,000 instances at 60 GB average size per instance might require up to 600 TB of snapshot storage just for that first, full snapshot across all the volumes. We say 'might' because blocks that have never been written to in the storage will not need to be copied during the snapshot operation.[23] If there is a 2% average daily change rate, then the daily incremental snapshots taken over their 32-day lifecycle will consume approximately 384 TB of storage.

Such a configuration will result in a combined 32-day rolling storage requirement of approximately 600 TB + 384 TB, or 984 TB. (Even if we assume for the initial snapshots that only 50% of each EBS volume was occupied with data, that rolling storage requirement would be 684 TB which is still a tangible cost.)

Bringing that down to an individual virtual machine, there could be almost 100 GB (98.4, to be precise) of snapshot data maintained per virtual machine over a 32-day rolling snapshot period for those short-term operational recoveries.

"Snapshot sprawl" isn't just about the number of snapshots that your environment may generate, but also the occupied storage. Returning to our 10,000 instances, consider a scenario where, say, 5% of instances per year are "lost"—developers or

---

23 Blocks that have been written to, and subsequently had data deleted however, will be indistinguishable to the snapshot system from blocks that have live data, and will be copied.

owners of the instances have left the company, and while the instance may be shut down, no one has done any cleanup of the snapshots or the storage.

This has direct parallels to large virtualization farms within many organizations—copies of virtual machines might be made for testing purposes, and the virtual machines might never be released when someone is done with their copy, or the owner of the virtual machine may depart, with no one taking responsibility for cleaning up virtual resources no longer in use out of concern they *might* be needed at a future point.

Now if an instance is no longer being used, at all, the daily snapshots over time will reduce to effectively zero occupied space, but those first full snapshots that are performed will still exist, or have been rolled forward to allow for volume recoverability; 5% of the full 600 TB snapshot is 30 TB, and again will have tangible impacts on billing within an environment.

In 2016, *RightScale* published an analysis of AWS costs and spend wastage where they noted:

> We found that unused cloud storage (including unattached volumes and old snapshots) represented **7 percent of cloud spend**. You can leverage automated tools to find and cleanup unattached volumes and old snapshots so that you never have to worry about waste.

> *Weins, K., "AWS Costs: How Much Are You Wasting?" RightScale,*
> *November 15, 2016, https://www.rightscale.com/blog/cloud-cost-analysis/*
> *aws-costs-how-much-are-you-wasting*

The 7% figure is rarely disputed, and can readily result in "quick wins" for bill analysis software and snapshot management systems within the public Cloud. AWS themselves quote the *RightScale* blog post in their regularly republished storage optimization whitepaper, where they write:

> Organizations tend to think of data storage as an ancillary service and do not optimize storage after data is moved to the cloud. Many also fail to clean up unused storage and let these services run for days, weeks, and even months at significant cost. According to this blog post by RightScale, up to 7% of all cloud spend is wasted on unused storage volumes and old snapshots (copies of storage volumes).

> *"AWS Storage Optimization," AWS Whitepaper, March 2018, https://docs.aws.*
> *amazon.com/aws-technical-content/latest/cost-optimization-storage-optimization/*
> *cost-optimization-storage-optimization.pdf.*

Earlier we noted that "under management" might be an overly-enthusiastic description of the process of maintaining snapshots. The reason for this is simple; ultimately, the automation and orchestration of snapshots in the public Cloud is *your* responsibility. Public Cloud providers such as AWS supply a myriad of ways in which you can take, access, and delete snapshots, but invoking those tools are your responsibility. You can invoke them from the web-based administration portal to your account, via command-line utilities, or even REST API interfaces, but you need to invoke them. In some senses, this is a little like a return to late-1980s/early-1990s backup and recovery on UNIX platforms; operating systems contained individual tools to collate files into an archive (e.g., "tar" and "cpio"), but the act of running those backups was up to the system administrator. This led to the proliferation of locally maintained scripts within businesses to run backups (not to mention manual processes for the deletion or overwriting of backups) until such time as enterprise backup and recovery products became more widespread. (More recently, Amazon has announced a basic snapshot management portal.)

When enterprise backup and recovery software was starting to make its mark on the computing industry, a common argument against it was, "our own staff can write and maintain a system for that." You will see similar arguments presented now for in-house development of processes around taking, managing and deleting snapshots, but the following question must be asked: is this "bread and butter" work for the business, or is the business better off directing energy and resources elsewhere? Just as the average business now does not invest time and effort into writing its own enterprise backup software for on-premises data protection, so too we might suggest that the average business making use of public Cloud resources should consider options other than "rolling their own" for ongoing snapshot management.

In a similar vein now, there is considerable proliferation of snapshot management systems for the public Cloud; these may be quite primitive (e.g., prebuilt commands available in online code repositories), basic (virtual machines deployed within the customer's public Cloud infrastructure—perhaps even from the Cloud provider's marketplace environment), and advanced (SaaS offerings, allowing subscription based snapshot management within minutes from signing up).

In all instances, we should note that these options will almost invariably make use of the public Cloud provider's own snapshot technology and operations—the purpose is not to supplant or *replace* the core process of the snapshot, but to supplement it with a better and more enterprise-appropriate management interface—and in some cases, functionality that meets more use cases than the public Cloud would otherwise provide.

We will review two standard approaches to providing an enterprise-grade snapshot management environment within a public Cloud environment.

CLOUD SNAPSHOT MANAGEMENT APPLIANCE

This approach is focused on making use of the *marketplace* that the public Cloud provider maintains for easy installation of third-party services and functions, and is shown conceptually in Figure 4.21. Like a smartphone application marketplace, the services or functions are typically bundled as deployable instances that may be downloaded and switched on with minimal configuration within the customer's Cloud environment.

Since this deployment methodology is the same one used by public Cloud consumer to access other generic, third-party helper appliances, it is a reasonably familiar process for businesses to follow.

Once the appliance has been deployed and activated, it can be configured to integrate into the public Cloud snapshot system to provide functions such as

- Scheduled and ad hoc snapshots
- Expiration of snapshots based on described retention times
- Recovery from snapshots

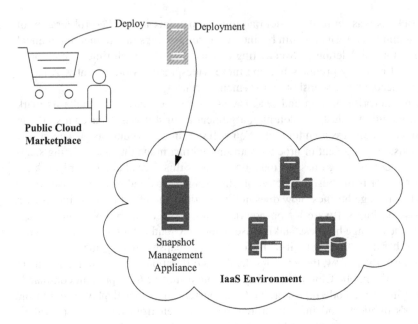

FIGURE 4.21 Deploying a snapshot management appliance from a Cloud provider's marketplace.

In this sense, it would be a very similar experience to deploying a virtual backup server within the public Cloud infrastructure, just with different data protection functionality.

One of the immediate challenges you might note from deploying a virtual machine within the public Cloud infrastructure itself is that this likely will limit the snapshot management it provides to that particular deployment, and that particular Cloud. As more businesses look toward multi-Cloud solutions, this model may create unnecessary segregation in a data protection solution, requiring multiple interfaces for the operation of snapshot activities across the Cloud providers chosen by the business. Businesses with, or planning to adopt, a multi-Cloud policy should carefully consider whether single-Cloud service appliances can be appropriately monitored and controlled in a centralized fashion when similar services are required in multiple public Clouds.

While the use of a virtual machine deployed within the infrastructure can be relatively straightforward, it does consume additional compute resources that you will have to pay for in order to operate (in *addition* to the charges associated with deploying the system from a marketplace, and potentially even ongoing subscription, or at least yearly renewal fees), and may result in fewer recovery options (without resorting to manual recoveries) in situations where there is an outage within your public Cloud infrastructure.

CLOUD SNAPSHOT MANAGEMENT PORTAL

While the marketplace deployment model is a relatively simple one, it's not the only option available. Another model is to use a *Software as a Service* (SaaS) portal for Cloud snapshot management. In other words, rather than deploying any infrastructure within the IaaS public Cloud environment, why not make use of another Cloud that's already running all the infrastructure required, in a multi-tenant subscription model?

The SaaS management subscription model offers some advantages over the first option. In this model, another vendor is running their own Cloud service (or using Cloud infrastructure to present a SaaS offering); your business will sign up to the SaaS offering from the other vendor, typically based on the number of virtual machines and/or databases that you intend to protect via snapshot operations.

The SaaS Cloud snapshot management system will then "plug in" to the public Cloud provider via documented API calls and authorised credentials—or potentially several different authorized credentials if the business has multiple public Cloud accounts. A conceptual view of this model is shown in Figure 4.22.

With this model, there is no infrastructure deployed within the public Cloud being protected; nor, in fact, does the subscriber need to deploy any infrastructure at all. The SaaS portal is accessed via a standard browser (usually any HTML5-compliant browser), and the system can be coordinating snapshots within minutes of subscribing. A benefit of this approach is that there are no systems to patch; when a new release of the portal is made, it is not the responsibility of the subscriber to perform any upgrades; instead, it is automatically upgraded by the company providing the subscription. In more advanced offerings, a REST API may also be available, allowing integration of functions into other workflows and control panels managed by the business.

This decoupling of the snapshot manager from the public Cloud provider also provides an additional benefit—the service might then provide additional functionality

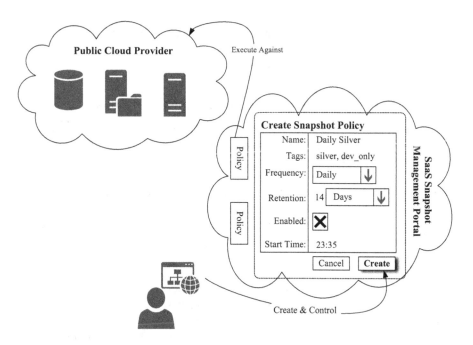

FIGURE 4.22 Conceptual view of SaaS portal for public Cloud snapshot management.

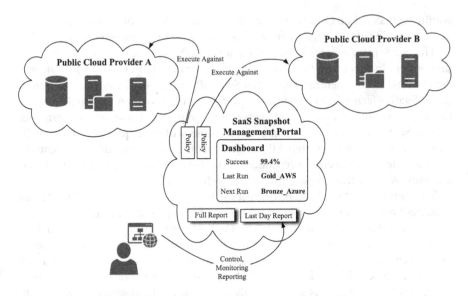

FIGURE 4.23   SaaS snapshot management portal with multi-Cloud support.

beyond the single public Cloud provider, such as providing snapshot management across multiple public Clouds, reducing or even eliminating the need for the staff within the business to perform snapshot operations, or learning the minutiae of different commands and options between the multiple Clouds. In particular, important in any enterprise, reporting and monitoring can also become multi-Cloud in such situations, providing operational control, visibility, and reporting for the business for its data protection operations regardless of which public Cloud provider it's running in. A conceptual representation is shown in Figure 4.23.

WHY USE THIRD-PARTY CONTROLS FOR CLOUD-NATIVE PROTECTION?

Public Cloud providers expose APIs and methods to perform native protection, such as snapshots. Why shouldn't they just be used? You might answer this question by asking a couple of other questions:

- Windows systems provide "copy," "xcopy," and "robocopy" commands, so why would you want to deploy a backup service in your organisation?
- Linux and UNIX systems provide commands such as "cp," "tar," "cpio," and so on, so why would you want to deploy a backup service in your organisation?

While in the 1980s and 1990s there was sometimes reluctance to deploy a commercial grade backup and recovery system on the basis of "we can roll our own," that mentality has largely fallen away. Enterprise backup environments—of the kind that provide surety and meet compliance requirements—are not just a series of cobbled together data copy commands that any company could write. Or rather, any company *could* write backup software, but why would they? While public Cloud and new methods of application development undoubtedly enable companies to develop bespoke software that meet their specific operational requirements, it doesn't follow that *everything* the company uses has to be developed in such a way. The business that turns to the public Cloud doesn't automatically also hire developers to write new word processors, spreadsheet packages, or operating systems, so why would comprehensive automation and enablement around Cloud-native data protection be any different? It has long been accepted that there is no business value in having individual system owners in the datacenter explicitly writing and managing their own data protection software, regardless of what tools the underlying operating systems come with. Likewise, the business turns to the public Cloud in order be more agile, more streamlined in repeatable operations. Having every developer responsible for managing their own virtual machine or database snapshots is, by and large, counterintuitive to the goals that a business has when moving into the public Cloud—and, humans being what they are, it's also unreliable and unpredictable.

Using a management layer on top of Cloud-native data protection isn't about running a Cloud the same way as a datacenter, but rather, ensuring that the Cloud experience is successful, adheres to appropriate levels of governance and accountability, and is cost-effective. Even if a public Cloud provider provides a native snapshot management console, it may still be worthwhile evaluating options provided by others to ensure that you can best meet your protection control, reporting, and monitoring requirements.

SUMMARIZING CLOUD-NATIVE DATA PROTECTION

Not all Cloud-native protection is exclusively snapshot-related. As mentioned previously, Microsoft Azure includes a basic backup and recovery service with limited OS and application support. As is the case for many Cloud services, the carrot is a cheap and simple entry point to the service, but the stick is the limited adaptability of the service, and the storage costs that it will consume over time. For example, some options do not support Linux, others do not support Oracle, there may be a limitation of no more than three backups per day of any individual system, and as mentioned previously, backups are simply compressed as they are written, achieving no high-level storage optimization compared to techniques such as deduplication.

In a similar vein to how a single data protection technique has overwhelmingly failed to supplant all others for all service-level objectives relating to granularity, recovery time/point objective, and retention levels, Cloud-native data protection will get your business *only so far* on the journey toward providing comprehensive protection of workloads in the public Cloud. While Cloud- native data protection methods may eventually provide sufficient scope and adaptability to meet all data protection requirements for all businesses, for now, a business placing workloads into the public Cloud should also strongly consider the options and capabilities provided by traditional backup and recovery services, running in and optimized for the public Cloud, to ensure that comprehensive protection is provided.

TRADITIONAL BACKUP AND RECOVERY IN THE PUBLIC CLOUD

Traditional backup and recovery solutions, normally seen in an on-premises datacenter, are increasingly gaining attention for running data protection in a public Cloud situations. While startup businesses that aim big without the legacy infrastructure might favor Cloud-native data protection, companies that are either just starting to move workloads into the public Cloud, or who are likely to continue to have their own datacenters for the foreseeable future, are likely to use at least a mix of both types of data protection. This will come from a variety of reasons:

- **Data protection in general:** Businesses that have run their own infrastructure appreciate and understand the concept of a data protection continuum, specifically, that data protection is not "one size fits all," and that a mix must be provided in order to achieve the protection and recovery granularity required for operational and compliance reasons.
- **Cloud-native data protection:** This has limits; it is designed to be consumed, en masse, in a very repeatable format. While this will suit some workloads, it will not suit all workloads. Businesses may desire to retain existing data protection models to ensure that protection adapts to the workload, rather than the workload adapting to suit the protection.
- **Investment protection:**
  - *Staff training and skills:* Over time, staff who manage on-premises infrastructure build up a wealth of knowledge and experience and throwing this away just because some workloads are being spun up in the public Cloud may be wasteful.
  - *Licensing:* Infrastructure vendors are offering increasingly flexible licensing constructs to allow businesses to move from hardware-based solutions to software-based solutions, and then to move software solutions back and forth between on-premises and public Cloud execution. Businesses that have these licensing constructs available to them will naturally seek to optimize their investments.
- **Operational consistency:** Businesses reduce risk and introduce cost savings by ensuring that processes are repeatable and consistent. The ability to run the same applications, and the same processes, regardless of whether a workload is running on-premises, or in the public Cloud, can keep the overall environment more manageable. This will apply in situations where a workload can be moved between the public Cloud and private infrastructure at a moment's notice, but it is still important when workloads are fixed in their locations but managed by the same teams, just simply to ensure that system management is simplified and less prone to human error.
- **Cost control:**
  - Cloud-native data protection is designed to be readily consumable; it doesn't promise to be *cheap*. Depending on workload types, operational requirements, and compliance retention needs, traditional backup and recovery solutions can offer cheaper solutions over longer periods of interest.

ARCHITECTURE MATTERS

It's crucial to understand, particularly for Infrastructure as a Service (IaaS) that just because a solution can run in a software-only configuration *does not mean* it is optimized for Cloud execution. This has been learned, disastrously in some cases, by businesses who aggressively lift entire datacenter workloads and move them into the public Cloud without any optimization or refactoring, consuming yearly IT budgets in just a few months, or even less.

This is equally true—perhaps, even, especially true—for backup and recovery solutions. The mere fact that a backup and recovery solution can be deployed as a software-only model and/or downloaded from a Cloud marketplace does not mean that it has been adequately architected for running in an environment with continuous billing. Backup and recovery solutions in particular have grown from on-premises infrastructure where the *goal* was to be a resource hog in places, so that processes would complete as quickly as possible. Optimization for running in an environment where every CPU cycle, megabyte of RAM, or byte of storage *is charged* is critical.

In the context of running backup and recovery services in the public Cloud, the architecture of the solution matters in that it *must* be cost-optimal. This comes from providing three types of efficiency:

- Storage
- Compute
- Transport

In this, we must return to the old adage about product purchasing; specifically, you can have good, cheap, or fast—pick two. In this case, though, the twist is that you want *good* and *cheap* most of all. In particular, simply "lifting and shifting" the approach used on-premises, or virtualizing a multinode appliance, may result in a fast deployment in the public Cloud, but at the risk of driving up ongoing operational and storage costs of the solution.

We will cover each of the architectural efficiency requirements below.

Storage Efficiency

There are two key areas in which storage efficiency is important in a backup and recovery solution within public Cloud:

- *Type* of storage consumed
- *Amount* of storage consumed

The first, the *type* of storage consumed, effectively covers whether the backup and recovery solution uses *block,* or *object* storage. While block storage can be directly attached to a running virtual machine in the public Cloud, it also costs considerably more than object storage to consume.

For instance, using the AWS Simple Monthly Calculator on July 29, 2018, and comparing EBS versus S3 Standard object storage costs for US West (northern California), a 10,000-GB (10-TB) volume of EBS storage would cost $540 (in

US dollars) per month, whereas 10,000 GB of S3 standard storage would yield a price of $260 per month. In both cases, additional costs have not been factored (for EBS, the cost of running compute services for the EBS volume, and for S3, gets/puts, etc.), and the costing was done without any free tier benefits or first-bill costs to keep the comparison as simple as possible. This yielded an effective pricing in EBS of 5.4¢/GB/month, and 2.6¢/GB/month for S3.

If we assume that the backup and recovery service will use the *same* 10,000 GB each month (i.e., storage consumed will not grow), and that the service is associated with a workload that will be run for 5 years, then the minimum storage costs over 5 years would be $32,400 on EBS or $15,600 on S3.

This is our first consideration with respect to running backup and recovery services in public Cloud situations, versus on traditional infrastructure. If the backup solution has not been refactored or developed to consume object storage, it will consume block storage in the way it might have done within a private datacenter.

Storage efficiency is not, however, as simple as a choice between whether object or block storage will be consumed. It is also about how *much* data need to be stored: in short, whether compression, or preferably, deduplication, is applied to the data storage.

To understand the implication of data storage efficiency, let us again consider our 10,000 GB consumed in order to provide the backup service. This might mean something as simple as 2500 GB (2.5 TB) of backup data generated each week, and 4 weeks of backup data retained.[24]

If the backup solution in place uses no compression, and no deduplication, then we have a linear cost model on storage consumed, using again our AWS July 29 2018 example for the US West, which might be $540 per month for EBS or $260 per month for S3.

If, on the other hand, the backup solution achieves a modicum of storage efficiency by compressing data before it is written to the protection storage, then we can potentially start to save costs. Our 10,000 GB now becomes the *logical* storage requirements, and the actual storage consumed will be lower. Let's assume the following for 4 weeks backup storage:

- 4 × full backups, with each full achieving 2:1 compression
- 24 × incremental backups, with each incremental achieving 1.5:1 compression

If the logical consumed storage per week (10,000 GB divided by 4) is 2500 GB, that alone doesn't tell us how big each individual full or incremental backup will be, so we'll assume that a full backup is 1920 GB, leaving 580 GB of incremental backups over a week – or approximately 96.67 GB incremental backup daily.

The net result then is that while the logical backup size over a 4-week period will be 10,000 GB, the storage consumed will be as follows:

---

24 For the purposes of simplicity, we will ignore any dependence tracking that might be performed on backups (e.g., between full and incremental backups) that require protection data to be retained for slightly longer than the 4 weeks.

- 4 × 1920 GB at 2:1 compression = 3840 GB
- 24 × 96.67 GB at 1.5:1 compression = 1546.72 GB
- Total storage consumed 5387 GB (rounded off)

Using the AWS cost estimator, with the same methods as before, this would bring EBS storage down to $290.90 per month, and S3 storage down to $140.07 per month, which is certainly a cheaper solution.

But what about deduplication? If we assume deduplication uses an efficient algorithm and is performed against the entire allocated storage pool being written to, it would not be unreasonable to assume a modest deduplication ratio of 10:1 compared to the logical data being generated and over the entire period of retention. Thus, the 10,000 GB in logical backup becomes 1000 GB of actual storage—$54 per month for EBS, or $26 for S3 storage.

Revisiting the three models and assuming no storage growth over that 5-year period of interest, we can see the following minimum storage costs as of the AWS simple monthly calculator for its US Western zone, in USD:

- Flat storage:
  - EBS: $540 per month; $32,400 for 5 years
  - S3: $260 per month; $15,600 for 5 years
- Compressed storage:
  - EBS: $290.90 per month; $17,454 for 5 years
  - S3: $140.07 per month; $8404.20 for 5 years
- Deduplicated storage:
  - EBS: $54 per month; $3240 for 5 years
  - S3: $26 per month; $1560 for 5 years

AWS and Azure, among others, offer "cold" object storage at substantially lower rates than regular object storage; for AWS, it is referred to as *Glacier*, and for Azure, it is *Azure Archive Storage*. While cheaper than a normal object, there can be other factors that influence their use: price to retrieve data, whether it can land immediately in that storage or needs to be staged, and the amount of data that can be retrieved in any given period of time (or delays that occur on retrieving that data). The most common assumption made by people who don't understand backup storage that any backup solution *must write to Glacier*, or chosen public Cloud equivalent, in order to be cost-effective. Using the previously stated cost calculator, though, 10,000 GB in Glacier in the AWS US Western zone would be $50 USD per month, or, achieving the same *compression* ratios as our example, $26.94 USD per month. However, by applying deduplication, a *cheaper* monthly cost can be achieved in Amazon S3 storage than in Glacier storage.

> **Aside:** *Why didn't we consider deduplication for Glacier?*
> Deduplication as a data efficiency format requires consistent *disk-like* access to the storage system in order to be useful. That may not necessarily have to be high-speed disk access—done correctly, deduplication can be applied to data stored in S3 storage, since the read penalty for any object in S3 storage will be effectively the same as any

other (particularly for storage in the same availability zone). The key aspect here is that the accessing system can at any point randomly request any block or chunk of data, and have that data returned in a reasonably responsive time. It does not matter whether a single object is requested, or a million objects are requested; the system will return them as and when they are requested.

However, since cold archive object platforms such as Glacier impose limits on the amount of data that can be pulled from the storage system at any given time and may impose delays on the retrieval of that data, this creates an inconsistent retrieval performance that prevents deduplication from operating efficiently. Such systems are designed for reasonably sequential access with potentially high latency between the read request and the data being returned; this is contrary to the requirements of deduplication—random I/Os with sufficiently low latency such that accumulated data can be retrieved and reconstructed in a timely manner.

Compression, on the other hand, applies to each atomic segment of data written (e.g., the full backup, or the incremental backup), and therefore can be applied to archival storage platforms such as Glacier. A read request can be issued, a long wait can be endured, and then as the data is sequentially read out of Glacier it can be decompressed by the system receiving the data.

Thus, we see the importance of storage efficiency; the pay per GB per month Cloud consumption model should encourage careful consideration of technology that favors object storage, and performs optimal deduplication against the data stored.

In the next subsection, on compute efficiency, we will see how storage efficiency will perhaps be the ultimate driver of cost consideration when understanding the architectural implications of in-Cloud data protection systems.

Compute Efficiency

Compute efficiency refers to the minimization of the chargeable compute- and RAM-associated resources to achieve an effective backup regime. Recall that when we reviewed the evolution of traditional, on-premises backup and recovery systems, the discussion relating to media servers, or storage nodes.

As such secondary-tier systems exist to funnel data from clients to protection storage via an indirect path, their CPU/RAM requirements can make a startling impact on the cost of running backup and recovery services in the public cloud. For instance, if running virtualized (an effective requirement in all except the most specific of instances in the public Cloud), one traditional backup and recovery vendor cites virtual system requirements of 128 GB RAM, 16 CPU cores, over 2TB of SSD, and 200 TB of backend storage in order to provide protection for 200-TB frontend system capacity with deduplication built into the media server.

Since public Cloud providers usually have tightly defined system types, you will seldom see a 1:1 correlation between a recommended system size for on-premises workloads and workloads that you can deploy in a public Cloud. For instance, as of August 2018, the AWS m5.4xlarge instance would provide 16 vCPU (but only 64 GB of RAM).

However, it is not just CPU and RAM that comes into play when considering virtual infrastructure within the Cloud to run backup and recovery services on; there will also be the storage that needs to be presented, of course, as discussed previously, but there will also be the *performance offering* for the virtual machine types. For instance, AWS provides a dedicated EBS bandwidth size for each type of virtual machine that you can deploy, and unless you're achieving data efficiency via source-based deduplication, this can make a significant impact on the resources you have to deploy. For example, that m5.4xlarge instance provides a dedicated EBS bandwidth of only 7000 Mbps, or 875 MB/s. This may sound sufficient, until we start calculating sustained read or write times. For instance, if a traditional, full backup of 100 TB is needed, 875 MB/s would result in a sustained transfer time of 36 hours and 37 minutes: hardly fast enough to achieve a backup within 24 hours. (We typically assume that any backup should complete within 24 hours; indeed, 8 hours is usually considered best practice.) Such EBS bandwidth limitations may result in the need to stripe data across multiple EBS volumes in order to achieve the desired throughput, rather than allocating a single larger volume.

Additionally, while AWS states that *network* performance for virtual machines may be (for instance), *up to 10Gbit*, it does not guarantee it, and lower performance virtual machines may not be able to achieve the same network throughput as higher performance instances, despite both being advertised as having network speeds of *up to 10Gbit*.

In addition to this having an impact on the overall cost, the way in which it is paid for will have an impact on the cost of the service, as well. Working on the basis of a reserved instance (since such a system should have a guaranteed level of resource availability), an m5.4xlarge system will have a tangible impact on run costs over either a 1- or 3-year period. Using AWS EC2 calculator [25] for the US West Coast zone on August 5, 2018, and running a Windows operating system, we can see costs such as the following (all monetary values are in US dollars):

- No upfront payment, standard 1-year term: $1027.84/month
- No upfront payment, standard 3-year term: $870.16/month
- Full up-front payment, standard 1-year term: $11,938/annum
- Full up-front payment, standard 3-year term: $31,846 USD for 3 years

The costs of those services over a 3-year period are $37,038.24, $31,325.76, $35,814, and $31,846, respectively. This may not seem a lot, particularly as a similarly scoped server for running on-premises will have a comparable price (and even, in fact, a similar scale of investment depending on whether the business wishes to buy the system outright, lease, or finance it over varying periods of time).

Except under very specific edge cases, compute resources are not particularly useful to operations without the underlying storage, so we also need to consider the storage that must still be attached to the system. Reverting to our prior example, that media server requires 400 GB OS region on SSD, 200 TB of general storage, and 2 TB of high-performance SSD. Using the AWS Simple Monthly Calculator again [26], for US West, we would need to provision:

- 1 × 2-TB provisioned IOPS io1 SSD volume with 20,000 IOPs.
- 13 × 16384-GB throughput optimized HDD volumes (following maximum EBS volume size of 16 TB).
- 1 × 400 GB general-purpose (gp2) SSD volume.

Such a sizing would add $14,494.22 *monthly* to the cost of running the media server, assuming that there was no way for it to address object storage instead of block storage.

Assuming a full up-front payment of 3 years for the virtual machine in order to minimize the overall cost, we would then see a combined total cost over 3 years of $554,637.92. Again therefore, we also see the importance of data efficiency in the overall design in the public Cloud. In actual fact, most businesses will instead settle for the recurring monthly charges rather than paying for up-front reservation over such a long period of time - but this serves as a good example of the *cumulative cost* that might be experienced.

A standard "lift and shift" approach to on-premises software solutions that have been designed around an architectural principal of sunk investment costs for hardware may protect data, but at an unmanageable cost. (An on-premises *scaleout* solution that is virtualized and moved into the public Cloud can usually result in an even *worse* cost explosion.)

Transport Efficiency

Finalizing our review of architectural considerations, backup environments that fully distribute deduplication to clients of the system, with data flowing directly to the protection storage can eliminate the need for large, complex media servers, allowing a reduction in the overall run cost of the environment when working in the public Cloud.

In a distributed deduplication environment, the individual hosts that are being protected will have the deduplication API installed directly. During the backup process, as data is read, it will be chunked and analyzed for uniqueness, with only new data being sent to the protection storage system. This has considerable advantages, including:

- Reduction in the CPU and memory requirements of the deduplication storage system to handle all data processing.
- Reduction in the network bandwidth required to achieve a full system backup.
- Reduction in the backup workload on the client.

It is the final point that is often considered counterintuitive. However, consider a simple example of a system that has 1 TB of data on it. During a full backup using conventional storage, or target-based deduplication storage, the entire 1 TB of data must be transferred from the client to the host handling the deduplication. However, if we achieve a 10:1 deduplication ratio during the backup process, and *source-based* deduplication is used, which would mean that a full backup would transfer only 100 GB of data, plus associated metadata used to determine data uniqueness. If this data can be sent directly from the client to the protection storage without any intervening systems, the data transport can be said to be maximally efficient.

For instance, if we can transfer data at 100 megabytes per second (MB/s), 1 TB of data will take approximately 2.8 hours (or 2 hours, 48 minutes) to transfer; however, if the 10:1 deduplication efficiency is being achieved prior to transfer, reducing the amount of data sent to 100 GB, this would require just 0.28 hours (16 minutes,

48 seconds) to complete. While the activities relating to deduplication may create a slight increase in the CPU and memory utilisation of each client, the *decrease* in impact by reducing the backup time, and the amount of data transferred, will far outweigh the cost.

To achieve data transport efficiency for in-Cloud backup and recovery services, we should consider the following goals:

1. Source side deduplication to reduce, to an absolute minimum, the amount of data that needs to be sent at any point in time.
2. Direct transmission from client to protection storage, without an intervening server.

Point 2 does not preclude a standard backup server; after all, something still needs to coordinate configuration, backup scheduling, recoveries, reporting, and so on. It's also important to note that it does not have to exclude *broker* servers. A broker server, in this instance, would be a server that enables the hosts being protected to communicate directly with object storage. (You might think of a broker server as an usher directing people as they enter a theater; the broker server points the backup clients at a specific address in object storage for backup, and similarly for recovery.) The important consideration in *both* however is they are *not part of the data path*.

Consider, then, the net impact to the overall environment: the CPU and RAM resources of the individual systems being protected are already being paid for—in fact, they're the core, accepted costs of running a workload in the Cloud, as they *are* the workload. So, rather than deploying a backup solution that utilizes intensive resources (CPU, RAM, or block storage) just to act as a funnel for intermediary processing before storing as deduplicated object, a more economical approach will leverage the "spare" computing on each of the systems being protected to distribute deduplication and minimise the *additional* resources required to coordinate backup and recovery services, and protection copy storage.

Ideal Architecture

If we consider the requirement for compute, storage, and data transport efficiency, an optimum architecture for traditional backup services in the public Cloud will exhibit the following key features:

- Use of object storage, wherever possible, for backup copies.
- Use of deduplication to reduce, wherever possible, the amount of data stored.
- Use of *source side* deduplication to reduce the amount of data that need to be transmitted.
- A direct path from client to deduplication storage in order to eliminate the need for media servers or secondary "funnel" systems that serve no point other than to receive, and send on, data.

In Figure 4.24 we see a representation of this style of architecture. Block storage is reduced to the essentials for the compute services required to run the environment

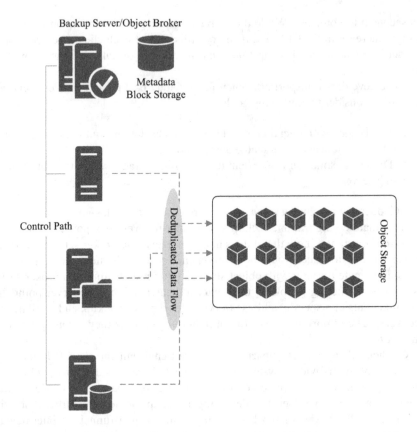

FIGURE 4.24   Optimum in-Cloud architecture for traditional backup.

(a backup server, and potentially an object broker service), and any metadata storage associated with the backup and recovery environment. Metadata storage would include configuration information, backup indices, and deduplication metadata, since storing the information relating to deduplicated data *in* object storage would render the service too slow. Ideally what we aim for here is an appropriate blending of block and object storage, with object storage being used for the bulk of the data, and block storage used for control, and the metadata required to rapidly access the exact data in object storage required.

The backup services effectively maintain control path connections only to the IaaS systems being protected; data do not flow through them for processing. Instead, the agents deployed on the in-Cloud virtual machines to facilitate backup will also incorporate the deduplication functionality required to send the minimum data required to object storage.

Ultimately, the goal here is to get the data from the source (the system being protected) to the most cost-optimised target storage with the minimum compute and network resources necessary, without compromising the overall protection and restoration performance required.

Considerations for On-Premises Backup of In-Cloud Infrastructure

We would be remiss if we did not mention an alternate option for providing backup services to infrastructure running in the public Cloud: leveraging existing on-premises infrastructure. For the most part, this will apply to protection of IaaS services in the public Cloud, although at times there may be options for PaaS and SaaS protection along a similar vein.

This option is going to be most available to organizations who have already made investment in on-premises backup and recovery solutions and see the public Cloud as an extension of existing datacenter strategies.

First, it is useful to consider some reasons why such an option might be considered by a business:

1. **Data copy ownership:** Some businesses have a legislative requirement to hold a copy of their data on-premises. When operating in the public Cloud, the simplest way to meet this requirement might be to ensure that backups are written to systems in a traditional datacenter.
2. **Existing on-premises investment:** Enterprise-grade data protection services, including high-capacity protection storage, are usually multi-year investments. A business that has invested significantly in on-premises data protection systems may wish to drive additional value from the investment by using it to protect in-Cloud infrastructure wherever possible.
3. **Rapid egress option:** Not all workloads that are deployed in a public Cloud environment stay there. Common factors for removing workloads from the public Cloud include data growth reducing the cost-effectiveness (consider Dropbox, for example, which built its own infrastructure and left AWS in 2017, saving $75 million over 2 years [27]), changing business priorities, or new legislative imperatives. An "all or nothing" exit from the public Cloud in a minimum period of time may incur steep data egress costs; however, daily transmission of deduplicated data from the public Cloud into the private datacenter may have a negligible impact on operational billing while providing a simple option for quickly turning off a workload by instantiating a private version of that workload with recovered data.
4. **Protection from Cloud shutdown:** An extension of the previous point: while this may not seem particularly relevant if using tier 1 public Cloud providers such as AWS, Azure, or Google, as discussed in the section titled "All Care, No Responsibility" (above, near beginning of the chapter), Cloud providers are businesses, too, and may shutter their services with minimum, or no notice.

Depending on the data size, network costs, and storage options, there are several ways a business can go down this path. By "network cost," we mean the cost of pulling data out of the public Cloud; some businesses will be able to arrange a link into a public Cloud that has no data egress fees associated, but usually Cloud customers will pay per kilobyte for data leaving the public Cloud provider. For storage costs, consider our prior discussions in this section, titled "Architecture Matters"—cost considerations may make storing protection data within a public Cloud environment unfeasible.

Just like any evaluation of backing up a remote branch or office back to a central datacenter, the business will have to evaluate any option with careful consideration around network bandwidth and network latency; specifically, the size of the data pipe and how long it takes for data to travel from one end to the other (influenced by network quality, distance, and intervening hops).

We will briefly discuss four options in the following subsections.

Everything in the Datacenter

In this model, the backup server(s) and protection storage are all within an on-premises datacenter, as shown in Figure 4.25.

In this model, the only backup-related components deployed in the public Cloud will be the individual agents (depicted by the letter "A") on each IaaS virtual machine. The backup services running on-premises will coordinate with the installed agent software to initiate backup operations (and coordinate recoveries), with the in-Cloud systems using the on-premises data protection storage.

This model effectively treats the protected systems within the public Cloud as if they were just part of the on-premises datacenter, and has the least public Cloud compute or storage costs of any IaaS protection model, although it does have to be planned carefully around network egress costs. It can be argued with a reasonable degree of confidence that these models can be cost-effective only when one or more (preferably all) of the following criteria are met:

- All data traffic exiting the Cloud is deduplicated *prior* to exiting the public Cloud.
- The subscription model to the public Cloud does not charge egress.
- The amount of data in the public Cloud requiring protection is reasonably minimal.

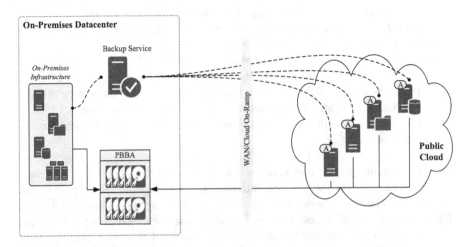

FIGURE 4.25   Backing up from the public Cloud to an on-premises datacenter.

Service in Datacenter, Protection Storage in the Public Cloud

This model has the backup server or services still running in the on-premises datacenter, as seen in Figure 4.25, but backups are written to protection storage provisioned in the public Cloud. This results in a topology such as that shown in Figure 4.26.

This model allows for a singular control interface for the backup process but eschews sending data out of the public Cloud service. Reasons why this model may be applicable include:

- **Cloud egress costs:** The cost of sending data out of the public Cloud may be deemed too high compared to the cost of storing the backup data within the public Cloud.
- **Backup volume:** The amount of data to be protected in the public Cloud may exceed the bandwidth capabilities of the link between the business and the public Cloud.

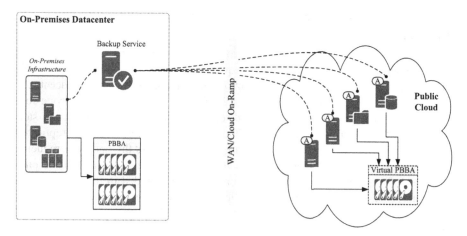

FIGURE 4.26 Running data protection services in the datacenter with protection storage deployed locally in the public Cloud.

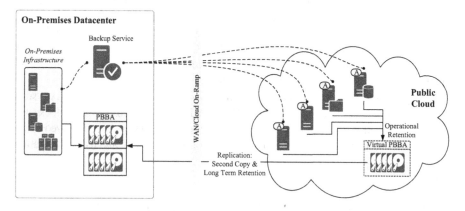

FIGURE 4.27 Backing up in the public Cloud with replication to on-premises storage.

- **Storage efficiency:** The backup system can write deduplicated data directly to object storage, resulting in a total cost that parallels any expansion requirement to the on-premises protection storage system.
- **Lower-value data:** Content being protected may have basic protection requirements, but the business can determine other mechanisms to extract the data from the public Cloud should it be necessary.[28]
- **No legal obligation:** The business has no obligation to keep an on-premises copy of the data being protected in public Cloud.

Like the previous model, this will create a hard dependency between the backup services in the datacenter being up, and the link between the datacenter and public Cloud available for data protection to successfully take place in the public Cloud. While that may be an acceptable dependence for backup operations, it is important to keep in mind that it will equally apply to *recovery* operations, as well.

Service in Datacenter, Protection Storage in Public Cloud and Datacenter

This model effectively merges the two previous model and in essence, closely aligns to a branch office scenario whereby a branch requires local recovery options for a relatively short retention time, while long-term retention data is retained in a larger datacenter.

This is shown conceptually in Figure 4.27. The on-premises backup service controls the backup for in-Cloud systems, directing those backups to protection storage that has been provisioned in the Cloud as well. Backups are then replicated to on-premises protection storage, which gives the business the option of reducing the retention time (and therefore, within reason, the required storage) in the public Cloud. For instance, 2 weeks' retention might be provided in the public Cloud for faster, data-line recoveries, with replicated data retained for longer in the on-premises protection storage—for both operational retention (e.g., another 2 weeks' retention) and long-term retention.

If investigating this option, it becomes essential to weigh up the costs of operating protection storage in the public Cloud that will be compatible, for replication purposes, with deployed protection storage on-premises. Ideally the in-Cloud system should use object storage, and realistically, the protection storage deployed on-premises will be block-based. If the two systems are not compatible for replication purposes, any deduplication done in the public Cloud will have to be "undone" for replication; that is, the data must be rehydrated and sent in its complete form across the link, potentially incurring time or egress costs.

More recently, options have become available for replication-compatible mixes such as we have described. For instance, Dell EMC Data Domain, which leverages block storage for its operational retention tier for on-premises deployments, can be deployed in the public Cloud with a modest block storage allocation for metadata, and its deduplication

---

28 It might be noted in this situation that an alternative approach would be to simply protect the content in the Cloud using a Cloud-native protection system such as snapshots.

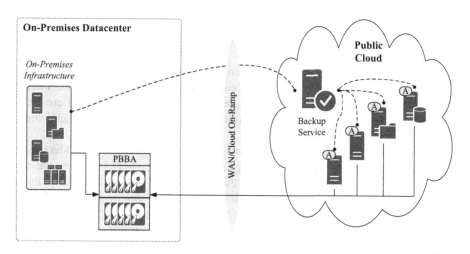

FIGURE 4.28 Backup service running in the public Cloud with protection storage in a datacenter.

pool landing directly in object storage. In such a situation, replication from the in-Cloud system to the on-premises system can take place entirely deduplicated.

Service in Public Cloud, Protection Storage in Datacenter

Our last example of options in this space sees the backup server provisioned in the public Cloud alongside workloads there, but backups directed to on-premises protection storage, as shown in Figure 4.28.

This option might be chosen in situations where there is a low latency link between the public Cloud and minimum, or no egress costs between the public Cloud and an on-premises datacenter.

The primary advantage of this option is that it allows a business to retain onsite ownership of backup data. As to the benefits of running the backup server in the public Cloud, we might consider the workload differences between the on-premises systems and the IaaS-deployed systems in the public Cloud; a highly virtualized datacenter can be protected under remote direction from a backup server with a relatively small number of proxies for image-based backup. Keeping in mind the likelihood that individual agents will be deployed on each IaaS virtual machine, there may be operational merits to having the backup server closer on the overall backup network to numerous individual agents than a small number of proxies, as long as the costs of extracting data from the public Cloud are considered manageable.

SAAS AND PAAS: NEW CHALLENGES

Once we leave IaaS behind and look at data protection for PaaS or SaaS, the level of access to the workload systems diminishes further. Unless a PaaS or SaaS provider has specifically made backup and recovery an exposed, accessible service, your options will be limited to one of the following two scenarios:

- Access to your data as a user
- Access to your data via an API[29] (e.g., a REST API)

To understand the difference between these options, consider a hypothetical online email service, *Ceres Messaging*. Ceres Messaging is a multitenant SaaS email system where businesses can sign up to host their own email within the Ceres ecosystem. Each business gets one administrative account in addition to the individual user accounts.

While the administrative user exists primarily to log into the Ceres Messenger console and perform user setup and other functions, this privileged user account can also be used to "impersonate" a regular user in the login process; that is, the login system allows superusers to provide their credentials but also specify an end user account to subsequently log in and access. While Ceres Messaging guarantees your emails are protected from any hardware fault within their environment, they do not provide any assistance for backup and recovery of any messages.

At some point, another company, Online Backup Inc., offers a backup and recovery service for Ceres Messaging. They make use of the superuser account to automatically log on to each user account in succession, doing a walk through the email account to find new messages and copy them to an alternate location.

This is effectively a user-only backup approach to a SaaS product. Without any API available, data access is done through an authenticated user account, via simulated activity – in this case, logging in to each account and accessing it, almost as if a high-speed read were being done by each user of her/his email.

There are three key issues with this approach:

1. **Efficiency:** While a "walk" through the email for each user will allow a scraping service to find emails received since the last backup, as a frontend access method, it is likely to be slower and perhaps even more interruptive to the overall service than a backend service.
2. **Security:** You'll note from the above description that the backup process relies on the *Online Backup Inc* service having access to the superuser account for the tenancy within *Ceres Messenger*. This is hardly ideal security.
3. **Reliability:** Any time you change the password for the superuser account, you'll need to change the copy held by *Online Backup Inc.*; otherwise backups will start failing.

Now let us consider an alternate approach: *Ceres Messaging* recognizes the importance of providing backup and recovery functionality to third-party services, and publishes an API for that. This is effectively a series of function calls that can be made by another system once it provides an authorization token that has been generated by the tenant administrator. This token is tied to specific functional permissions: while it grants the permission to query for email for a user, for instance, it does not grant permission to create a new user or delete an existing one. It is also

---

29 Application programming interface.

tied to a specific service; for example, the token issued and authenticated for use is a combination of a locally issued key and a key issued by the backup provider, thereby locking the authorized access down to *just* the backup service provider that has been subscribed to.

The function calls are then specifically limited to what is required for backup and recovery. This might, for instance, include the following (where "TOKEN" is the security token that has been generated out of the email platform and provided to the backup system):

- User_List(TOKEN): Retrieves a list of users on the system.
- New_Messages(TOKEN,User,Date): Retrieves a list of all messages for the nominated user account created (i.e., received) since the given date.
- Read_Message(TOKEN,User,MessageID): Retrieves a specific message for the nominated user based on a message ID received back from New_Messages.
- Read_Messages(TOKEN,User,List): Does a 'bulk' retrieve of all messages for a nominated user based on the list of Message IDs supplied to the function.
- Write_Message(TOKEN,User,Path,Message): Saves into the nominated User email account, at the specified path (e.g., Inbox, Vendors/Ceres Messaging/Recovered) the given message.
- And so on.

This list is an example only, and for a SaaS service would typically be accessed via a REST API—effectively, encapsulated as HTTPS Get/Put calls.

There are several advantages of this approach over the user-based approach:

1. **Security:** Since the access is provided by a mechanism other than a user account, or a super–user account, the security of the backup/recovery service has less impact on the security of the subscribed service, particularly in relation to user authentication/password changes and so on. It can also be revoked instantly by deleting the authentication token, rather than having to change passwords and so forth. Additionally, the access is granted *only* to the specific authorized functions, avoiding abuse of privilege.
2. **Functionality:** Since the service has had backup and recovery built into its offering, there is less risk of changes to the service resulting in the backup/recovery service no longer working. (For instance, the user-based access process may literally simulate a walk of user accounts by using the webmail portal. A change in design for the webmail portal might break the backup and recovery service.)
3. **Efficiency:** With backup and recovery functionality integrated, the process of retrieving new messages in particular might be faster; rather than a web-based walk of the email folders, a server back-end process might poll the mail database or mail filesystem by date. Likewise, a streamed retrieval of multiple email messages could be engineered to be faster than atomic message retrieval.

Such access also opens the possibility not just for a SaaS-based backup and recovery mechanism, but integration into traditional, on-premises backup and recovery solutions that the business might also be making use of, although, as we will review below, this may not actually be as desirable as you may think.

Particularly when reviewing options for SaaS and PaaS backup and recovery services, there are several considerations that you should pay special attention to. We will outline these below.

SECURITY

The simplest form of access to a SaaS or PaaS service is via an authenticated administrative account. However, as we covered in our example, this may not be ideal from a security perspective, particularly if there is limited granularity available in user account permissions. Additionally, this injects typical password management concerns into the security model, which may result in configuration options that do not follow business or industry best practices on security.

Ideally, the access mechanism used will not require a specific user account and will be locked down to *exactly* the permissions required in order to meet service objectives.

DATA SOVEREIGNTY

Data sovereignty typically refers to *where* your data is. For some businesses, there may be a mandated requirement to retain a copy of data on-premises; if so, that will provide very strict guidance on what type of data protection service can be used. (That being said, such requirements should be confirmed as necessary from a legal perspective, or simply mandated as a security process that can be reevaluated in light of a shift to the Cloud.)

The other side of data sovereignty is which legal jurisdiction the backup data is held in. For instance, in Australia, many types of government data must not be stored outside the country. If a SaaS backup provider stores data in only, say, the United States, then it might be automatically excluded from consideration due to data sovereignty requirements.

An additional consideration related to data sovereignty is where the *protected* data resides (in addition to where the protected copies reside). It is not unheard of, for instance, for businesses to vehemently assert data sovereignty requirements for protection copies (e.g., backups), only to realize that the *actual* data they wish to copy are already being stored in a location outside the mandated space. In this sense, planning data protection for SaaS and PaaS workloads can be a good trigger point for reevaluating whether the data sovereignty requirements for the workload are, in fact, being sufficiently met.

INFRASTRUCTURE REQUIREMENTS

What, if any, infrastructure must be deployed (either on-premises, or in a public Cloud IaaS environment) to provide the protection services?

When we are providing backup and recovery services for on-premises workloads, it is typically expected that there'll be some form of infrastructure requirement associated with that protection. However, consider one of the reasons that often drive public Cloud adoption: reducing, or even eliminating infrastructure that must be managed by a dedicated IT team. Particularly as workloads step up the Cloud service layer into PaaS or SaaS, deploying in-Cloud or on-premises infrastructure just to provide a protection service may run counter to the business objectives. Therefore, in such situations, subscription based SaaS services may have greater appeal and applicability.

Conceptually, this might resemble a configuration such as shown in Figure 4.29. In such an environment, the SaaS or PaaS environment is protected by a service running from another SaaS provider, which avoids the need for the subscribing business to stand up or manage any infrastructure themselves. (It also ensures they are always running the most up to date copy of the service.)

Administrative users connect to the backup service as they would to any other SaaS application: via a web-based interface. This gives access to configuration, monitoring, and reporting in a multitenant environment and partitioning subscribing businesses from one another in the way any other SaaS or PaaS service would. The backup service itself will be split into two components—storage (likely object storage) and compute—which may be IaaS at the backend or may be a fully Cloud-native application instead. Whenever a backup or recovery is required, the service will reach into the protected service and the object storage, orchestrating the copy of data accordingly.

SERVICE GRANULARITY/FUNCTIONALITY

This is effectively where normal backup/recovery service functionality questions come into play; specifically, does the protection service for your SaaS or PaaS

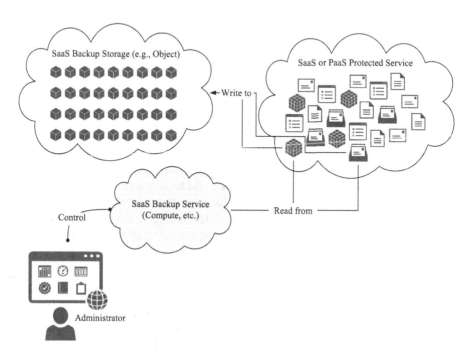

FIGURE 4.29   Conceptual SaaS/PaaS backup via a SaaS subscription.

environment offer the required (or an acceptable) level of functionality and granularity? For instance, when evaluating backup options for SaaS email systems such as Office 365, you'll want to ensure that you can achieve individual message-level backup and recovery; if the only way you can recover a user's email is to recover the entire account, or all email for all users in the business, it will be unlikely to meet standard operational requirements.

Cost

How is pricing determined for the backup service? There are three typical models:

1. Per user account
2. Backup storage consumed
3. Both 1 and 2

(Ideally one of the first two options should be the goal, rather than a combination charge.)

User Enablement

When moving workloads into the public Cloud, another factor for consideration is whether it improves the user experience. For instance, when moving email from an on-premises solution to public Cloud SaaS, this might allow for a variety of additional functions for users that had not been enabled (or available) in the on-premises solution, including the following:

- Additional email storage capacity
- Access without VPN
- Greater collaboration options

Likewise, when evaluating a backup product or SaaS or PaaS, consider whether it further extends the user experience. Again, considering email, a variety of on-premises backup and recovery services for email allow for granular recovery, down to the individual message level, but this must be done by an administrative user, resulting in many businesses not making this functionality available to end users to avoid flooding help desks. However, SaaS based backup services may provide an easy-to-use portal for end users to access (perhaps even integrating as a plugin to the protected service web portal) to perform data recovery. This could represent a substantial leap forward to end users and benefit the net employee satisfaction with IT systems within the business.

Supportability

As we've established, ideally services should interact via APIs. This is not just from a security perspective, however, but also from a supportability perspective. Consider a system that has both a CLI and an API, and that each has a function to retrieve a list of user accounts. The CLI might see this performed as follows:

```
# get-users-all
  andyp (Andy Patrick)
  joeyd (Joey Denver)
  marys (Mary Stuart)
  niamho (Niamh O'Reilly)
  xavierh (Xavier Hollander)
```

Equally, an API available to a developer for the system might include a function called get_users_all() that returns a dictionary, or a hash of users, that is, populating a variable with content such as the following:

```
$users{"andyp"} = "Andy Patrick"
$users{"joeyd"} = "Joey Denver"
$users{"marys"} = "Mary Stuart"
$users{"niamho"} = "Niamh O'Reilly"
$users{"xavierh"} = "Xavier Hollander"
```

Now, theoretically a developer wanting to access a list of all users for the system could get that list *either* via the API, *or* via the CLI. However, CLIs for the most part are designed to produce output in human-readable format, so what happens to the software built around an expectation of receiving a user list in the format of "tab useraccount (username)" when the vendor releases an update such that the output is changed to:

```
# get-users-all
  Andy Patrick: andyp
  Joey Denver: joeyd
  Mary Stuart: marys
  Niamh O'Reilly: niamho
  Xavier Hollander: xavierh
```

This is a fundamental aspect about supportability; if we think about our *Ceres Messaging* example earlier, backup software built around running a series of CLI commands would need to be comprehensively updated any time the output format from a CLI is changed. By comparison, APIs are changed more cautiously by vendors, with the nature of the changes usually carefully announced.

The other fundamental consideration around supportability is whether the APIs that are used are public or private. A *public* API function is one that is documented and supported by the vendor; a *private* API function can refer to functionality that the vendor has chosen not to formally expose or has even taken steps to hide. *Ceres Messaging* may have a bulk_copy(source-user,target-user) API call which is undocumented and meant only to be used by one of its own utilities. If *Online Backup Inc.* makes use of this private API call, it could be putting its subscribers at risk: either of data corruption/loss (e.g., a future update might see Ceres Messaging reverse the source and target user in the API call without announcing it, since it's private and no one should be using it), or service loss (e.g., a future update might see Ceres Messaging change the API to expect three arguments: source user, target user, and a flag for merge or overwrite, resulting in third-party calls with only two arguments failing after the update).

Sensible SaaS and PaaS backup products then will be built with supportability in mind: using APIs to extract content in a predictable, machine processable format, and using only public APIs, so there is minimal risk that a core service upgrade will disrupt the backup services.

LEGAL HOLD IS NOT A BACKUP METHOD

Particularly when we consider email or document collaboration SaaS services such as Office 365, a common objection to using a fully functional backup and recovery service is "But we can use legal hold" for this.

Legal hold is a function provided in some services to extend protection of data. For instance, a user can delete an email at any point in time, sending it to the "Trash" folder. A user who really wants the email deleted could empty the trash, deleting it permanently. However, if the administrator doesn't want this happen (for legal reasons), then she might have enabled legal hold, thereby capturing any deleted message and saving a copy elsewhere—or, indeed, saving a copy of all emails received by the system in another location.

Legal hold *technically* ensures that there is a secondary copy of the content, but that secondary copy is locked within the primary service, which potentially locks your business to that service as well. It is also very much an administrative function, and for many services is unlikely to work in such a way that it allows individual end users to still retrieve their email. Depending on the service, it may also require you to continue to pay a subscription for that end user regardless of whether they are still employed by the company.

When the backup and recovery service is divorced from the service being protected, however, there is greater flexibility: user self-service, keeping backup data without retaining the original account that was being protected, and having that backup data *outside* the protected service. All these options should be very carefully considered rather than just buying into the idea that legal hold, if offered, is *minimally functional*. (After all, there is significant difference between minimal and sufficient functionality, without even considering optional functionality.) It should also be noted that in popular systems such as Office 365 SaaS email, accessing email that has been placed in Legal Hold is a fiddly task, accessibly only to administrators. This may serve a protection purpose, but leave the company exposed to delays in bulk extraction of email when required, and leave end-users no better off than they had been with an on-premises solution.

CHOOSING A PROTECTION METHODOLOGY IN THE PUBLIC CLOUD

When we look at selecting and deploying protection services for workloads running in a public Cloud, four key factors need to be considered, which we will outline in this section.

DATA PROTECTION IS A CONTINUUM OF ACTIVITIES

Data protection is not a singular activity. Not even considering privacy and security, the protection of stored data from failure or loss is a multidisciplinary process comprising potentially multiple types of activity.

"When all you have is a hammer, everything looks like a nail." There are some who suggest that a single type of data protection can provide all the answers, meeting all business requirements. Such solutions ultimately become costly, unwieldy, and prone to vendor lockin. While the thought of vendor lockin has become less of a concern for many businesses, businesses turning to a public Cloud may encounter a more vexing issue: becoming a 'data hostage'. As you may imagine, that happens when you have to pay a "ransom" to get your data out of the public Cloud. Obviously, it isn't *technically* a ransom, since the egress costs from the public Cloud are well documented, but if a business organically grows its public Cloud workloads without evaluating exit costs, there can come a time when the cost of exiting the Cloud makes it unpalatable, even if it is desired (or required).

In the datacenter, some businesses have signed themselves up to vendor lockin by using entirely *on-platform* data protection—for example, relying exclusively on snapshot and replication processes instead of considering backup and recovery systems with long-term retention capability. While this can *seemingly* reduce operational complexity, if the business makes a strategic decision to switch to another storage provider, they can find themselves locked into long-term maintenance costs on their previous storage supplier, or migration projects orders of magnitude more expensive, just because they have locked up their long-term retention into the storage platform that they want to replace.

Likewise, the same challenge can occur within the public Cloud; you may be able to shoehorn your requirements into a single type of data protection, but at what future cost?

With this in mind, we will consider the choice of a protection methodology within the public Cloud in three discrete sections: disaster, operational recovery, and long-term recovery.

Disaster Recovery

Since disaster recovery is focused on getting systems back up and running after a reasonably significant failure (within the scope of either a single system, a business function, or the entire business), your primary consideration when choosing a disaster recovery mechanism in the public Cloud is to ensure that it's going to offer you the fastest potential service restoration time for your available budget.

The same as for on-premises datacenters, protection techniques such as snapshots are going to be important from a disaster recovery perspective. The goal of a snapshot is not just a quick point-in-time copy of the data, but also to allow for faster recovery than might be possible from traditional backup and recovery services. Consider, for instance, the recovery process from an AWS snapshot of block storage (e.g., the virtual hard drive attached to an EC2 instance) [30]:

New volumes created from existing EBS snapshots load lazily in the background. This means that after a volume is created from a snapshot, there is no need to wait for all of the data to transfer from Amazon S3 to your EBS volume before your attached instance can start accessing the volume and all its data. If your instance accesses data that hasn't yet been loaded, the volume immediately downloads the requested data from Amazon S3, and continues loading the rest of the data in the background.

While this isn't an instantaneous copy process, it's an *instant access* process (or as near as you can get). There will be a performance penalty, of course, if the instance is started up from snapshot and you start performing large amounts of read triggering recall from S3, but the service *is* back up and running at a faster rate than, say, creating a "base" instance from a template, installing the backup/recovery agent, and recovering the data.

An emerging area to watch for in this space, though, is either *nested* or *hosted* virtualization. For instance, the VMware Cloud on AWS (VMC) is a VMware Cloud environment running on physical systems hosted within AWS environments.[31] In this scenario, the environment *partially* exposes the hypervisor to the tenant within the public Cloud environment. While we have talked at length about backup and recovery of IaaS requiring agent-based backups within each public Cloud guest, the conversation does, in fact, change a little when considering options such as VMC. Where this exposes the potential to perform image-based backup and recovery, there may be holistic recovery processes available that are *faster* than a recovery from snapshot. (For example, it may be possible to leverage changed block tracking for an overwrite recovery of a virtual machine; in this scenario, the backup software only has to retrieve from production storage the content that had been overwritten or altered within the virtual machine since the last backup. A multi-TB virtual machine that has been corrupted by the misapplication of a patch may need only a few gigabytes recalled from protection storage and written back to the image.)

An additional consideration from a disaster recovery perspective is recovery across geographic locations and redundancy within those locations. The public Cloud is not a single datacenter: your public Cloud provider will have multiple datacenters in multiple locations.

If we consider AWS, for instance, geographic locations are referred to as *regions* and redundancy can be provided within those regions via *availability zones*. AWS cautions that your public Cloud resources "aren't replicated across regions unless you do so specifically" [32]. The same document points out that while their datacenters are engineered to be highly available, there is always the risk of a failure that affects access to an availability zone, so AWS cautions: "If you host all your instances in a single location that is affected by such a failure, none of your instances would be available" [33].

Just the same way that you must carefully plan failover options between datacenters in an on-premises environment, there are planning and design requirements around ensuring that a workload you place in the public Cloud can survive the failure of an availability zone or an entire region. For example, when copying a snapshot from one AWS region to another, the first copy always must be a full copy, which obviously has implications on your S3 storage utilization. Further, AWS does charge for data traffic *between* regions. Depending on the nature of the workload, your ability to fail over the workload from one availability zone to another, or one region to another, may be something that can be automatically architected within AWS itself, or it may be something that your organization has to develop into the application design and operation (or, indeed, a combination of the two).

---

31 In this scenario, VMware systems run on 'bare metal' within the AWS datacenter, so there is no 'nesting' of hypervisors.

Whether you even *provide* cross-region recoverability will depend not just on the nature of your budget but also the *workload* you're providing. For instance, a business using the AWS Sydney region to provide Virtual Desktop Infrastructure (VDI) to its East Coast Australian users (e.g., Sydney, Melbourne, and Brisbane) could in theory ensure the VDI environment is protected against regional failure by designing failover capabilities to the AWS Singapore region, but given the physical distance involved, latency is likely to render the service inoperable.

Operational Recovery

While disaster recovery is concerned with getting an entire system, service, or collection of services back up and running as quickly as possible, operational recovery may not always leverage the same techniques (although in the reverse, there are many instances where the processes you use for operational recovery can also be leveraged as part of a disaster recovery process).

Consider, for instance, snapshots, which are particularly pertinent given their popularity within public Cloud environments.

While the public Cloud does not require you to necessarily invest in significant amounts of infrastructure upfront like a traditional capital-expenditure model does, the ongoing operational charges should also be considered as part of the planning around data protection. For instance, consider our example in the section (containing Figure 4.19) titled "Making Use of Cloud-Native Data Protection" of protecting 10,000 instances with an average EBS volume size of 60 GB using Cloud-native snapshot technology. As you'll recall, we suggested that a rolling 32-day protection cycle of snapshots across all those instances could theoretically consume up to 984 TB of object storage on an ongoing basis. In reality, though, while snapshots provide a means of quickly achieving operational recovery, they may not represent the most storage-efficient technology in terms of longer-term operational retention compared to deduplicating backup technology. For instance, those 10,000 instances averaging 60 GB of storage each might have a reasonable degree of commonality between the systems, resulting in a 20:1 deduplication ratio (or even higher).

If we take a full backup and 31 incremental backups at 2% change rate (the same as used in the example in the "Making Use of Cloud-Native Data Protection" section), mimicking the 32-day cycle, then at 20:1 deduplication the object storage requirements come down from a maximum of 984 TB on a rolling 32-day cycle to just 48.6 TB instead. Even if we say that, as a result of backup dependencies we won't delete the first full backup until all the dependent incremental backups are expired (thereby doubling the length of time backups are stored for), using a deduplicating backup system that writes to object storage, we could achieve arguably better granularity recovery consuming just under 97.2 TB of object storage, versus 984 TB of object storage. (Of course, it wouldn't be a straight doubling of storage requirements in that situation; deduplication would result in considerable storage savings between the first, and the second full backup.) Therefore, it may be deemed far more appropriate to consider a cycle such as the following:

- Daily snapshots, retained for 5 days
- Ongoing 32-day backup cycle

Such a configuration would in a worst-case scenario require 600 TB of object storage for the full-copy snapshots, 60 TB of object storage for the 5-day 2% daily change snapshots, and another approximately 97 TB of storage for backups (assuming dependence cycle requirements), resulting in an overall object storage requirement of approximately 757 TB, instead of 984 TB.

Part of the process of moving into the public Cloud should be to plan how growth is handled. While It may be acceptable to focus initially on a single form of data protection (for example, snapshots), as the environment grows, the limitations and costs associated with that single form of data protection could adversely skew the cloud experience for the business. If the business intends to deploy 10 EC2 instances initially, but projections show there to be 500 EC2 instances by the end of the first year, there should be an understanding of how data protection will grow and adjust with the additional workloads, not just an assumption that the lowest-cost option for protecting 10 workloads will still be lowest-cost option for protecting 500, 1000, 10,000, or more workloads.

It's very easy when moving into the public Cloud to assume that "the old way" is not the most efficient approach. Yet, efficiencies come in many forms, and when you have to pay (and pay again, every month) for every gigabyte of data consumed in the public Cloud, your business must not allow itself to become blinkered against tried and trusted approaches to protecting data, just because they originated in traditional datacenter environments.

Long-Term Recovery

The retention window for operational recovery is (for most businesses) somewhere in the order of 30–90 days, tending more toward the lower than the higher number. Long-term, or compliance retention, though, might range anywhere from a few months to decades. Even businesses that do not have a compliance requirement (or believe that they do not have a compliance requirement) to keep truly long-term copies of their data will often still retain at least a few monthly backups simply for additional redundancy.

It is up to your business, of course, to determine the level of long-term data that you must keep, and the granularity of that data. A common long-term retention period in many countries of 7 years can still yield different levels of retention within businesses; some may opt for keeping monthly backups for the full 7 years (effectively, 84 monthly backups), while others might instead opt for keeping 12 or 13 monthly backups, and either 7 annual backups, or 14 half-yearly backups. This can obviously make a substantial difference on the amount of data to be retained. Just like any fundamental storage or infrastructure transition that takes place *on-premises*, a move into the public Cloud should see existing retention requirements revalidated to ensure data is:

- Kept long enough
- Not kept for long
- Retained with the required granularity

Now, consider a workload running in the public Cloud with long-term retention requirements: for legal compliance reasons, you must retain monthly copies of the data for say, 7 years. If you're only approaching things from the perspective of snapshots, that implies keeping a snapshot taken monthly for 84 months. If at some point you want to pull the workload *out* of the public Cloud, you have to consider not only the workload itself, but all those snapshots. Do you restore each required snapshot and copy it out of the Cloud, or do you just keep on paying a diminishing monthly bill for that workload for up to 7 years after?

This is a challenge that many companies have found themselves in when they stick to a purely *on-platform* data protection strategy but years later decide to change their primary storage platform.

Your choice for operational retention in the public Cloud will be governed by the speed with which you can get the data back; your choice for long-term, or compliance, retention in the public Cloud should be focused on data efficiency and data portability. As we have established previously, long-term retention can make a substantial impact on the amount of data that you have to store, so minimizing its size wherever possible is essential. But equally, you must think ahead: what happens if the business decides to either exit the public Cloud altogether, or at least switch public Cloud providers? If you do intend to store long-term retention protection data in the public Cloud, it's essential you have plans regarding that strategy changing, or else the business may be left in the lurch, either financially, or from a legal compliance perspective.

For this reason we can again see tangible benefits to using some form of backup system, with efficient deduplication services, particularly if that system can be run on-premises as well and can replicate without rehydration. If you *do* have to extract your long-term retention data from the public Cloud, would you prefer to be faced with egress charges for 10 PB of data, or 400 TB of data at a 25:1 deduplication ratio?

Most public Cloud providers offer a service where you can ship a bulk copy of your data directly to one of their datacenters, for example, on a hard drive, multiple hard drives, or even an "object storage in a box" system, to speed up the *ingress* option. For example, Amazon refers to this as their *Snowball* service. While most of the time *Snowball* is considered as an ingress service, it can be used for data *egress* as well. As of September 29, 2018, the data egress fee via Snowball for the Sydney region, for instance, was $0.04/GB [34], plus shipping. If bulk shipping-based export of data is available in a region that you require, it can be factored into exit considerations for long-term retention plans, but even still, driving data efficiency can remain an important cost consideration. Using our previous example, exporting 10 PB via Snowball would see a per-GB cost of $400,000; yet if the same logical data could be extracted, deduplicated at 25:1, 400 TB would cost a mere $16,000 in per-GB fees by comparison.

You might wonder why such services aren't used for regular transfer of long-term retention data from the public Cloud into a private datacenter; while there may be other reasons, the core one would be the fussiness of such a solution; it requires multiple manual interventions at both ends, and while it may have functional elements that are susceptible to automation, it will require end-to-end oversight. While this can be readily accepted as part of an overall exit strategy, something that will be done only once, or at most, a few times, it would prove troublesome and unreliable to be executing on a monthly process.

MONITORING AND MANAGEMENT

"Single pane of glass" is a common trope in the data protection industry. In reality, it is rarely achieved outside of monolithic, largely homogenous environments, and often purely as a sleight of hand. One might even suggest that businesses can paint themselves into a corner when they pursue "single pane of glass" to the exclusion of required functionality elsewhere. Data protection is an important function, of course, but equally as, if not more, important are the actual business functions that data protection safeguards.

As the number of business functions increases, so, too, does the number of workloads to support those functions, and in turn, the applications that run those workloads. Cloud does not remove this challenge, and in fact is more likely to extend it—workloads can run in multiple locations, they can run in multiple different ways, and it can even generate a shift away from a relatively small number of large, complex-functioning workloads to a large number of small, highly tailored workloads.

While being able to monitor, or manage, every aspect of data protection from a single console is, of course, desirable, we also have to consider that it may not be an operational practicality—either at all, or without local customisation. One might suggest that this is something, that the entire agile, DevOps process can enable; businesses can leverage REST APIs across the entire fleet of workloads maintained in order to deliver a central, customized, or even bespoke portal for monitoring, or for monitoring and management.

Therefore, unless your business is unique, or your workloads are practically singular, you should not expect that the public Cloud, in and of itself, will solve the "single pane of glass" problem. The significant difference between on-premises solutions and the public Cloud, between IaaS and SaaS, between PaaS and IaaS, and the *different services you use in each vertical* may indeed create a sufficiently unique combination that there will exist no "out of the box" solution that immediately provides you a comprehensively complete portal for monitoring and management of your data protection needs across the entire spectrum.

That solution, then is likely to resolutely remain within rather than without.

IN CONCLUSION

There is no objective, universally "right" set of data protection options that can and should be deployed in all circumstances for all businesses. Instead, there are perhaps a number of general guidelines that one should keep in mind when planning data protection services in a public Cloud environment. In no particular order, these guidelines include the following:

- **Architecture matters:** Your data protection solution must be efficient under three essential criteria: compute, transport, and storage. This is always desirable in on-premises solutions but becomes more critical when you pay for the consumption of these continually.
- **"One size fits all" is another way of saying, "jack of all trades master of none":** In a fully fleshed-out public Cloud environment you are likely to have a variety of workloads running under a number of *aaS* models; this may

require a number of specific data protection functions that each significantly or completely meet a subset of your requirements rather than a single data protection function that requires you to compromise for all of your workloads.

- **The fundamental best practices to data protection remain the same regardless of where your workload and data resides:**
  - Continuing the prior point, even the different recovery point and recovery time objectives that your business requires may drive different data protection functions, or a mix of them. It is, in fact, quite rare to use only a *single* form of data protection for any specific enterprise workload.
  - Data protection should not introduce the potential for a single point of failure within the business; this means that the copies you take should be replicated, and at least some of those copies should exist outside the original location; thus there should be off-platform copies as well.
  - If you want to make assumptions about data being protected, it's best to assume that they are not protected.
  - While you perform data protection, you must always remain cognizant of the requirement for *workload* protection.
  - Part of the process of planning for data protection is also understanding your data availability requirements; the public Cloud does not guarantee data and systems availability; the onus still falls onto your organization to architect it appropriately.
  - The bulk of your data footprint will reside in data protection, so every lifecycle management remains an integral guiding force to public Cloud data protection; every terabyte that you eliminate from primary systems may save you 20, 30, or more TB from data protection systems.
- **Have an exit plan:** This doesn't have to be fully fleshed out, but going into the public Cloud should trigger careful consideration of what you would do to *exit* the public Cloud, and that consideration must apply as much to data protection as it does to the actual workloads themselves. (Ideally, the documented architecture for a public Cloud workload should include preferred and considered options for both extracting the workload from public Cloud, and moving it to another public Cloud provider.)

The public Cloud does not exist in a vacuum; the ways in which you integrate with it do not stop at the firewalls of your business. In the next section, we will cover some additional considerations for extending on-premises data protection (either existing, or net new) through the use of the public Cloud. However, the above guidelines will still be valuable regardless of how blurred the boundary is between your on-premises and public Cloud workloads.

EXTENDING ON-PREMISES DATA PROTECTION INTO THE CLOUD

Not all workloads solely exist either on-premises, or in a public Cloud. While some businesses adopt Cloud-like automation and orchestration tools on modern equipment, thereby creating a *private* Cloud experience in their own datacenters, there is a growing tendency to consider how to best mix on-premises and public Cloud processes into a seamless (or as seamless as possible) experience for the business.

In this section, we will consider three common techniques of extending on-premises data protection into public Cloud.

Hybrid Cloud Solutions

Whereas a *private* Cloud attempts to emulate much of the functionality of *public* Cloud on-premises, a *hybrid* Cloud solution is premised around stretching between private and public Cloud options, attempting as much as possible to create a seamless experience that offers the best of both worlds.

There are essentially three approaches to developing a hybrid Cloud solution:

- Using a portal (either bespoke or purchased) that provides a single pane of glass over the private Cloud experience as well as one or more public Cloud options. This may simply act as an overarching management/monitoring console, with public and private Cloud resources completely separated, or it may also incorporate capabilities around migrating workloads between the private and public Cloud experiences.
- Bring public Cloud infrastructure on-premises, such as with Azure Stack. In this mode, hybrid applications and services can be developed on essentially the same infrastructure and deployed where needed.
- Using private Cloud infrastructure that offers bridging into the public Cloud, such as VMware vCloud (on-premises) reaching out to VMware Cloud for AWS.

Regardless of which option is chosen, an essential part of a safe hybrid Cloud deployment will be to ensure that data protection services are available for workloads, no matter where those workloads reside.

To ensure data protection for the hybrid Cloud, there are four essential considerations, described in the following subsections.

Impact of Data Protection Requirements on Workload Placement

Perhaps the most serious consideration is whether the data protection requirements (either assigned or selected) for a workload effectively govern *where* the workload can be deployed in the first place.

For the most part, if there are specific requirements around data protection that mandate a workload placement, that placement is likely going to be mandated to be the private Cloud environment. Examples of where this may occur include, but are not necessarily limited to:

1. **Data sovereignty:** The business may have a legal requirement to retain at least one copy of the data on-premises. In such a case, this may either force the workload to stay on-premises or might simply be handled by backing up from the public Cloud into the on-premises solution.
2. **Performance:** Some workloads may require specialist data protection solutions that cannot be serviced adequately within a public Cloud environment.

A prime example of such a workload will be a large database that requires Storage Integrated Data Protection (SIDP) where the SLAs (either for backup, or recovery) cannot be met using public Cloud techniques, or virtualized IaaS data protection services. For instance, such techniques may integrate primary storage arrays, protection storage, and the native application protection tools (e.g., Oracle RMAN) to create protection copies within seconds via snapshots, with automatic transfer of the data to protection storage. (This can sometimes be known as *convergent data protection*, since it typically mixes multiple data protection techniques, such as snapshot and backup, into an integrated process.)

More generally, the mandating will happen when data protection requirements can be met by only one of the available Cloud options; a business that has started with a traditional infrastructure and modernized it to a private Cloud may already have the technical capabilities of running something with continuous storage availability across on-premises datacenters, and therefore deem refactoring of applications to achieve a similar result in the public Cloud too expensive. Conversely, a business that could never afford that style of on-premises infrastructure may be left with no option other than to deploy such requirements within the public Cloud with appropriate safeguards built into the application and deployment model.

When planning a hybrid Cloud environment, the business will need to establish clear models of when and where data protection requirements might force workload locality.

Data Protection Portability

If a workload is designed to be portable, that is, be moved between the private and public Cloud aspects of the environment, there should also be consideration of whether the data protection for the workload is similarly portable.

There are a few essential options here, including the following:

- When the workload shifts between an environment, the data protection is "restarted" in the new environment.
- When the workload shifts between an environment, any common data protection (e.g., backup) is "copied" into the new location as well (e.g., a workload previously running on-premises might be moved into the public Cloud, and the backups that had been performed for it replicated into a backup server that protects the region of the public Cloud that the workload has moved into).
- Does operational recovery (i.e., short-term retention) adjust to suit the infrastructure options (private infrastructure vs. public Cloud), with long-term retention handled separately?

In fact, it may be worthwhile (as we will note in the next subsection) that long-term retention be handled separately from operational recovery retention regardless of how portable the operational data protection is.

If the operational recovery process alters between private infrastructure and the public Cloud, or if the operational recovery processes are restarted when the workload is shifted, it will, of course, be necessary to meet agreed-to SLAs with the business (or that are legally required). That is, if the business has a 4-week retention time on short-term backups, then just because the workload moves to a different location doesn't mean that the old backups can be instantly deleted; instead, there will likely need to be an overlap period where backups are held in both locations to ensure that recovery targets can be met.

Long-Term Retention Mobility

If you need to provide long-term retention, do you try to move that with the work-load, or do you have a blanket rule that long-term retention remains in one location? If it remains in one location, your options will effectively be one of the following:

- Same location as where workload was initially deployed
- Always on-premises
- Always public Cloud

As is always the case with long term retention, the challenge is the amount of data that might be stored. Disregarding annualized growth, a workload that receives weekly full backups, daily incrementals with a 2% daily change rate, and monthlies retained for 7 years will, over the course of the 7 years, see long-term, or compli-ance retention backups consume almost 95% of the backup storage requirements. Given the cost of egressing data from the public Cloud, not to mention the amount of time it might take to replicate such data, deciding upfront to move long-term reten-tion when a workload is moved could have very costly implications, particularly for larger datasets.

An alternative, of course, in a hybrid Cloud environment might be to treat the private and public Cloud components as separate datacenters, that is, replicate on-premises backup data into the public Cloud, and similarly replicate in-Cloud backup data back to an on-premises vault. In this way, portability of long-term retention backups (as well as operational retention backups) becomes automatic, although this does create additional cost considerations for data storage in the public Cloud, in addition to egress fees from the public Cloud.

Mapping Data Protection Methodologies from a Service Catalog

Since key aspects of a Cloud environment include automation and repeatabil-ity, Cloud workload deployment options are usually handled by a management portal that maps service catalog options and descriptions to the actual technical requirements.

When a hybrid Cloud user elects to activate a workload that can run *only* in the public Cloud or on the private infrastructure, the data protection assignment should be reasonably simple. However, when a user indicates s/he wants "gold"-level data-base protection for a new workload being provisioned that might start on-premises *and* can be moved into the public Cloud, this effectively necessitating *two* data pro-tection options: one for when the workload runs on private infrastructure, and the other for whenever the workload is moved into the public Cloud.

Depending on business requirements, this might be handled in one of the following ways:

- The user requesting resources for a new workload might be required to explicitly request a protection option for on-premises, *and* a protection option for the public Cloud.
- Each data protection option presented may be a "meta"option that maps to two data protection options: one for on-premises and one for the public Cloud.

While the first option may appeal from a development simplicity perspective, it does increase the requirements for the Cloud consumer to *understand* the different technical options, which effectively runs counter to the standard goal of simplicity of consumption. An example of the second option is shown in Figure 4.30.

Summarizing Hybrid Cloud Data Protection

Hybrid Cloud environments offer considerable potential for businesses to get the most out of a combined on-premises and public Cloud infrastructure experience, and are likely to become increasingly common as businesses modernize their private infrastructure, invest more into virtualization across the entire datacenter, and adopt more converged, and hyperconverged infrastructure.

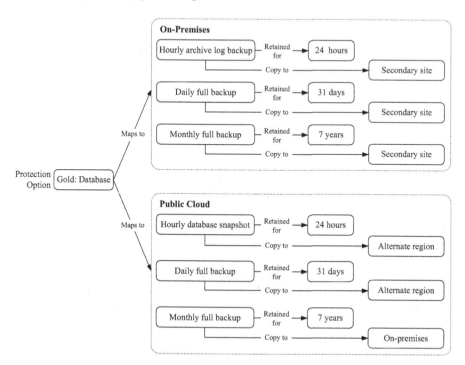

FIGURE 4.30 Mapping protection options for portable workloads in a hybrid Cloud environment.c

Ensuring that data protection works seamlessly across the private and public Cloud aspects of a hybrid Cloud environment will be a critical factor in the overall success of a hybrid Cloud. From a day-to-day perspective, the principles of data protection will be largely unchanged in a hybrid Cloud; either the appropriate private Cloud data protection will be used, or the appropriate public Cloud data protection will be used. What will require greater attention to detail will be the planning of workload mobility, service catalog selection, and the where or when of data protection for any specific workload that is transitioned between the private and public infrastructure.

LONG-TERM RETENTION

While businesses typically aim to have protection data that they use for operational recovery (i.e., short-term retention data) close by, in terms of connective bandwidth to the systems being protected, long-term retention is usually an entirely different scenario.

We can say that, in general, key characteristics of recovery from operational retention data are as follows:

1. **Not queued:** Once data have been selected for recovery and the recovery initiated, data should start streaming back immediately, or as soon as possible. (This, in fact, is a significant contribution in the demise of tape: recoveries being queued waiting for tape drives to be freed up, or tapes to be returned from off site.)
2. **Fast:** When you need to get data back for the purposes of operational recovery, whether it's a single file, complete virtual machine, or a database, you'll want it back quickly. The nature of the recovery suggests that users, or customers, are unable to do what they need to do until the recovery completes. The number of people inconvenienced until the recovery is complete usually just increases the urgency of the recovery speed.
3. **Flexible:** If a user loses a single file, you don't want to overwrite the entire corporate file server to return the data. If a single table is corrupted in a database, it might be preferable to recover just that table, rather than the entire database. Operational retention backups should offer the best possible flexibility in terms of granularity for recovery purposes, wherever possible.

Note that the other operational requirement for recovery from operational retention is "reliable" or "accurate"; however, this is the same for both operational and long term retention.

In terms of long-term retention, our goals shift. The characteristics of what we require from operational retention all come at a price; speed, flexibility, and instant start are all drivers on the types of technology used, and the level of effort that goes into its development. Generally speaking, businesses are prepared to pay more for these features because of the urgency associated with operational recoveries.

One of the most common characteristics of recoveries from long-term retention is the relative infrequency with which they are done. Large enterprises protecting multiple petabytes of data might perform one or two recoveries from long-term retention a year, or perhaps fewer. The concept of "write-only memory" (WOM) has existed as a joke since as far back as the 1970s, but for many businesses, long-term retention is almost WOM-like.

Since long-term retention data are rarely recovered from, the economics of it shifts:

- Users almost naturally expect that data retrieved from a much older backup will take longer to recall (certainly, even when users don't expect it, the business almost invariably accepts it as an operational difference to standard recoveries).
- It is more important that the storage be dense and cheap in terms of cents per gigabyte than fast.

Herein is the appeal of object storage.

While the reliability targets on block storage in the public Cloud are no different (or sometimes are less) than what can be achieved with on-premises storage systems, object storage provides high degrees of reliability (or durability). The AWS durability design goal for S3 is 99.999999999%, which, according to AWS, means that "If you store 10,000 objects with us, on average we may lose one of them every 10 million years or so" [35].

It's important to note here that *durability* does not mean the same thing as *availability*. Durability effectively refers to the chance of data corruption or loss; availability refers to whether you can access it when you want to. The AWS *Availability* SLA for S3 storage is just 99.9% on the basis of being designed for 99.99% availability. 99.99% availability allows for content being unavailable for 52 minutes, 35.7 seconds per annum; 99.9% availability, on the other hand, allows for 8 hours, 45 minutes, and 57 seconds of unavailability per annum. The availability SLA for S3 infrequent access (IA), by the way, is 99%, which allows for the service being unavailable for up to 3 days, 15 hours, 39 minutes, and 29.5 seconds per annum. (In this sense, while it might be "cheap" to deploy *operational* protection that uses S3-IA, it must be done with the understanding there *might* be some significant downtimes over the course of a year.)

Since we typically accept a longer SLA on recovery time from long-term retention backups, the potential for lower availability on the storage medium is not so much of an issue as long as there is a high degree of reliability on the data being retrieved without corruption.

Businesses wishing to shift to object storage for long-term retention may find natural advantages in using the public Cloud to do so, including the following:

1. **Speed of adoption:** With nothing to stand up in private infrastructure, object storage in the public Cloud can minimize the time to readiness.
2. **Minimization of on-premises infrastructure:** Businesses wishing to avoid further deployments, either of storage, or in general any infrastructure within their datacenter environments, can adopt public Cloud object storage and potentially reduce their datacenter footprint (e.g., by removing physical tape libraries).

3. **No minimum entry size:** Like any other storage array, on-premises object storage systems will have a minimum configurable size. If this size is substantially in excess of the projected long-term requirements for a business, it may be impractical to consider private object storage. Software defined object storage systems may mitigate the initial entry size requirements of physical storage appliances.

4. **Operational expenditure:** Because the public Cloud is a "pay as you go" system, businesses seeking to avoid capital expenditure purchases may be happy with the projected cost of long-term retention in the public Cloud even if the cumulative operational expenditure spend is higher.[36]

Ideally, extension to the public Cloud in this form should be achieved as a seamless form of tiering between the operational retention storage for the backup environment and the public Cloud object storage; as data age from the on-premises protection storage, it is eventually moved ("tiered") out to the Cloud. In this way, long-term retention data stay within the control and visibility of the data protection product. When or—more correctly—*if* a recovery is requested from long-term retention data that have been tiered out to public Cloud object storage, it can be "recalled" by the backup system to be used.

As has been discussed previously with long-term retention data, optimally the data that is tiered out should be deduplicated to reduce the overall storage requirements (and therefore cost).

DISASTER RECOVERY AS A SERVICE

Whenever we consider disaster recovery, it's important to step back first and understand that disaster recovery is only the *technical*, or *IT*, aspect of a much more complex process referred to as *business continuity*. Business continuity is the end-to-end process covering keeping the business (or a part of the business) running; business continuity processes will invoke disaster recovery plans as needed.

Providing disaster recovery services for the business can be a reasonably expensive process, particularly for smaller businesses. While an enterprise may readily have budget available to maintain systems ready to enable transition from one datacenter to another in the event of a catastrophic failure, keeping disaster recovery systems available 24×7 for the *chance* they are required is sometimes too expensive a proposition for smaller companies.

Sometimes, this results in running active/active datacenters—rather than keeping a datacenter idle in the event that it is needed, workloads are distributed between the company's datacenters while ensuring that there are sufficient processing and storage capabilities to run the *entire* production workload requirements within a single datacenter. Even this, however, can be expensive; many businesses have found when conducting disaster recovery tests (or worse, real disaster recovery processes) that interdatacenter dependences had crept in, resulting in a nonfunctional environment without *both* datacenters available.

---

36 Although, depending on the scale, many vendors can present OpEx models to customers for less than the OpEx expenditure offerings from public Cloud providers.

An emerging process for mitigating this cost is *Disaster Recovery as a Service* (DRaaS). In this situation, the business deploys technology and processes that allow it to failover an on-premises workload into the public Cloud in the event of a local systems failure or outage. Such failover may not be immediate, but businesses seeking this approach will usually endure longer outages to keep the overall disaster recovery cost down.

There are several different ways this can be achieved, but one is to leverage the backup and recovery services in place. As backups are completed, select backups designated for disaster recovery consideration will be copied out into public storage. This might be done in one of two different ways:

- **A literal copy between compatible backup systems:** The business might have a hardware-based backup and recovery service on premises, and use a software-defined solution of the same components running in the public Cloud.
- **An extraction of backup content:** Alternatively, backups might be extracted and stored in a different format in the public Cloud (e.g., object storage) in order to minimize the amount of infrastructure that needs to be continuously running in the public Cloud.

Regardless of the copy process, we must keep in mind that there will usually be a need for a *conversion* process between the format of the on-premises systems and the virtualization used by the public Cloud provider. (For example, a VMware virtual machine may need to be converted to AWS AMI format.) Obviously, there will likewise need to be a process to convert the disaster recovery system *back* to on-premises format when the local datacenter facilities are ready to take over the running of the system again.

The appeal of approach is almost purely economic. Between rack rental space, equipment costs, power, cooling, administration and maintenance effort, maintaining an on-premises disaster recovery service may cost even small businesses many hundreds of thousands of dollars per annum. While there will undoubtedly be costs in running workloads that have not been refactored for optimized execution in the public Cloud, the number of times this expenditure is required per annum may be quite low. Being *as a service*, the disaster recovery components *available* in public Cloud under this model will be spun up (and sometimes, only be *created*) only as required. Particularly for smaller businesses, this might make DRaaS orders of magnitude cheaper than running a full disaster recovery datacenter.

A conceptual overview of DRaaS is shown in Figure 4.31.

The DRaaS machine conversion process will transform a virtual machine that had been running on premises to one that can run in the native format of the Cloud service provider. There are two key models that might be used for this conversion process:

- **Immediate:** Once the required data have been copied into the public Cloud (or even while they are being copied into the public Cloud), the data format is converted to be compatible with public Cloud execution. The resulting virtual machine will be left powered off until it needs to be used.

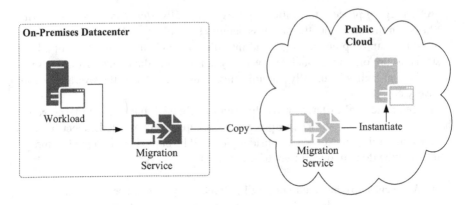

FIGURE 4.31   Conceptual DRaaS failover.c

- **On-demand:** The required data is likely to be copied into object storage; when a disaster event is triggered, the in-cloud resources for DRaaS will read the data out of object storage and instantiate a new virtual machine with the appropriate configuration and data.

It should be noted that neither option can realistically provide the same sort of failover options as can traditional, on-premises infrastructure. In a traditional active–active or active–passive datacenter configuration, a virtual machine could be maintained synchronously between two LAN or MAN[37] connected datacenters, and in the event of the primary instance failing, the secondary instance could be started in seconds. While there will still be a service disruption in such a scenario, it will be far shorter than can be reasonably expected in a DRaaS configuration.

The on-demand DRaaS option outlined above will require the following steps:

- (Prefailover) Copying data from on-premises to the public Cloud.
- (Failover) Reading data and instantiating the public Cloud virtual machine required.
- (Failover) Starting the virtual machine.

The immediate DRaaS option outlined above will require the same steps, but as follows:

- (Prefailover) Copying data from on-premises to the public Cloud.
- (Prefailover) Reading data and instantiating the public Cloud virtual machine required.
- (Failover) Starting the virtual machine.

---

37 LAN = local-area network, perhaps between two datacenters on the same campus. MAN = metropolitan-area network, usually indicating greater physical separation between datacenters within the same city, but still close enough to allow synchronous replication.

In both cases, the steps involved will take time; copying the data from an on-premises location to the public Cloud will be limited to available bandwidth and the amount of data to be copied. Within the public Cloud, if the data is not converted inline to virtual disk format as it is received, there will be a read-and-conversion process that needs to take place either immediately after all data has been received, or on-demand when a disaster is invoked.

While on-premises disaster recovery failover can offer a recovery-time objective (RTO) of just seconds, it is more likely the case that DRaaS will offer *at best* RTOs of many minutes, or even an hour or more depending on the amount of preparation done in the public Cloud prior to invoking recovery, and the size of the data involved.[38] However, for smaller businesses, and the lower-tier workloads of larger businesses, a higher RTO may be seen as a significantly lower price to pay compared to a permanently provisioned failover datacenter.

Few, if any, disaster services are worthwhile unless they offer a means to fail back as well. Usually therefore DRaaS will offer a reverse transfer option, transferring the workload *back* from the public Cloud and into the private infrastructure when the failed system(s) have been repaired, and are able to host the workload again. This transfer back will similarly involve a copy of the virtual systems, and then conversion to an on-premises compatible virtualization format. (Traditional, on-premises failover and failback might be able to make use of changed block tracking, volume bitmaps or other technologies that enable an "incremental" copy—this is less likely to be available for failback from DRaaS because of the standard limitations posed on access to content at a hypervisor level, and the different virtual machine formats that will be encountered.)

> **Note:** You may wonder why migrator services are required in the public Cloud, since they will obviously consume some resources; however, think about the overall purpose of DRaaS: to provide the ability to failover workloads in the event of a disaster in the local datacenter. That disaster might be limited to a single machine, or it might impact the entire datacenter itself. If the DRaaS management systems are available only in the on-premises environment, this would significantly limit the utility of DRaaS should a full disaster take place; data might be fully replicated and available in the public Cloud, but there would be no way to initiate the process of activating those DR systems.

USING THE CLOUD FOR DATA PROTECTION

Sometimes the workloads that are placed into the public Cloud *are* the backup workloads. This may be the case for organizations that are just starting to explore the public Cloud as a means of shifting or reducing operational cost of IT services to the business.

---

38 Even if immediate instantiation is performed once data is received, the amount of time that instantiation takes, coupled with the original data copy speed acts as an inhibitor on the lowest possible RTO that the service can deliver to the business regardless.

As is the case for most Cloud-related functions, such an option gets an *aaS* moniker, in this case, Backup as a Service (BaaS). We will explore two common uses of BaaS in this section.

BaaS as a Replacement for Datacenter Data Protection

BaaS for datacenter workload protection primarily grew out of telecommunication companies, and Internet service providers, looking for "value add" for their business subscribers. The idea is simple; rather than businesses needing to deploy their own infrastructure to protect their on-premises workloads, they could back up to a multitenant environment hosted by the backup service provider. Over time, various degrees of public Cloud providers have also evolved services along a similar line.

The multitenant environment might be a true multitenancy configuration built from the ground up to support multiple businesses protecting their data through a single software/hardware deployment, or multiple hardware and/or software deployments where there is some degree of physical separation, but cost control is achieved by licensing and hardware deployment agreements between the BaaS provider and its vendor(s).

A conceptual view of a BaaS environment is shown in Figure 4.32.

Just as bandwidth of the LAN had been a perennial problem for backup functions within the datacenter, bandwidth between the individual BaaS subscribers and the BaaS provider is also a fundamental aspect of enrolling in such services. In particular, source-side deduplication will most likely become a critical consideration, since for many businesses their links to the public Internet, or their Internet service provider (ISP) (when the service is being provided there) may be orders of magnitude slower than internal LAN performance.

If you are planning to use a BaaS provider, there are several key factors to consider before enrolling. These are described in the following subsections.

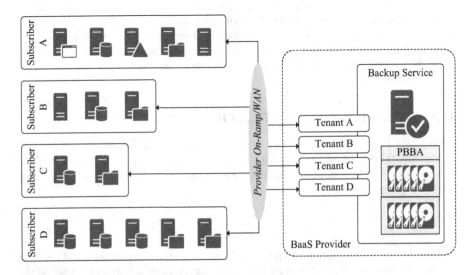

FIGURE 4.32 Conceptual overview of BaaS.

Charging Mechanism

There'll be a fee associated with BaaS, of course, but it's the nature of the fee—how it is calculated and what modifiers are placed on the fee on the basis of service usage or data volume, which may have substantial impact on the cost of the service to the business.

First, consider how you might be charged for the volume of data. The BaaS provider will more than likely draw upon one of two common charging methods for accessing the service, or perhaps even a combination of both:

- **FETB (Frontend TB):** This is usually stated as "if you did a full backup of everything you are protecting, how much data would it be?" For example, if you had 100 virtual machines to protect and each virtual machine was 100 GB, then you would potentially be facing a FETB size of 10 TB. FETB is typically *not* affected by the number of backups you perform.
- **BETB (Backend TB):** This is effectively a calculation of the total amount of backend protection storage occupied by *all* the backups that you have performed. This will create an immediate follow-up question for consideration: Will you be charged by physical capacity occupied, or logical data stored? (This may be different if deduplication is used.) A challenge here is that on a daily basis, as the relative deduplicability of data changes, so, too, will the BETB sizing.

Some BaaS providers will have contractual modifiers on charge rates based on a variety of factors, and you should make yourself aware of them. These may include considerations such as:

- Number of backups executed within a given period (e.g., maximum of two per day per host before additional charges).
- Number of recoveries executed per day (alternatively, recoveries may simply be charged separately).
- Whether the data meet the minimum deduplication ratios.

The final point is typically a service providers mechanism to protect themselves from customers who sign up to a BaaS but then back up content that has a deleterious effect on the BaaS environment. For instance, a 10:1 deduplication ratio may be required in order to meet standard pricing; a deduplication ratio of 5:1 to less than 10:1 might imply more database data than anticipated, or data that has a much higher change rate than anticipated. Data that consistently yields less than a 5:1 deduplication ratio may be precompressed or preencrypted data, which would have even more potential to skew storage efficiency at the backend. Astute service providers will have these caveats to either reduce the chance of a subscriber overusing or abusing the service— and if they do either, ensure that there is a financial penalty that allows the service provider to recoup the additional running costs incurred.

Compatibility

If you are replacing an on-premises backup solution with one that is run by a service provider, be sure that you don't make any assumptions when it comes to compatibility offered by the BaaS provider versus the compatibility that you have within your own environment. In particular, be sure to confirm the following options:

- Operating system compatibility
- Application and database compatibility
- Time-to-currency

The first two options will determine whether the BaaS is technically suitable for your business *now*; the third option will determine whether the BaaS offers sufficient adaptability to meet the changing requirements of your business. For example, if an operating system upgrade is issued by a currently supported vendor, how long will the BaaS provider take before they support that OS? Likewise for databases and applications. Will the BaaS enable you to upgrade within your normal timeframes, or will it act like an anchor, holding you in place and slowing or preventing required innovation within the business? While this will partly be dependent on the speed at which these updates are provided by the backup software/hardware vendor, it will also be impacted by the frequency with which the BaaS provider updates the components that deliver the service.

Service Levels

There is no guarantee that the service levels offered by the BaaS provider will *exactly* match the service levels that you currently have with your business for backup and recovery. As part of the planning process, then, it will be important to very carefully map out what the BaaS providers service levels are in terms of backup runtime and recovery time, whether backups are duplicated to another location, whether backups are eligible for long term retention, and so on.

Recovery time in particular is difficult to guarantee in any backup service because of a large number of contributing factors, and BaaS is no different; instead, most recovery service agreements will focus on the time taken between when a recovery is initiated, and when return of restored data to the host that requested them begins.

As is the case with any managed service environment, subscribers should be cautious to ensure that there are *some* service guarantees relating to data recovery. It is less likely to get a guaranteed recovery time (e.g., "tier 1 systems will be recovered within 15 minutes")—instead, the guarantees should be around ensuring that the data that has been backed up *is* recoverable.

Service Availability and Redundancy

Another factor for consideration is what guarantees or SLAs the BaaS provider makes regarding *their* service being available, and what level of redundancy is offered for backups.

Just as for on-premises backup systems, you'll need to consider factors such as the following:

- If the BaaS providers backup server fails, will backups:
  - Be placed on hold until such time as the service is restored in place?

- Continue to run on a failover backup server?
- Have a mix of both, depending on what service level you've assigned to the backups? (For example, "gold" might continue to run on a failover server, while "bronze" may have to wait for the original server to be repaired.)
- Are the backups themselves a single point of failure?
  - Does the BaaS provider replicate backups automatically to a secondary location in case there is a in issue in the first location?
  - Are all backups replicated, or just specific backups based on the assigned service tier? (For instance, "gold" and "silver" backups might be replicated to another location, but "bronze" backups might not.)

Security and Encryption

At bare minimum, from a security perspective, you will want to know that the solution features end-to-end encryption; that is, data is sent from your servers to the BaaS storage encrypted, and data is stored in an encrypted format. Some solutions may allow you to choose an encryption key that the business itself manages, thereby denying the ability to decrypt from the service provider. Alternately, if you require such a level of control, the service provider may deploy dedicated systems for your service (perhaps even via software-defined solutions).

In a multitenant environment, the administrators you assign to work on backup and recovery operations are unlikely to have the highest privileges within the environment. For instance, one common style of multitenancy has the following levels:

- Service administrator
  - Tenant administrator
    - Tenant user

In such situations you will want to ensure that the service provider includes the capability for you to review appropriate access, configuration, and recovery logs so that you can prove, to both your own security teams and any auditors, that no one outside authorized company representatives have performed sensitive actions within the backup and recovery environment.

Flexibility

As part of a move toward BaaS, it is important that the business first conduct a review of all the "non-standard" ways in which it uses its current backup and recovery systems and thoroughly documents the way in which current systems are protected.

From this review, it will be possible to determine what levels of flexibility are required in the service, *or*, what changes to operational practices are required to adjust current processes to meet data protection requirements within less flexible systems. For example:

- Do database servers get multiple transaction log backups during the day? Is this supported by the BaaS provider?
- Do some hosts or datasets within the environment get backed up outside of the backup server job scheduler?

- Are there pre- and post-backup commands executed on some systems?
- Do any scheduled maintenance jobs on any systems assume scripted access to the backups?

It is entirely possible, of course, that the BaaS provider will use a backup and recovery service that is completely different from the one that the business has previously run within its own datacenters, which will result in immediate changes to use, but the above scenarios may represent levels of flexibility that are not offered by a BaaS provider, or that come at a premium.

Long term versus Operational Retention

It is not uncommon to see BaaS providers *only* offering operational retention periods—for example, 30 or 60 days of backups kept, with no older backups retained.

Just because your business moves to a service provider for backup does not affect your compliance requirements for longer-term retention of data; nor does it shift the onus of compliance onto the BaaS provider. If a chosen BaaS provider does not include facilities to store long-term retention backups (e.g., monthlies for 12 months, yearlies for 7 years), then you would need to still run your own backup service to meet these requirements *or* adjust your operational processes and applications to handle long-term retention by keeping data online (e.g., having a no-delete policy, append-only databases). Since radically altering operational processes and applications to enforce long-term retention at that layer is seldom feasible and running your own backups for long-term retention may invalidate any cost savings that might have been made otherwise, this may require a reevaluation of which BaaS providers can meet the business's long-term data retention requirements as part of their service.

Egress

Consider the example we raised in the section titled "All Care, No Responsibility" (the next main section after the Introduction at the beginning of the chapter)—that of CIOs facing service provider shutdown of days, or weeks. Or perhaps simply consider a situation where the business decides that it no longer wishes to subscribe to a BaaS, but instead wants to return backup services to the datacenter.

In either situation, it will be necessary to have at least some basic plans in place for exiting a BaaS whenever you have long-term retention backups stored with the provider. In most circumstances the effort of extricating short-term (operational) retention backups from a third-party provider will outweigh simply continuing to pay for the service for that duration after the last backup has been completed. (For example, if operational recovery backups are retained for only 30 days, you might simply factor in paying an additional month's subscription to the service to allow exit without compromising operational recoverability.)

Long term retention backups clearly pose a larger challenge. Particularly in situations where monthly backups are retained indefinitely, or for a full 7+ years, this may represent a large amount of data to be extricated from the BaaS provider. If you are going to use long-term retention with a BaaS provider, be sure to understand what your egress options are if or when you exit the service. Keep in mind here, of course, that if you simply stop paying your monthly bill, the data being stored will eventually cease to exist. (The BaaS provider is not obligated to keep your data when you stop paying for it.)

Final Thoughts on BaaS for Datacenter Protection

There is always room for additional considerations when searching for or enrolling with a BaaS provider, but the ones we've covered thus far will likely serve as a good introduction to the sorts of factors that you'll want to keep in mind.

There is, perhaps, one more consideration that should come into play: your understanding of the cost of the environment. Presumably the business wants to adopt BaaS to either recoup costs of running a local backup environment or redirect IT efforts to areas deemed more profitable or useful to the business.

Regardless of the reasons for adopting BaaS, you should build up a cost model to determine whether it is financially feasible, based on the advertised and agreed-to rates (and modifiers), and any soft-costs internal to the business (reduction of one FTE, retirement of infrastructure, etc.)

If the cost model demonstrates that the BaaS is worth moving to, then as BaaS adoption progresses, you should be prepared to regularly revisit the cost model against the actual charges incurred and refine the accuracy of the model. This should allow you to determine whether you are meeting your cost objectives. If you are not meeting those objectives, the cost model gives you the parameters to evaluate against where you are seeing price skews and to determine whether it is worthwhile to continue with the BaaS. Companies that approach BaaS without developing their own cost models and evaluating actual costs to the predicted ones will be more at risk of suffering cost overruns.

BaaS is by no means "doom and gloom," however, but—like everything to do with public Cloud services—it's important to fully appreciate not only what you *gain* but also what you *pay* in order to use the service.

BAAS FOR DESKTOP/LAPTOP DATA PROTECTION

Backup for desktop and laptop systems within businesses have traditionally presented several problems, such as the following:

- **Availability:** Datacenter-based backup and recovery is premised on knowing that the systems being backed up are always on. This is not the case with desktops or laptops within the organization.
- **Execution window:** Datacenter-based backup and recovery is equally premised on running "out of hours" compared to when the highest volume of users (or at least internal business users) are likely to be accessing the systems—for example, between 6 p.m. and 6 a.m. In much the same manner as the above point, such timing might be a complete anathema to desktop and laptop users.
- **Reliability:** Datacenter backup products are oriented toward achieving 100% (or as near as possible) success rates; this requires a different approach with laptop and desktop backups—otherwise, based on availability and execution windows, wholesale execution of backup groups or

sets containing hundreds or more laptops/desktops might result in 50%, 70%, or even 90% failure rates regularly, making analysis of performance challenging.

- **Data storage requirements:** With the growth in data storage capabilities at the endpoint, the amount of storage potentially provisioned across desktops and laptops may be orders of magnitude larger than that within the datacenters themselves, albeit considerably more distributed. (For example, a business with 1000 desktop users and 1000 laptop users might have desktop systems with 1 TB drives in each, and laptops with 0.5-TB drives in each, resulting in distributed storage of 1.5 PB.) This usually creates a requirement for *inclusive* rather than *exclusive* backup policies.[39]
- **Connectivity:** Particularly for laptop users, connectivity becomes a challenging coordination issue; roving users may not always be connected to a corporate network (which may be required in order to connect to the backup service), and when they are connected, it might be over lower bandwidth links (e.g., via VPN) than would normally be desired for backup purposes.

In short, laptop and desktop backup is usually considered a sufficient a headache in most organizations that policies are enacted to avoid, rather than allow. The following are examples of such policies:

- Mandating use of centrally provisioned storage.
- Limiting the amount of storage that can be consumed on the laptop or desktop.
- Explicitly pointing out that anything stored on a laptop/desktop is considered expendable and is not protected.
- Using thin client technology (particularly to replace desktops) to prevent users from having any local storage at all.

Yet, except in environments with the most rigorously enforced storage policies, users *do* store content on their laptops and desktops. Where the business avoids approaching this issue, users might manage their own backups (e.g., to an external hard drive), try to remember to copy files and data back to a file server regularly, or simply not do anything at all. Even if users try to enact their own data protection, the storage medium that they use may not be configured with sufficient security (e.g., encryption, particularly for portable storage) compared to the data being protected.

Self-enacted backup regimes are rarely desirable for a business; after all, they place data that belong to the business out of control of the business. For example, a dismissed employee with a self-enacted backup policy will potentially retain business-sensitive

---

39 An inclusive backup policy only backs up the data that has been explicitly included in a list of datasets. An exclusive backup policy, on the other hand, backs up everything except data that has been explicitly excluded. The exclusive approach is best practice for servers and systems within the datacenter. Following an exclusive approach to desktop/laptop, backups may result in excessive, and costly, data protection storage utilization.

information simply because the business did not know about the copy in the first place. When a user is mobile, this becomes an ongoing security issue if they have failed to secure their selected backup medium sufficiently in the first place.

Furthermore, we must also revert to a truism of data protection; if you rely on the user to start the backup, the backup won't start. In other words, such user-controlled systems may or may not even be particularly reliable, depending on how the user has configured them.

An increasingly common mistake appearing in corporate IT environments is to allow access to appropriately secured Cloud drive systems, such as Google Drive, OneDrive, OneDrive for Business, and Dropbox. IT departments might even *replace* existing backup and recovery services for end-user systems with such Cloud drive services, announcing to end users that they can protect their content by copying the content across to such a storage facility.

Such decisions are fundamentally flawed. Cloud drive storage such as the ones mentioned are designed to effectively act as a replacement to primary storage on the end-user system. They may store a local copy on the end-user system, but that copy is "mirrored" to the Cloud storage system. For example, Microsoft's OneDrive service creates (unless directed otherwise on initialization) a direc-tory, "OneDrive," within the user's folder (e.g., "C:\Users\preston\OneDrive"). If a user saves a document into this directory, that document is automatically copied into the OneDrive Cloud storage, when that storage is available. Such a process is shown in Figure 4.33.

But equally, if a user *deletes* a document from that directory, or ransomware *encrypts* the entire content of that directory, then the changes are replicated, for good or ill, into the OneDrive Cloud storage. The only way to avoid this unfortunate scenario is if the user keeps a *secondary* copy of her/his documents in another location on the laptop—at which point, refer to the truism about users being responsible for their own backups, not to mention the reality that this still does not protect users against encryption or deletion malware running on their systems. (Alternately, the business should subscribe to a service that allows *them* to back up the Cloud storage environment.)

Businesses wishing to deploy true endpoint data protection for laptop/desktop users, without introducing additional overhead on datacenter backup and recov-ery services, can therefore consider dedicated Cloud based services that provide this type of protection. (Such services may also provide protection for server data as well, although the practicality may lesson unless such systems are quite remote, with poor inbound connections to the datacenter but *good* public Internet connections.)

Businesses seeking to provide this form of endpoint data protection should look for, or at least carefully weigh up, the pros and cons of making use of the following types of functionality:

1. **User self-service:** This will remove overhead from the IT helpdesk for the business. This may be limited to simple file-level recovery, but even in that is usually more than enough for an end user's needs.
2. **Integration with corporate authentication:** Integrating with corporate authentication services (e.g., Microsoft Active Directory, LDAP) allows the

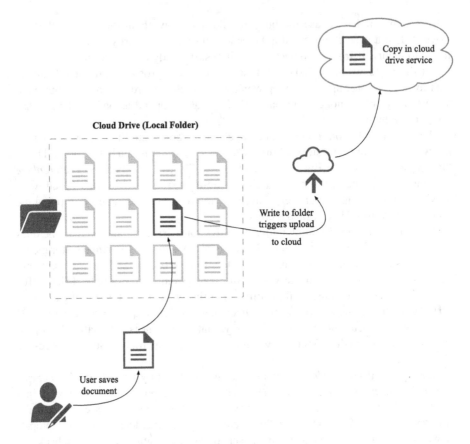

FIGURE 4.33   Conceptual process for writing to a Cloud drive.

business to integrate access controls, and automatically cancel or lock down services for users who are flagged as having left the company—effectively increasing capabilities around compliance.

3. **End-to-end encryption:** Where a Cloud backup service is used, particularly an endpoint backup service, data is likely to travel over the public Internet. This increases security considerations, and most businesses will require encryption, not only of the in-flight data, but the data as it is stored in the public Cloud provider. Astute businesses will require control over the encryption/decryption keys associated with that data, so that the Cloud backup provider cannot decrypt the data themselves.

4. **Reporting:** If endpoint data protection is to be provided, it logically follows that the service owner (e.g., the IT department) should be able to report on backup and recovery operations, including understanding which users have not had a successful backup recently, or who recovered what data.

5. **Lockdown of storage options:** Many backup services will allow for backup to local storage (e.g., a USB drive). Businesses with higher security considerations will want the option of either disabling this feature, or mandating a high encryption level with security keys owned by the business.

6. **Lockdown of backup selections:** Since public Cloud storage is charged, businesses will likely want to be able to set limits on what users may protect (in terms of either data volume, data type, or both); otherwise, enterprising users may very well end up backing up their entire digital media library via the service.

7. **Compression or deduplication:** Again, since public Cloud storage is charged, businesses will want to ensure that a minimum of Cloud data storage is used. This might be through compression or deduplication. While deduplication might be preferred, the logistics of deduplication on endpoint systems with potentially low-speed connections to the backup service may make this more challenging, and usually when deduplication is available in such circumstances, it is at a per-device level.

8. **Legal hold:** While the business might normally mandate a retention regime of 30 days, or maybe no more than seven copies of each document, there may be times when the business will need to ensure that certain backups don't get deleted, for legal or compliance reasons. In this case, some form of legal hold allowing for override of retention policies will be essential.

While this is not an exhaustive list, it does set the scene for the types of considerations that should come into play when planning to backup laptop and desktop systems to a public Cloud backup service.

IN CONCLUSION

Perhaps unsurprisingly, planning and executing a comprehensive data protection strategy in or even involving public Cloud requires two considerations:

1. Risk – What likely risks does the business have to plan for?
2. Cost – What is the cost of providing the solution?

In fact, you might say that it's risk and cost squared, because you *also* have to keep in mind:

1. What are the risks to the business of *not* protecting the environment successfully?
2. What is the cost to the business of *not* protecting the environment successfully?

The simple reality is that the same challenges that a business must keep in mind when planning and executing a comprehensive *on-premises* data protection strategy apply when the public Cloud is involved. The public Cloud introduces the capability of solving many conventional business/IT challenges, but the challenges around data protection are *not* inherently solved just because a workload moves from the datacenter to the public Cloud, or is born in the public Cloud rather than the datacenter.

In this, businesses should always be cautious to consider the axiom, "all care, no responsibility" when it comes to public Cloud: there is no excuse to *assume* your data, and your workloads are protected just because they're running on someone else's infrastructure. In fact, if you are to make any assumptions, you're best off assuming that your data and workloads *aren't* protected. It's far more likely to be an *accurate* assumption. So, regardless of whether you move a workload into the public Cloud, or you create a new workload in the public Cloud, *you* have to come up with the data protection strategy for it. Ideally as your business plans its move into the public Cloud, or adds maturity around its public Cloud utilization, there will be architectural models and standards established on ensuring that your data stay protected for both operational and long-term/compliance needs throughout their entire lifecycle.

The traditional datacenter purchase model for infrastructure, namely, capital expenditure, paying in advance for a specific period of interest (e.g., 3 or 5 years), is fundamentally turned on its head in the public Cloud. Yet, astute businesses who achieve optimal gain from the public Cloud recognize that you don't automatically save money by flipping to a pay-as-you-go model while continuing to do things in exactly the same way. In fact, some of the worst cost-related failures in the public Cloud have happened exactly when companies have assumed that they can switch to pay-as-you-go without adjusting, well, *how they go.*

Again, we have similar considerations to protecting data on-premises, but these are magnified in the public Cloud:

- **Architecture matters:**
  - Just because data protection functions that run on-premises can be *software defined*, that is, run in a virtual fashion, does not guarantee they will run *efficiently* in the public Cloud, where you are charged for resources on a continuous basis. This covers compute, data storage, and data transport.
  - Object storage is an important factor in reducing your Cloud data protection costs.
  - Deduplication is *essential* for reducing your overall Cloud data protection costs.
- **Long-term retention has a substantial cumulative impact** on the cost of your data protection storage requirements; particularly for greenfield use cases in the public Cloud, these costs may seem trivial at first, but the cumulative cost over the entire data lifecycle (often 7+ years) must be calculated for the business to make intelligent long-term decisions.

The term *public Cloud* can mean many different things to many people. Some businesses might see it as being synonymous with a single large-scale public Cloud vendor, such as AWS, Azure, or Google. Yet, it can encompass a staggering number of different platforms and workloads, and each of those platforms and workloads will need data protection consideration. As we noted when discussing the differences between IaaS, PaaS, and SaaS, the type of service that you subscribe to or use in the public Cloud will directly affect the flexibility and capability that you will have around protecting those data. What's more, public Cloud adoption allows for a much broader scope of service providers and service types being used by the business to facilitate many more workloads, or even a myriad of *micro-workloads*. This alters the dynamic on how you plan, manage, and monitor your data protection activities across traditional datacenters and potentially a number of different public Cloud stacks. In essence, the onus on centralized visibility and control shifts from an individual vendor to *you*, as a business.

Just as in the datacenter, a fully formed data protection solution does not come from a single product; it requires a mix of on-platform and off-platform protection functions, or solutions, that allow the business to meet a variety of recovery time and recovery point objectives, at the appropriate level of granularity, and cost-constrained within the budgetary limitations and requirements of the business.

We started this chapter with the cautionary tale of Icarus and Daedalus, and it is fitting to reflect on that as we complete our discussion around data protection in the public Cloud; it is indisputable that the public Cloud can provide almost unparalleled freedom of operation to a business, but we must always keep in mind that operational freedom does not imply freedom from operational risk. Businesses that fail to approach the public Cloud with a healthy set of processes around data protection may find themselves figuratively sharing the fate of Icarus.

SOURCES

1. http://www.gutenberg.org/files/9313/9313-h/9313-h.htm#link2H_4_0007
2. https://www.microsoft.com/en-au/servicesagreement/
3. https://aws.amazon.com/agreement/
4. June 29, 2016: https://cloud.google.com/docs/compare/aws/storage
5. https://cloud.google.com/terms/service-terms
6. https://azure.microsoft.com/en-au/support/legal/subscription-agreement-nov-2014/
7. https://www.digitalocean.com/legal/terms/
8. https://www.networkworld.com/article/3263742/business-continuity/what-to-do-if-your-cloud-provider-stops-offering-its-services.html
9. https://diginomica.com/2015/01/06/cios-worst-nightmare-cloud-provider-goes-bankrupt/
11. Sharwood, S., "Google cloud VMs given same IP addresses...and down they went," *The Register*, June 17, 2018 (available online at https://www.theregister.co.uk/2018/06/17/google_cloud_vms_given_same_address_outage/).
12. https://www.helpnetsecurity.com/2014/03/24/10000-github-users-inadvertently-reveal-their-aws-secret-access-keys/
13. https://www.zdnet.com/article/security-lapse-exposes-198-million-united-states-voter-records/
14. https://www.theregister.co.uk/2017/01/09/mongodb/
16. https://exchange.telstra.com.au/latency-milliseconds-matter-virtual-life-death/
19. https://www.cnbc.com/2016/02/16/the-hospital-held-hostage-by-hackers.html
20. https://www.cyberscoop.com/hancock-hospital-ransomware/
22. "Working with Backups," AWS Documentation (available online at https://docs.aws.amazon.com/AmazonRDS/latest/UserGuide/USER_WorkingWithAutomated Backups.html).
25. https://aws.amazon.com/ec2/pricing/reserved-instances/pricing/
26. https://calculator.s3.amazonaws.com/index.html
27. https://www.geekwire.com/2018/dropbox-saved-almost-75-million-two-years-building-tech-infrastructure/

30. AWS Documentation, "Restoring an Amazon EBS Volume from a Snapshot" (available online at https://docs.aws.amazon.com/AWSEC2/latest/UserGuide/ebs-restoring-volume.html).

32. AWS Documentation, "Regions and Availability Zones" (available online at https://docs.aws.amazon.com/AWSEC2/latest/UserGuide/using-regions-availability-zones.html).

33. Ibid.

34. https://aws.amazon.com/snowball/pricing/.

35. Barr, J., "Amazon S3 Reduced Redundancy Storage," May 18, 2010 (available online at https://aws.amazon.com/blogs/aws/new-amazon-s3-reduced-redundancy-storage-rrs/).

5 The Update from the First Version

So far in this book, we have covered a lot of ground when it comes to the Cloud. Thus far, we have examined the following integral pieces of any Cloud-based deployment:

Chapter 1—Introduction to the Cloud Computing Environment

Evolution to the Cloud: The Mainframe
Evolution to the Cloud: The Personal Computer
Evolution to the Cloud: The Wireless Network
The Last Evolution to the Cloud: The Smartphone
Evolution of the Cloud
Evolution of Cloud Computing Infrastructure
The Basic Concepts and Terminology Surrounding Cloud Computing
The Challenges and Risks of Cloud Computing
The Functions and Characteristics of Cloud Computing
Cloud Computing Delivery Models
Cloud Computing Deployment Models
Security Threats Posed to Cloud Computing
Cloud Computing Cost Metrics and Service

Chapter 2—An Overview of the Evolution of Amazon Web Services

Major Components of Amazon Web Service
A Review of the Amazon Elastic Cloud Compute (EC2)
A Review of the Amazon Simple Storage Service (S3)
A Review of AWS Security Services

Chapter 3—Threats and Risks to Cloud Infrastructure and Risk Mitigation Strategies

Cyber Threats to the Cloud
Spear Phishing
An Incident Response Playbook for a Phishing Attack
Malware Injection Attacks
Threat and Risk Management Strategies for a Cloud Computing Infrastructure

Chapter 4—Cloud Data Protection

All Care, No Responsibility
Your Business Is Not Unique
A Data Protection Primer

DOI: 10.1201/9781003459569-5

5.1 THE UPDATE FROM THE FIRST VERSION

As one can see, the first of the book "Protecting Information Assets and IT Infrastructure in the Cloud" primarily dealt with the basic Cloud concepts, as well as the backup and recovery strategies that can be used into it. Also, the primary focus was on the Amazon Web Services, also known as the "AWS" for short. At the writing of the first edition of this book, the AWS was the primary juggernaut Cloud provider.

But ever since COVID-19 pandemic hit the United States and the world hard back in late 2019, many new advances in Cloud technology have evolved. A lot of this was spawned because of the remote workforce which had evolved at the time. Of course, there is nothing new to remote work, but the way it precipitated and evolved took the whole world by surprise. For example, the notion of a near 99% remote workforce was thought to happen later this decade.

But rather, it happened in a very short time span of three months. Also, video-conferencing became a huge tool as well, as nobody had any real direct contact with each other. Thus, the tool of choice to use at that time was Zoom. But because of its heavy usage, it quickly showed its weaknesses and vulnerabilities. Thus, Corporate America started to look for other alternatives, such as WebEx, and especially Microsoft Teams. Over time, and especially after the COVID-19 pandemic, Microsoft Teams has gained in huge popularity and usage.

In fact, the entire Cloud platform from Microsoft, which is known as "Azure", has also gained huge acceptance and adoption when compared to the AWS. In fact, it is now the predominant choice for the small- to medium-sized business (SMB) market, and even the nonprofit organizations. It is now a very strong foe and competitor to the AWS, by its continual research and development efforts and introducing new products to the marketplace, namely, that of the M365 platform.

But probably one of the biggest areas in which Azure has made its mark has been in the world of artificial intelligence and machine learning, also known as "AI" and "ML", respectively, for short. This platform, when compared to the AWS, has also made huge strides in working closely with the United States Federal Government, especially when it comes to the close partnership with the Department of Defense (DoD) and the Cybersecurity Maturity Model Certification, which is also known as the "CMMC". This is where the Defense Industrial Base (also known as the "DIB") must come into compliance by achieving a certain level of certification from the DoD, before the defense contractors and their respective subcontractors are allowed to bid on contracts, or even possess controlled unclassified information and federal contract information (also known as the "CUI" and the "FCI" datasets for short, respectively) into their databases.

Thus, the second edition of this book is to provide an update to the first edition. But this time, the main focus will be upon Microsoft Azure, its components, the various AI and ML tools it has. But even more importantly, another area of focus for this second edition will be upon the business relationship that Microsoft has with OpenAI, the organization that has developed the game changer AI platform known as "ChatGPT".

5.2 THE MAJOR COMPONENTS OF MICROSOFT AZURE

But as introduction to the massive Azure Cloud Platform, in this part of the chapter, we provide an overview into all of its major components.

5.2.1 THE COMPUTE RESOURCES

Microsoft Azure has an entire array of tools and technologies that comes with it, in a manner similar to that of the AWS. The first area to be examined is that of the compute resources. This primarily includes the virtual servers, which are at the heart of any Cloud-based deployment.

Service	Overview	Azure Name
Virtual Servers	* Users can deploy, manage, and maintain OS and server software; instance types provide configurations of CPU/RAM.	* Virtual Machines * Virtual Machine Images
Container Management	* It Supports Docker/Kubernetes containers and allows users to run applications on managed instance clusters. * Can store Docker formatted images. * Can container instances without any additional installation of underlying infrastructure or hosts.	* Container Service * Container Service Kubernetes * Container Registry * Container Instances
Microservice-Based Applications	* Manages the execution, lifetime, and resilience of complex, interrelated code components that can be either stateless or stateful.	* The Service Fabric
Backend Process Logic	* This integrates systems and runs backend processes in response to events or schedules.	* Functions * Event Grid
Job Orchestration	* This tool orchestrates the tasks and interactions between compute resources.	* Batch
Scalability	* The end users set defined metrics and thresholds that determine if the platform adds or removes instances.	* Virtual Machine Scale Sets * App Service Scale Capability * AutoScaling
Predefined Templates	* These are templates for creating and deploying virtual machine-based solutions.	* QuckStart Templates and Blueprints
Time Sync	* This enables the end user to access time servers from time sync service within the Cloud network.	

5.2.2 THE STORAGE

These are the features that allow you to store all of kinds of information and data in Azure.

Service	Overview	Azure Name
Object Storage	* This is for use cases including Cloud apps, content distribution, backup, archiving, disaster recovery, and big data analytics.	* Storage—Block Blob
Virtual Server Disk Infrastructure	* This is SSD storage optimized that is used for I/O intensive read/write operations.	* Page Blobs * Premium Disk Storage
Shared File Storage	* This is an interface to create and configure file systems as well as share common files.	* Files
Archiving—Cool Storage	* This is for storing data that is infrequently accessed and long-lived.	* Storage: Hot, Cool, Archive Tier
Backup	* These are the solutions that allow files and folders to be backed-up and recovered from the Cloud and provide off-site protection against data loss.	* Backup
Hybrid Storage	* This integrates on-premises IT environments with Cloud storage.	* StorSimple
Bulk Data Transfer	* This is a data transport solution that uses secure disks and appliances to transfer substantial amounts of data, ranging from Petabytes to Exabytes.	* Import/Export * Databox
Disaster Recovery	* This automates the protection and replication processes of virtual machines with health monitoring, recovery plans, and recovery plan testing.	* Site Recovery

5.2.3 THE NETWORKING

This is the part of Azure in which you configure and deploy your entire networking infrastructure. Technically, these are known as "VNets".

Service	Overview	Azure Name
Cloud Virtual Networking	* This is an isolated, private environment in the Cloud.	* Virtual Network
Cross-Premises Connectivity	* This allows for the connection Azure virtual networks to other Azure virtual networks or customer on-premises networks. It also supports VPN tunneling.	* VPN Gateway
Domain Name System Management	* This manages the DNS records for a particular domain. * This is a service that hosts domain names, routes users to Internet applications, and manages traffic to apps.	* DNS * Traffic Manager
Content Delivery Network	* This is a global content delivery network that transfers audio, video, applications, images, and other files.	* Content Delivery Network
Dedicated Network	* This creates a dedicated, private network connection from a location to the cloud provider.	* Express Route
Load Balancing	* This distributes incoming application traffic to add scale, handle failover, and route to a collection of resources.	* Load Balancer * Application Gateway

5.2.4 THE DATABASE

Azure hosts a wide array of databases, which include the following:

- SQL Server
- Cosmos DB
- Oracle
- PostGRESql
- MySQL

This is where you can custom create your databases to store, transact, process, and archive all of your datasets in a very secure environment.

Service	Overview	Azure Name
Relational Database	* The SQL Database is a high-performance, reliable, and secure database you can use to build data-driven applications and websites.	* The various SQL Databases, including MariaDB
NoSQL—Document Storage	* This supports multiple data models: key-value, documents, graphs, and columnar.	* Cosmos DB
NoSQL—Key/Value Storage	* This is a non-relational data used for storing for semi-structured data.	* Table Storage
Caching	* This is an in-memory–based, distributed-caching service that provides a high-performance store which offloads non-transactional work from a database.	* Redis Cache
Database Migration	* This transfers the database schema and data from one database format to a specific database technology in the cloud.	* Database Migration Service * Data Migration Assistant

5.2.5 THE ANALYTICS AND BIG DATA

What exactly is Big Data? It can be defined technically as follows:

> Big data is a combination of structured, semi structured and unstructured data collected by organizations that can be mined for information and used in machine learning projects, predictive modeling and other advanced analytics applications.

Systems that process and store big data have become a common component of data management architectures in organizations, combined with tools that support big data analytics uses. Big data is often characterized by the three Vs:

- the large **volume** of data in many environments;
- the wide **variety** of data types frequently stored in big data systems; and
- the **velocity** at which much of the data is generated, collected and processed.

(SOURCE: www.techtarget.com/searchdatamanagement/definition/big-data)

Azure has more than enough processing to handle this kind of data load. The exact components of the Big Data part of Azure is illustrated in the matrix below:

Service	Overview	Azure Name
Elastic Data Warehouse	* This is a fully managed data warehouse that analyzes data using business intelligence tools.	* SQL Data Warehouse
Big Data Processing	* This breaks up large data processing tasks into multiple jobs and then combines the results to enable massive parallelism.	* HDInsight
Data Orchestration	* This processes and moves data between different compute and storage services. * It is also a Cloud-based ETL/data integration service that orchestrates and automates the movement and transformation of data.	* Data Factory * Data Factory + Data Catalog
Analytics	* This is a storage and analysis platforms that create insights from massive quantities of data.	* Stream Analytics * Data Lake Analytics * Data Lake Store
Streaming data	* This allows for the mass ingestion of small data inputs, typically from devices and sensors, to process and route data.	* Event Hubs * Event Hubs Capture
Visualization	* These are business intelligence tools that build visualizations, perform ad hoc analysis, and develop business insights from data. * It also allows for the visualization and data analysis tools to be embedded in applications.	* Power BI * Power BI Embedded
Search	* This is a scalable search server based on the Apache Lucene. * This delivers full-text search and related search analytics and capabilities.	* Marketplace—Elastisearch * Search
Machine Learning	* This produces an end-to-end workflow to create, process, and publish predictive models from complex and large datasets.	* Machine Learning Studio * Machine Learning Benchwork
Data Discovery	* This provides the ability to better understand and consume data sources. * This is a serverless query service that uses standard SQL commands for analyzing databases.	* Data Catalog * Data Lake Analytics

5.2.6 The Internet of Things

The Internet of Things is where all of the objects that you interact with on daily basis, both in the real and virtual worlds, are all interconnected together.

A technical definition of it is as follows:

> The Internet of Things (IoT) describes the network of physical objects—"things"—that are embedded with sensors, software, and other technologies for the purpose of connecting and exchanging data with other devices and systems over the internet. These devices range from ordinary household objects to sophisticated industrial tools.

With more than 7 billion connected IoT devices today, experts are expecting this number to grow to 10 billion by 2020 and 22 billion by 2025.

(SOURCE: www.oracle.com/internet-of-things/what-is-iot/)

The components that make up the Internet of Things (IoT) in Azure are as follows:

Service	Overview	Azure Name
Internet of Things Streaming Data	* This is a preconfigured solution for monitoring, maintaining, and deploying common IoT scenarios. * This is a gateway in the Cloud for managing bidirectional communication with billions of IoT devices securely and at scale. * This is used to create IoT gateway solutions. * This triggers a specific function to perform a certain action. * This secures all of your IoT devices * This provides advanced data analytics from all of your IoT devices. * This allows for the mass ingestion of small data inputs, from devices and sensors.	* The IoT Suite * The IoT Hub * The IoT Edge * Functions + Logic Apps * Security Center * Time Series Insights + ML + Stream Analytics * Event Hubs * Event Capture

5.2.7 THE MANAGEMENT AND MONITORING

This service from Azure provides visibility into the health, performance of all of your Cloud-based applications. The exact components of it are as follows:

Service	Overview	Azure Name
DevOps	* These are services to generate, monitor, forecast, and share billing data. * This is a unified management console that simplifies building, deploying, and operating cloud resources. * This is an authenticated, browser-based shell experience that's hosted in the cloud and accessible from anywhere in the world.	* Billing API * Azure Portal * Cloud Shell
Administration	* This provides deeper insights into event logs and more. * This enables for continuous IT services and compliance. * This provides for the detailed information about the health of all of your Azure resources. * This is a standalone app from Microsoft that allows you to easily work with Azure Storage data on any kind of OS.	* Log Analytics in Operations Management Suite * Microsoft Operations Management Suite— Automation and Control * Resource Health * Storage Explorer

5.2.8 THE MOBILE SERVICES

These are the services from Azure that allow you to create all kinds of mobile apps for your own organizations, as well as your customers. It gives you the ability to connect to just about any kind and type of wireless device.

Service	Overview	Azure Name
Pro App Development	* This provides for rapid development of mobile solutions. * This offers the technology to build cross-platform and native apps for mobile devices. * This allows for authentication capabilities into mobile application.	* Mobile Apps * Xamarin Apps * Mobile Apps * AAD B2C
App Testing	* These are services to support the testing of mobile applications.	* Xamarin Test Cloud
Analytics	* This is for the debugging and the analysis of a mobile application.	* Hockey App * Application Insights
Enterprise Mobility Management	* This provides mobile device management and mobile application management.	* Intune
Real-Time Data Queries	* This provides GraphQL service for real-time data queries, sync, and offline features.	* Mobile Apps

5.2.9 THE SECURITY, IDENTITY, AND ACCESS

Cloud security is a huge issue today, and Azure has all of the tools available in order to ensure that you have a robust and secure Cloud deployment. Typically this falls under the realm of Identity and Access Management (IAM). This is technically defined as follows:

> Identity and Access Management (IAM) is the branch of IT concerned with verifying users' identity and controlling their access to digital resources. Or, as Gartner defines it: "IAM is the discipline that enables the right individuals to access the right resources at the right times for the right reasons".
>
> *(SOURCE: https://auth0.com/blog/what-is-iam/)*

The components that make this up in Azure are as follows:

Service	Overview	Azure Name
Security	* This is an automated security assessment service that improves the security of all of your applications. * This allows for end users to create, manage, and consume certificates in the Cloud. * This is a threat detection service that provides protection on a real time basis.	* Security Center * App Service Certificates * Security Center
Authentication and Authorization	* This provides for a way to securely control access to services and resources. * This allows for security policies and role management to be enforced for multiple accounts. * This safeguards access to data and applications while delivering a range of verification options.	* Active Directory * Active Directory Premium * Managed Service Identity * Subscription and Service Management + RBAC * Multi Factor Authentication
Information Protection	* This secures email, documents, and sensitive data shared outside of the business.	* Information Protection
Encryption	* This helps protect and safeguard data. * This provides a way to manage, create, and control encryption keys stored in hardware security modules.	* Storage Service Encryption * Key Vault
Firewall	* This device protects web applications from common web exploits.	* Application Gateway Web * Application Firewall
Directory Services	* This is a Cloud solution that provides a robust set of capabilities to manage users and groups. * This is an IAM service for consumer-facing applications that scales to hundreds of millions of identities. * This supports Active Directory in the Cloud.	* Active Directory Domain Services + Windows Server on the IaaS * Active Directory B2C * Windows Server Active Directory
Compliance	* This provides access to audit reports, compliance guides, and trust documents that are stored in the Cloud.	* Microsoft Service Trust Portal
Security	* This provides protection to your Cloud deployment from Distributed Denial of Services attacks.	* Marketplace—Security

5.2.10 THE DEVELOPER TOOLS

It is important to keep in mind that Azure is not all about moving an on-premises infrastructure to one that is in the Cloud, or simply for data storage to keep in compliance with the data privacy laws such as the GDPR, CCPA, HIPAA, etc. Azure is also a great way to build and deploy new types of software applications, especially if they are web based. The matrix below demonstrates all of the tools that are available in this regard.

Service	Overview	Azure Name
Media Transcoder	* This offers broadcast-quality video streaming, including transcoding.	* Media Services
Media Encoder	* This enables the end user to execute video processing.	*
Email	* This allows for the integration of email functionality into web-based applications.	* Marketplace—Email
Workflow	* This service connects apps, data, and devices anywhere in the world.	* Logic Apps
API Management	* This is a turnkey solution for deploying and publishing APIs into web-based applications.	* API Management
Enterprise App Integration	* This provides for partner management, Cloud to on-premises, and line-of-business application integration for SAP, Oracle, and SQL Server.	* Logic Apps
Backend Process Logic	* This provides for a way to run scripts or programs as background processes.	* Functions
Application Development	* This allows for Azure to connect to Salesforce, Office 365, Twitter, Dropbox, Google Services, and more. * These are managed hosting platforms for deploying and scaling web applications and services. * Developer tools for scripting application deployment. * These are tools for building, debugging, deploying, diagnosing, and managing web-based apps. * This connects various data sources together by using a visual designer.	* Logic Apps * Web Apps * Cloud Services * API Apps * Visual Studio Team Services * Developer Tools * Power Apps
App Testing	* This is a tool for testing cross-platform functionality to dev/test environments.	* DevTest Labs
DevOps	* This is a service that supports continuous integration and deployment (CI/CD).	*Visual Studio Team Services
Backend Process Logic	* This is a Cloud-based technology to build distributed web-based applications.	* Logic Apps
Programmatic Access	*This is a command-line tool to create and automate solutions.	*Command Line Interface *Power Shell

5.2.11 The Enterprise Integration

This is the part of Azure that allows you to build and deploy B2B workflows to integrate with other third software packages, on-premises apps, and even those in the Cloud. The components for this are as follows:

Service	Overview	Azure Name
Enterprise App Integration	* This connects apps, data, and devices anywhere Salesforce, Office 365, Twitter, Dropbox, Google services, and more.	* Logic Apps
Enterprise Application Services	* This is a CRM with five modules: Sales, Customer Service, Field Service, Project Service Automation, and Marketing. * This is a Cloud service providing communications, email, and document management for iOS and Android based devices.	* Dynamics 365 * Office 365
Content Management in the Cloud	* This is a tool for the discovery, sharing, and collaboration on content.	* SharePoint Online
Commercial PaaS-IaaS-DBaaS Framework	* This lets users deliver Azure services from an On Prem datacenter.	* Stack
Messaging	* This offers queuing services for the communication between decoupled application components. * This supports a set of Cloud-based, message-oriented middleware technologies. * This is a messaging service for distributed systems and serverless applications.	* Queue Storage * Service Bus Queues and Relays * Azure Event Grid

(*Source*:   Azure Account Subscription)

5.3 MORE ABOUT MICROSOFT AZURE

So far in this chapter, we have covered the major components of Azure in great detail. But keep in mind that this list is not totally inclusive, Microsoft is coming out with many newer tools in order to meet the needs of both individuals and end users. In this next section, we provide an overview of some of the major activities that can take place in Azure.

To download the resource in which you can actually do these activities, copy and paste the following link into your web browser:

http://cyberresources.solutions/Cloud_Update_Book/Azure_Activity_eBook.pdf

Here is a listing of the major activities that you can do in Azure:

5.4 THE ACTIVITIES THAT CAN BE DONE IN AZURE

5.4.1 Getting Started with Azure

- Using the Resource Manager
- Using PowerShell
- Deploying Role Based Access Control

- Learning How to Use the Azure Portal
- Managing Your Subscriptions and Billing

5.4.2 THE AZURE APP SERVICE AND WEB APPS

- Creating and Deploying a Web App in the Cloud
- Scaling and Configuring Your Web-based Apps

5.4.3 THE VIRTUAL MACHINES (VMS)

- Understanding the Components of a Virtual Machine
- How to Create a Virtual Machine
- How to Connect a Virtual Machine to Other Azure-based Services
- Learning How to Configure and Scale Your Virtual Machines

5.4.4 THE AZURE STORAGE

- Understanding the Types of Various Storage Mechanisms
- How to Deploy Security for Your Storage
- How to Create and Manage Your Storage Mechanisms

5.4.5 THE AZURE VIRTUAL NETWORK

- Understanding and Deploying Network Security Groups
- Making Use of Point to Site Networks

5.4.6 THE AZURE DATABASE

- Understanding the SQL Server (Azure) Database
- How to Connect a Web App to an Azure Database
- How to Deploy an Azure Database into a Virtual Machine

5.4.7 THE AZURE ACTIVE DIRECTORY

- Understanding the Azure Active Directory
- How to Create and Deploy a Directory
- How to Create and Implement User Groups and Associated Policies

5.4.8 THE MANAGEMENT TOOLS

- Making Use of the Azure Software Development Kit (SDK)
- Understanding PowerShell
- Understanding the Azure Power Shell

5.5 THE NEXT CHAPTER

In the next chapter, we do a deeper dive into what artificial intelligence (AI) and machine learning (ML) are all about and the major tools that are associated with them in Azure.

6 Introduction to Artificial Intelligence

In the last chapter, we provided a deep dive into the major inner workings of Microsoft Azure, and we also outlined some of the major activities that a business or even an end user can do, in order to come out with the app that they are trying to build, or simply use Azure as a way for storing large amounts of data. But of course, Azure is so much more than that.

As also mentioned in the last chapter, Microsoft has spent a lot of money and time into its research and development in order to come up with the latest innovations. One such area is that of artificial intelligence (AI) and machine learning (ML). There is no doubt that these are the big buzz words of today, but the bottom line is that this is where businesses will go to, especially when it comes to automation.

A technical definition of AI is as follows:

Artificial intelligence (AI) makes it possible for machines to learn from experience, adjust to new inputs and perform human-like tasks. Most AI examples that you hear about today—from chess-playing computers to self-driving cars—rely heavily on deep learning and natural language processing. Using these technologies, computers can be trained to accomplish specific tasks by processing large amounts of data and recognizing patterns in the data.

(SOURCE: www.sas.com/en_us/insights/analytics/
what-is-artificial-intelligence.html)

An example of AI is illustrated below:

Probably some of the best examples is robotic process automation, also known as "RPA" for short. The technical definition of it is as follows:

Robotic process automation (RPA), also known as software robotics, uses automation technologies to mimic back-office tasks of human workers, such as extracting data, filling in forms, moving files, et cetera. It combines APIs and user interface (UI) interactions to integrate and perform repetitive tasks between enterprise and productivity applications.

(SOURCE: www.ibm.com/topics/rpa)

A real world example of this being used is in the creation of electronic devices. An example of this is illustrated below:

DOI: 10.1201/9781003459569-6

Another area where AI works great for automation is when it comes to the world of cybersecurity. As most of us know, the IT Security team of today is completely inundated with alerts, warnings, and other similar messages. Because of this huge influx, no human being has the time to filter through all of this, to see what is legitimate and what is not. And by the time a real warning has been found, it probably would have been too late to do anything about remediating it.

This is where AI can also come in. It can automate these mundane tasks very quickly, but it can alert the IT Security team of what is real and what is not in just a

matter of seconds. This will then allow them to respond quickly, and remediate the threat that exists before it spreads all over the IT and Network infrastructure of a business. Another huge advantage of this is that it prevents the problem from "Alert Fatigue" in happening, which is a huge cause of employee burnout.

Another area in cybersecurity where AI is starting to see heavy use is in both penetration testing and threat hunting. Even when conducting these kinds of exercises, there are a lot of repetitive tasks that need to be done, and if these are automated, it will allow for the penetration testing or threat hunting team to focus on the bigger picture, where human intervention is required.

An example of how AI can be used in cybersecurity is illustrated below:

In the end, the ultimate goal of AI is to mimic the human brain, especially when it comes to the thinking and reasoning processes of it. But truth be told, the human brain is a very complex organism. In fact, it is probably the most complex that resides in the human body. At best we will only understand 0.5% of how it actually works.

Another very important thing to be kept in mind about AI is that it is only as good as the data receives. In other words, it is a purely "Garbage In and Garbage Out" method of getting your output. So for this very reason, you want to make sure that whatever datasets you feed it, it must be cleansed and optimized on a $24 \times 7 \times 365$ basis. If your datasets are skewed in any way, shape, or form, your output will be skewed as well. Thus, the field of data science in AI is a very important one, and we provide much more detail into it in the next section.

6.1 THE IMPORTANCE OF DATA IN ARTIFICIAL INTELLIGENCE

So far in this chapter, we have examined in great detail what artificial intelligence is, what its subcomponents are, as well as provided a very strong foundation in terms of the theoretical and practical applications of it that has led to the powerhouse that it is today in cybersecurity. In this part of the chapter, we now focus upon the key ingredient that drives the engines of artificial intelligence today—the data that is fed into it, and the feeds from where it comes from.

We all obviously have heard of the term "Data" before. This is something that has been taught to us ever since we started elementary school. But what really is data? What is the scientific definition for it? It can be defined as follows:

> In computing, data is information that has been translated into a form that is efficient for movement or processing. Relative to today's computers and transmission media, data is information converted into binary digital form.

> *https://searchdatamanagement.techtarget.com/*
> *definition/data*

So as this can be applied to artificial intelligence, the underlying tool will take all of the data that is fed into it (both numerical and non-numerical based), convert it into a format that it can understand and process, and from there provide the required output. In a sense, it is just like garbage in/garbage out, but on a much more sophisticated level.

This section will cover the aspect of data and what it means for artificial intelligence from the following perspectives:

- The fundamentals of data basics;
- The types of data that are available;
- Big Data;
- Understanding preparation of data;
- Other relevant data concepts that are important to artificial intelligence.

6.1.1 THE FUNDAMENTALS OF DATA BASICS

Let's face it, everywhere we go, we are exposed to data to some degree or another. Given the advent of the smartphone, digitalization, wireless technology, social media, the Internet of Things (IoT), etc., we are being exposed to it every day that we are even cognizant of. For example, when we type in a text message, or reply to an email, that is actually considered to be data, but more of a qualitative kind. Even videos that you can access on YouTube, or even podcasts can also be considered as well.

It is important to keep in mind that data does not have to be just the numerical kind. If you think about it, anything that generates content, whether it is written, in the form of audio or video, or even visuals, are all considered to be data. But in the word of information technology, and even to that of a lesser extent in artificial intelligence, data is much more precisely defined and, more often than not, symbolically represented, especially when the source code compiles the datasets that it has been given.

In this regard, the data that is most often used by computers are those of the binary digits. It can either possess the value of either 0 or 1, and in fact, this is the smallest piece of data that a computer will process. The computers of today can process at least 1,000× data sizes more than that, primarily because of the large amounts of memory that they have and very powerful processing capabilities.

In this regard, the binary digit is very often referred to merely as a "bit". Any data sizes larger than this are referred to as a "byte". This is illustrated in the table below:

Unit	Value
Megabyte	1,000 Kilobytes
Gigabyte	1,000 Megabytes
Terabyte	1,000 Gigabytes
Petabyte	1,000 Terabytes
Exabyte	1,000 Petabytes
Zetabyte	1,000 Exabytes
Yottabyte	1,000 Zetabytes

6.1.2 THE TYPES OF DATA THAT ARE AVAILABLE

In general, there are four types of data that can be used by an artificial intelligence system. They are as follows:

1) *Structured Data*:

These are datasets that have some type or kind of preformatting to them. In other words, the dataset can resides in a fixed field within a record or file from within the database that is being used. Examples of this typically include values such as names, dates, addresses, credit card numbers, stock prices, etc. Probably some of the best examples of structured data are those of Excel files and data that is stored in a SQL database. Typically, this type of data accounts for only 20% of the datasets that are consumed by an artificial intelligence application or tool. This is also referred to as "quantitative data".

2) *Unstructured Data*:

These are the datasets that have no specific, predefined formatting to them. In other words, there is no way that they will fit in nicely into an Excel spreadsheet or even an SQL database. In other words, this is all of the data out there in which its boundaries are not clearly defined. It is important to keep in mind that although it may not have the external presence of an organized dataset, it does have some sort of internal organization and/or formatting to it. This is also referred to as "qualitative data", and the typical examples of this include the following:

- Text files: Word processing, spreadsheets, presentations, email, logs.
- Email: Email has some internal structure thanks to its metadata, and we sometimes refer to it as semi-structured. However, its message field is unstructured, and traditional analytics tools cannot parse it.
- Social Media: Data from Facebook, Twitter, LinkedIn.
- Website: YouTube, Instagram, photo sharing sites.
- Mobile data: Text messages, locations.
- Communications: Chat, IM, phone recordings, collaboration software.
- Media: MP3, digital photos, audio and video files.
- Business applications: MS Office documents, productivity applications.

These kinds of datasets account for about 70% of the data that is consumed by an artificial intelligence tool.

3) *Semi-Structured Data*:

As its name implies, there is no rigid format into how this data is typically organized, but either externally or internally, there is some kind of organization to it. It can be further modified so that it can fit into the columns and fields of a database, but very often, this will require some sort of human intervention in order to make sure that it is processed in a proper way. Some of the typical examples of these kinds of datasets include that of the "extensible markup language", also known as "XML" for short. Just like HTML, XML is considered to be a markup language that consists of various rules in order to identify and/or confirm certain elements in a document. Another example of semi-structured data is that of the "JavaScript Object Notation", also known as "JSO" for short. This is a way in which information can be transferred from a web-based application to any number of application protocol interfaces (also known as "APIs" for short) and, from there, to the server upon which the source code of the web-based application resides upon. This process can also happen in the reverse process as well. These kinds of datasets account for about 10% of the data that is consumed by an artificial intelligence tool.

4) *Time Series Data*:

As its name also implies, these kinds of datasets consist of data points that have some sort of time value attached to it. At times, this can also be referred to as "Journey" kind of data, because during a trip, there are data points that can be accessed throughout the time from leaving the point of origination to finally arriving at the point of destination. Some typical examples of this include the price range of a certain stock or commodity as it is traded on an intraday period, the first time that a prospect visits the website of a merchant and the various web-based pages they click on or materials that they download until they log off the website, etc.

Now that we have defined what the four most common datasets are, you may even be wondering at this point, just what are some for them? Examples of this include the following:

For Structured Datasets:

- SQL Databases;
- Spreadsheets such as Excel;
- OLTP Systems;
- Online forms;
- Sensors such as GPS or RFID tags;
- Network and Web server logs;
- Medical devices.

For Unstructured Sets:

Source	Example
Social Media	Facebook, LinkedIn, Instagram, Twitter, YouTube, Pinterest
Location & Geo Data	GPS Systems
Machined Generator & Sensor Based	Web Server files, Smart Meters, Manufacturing Sensors, Equipment Logs, Trading Systems, Data Records
Digital Streams	Video, Audio, and Images
Text-based Documents	Email, PowerPoint, Spreadsheets, Word Processing
Logs	Server Logs, Clickstream
Transactions	Data from CRM Systems, Ecommerce Store Interactions, Transactional Data from ERP Systems
Micro Blogging	Twitter, Customer Feedback Streams

For Semi-Structured Datasets:

- Emails;
- XML and other markup languages;
- Binary Executables;
- TCP/IP packets;
- Zipped Files;
- Integration of data from different sources;
- Web Pages.

(SOURCE: 11)

For Time Series Datasets:

- Statista;
- Data-Planet Statistical Datasets;
- Euromonitor Passport;
- OECD Statistics;
- United Nations Statistical Databases;
- World Bank Data;
- U.S. Census Bureau: International Data Base;
- Bloomberg;
- Capital IQ;
- Datastream;
- Global Financial Data;
- International Financial Statistics Online;
- MarketLine Advantage;
- Morningstar Direct.

As it was mentioned earlier, it is the unstructured datasets that account for a majority of the datasets that are fed into an artificial intelligence application, and this is the beauty about them. They are so powerful that they can take just about any kind or type of dataset that is presented to them, literally digest into a format that can understand it, process it, and provide the output or outputs that are required. In other words, there are no limiting factors with regards to this, and as a result, they can give just about any kind of prediction or answer that is asked of it.

6.1.3 Big Data

As also previously reviewed, the size and the number of datasets are literally growing at an exponential clip on a daily basis, given all of the technological advancements that are currently taking place. There is a specific term for this, and it is called "big data". The technical definition of it is as follows:

> Big data is larger, more complex data sets, especially from new data sources. These data sets are so voluminous that traditional data processing software just can't manage them. But these massive volumes of data can be used to address business problems that wouldn't have been able to be tackled before.

(SOURCE: www.oracle.com/big-data/what-is-big-data/)

In a way, this can also be likened to another concept known as "data warehousing".

There are three main characteristics that are associated with "big data", and they are as follows:

1) *Volume*:

   This refers to sheer size and scale of the datasets. Very often, they will be in the form of unstructured data. The dataset size can go as high as into the terabytes.

2) *Variety*:

   This describes the diversity of all of the datasets that reside in the Big Data. This includes the structure data, the unstructured data, the semi-structured data, and the time series data. This also describes the sources from where all of these datasets come from.

3) *Velocity*:

   This refers to the rapid speed at which the datasets in the Big Data are actually being created.

4) *Value*:

   This refers to just how useful the Big Data is. In other words, if it is fed into an artificial intelligence system, how close will it come to in giving the desired or expected output?

5) *Variability*:

   This describes how fast the datasets in the Big Data will change over a certain period of time. For example, structured data, time series data, and semi-structured data will not change that much, but unstructured data will. This is simply due its dynamic nature at hand.

6) *Visualization*:

   This is how visual aids are used in the datasets that are in the Big Data. For example, these could be graphs, dashboards, etc.

6.1.4 Understanding Preparation of Data

As it has been mentioned before, it is the data that drives the artificial intelligence application to do what it does. Meaning, it is like the fuel for it to run. Although these are quite robust in providing the output that is asked of it, it is still viewed as "Garbage In and Garbage Out" process. Meaning, the quality of outputs that you are going to get is only going to be as good as the data that is put into it.

Therefore, you must take great effort to make sure that the datasets that you are feeding into your Artificial Intelligence systems are of a very robust and will meet the needs of you are wanting in terms of what you want the desired outputs to be. The first step in this process is known as "data understanding":

1) *Data Understanding:*

   In this regard, you need to carefully know where the sources of your data and their respective feeds are coming from. Depending upon what your exact circumstances and needs are, they will typically come from the following sources:

- *In-House Data*:
    - As its name implies, these are the data points that are actually coming into your business or corporation. For example, it could be data that originates from your corporate intranet, or even your external website, as customers and prospects download materials from your site or even fill out the contact form. Also, it could be the case that you may have datasets already in your organization that you can already use.
- *Open Source Data*:
    - These are the kinds of data that are freely available from the Internet, especially when you are using Google to find various data sources. For example, the federal government is a great resource for this, as well as many private enterprises (obviously, you will have to pay for this as a subscription, but initially, they will more than likely offer a free trial at first to test drive their respective datasets). This would be a great opportunity to see if what they are offering will be compatible to your artificial intelligence system and if it will potentially yield the desired outputs. These kinds of datasets will very likely use a specialized application protocol interface (API) in order to download the data. Other than the advantage of being free, another key advantage of using open source data is that it already comes in a formatted manner that can be uploaded and fed into your artificial intelligence system.
- *Third Party Data*:
    - This is the kind of datasets that are available exclusively from an outside vendor. Examples of these can be seen in the last subsection of this chapter. The primary advantage of obtaining data from these sources is that you can be guaranteed, to a ce rtain degree, that it has been validated. But the disadvantage of this is that they can be quite expensive, and if you ever need to update your datasets, you will have to go back to the same vendor and pay yet another premium price for it.

According to recent research, about 70% of the artificial intelligence systems that are in use today make use of in-house data, 20% of them use open source data, the remaining 10% comes from the outside vendors. In order to fully understand the robustness of the datasets you are about to procure, the following must first be answered:

- Are the datasets complete for your needs and requirements? Is there any missing data?
- How was the data originally collected?
- How was the data initially processed?
- Have there been any significant changes made to it that you need to be aware of?
- Are there any quality control (QC) issues with the datasets?

2) *The Preparation of the Data*:
   This part is often referred to as "data cleansing", and it requires the following actions that you must take before you can feed the data into your artificial intelligence system:

- *Deduplication*:
  - It is absolutely imperative to make sure that your data does not contain duplicate sets. If this is the case, and it goes unnoticed, it could greatly affect and skew the outputs that are produced.
- *Outliers*:
  - These are the data points that lie to the extremes of the rest of the datasets. Perhaps they could be useful for some purpose, but you need to make sure first if they are needed for your particular application. If not, then they must be removed.
- *Consistency*:
  - In this situation, you must make sure that all of the variables have clear definitions to them and what they mean. There should be no overlap in these meanings with the other variables.
- *Validation Rules*:
  - This is where you try to find the technical limitations of the datasets that you intend to use. Doing this manually can be very time-consuming and laborious, so there are many software applications that are available that can help your determine these specific kinds of limitations. Of course, you will first need to decide and enter in the relevant permutations, and these can be referred to as the "thresholds".
- *Binning*:
  - When you procure your datasets, it may also be the case that you may not need each and every one to feed into your artificial intelligence system. As a result, you should look at each category and decide the ones that are the most relevant for the outputs that you are trying to garner.
- *Staleness*:
  - This is probably one of the most important factors to consider. Just how timely and relevant are the datasets that you are using? For an artificial intelligence, it is absolutely crucial that you get data that is updated in real time, if your desired output is to predict something into the future.
- *Merging*:
  - It could be the case that the two columns in your datasets could contain very similar pieces of information. If this is the case, you may even want to consider bringing these two columns together by merging them. By doing so, you are actually using the processing capabilities of your artificial intelligence much more efficiently.
- *One Hot Encoding*:
  - To a certain degree, it may even be possible to represent qualitative data as quantitative data, once again, depending upon your needs and requirements.
- *Conversions*:
  - This is more of an aspect of formatting the units as to how you want your outputs to look like. For example, if all of your datasets are in a decimal-based system, but your output calls for the values to be in the metric system, then using this technique will be important.

- *Finding Missing Data*:
  When you are closely examining your datasets, it could quite often be the case that ther0e may some pieces that are missing. In this regard, there are two types of missing data:
  - Randomly missing data: Here, you can calculate a median or even average as a replacement value. By doing this, it should only skew the output to a negligible degree.
  - Sequentially missing data: This is when the data is missing in a successive fashion, in an iterative manner. Taking the median or average will not work because there is too much that is not available in order to make a scientific estimate. You could try to extrapolate the preceding data and the subsequent data to make a hypothesized guess, but this is more of a risky proposition to take. Or you could simply delete those fields in which the sequential data is missing. But in either case, the chances are much greater that the output will be much more skewed and not nearly as reliable.
- *Correcting Data Misalignments*:
  - It is important to note that before you merge any fields together in your datasets that the respective data points "align" with the other datasets that you have. To account and correct for this, consider the following actions that you can take:
    - If possible, try to calculate and ascertain any missing data that you may have in your datasets (as previously reviewed);
    - Find any other missing data in all of your other datasets that you have and intend to use;
    - Try to combine the datasets so that you have columns which can provide for consistent fields;
    - If need be, modify or further enhance the desired outcome that the output produces in order to accommodate for any changes that have been made to correct data misalignment.

6.1.5 OTHER RELEVANT DATA CONCEPTS THAT ARE IMPORTANT TO ARTIFICIAL INTELLIGENCE

Finally, in this subsection we examine some other data concepts that are very pertinent to artificial intelligence systems and are as follows:

1) *Diagnostic Analytics*:
   This is the careful examination of the datasets to see why a certain trend has happened the way it did. An example of this is discovering any hidden trends which may not have been noticed before. This is very often done in data warehousing or big data projects.
2) *Extraction, Transformation, and Load (ETL)*:
   This is a specialized type of data integration and is typically used in, once again, data warehousing applications.
3) *Feature*:
   This is a column of data.

4) *Instance*:
   This is a row of data.
5) *Metadata*:
   This is the data that is available about the datasets.
6) *Online Analytical Processing (OLAP)*:
   This is a technique which allows you to examine the datasets from types of databases into one harmonized view.
7) *Categorical Data*:
   This kind of data does not have a numerical value per se but has a textual meaning that is associated with it.
8) *Ordinal Data*:
   This is a mixture of both categorical data and numerical data.
9) *Predictive Analytics*:
   This is where the artificial intelligence system attempts to make a certain prediction about the future (this is displayed as an output), based upon the datasets that are fed into it.
10) *Prescriptive Analytics*:
    This is where the concepts of Big Data (as previously examined) are used to help make better decisions, based upon the output that is yielded.
11) *Scalar Variables*:
    These are the types of variables that hold and consist of only single values.
12) *Transactional Data*:
    These are the kinds of datasets that represent data to actual transactions that have occurred in the course of daily business activities.

An example of data science is seen below:

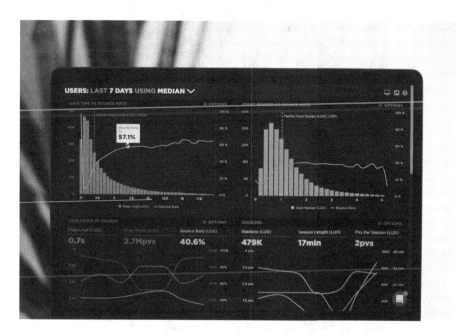

6.2 AN INTRODUCTION TO MACHINE LEARNING

A subfield of AI is that of machine learning, also known as "ML". Rather than doing the proverbial "Garbage In and Garbage Out" process like that of AI, ML tries to emulate the thinking process of the human brain, in order to come up with a range of possible answers. A technical definition of ML is as follows:

> Machine learning is an application of AI that enables systems to learn and improve from experience without being explicitly programmed. Machine learning focuses on developing computer programs that can access data and use it to learn for themselves.

> *(SOURCE: www.expert.ai/blog/machine-learning-definition/)*

So as one can see, a key difference between ML when compared to that of AI is that it requires not so much intervention when it comes to getting the desired output. Rather, the ML system tries to learn on its own based from previous outputs it has computed. From here, it then tries to extrapolate future outputs. An illustration of ML is below:

But unlike AI, ML follows a distinct and established process not only to achieve the desired output but to also help it learn in the process. This is further discussed in the next subsection.

6.2.1 THE MACHINE LEARNING PROCESS

When you are applying machine learning to a particular question that you want answered or to predict a certain outcome, it is very important to follow a distinct process in order to accomplish these tasks. In other words, you want to build an effective model that can serve well for other purposes and objectives for a subsequent time down the road. In other words, you want to train this model in a particular fashion so that it can provide a very high degree of both accuracy and reliability.

This process is depicted below:

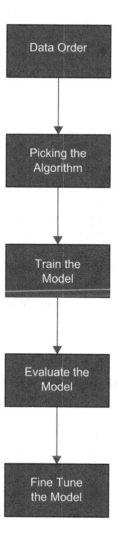

6.2.1.1 Data Order

In this step, you want to make sure that the data is as unorganized and unsorted as possible. Although this sounds quite contrary, if the datasets are by any means sorted or organized in any way, shape, or form, the machine learning algorithms that are utilized may detect this as a pattern, which you do not want to happen in this particular instance.

6.2.1.2 Picking the Algorithm

In this phase, you will want to select the appropriate machine learning algorithms for your model. This will be heavily examined in this part of the chapter.

6.2.1.3 Training the Model

The datasets that you have will feed into the machine learning system, in order for it to learn first. In other words, various associations and relationships will be created and examined so that the desired outputs can be formulated. For example, one of the simplest algorithms that can be used in machine learning is the linear regression one, which is represented mathematically as follows:

$$Y = M*X + B$$

Where:

M = The slope on a graph;

B = Is the Y intercept on the graph.

6.2.1.4 Model Evaluation

In this step, you will make use of a representative sample of data from the datasets, which are technically known as the "test data". By feeding this initially into the machine learning system, you can gauge just how accurate your desired outputs will be in a test environment before you release your datasets into the production environment.

6.2.1.5 Fine-Tune the Model

In this last phase, you will adjust the permutations that you have established in the machine learning system so that it can reasonably come up with desired outputs that you are looking for.

6.2.2 THE MACHINE LEARNING ALGORITHM CLASSIFICATIONS

There are four major categorizations of the machine learning algorithms, and they are as follows:

1) *Supervised Learning*:
   These types of algorithms make use of what are known as "labelled data". This simply means that each dataset has a certain label that is associated

with them. In this instance, one of the key things to keep in mind is that you need to have a large amount of datasets in order to produce the dataset you are looking for when you are using algorithms based from this category. But if the datasets do not come already labelled, it could be very time-consuming to create and assign a label for each and every one of them. This is the primary downside of using machine learning algorithms from this particular category.

2) *Unsupervised Learning*:
   These kinds of algorithms work with data that is typically not labelled. Because of the time constraints it would take to create and assign the labels for each category (as just previously mentioned), you will have to make use of what are known as "deep learning algorithms" in order to detect any unseen data trends that lie from within all of your datasets. In this regard, one of the most typical approaches that are used in this category is that of "clustering". With this, you are merely taking all of the unlabelled datasets and use the various algorithms that are available from within this particular category is to put these datasets into various groups, which have common denominators or affiliations with them. To help out with this, there are a number of ways to do this, which are the following:

   - *The Euclidean Metric*:
     - This is a straight line between two independent datasets.
   - *The Cosine Similarity Metric*:
     - In this instance, a trigonometric function known as the "Cosine" to measure any given angles between the datasets. The goal here is to find any closeness or similarities between at least two or more independent datasets based upon their geometric orientation.
   - *The Manhattan Metric*:
     - This technique involves taking the summation of at least two or more absolute value distances from the datasets that you have.
   - *The Association*:
     - The basic thrust here is that if a specific instance occurs in one of your datasets, then it will also likely occur in the datasets that have some sort of relationship with the initial dataset that has been used.
   - *The Anomaly Detection*:
     - With this methodology, you are statistically identifying those outliers or other anomalous patterns that may exist from your datasets. This technique has found great usage in cybersecurity, especially when it relates to filtering out for false positives from the log files that are collected from the firewalls, network intrusion devices, and routers, as well as any behavior that may be deemed too suspicious or malicious in nature.

- *The Autoencoders*:
  - With this particular technique, the datasets that you have on hand will be formatted and put into a compressed type of format, and from that, it will be reconstructed once again. The idea behind this is to detect and find any sort of new patterns or unhidden trends that may exist from within your datasets.
- *The Reinforcement Learning*:
  - In this instance, you are learning and harnessing the power of your datasets through a trial and error process, as the name of this category implies.
- *The Semi-Supervised Learning*:
  - This methodology is actually a mixture of both supervised learning and unsupervised learning. However, this technique is only used when you have a small amount of datasets that are actually labelled. Within this, there is a sub technique which is called "pseudo-labelling". In this regard, you literally translate all of the unsupervised datasets into a supervised one state of nature.

6.3 AZURE, ARTIFICIAL INTELLIGENCE, AND MACHINE LEARNING

As stated earlier in this chapter. Microsoft has now been on the cutting edge of both AI and ML technologies. In fact, when compared to some of the other Cloud service providers (as the Amazon Web Services, Google Cloud Private, etc.), they offer some of the most advanced tools available in order to create both AI and ML based apps that are not only scalable but can be created and deployed quickly. The next subsection outlines the major AI and ML components that can be found in Azure.

6.3.1 THE MAJOR COMPONENTS

The matrix below describes the major AI and ML tools that are available in Azure.

Service	Description	Azure
Conversational UI/ UX Virtual Personal Assistant	*This is a suite that covers intelligence cognitive services, machine learning, analytics and more. *This creates and connects intelligent bots that interact with end users via text messaging, Teams, Slack, Twitter, etc.	*Cortana Intelligence Suite *Microsoft Bot Framework + Bot Service

(Continued)

Service	Description	Azure
Speech Recognition	* This is an API that can convert speech to text, understand end user intent, and converting text back to speech for natural responsiveness. * This allows for applications to understand end user commands contextually. * This gives the app the ability to recognize individual speakers and/or users. * This is a fine-tuning mechanism to eliminate extraneous variables such as speaking style, background noise, and vocabulary.	* Bing Speech AI * Language Understanding Intelligent Service * Speaker Recognition API * Custom Recognition Intelligent Service
Text to Speech	* This converts speech to text.	* Bing Speech API
Speech to Text	* This converts text to speech.	* Bing Speech API
Text Translation	* This allows for automated language translation.	* Translator Text API + Emotions API
Text analysis	* This allows for such functionalities as key phrases, languages and sentiment.	* Text Analytics API
Visual Recognition	* This extracts information images, generates captions, and identifies objects in images. * This mechanism detects, identifies, analyzes, organizes, and tags faces in photos. * This mechanism recognizes emotions in images. * This is a video processing mechanism which produces stable video output, detects motion, creates intelligent thumbnails, detects and tracks faces.	* Computer Vision API + Face API * Face API * Emotions API * Media Analytics + Video Indexer

6.3.2 THE AZURE MACHINE LEARNING

Along with the AI tools just depicted in the matrix above, Azure also has a platform called "Azure Machine Learning". Essentially, this is where data scientists and their teams create extremely powerful ML apps in a very easy fashion. In technical terms, the Azure Machine Learning is defined as follows:

> Azure Machine Learning is a cloud service for accelerating and managing the machine learning project lifecycle. Machine learning professionals, data scientists, and engineers can use it in their day-to-day workflows: Train and deploy models, and manage MLOps.
>
> You can create a model in Azure Machine Learning or use a model built from an open-source platform, such as Pytorch, TensorFlow, or scikit-learn. MLOps tools help you monitor, retrain, and redeploy models.

(SOURCE: https://learn.microsoft.com/en-us/azure/machine-learning/ overview-what-is-azure-machine-learning?view=azureml-api-2).

The Azure Machine Learning Project Lifecycle is illustrated below:

It should be noted that MLOps is really nothing but the concepts of DevOps implemented into the world of machine learning. This is illustrated below:

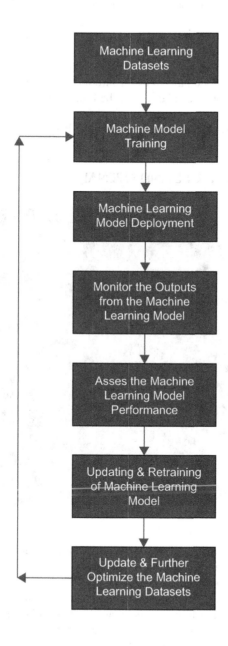

It is important to note that in order to launch any kind of ML project, you also need to have the Azure Machine Learning Studio. For more information about this and how to use this tool, click on the link below:

http://cyberresources.solutions/Cloud_Update_Book/Azure_ML_Studio_
    eBook.pdf

Although we have provided an overview into the AI and ML tools in Azure, much more detailed information can be seen at the link below:

http://cyberresources.solutions/Cloud_Update_Book/Azure_ML_eBook.pdf

6.4 MICROSOFT AZURE AND OPENAI

As it was mentioned earlier in this book, artificial intelligence and machine learning is now the craze in today's times. But really, there is nothing new about these technologies. They have been around since the 1950s and have evolved into sophistication ever since then. The major catalyst for its explosive growth now has been primarily due to the launch of what is known as "ChatGPT". This is an IT extensive platform, and all the end user has to do is merely ask it a question, and it will appear with the right answer to the query.

But it has more sophisticated uses, such as creating code and even content generation. Since ChatGPT is being used to create something new, a new term has thus evolved, which is technically known as "Generative AI". Microsoft has had a huge hand in the evolvement, and in the next subsection, we will take a closer look at the relationship between Microsoft and OpenAI, the creator of ChatGPT.

6.4.1 THE BUSINESS RELATIONSHIP BETWEEN MICROSOFT AND OPENAI

This relationship between the two entities goes as far back as 2019. Consider these trends:

- Microsoft made its first investment into OpenAI with just $1 Billion. Seems like a small investment to Microsoft, but who knew at the time what AI and ML would be like today?
- This small investment from Microsoft has given birth to a new industry trend called "Generative AI", as just reviewed.
- Now in 2023, the market value of OpenAI is at well over $13 billion, and its current valuation is now at well over $13 billion.
- Azure has now become the main platform for ChatGPT. For example, it is now providing all of the resources and computing power for all of the research, new product lines, as well as the programming interfaces (also known as APIs) that are coming out or that are being planned by OpenAI.
- Microsoft has become the largest integrator of ChatGPT into its own product line. For example, it is being used in the Bing Search Engine and even its entire M365 product line, most notable those of Word, PowerPoint, and Excel.
- Microsoft is also using ChatGPT for its marketing platforms and even all of the coding tools that are used by GitHub.
- Many financial analysts say the relationship could bring in an additional $30 billion of new revenue, primarily coming from Azure and ChatGPT.
- OpenAI was first launched as a not-for-profit company back in 2015, with Open Source Software being its prime business model. This was done to counter the market size and effects brought by the Open Source Software from Google.
- This relationship has been viewed to counter the ill-fated AI and ML projects that were launched by Microsoft. This includes the "Clippy" from Word, the Cortana Virtual Personal Assistant, and the Ty Chatbot that it deployed on Twitter.
- The AI and ML algorithms that drive ChatGPT will also be deployed in the Edge web browser, from Microsoft.
- Microsoft has full exclusive rights to the latest large language model (LLM) models from OpenAI, as well as the latest ChatGPT algorithm, which is called "GPT-4".
- Earlier this year, Microsoft and OpenAI just announced that they are planning to not only extend their relationship but to deepen it as well. Following are some examples of this:

- Microsoft will create new supercomputer facilities based off of the Azure Platform. This will allow for OpenAI to create not only new and innovative AI and ML products, but they will be able to further enhance the strength of ChatGPT, thus making it still the market leader in the foreseeable future.
- As mentioned also, Microsoft will now deploy the algorithms from ChatGPT across all its product lines, which include those in both Azure and M365.
- Azure will now become the sole Cloud Provider for OpenAI and ChatGPT. This means that Azure will now be the powerhouse for all of OpenAI's research and development, product and service lines, and even its APIs.
- It is hoped that this deepened relationship in the coming years will lead to a new revolution in both AI and ML, which is called the "artificial general intelligence", also known as "AGI" for short. This is where these two tools can solve a much wider and broader scope of both problems and issues to be solved. This stands in opposition to what is known as "artificial narrow intelligence", also known as "ANI" for short. This the current state of AI and ML, where they are used to solve much narrower problems and issues.
- One of the biggest accomplishments of this renewed relationship between Microsoft and OpenAI is the creation of what is "Azure OpenAI". This is where data scientists, software developers, and anybody else involved in ML and AI can gain direct access to the algorithms from Open AI. At the present time, this includes both GPT-3 and GPT-4. However, access for this new service is extremely limited, and more information about it can be seen at these three links:

  https://learn.microsoft.com/en-us/azure/cognitive-services/openai/overview

  https://learn.microsoft.com/en-us/azure/cognitive-services/openai/concepts/models

  http://cyberresources.solutions/Cloud_Update_Book/OpenAI-cheatsheet.pdf

  (NOTE: The above link is a step by step guide into actually using Azure OpenAI)

6.5 THE MICROSOFT COPILOT

As it was discussed in the last subsection, the relationship between Microsoft and OpenAI has become much stronger and fortified in the recent years. Part of this has been the ability for end users, data scientists, and software developers to gain access to the technologies of OpenAI in a much easier fashion than what it normally would have been. Also, Microsoft is going to be implementing these technologies as well into their own product lines, most notable that of M365.

One of the best examples of this is the new product from Microsoft which is called "CoPilot". The premise behind this is to further enable the use of AI technology into its entire portfolio suite. The main access point of this will be through a new service called "Microsoft Graph". The company views this as the primary gateway to gain access to AI tools that are devoted exclusively to M365. Also, they will be leveraging the large language model (LLM) toolset that OpenAI has developed and deployed.

Here are some examples of where CoPilot will come into use:

1) *Microsoft Word*:

It can write, edits, summarizes, and creates right alongside you. With only a brief prompt, Copilot in Word will create a first draft for you, bringing in information from across your organization as needed.

(SOURCE: www.microsoft.com/en-us/microsoft-365/blog/2023/03/16/ introducing-microsoft-365-copilot-a-whole-new-way-to-work/)

2) *Microsoft Excel*:

It will work alongside you to help analyze and explore your data. Ask Copilot questions about your data set in natural language, not just formulas. It will reveal correlations, propose what-if scenarios, and suggest new formulas based on your questions—generating models based on your questions that help you explore your data without modifying it.

(SOURCE: www.microsoft.com/en-us/microsoft-365/blog/2023/03/16/ introducing-microsoft-365-copilot-a-whole-new-way-to-work/)

3) *Microsoft PowerPoint*:

It can turn your ideas into stunning presentations. As your storytelling partner, Copilot can transform existing written documents into decks complete with speaker notes and sources or start a new presentation from a simple prompt or outline.

(SOURCE: www.microsoft.com/en-us/microsoft-365/blog/2023/03/16/ introducing-microsoft-365-copilot-a-whole-new-way-to-work/)

4) *Microsoft Outlook*:

It works with you in your inbox and messages so that you can spend less time on email triage and more time on communicating—better, faster, and more easily. Summarize lengthy, convoluted email threads with multiple people to understand not only what has been said, but the different viewpoints of each person and the open questions that have yet to be answered. Respond to an existing email with a simple prompt or turn quick notes into crisp, professional messages—pulling from other emails or content that you already have access to from across Microsoft 365.

(SOURCE: www.microsoft.com/en-us/microsoft-365/blog/2023/03/16/ introducing-microsoft-365-copilot-a-whole-new-way-to-work/)

5) *Microsoft Teams*:

Copilot helps you run more effective meetings, get up to speed on the conversation, organize key discussion points, and summarize key actions so that the entire group knows what to do next. In your chat, Copilot gets you answers to specific questions or catches you up on anything you've missed, all without interrupting the flow of discussion.

(SOURCE: www.microsoft.com/en-us/microsoft-365/blog/2023/03/16/ introducing-microsoft-365-copilot-a-whole-new-way-to-work/)

6) *Microsoft Viva Engage*:
It equips leaders with insightful conversation starters based on sentiments and trending topics across workplace communities and conversations. Copilot will offer leaders suggestions as they draft more personalized posts, with options to add images and help adjust the tone to enrich conversations.

(SOURCE: www.microsoft.com/en-us/microsoft-365/blog/2023/03/16/ introducing-microsoft-365-copilot-a-whole-new-way-to-work/)

An example of Microsoft CoPilot is illustrated below:

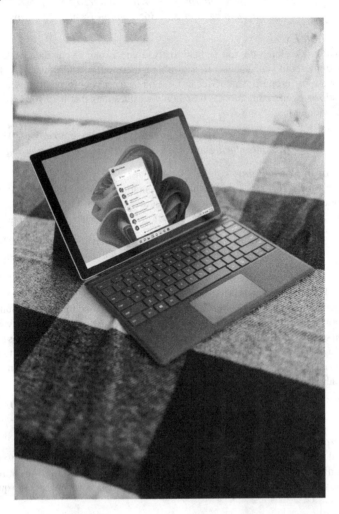

6.6 AN OVERVIEW INTO CHATGPT

For the most part, we are all familiar with chatbots. These are the dialog boxes that usually appear in the lower right-hand side of your web browser. Through this, one is able to chat with what is known as a "virtual agent" in real time. This is the look and feel as if you are talking to a real human being (and in some cases, you actually are—it's hard to know). But over time, the chatbot technology has greatly advanced to the point where it can now pull up the profile of an end user, based on previous conversations.

From there, it can provide rather intelligent answers to the end user based upon the questions that are being asked of it. A lot of this is done through neural network technology, as reviewed earlier in this whitepaper. For chatbots, it is "natural language processing", or "NLP" that is most commonly used. But just recently, a very sophisticated form of chatbot came out in the marketplace. This is known as "ChatGPT", and it is making waves across all industries.

6.6.1 THE ORIGINS OF CHATGPT

This platform was originally developed by an organization known as "Open AI". It first came out in November 2022, so it is still a fairly new application. Technically, ChatGPT is built upon Open AI's GPT-3.5 and GPT-4 algorithms of what are known as the large language models, also known as "LLMs". Further, these specific algorithms were optimized using both supervised and unsupervised AI learning techniques. However, as of March 2023, ChatGPT is now powered by the GPT-4 algorithm, which is the latest release from Open AI.

6.6.2 THE TECHNICALITIES BEHIND CHATGPT

ChatGPT comes from the family of generative pre-trained transformer language models (This is where the "GPT" part of the name comes from). As just mentioned, it uses both supervised and unsupervised learning. It should be noted that human intervention was needed to help optimize the performance of ChatGPT. In terms of the former, the model was given real life conversations in which the developers played both sides of the fence: the end user as well as the virtual assistant.

With the latter, the developers created ranked responses that the model had formulated based upon previous conversations. From here, these quantitative based rankings were then used for the development of the "reward models". These were eventually used to further optimize the model by making use of proximal policy optimization algorithms, also known as the "PPO".

At the present time, OpenAI collects information and data from the many ChatGPT end users as feedback. This is then used to train and optimize the back-end algorithms even more. With this mechanism, the end user can either "upvote" (positive) or "downvote" (negative) the responses they receive from ChatGPT and how useful it was for them in the project that they were trying to accomplish.

6.7 THE ADVANTAGES AND THE DISADVANTAGES OF CHATGPT

6.7.1 THE ADVANTAGES

The primary thrust of ChatGPT is to provide a chatbot that is much more sophisticated than the others that are currently being used right now. In other words, rather than appearing to display canned answers, Open AI wants their chatbot to be as conversational as possible, with having the same experience as you would with having a conversation with a real human being. But given how sophisticated this platform has become, ChatGPT can now serve an entire host of other applications, some of which include the following:

- It is used quite heavily for content generation. For example, rather than taking the time to create their own content, many writers are now using ChatGPT to compose an entire book for them. The publishing industry is quite aware of this and in fact are now cracking down on authors that use this method. In fact, Kindle Direct Publishing (KDP) of Amazon (the largest self-publishing platform) has taken a harsh stance against this.
- Create and compile source code for a web-based application.
- Can emulate heavy gaming applications.
- The Financial Sector:
  - Providing financial advice;
  - Detecting any sort of fraudulent transactions;
  - The creation of legal documents and contracts between banks, brokerage firms, etc.
- Sales and Marketing:
  - SEO;
  - Keyword research;
  - Creating customer feedback forms.
- The Healthcare Industry:
  - Medical transcription;
  - Triaging of patients in the ER;
  - Creating virtual agents for the purposes of scheduling medical appointments.
- It is now becoming a strong alternative to the Google Search Engine.
- It can also be used for language translation, for example converting an English book into Spanish, and many other languages.
- The Educational Sector:
  - Resume writing/proofing/editing;
  - Recruiting and even interviewing candidates.

But of course, as the sophistication of the algorithms in ChatGPT grows even more sophisticated, the applications it will serve will also explode.

6.7.2 The Disadvantages

Despite the advantages of ChatGPT, it also suffers from a number of limitations as well, some of which are as follows:

- The output is not what the end user is expecting (but this is true of all AI apps—a lot of this depends upon the data that is fed into it). In technical terms, with regards to large language modeling, this is also known as "Hallucination".
- It is also the case that in the efforts to make ChatGPT as humanlike as possible, it is possible that it can become too overtrained and not give the correct, or expected, out. In technical terms, this phenomenon is also known as "Optimization Pathology", which is also known more commonly as Goodhardt's Law.
- It is prone to "Algorithmic Bias". This is where the algorithms that drive ChatGPT cerates unfair outcomes, in which one output is highly favored over the alternatives.
- ChatGPT cannot connect to the Internet, thus it is unable to provide answers on a real-time basis. For example, if you ask it to give you the temperature and weather conditions at this very moment, it will not be able to do it.
- It can only accept inputs from the end user in a text-only version. It cannot pull in resources from other areas, such as websites, videos, and images.
- It is unable to multitask. This simply means that you can only present one query at a time to it.
- Because of the sophistication of its algorithms, it takes a lot of overhead in terms of both computing and processing power in order to come up with answers to the queries that it is posed with.
- AI algorithms can go "stale" quickly over a short period of time. Therefore, there is the constant need to keep them updated, refined, and optimized at all times.
- There have been complaints that ChatGPT can be very wordy in terms of its answers and usually not enough detail is provided, especially for complex queries.

6.8 THE NEXT CHAPTER

Overall, this chapter has provided a high level overview of what artificial intelligence (AI) and machine learning (ML) are all about. There was also an extensive review into the AI and ML components, and the business relationship between Microsoft and OpenAI. Finally, this chapter also examined how Microsoft intends to leverage the AI technology from OpenAI into its M365 portfolio, via the new product that will be offered called Microsoft CoPilot.

In the next chapter, we will do a deeper dive into the social implications of AI.

7 Conclusion

So far in this book, we have examined the structure of the Cloud model from different angles as well as perspectives. We have examined both the Amazon Web Services (AWS) and Azure and the rapid developments that have been made in both artificial intelligence (AI) and machine learning (ML). Then eventually, the book made the transition to both of these topics and how Microsoft has made rapid advances in these fields, primarily fueled with its partnership with OpenAI, the creators and developers of ChatGPT.

As also previously mentioned, there is really nothing new about the science of AI and ML. It has its roots back as early as the 1950s, and it has evolved ever since then. But the implications of it are being felt the most today, from both a technological and social perspective. This once again has been brought on primarily by the ChatGPT.

For example, many people around the world hold this platform in pure wonderment and even dream of the day when it will evolve to the point that everything will be automated, much in a way like you see in science fiction movies and programs (especially that of *Star Trek: The Next Generation*). But this has been hugely offset by the fears that it has also brought upon the American society.

Some of these include the following:

- The overall effects of AI on the general American society.
- The fear of the misuse of personal information and data.
- The fear of Big Brother watching, especially by government agencies at the federal, state, and local levels.
- The angst of covert surveillance, especially when computer vision (a subset of AI) is implemented into CCTV camera technology.
- Probably the biggest fear right now in the United States is how AI will impact the workforce. For example, many labor-related jobs (such as working in a warehouse, factory, car assembly plant, etc.) require conducting ordinary and routine tasks. While AI can be advantageous here, there is the huge fear that it will totally lead to human worker replacement, resulting in large job losses.
- There is also fear in the marketing and content generation industries. For example, ChatGPT can be used to create marketing campaigns and even write an entire book. This has led to a huge amount of angst as well among writers and other marketing professionals that their services will no longer be required, as AI could possibly do the same, possibly even better and even cheaper.
- This fear even holds true with the software development industry. ChatGPT can be used to varying degrees to create and compile source code in a very quick fashion and, in some cases, even faster than human beings. Will this lead to a total automation of software development?
- Probably one of the biggest fears is that ChatGPT and AI in general can be used for nefarious purposes, especially by that of the Cyberattacker.

DOI: 10.1201/9781003459569-7

For example, malicious code can be compiled in just a matter of a few minutes to launch new brands of Ransomware and other similar types of large-scale attacks, especially that on the critical infrastructure. Although OpenAI has claimed that there are safeguards in place to mitigate this from happening as much as possible, there is no concrete proof yet to substantiate this claim.

From the above, the list can go even further. Only the ones that are prevalent today have been highlighted.

7.1 THE RESPONSE

In an effort to quell these fears here at least in the United States, the Biden administration has introduced legislation into both the House and Senate addressing the specific fears of AI that the American public has and ways as to how the rapid evolvement of AI and ML should be slowed. This is an effort to help slow down its rapid pace of development, in an effort for the American society to take a moment of pause and understand to a better degree what the implications of AI, especially that of ChatGPT, will bring to them.

One such work is the "AI Bill of Rights", which will be examined in more detail later in this chapter. But in the meantime, the United States federal government has also come out with a special whitepaper on what the implications of AI means to the American worker. This will be the social implication feature of this chapter. We now examine some of the critical sections of this whitepaper.

7.2 THE WHITEPAPER

The exact title of this whitepaper is as follows: "THE IMPACT OF ARTIFICIAL INTELLIGENCE ON THE FUTURE OF WORKFORCES IN THE EUROPEAN UNION AND THE UNITED STATES OF AMERICA".

7.2.1 THE ADVENT OF COMPUTER VISION

One of the first topics to be covered by it is the recent progress made in AI. Of course, one of the topics pointed out is the evolution of ChatGPT. But other than that, the whitepaper points out that the latest developments in AI have been in respect to those of what is known as "Computer Vision" (as just examined).

This is the field of AI where the vision process of the human eye to the human brain is attempted to be manipulated. But taking it even further, it is also the goal of Computer Vision to try to replicate how the human brain processes the visual data that it receives from the eye and how it is used to make rational judgements and how it works in the overall thought processes of a human being.

Although computer vision is still relatively in its infancy, it has started to make its mark in applications, especially when it comes to the realm of Physical Security. In this regard, this technology is being used in conjunction with facial recognition, in an effort to positively identify any wanted suspects or fugitives that may be walking around certain premises. Computer vision can also be used to help manipulate any images or video that is captured by the CCTV system which is non-discernable.

The biggest fear now with computer vision is that it could potentially be used on social media sites (especially those of Facebook and Twitter) in a very covert fashion, without first obtaining authorization or permission from the subscriber.

7.2.2 THE PRESENT STATE OF AI

The whitepaper even ventured on to examine the current state of AI in the American society today. The writers of it first noted that since the 1950s, the evolution of AI and its subfields (most notable those of machine learning, neural networks, and computer vision) has happened in spurts. This is has been brought on by new innovations as they have occurred, and from there, this has spurred on public interest.

But as the interest waned over time, so did the innovation cycle of AI in terms of research and development. These peaks and valleys in AI have also been referred to as "AI Spring" and "AI Winter", respectively. Because of the huge growth rate that has been brought on by ChatGPT, many experts now view that the United States is in a "AI Spring". But there is speculation that further interest into ChatGPT could wane in the future, and eventually leading a proverbial "bursting of the bubble", much like what we saw in the Internet boom of the late nineties.

But people are stating that despite this expected decline, there will be two new emerging trends that will emerge from ChatGPT:

- The growth of what is known as "artificial general intelligence", also known as "AGI" for short. As stated earlier in this book, this is where AI will be able to solve macro-based issues and problems, rather than using the narrow focus that is has now. In fact, this is an area that OpenAI is actively working on at the present time. The primary goal here is to mimic and even exceed the reasoning powers of the human brain.
- The further expansion of what is known as the "invention of the method of invention", also known as "IMI" for short. This is where AI can be used to further stimulate the process of the current pace of innovation and perhaps even introduce new processes to speed up and accelerate the growth of research and development.

7.2.3 THE FUTURE CHALLENGES OF AI

The whitepaper even mentions the fact that trying to quantify the potential benefits that AI can bring to the American society is very difficult at this point. The primary reason for this is that AI can be embedded into tools that are both free (for example, those that make use of open source platforms) and subscription based (this is where the American consumer will have to pay for a product or service that has AI embedded into it). To this end, social science researchers have even proposed creating a new metric that can be added onto the overall GDP number, called the "GDP-B".

But the negative implications of AI are also well noted, apart from the ones just discussed in the last section. These include the following:

- The violation of privacy rights
- The creation of anticompetitive environments amongst corporations
- The nefarious manipulation of human behavior brought on by ML
- The imbalance of automation and staff augmentation in the American workforce
- The issues of racial discrimination and profiling
- The huge spread of misinformation, especially those on the social media platforms

Interestingly enough, the whitepaper makes the conclusion that the mentioned after-effects are not borne by AI itself, but rather the choices that are made by using the technology. It even mentions the fact that the United States federal government will have the ultimate responsibility when it comes to finding the right balance of the usage of AI in American society.

7.2.4 THE ADOPTION RATE OF AI IN THE UNITED STATES

The whitepaper even addresses how well AI had been adopted in the US. It does not look at it from the level of microeconomics, such as how much of the American population is currently using ChatGPT, but rather, it takes the perspective from a macroeconomic perspective. Here are some of the findings:

- The overall rate of adoption of AI in corporate America is actually rather low. It is not really the Fortune 500 per se that makes use of it on an extensive basis, but rather, it is being used extensively by larger companies that are owned by younger people.
- These business owners have more formal education and have more experience with using AI.
- Only 2.9 of companies in the United States make use of machine learning, 1.8% use computer vision, and a mere 1.3% make use of natural language processing algorithms (also known as "NLPs"; these are heavily used in chatbots).
- Recently, about 12.8% of the American workforce are employed by a company that makes exclusive use of AI.
- The industries that are most likely to make use of AI include the following:
  - Information Technology;
  - Professional Services;
  - Financial and Brokerage-based forms;
  - Management Consulting Firms.

But in terms of the exposure rate, workers who use AI will most likely be found in the following industries:

- Retail;
- International Trade;

- Utilities;
- Food Service.

- American businesses that are funded with venture capital money are most likely to be adopting AI technology.
- If a company were to adopt AI, the following statistics have been cited:
  - 80% of organizations use AI to improve their current product and service lines;
  - 65% of businesses use AI to improve their existing processes (both business and technological);
  - 54% of them use it for automation purposes.
- The use of virtual personal assistants ("VPAs") has reached a climax of a 72% adoption rate in the United States.

7.2.5 The Adoption Rate of AI in the European Union

It is also important to examine the trends of AI adoption in the EU as well. Here is what the whitepaper noted:

- Similar to the United States, businesses that are EU based use AI to a larger degree. But it seems here that the adoption rate is higher pegged at 28%.
- The firms in the EU that make use of AI also make heavy usage of ML, NLP algorithms.
- AI has been heavily used for the analysis of big data and chatbots.
- The EU countries with the most levels of AI adoption include the following:
  - Denmark at 28%;
  - Portugal at 17%;
  - The Netherlands at 13%.
- EU-based businesses also make heavy use of robotic process automation ("RPA"), which is also a subset of AI.

7.2.6 The Impacts of AI in the American Workplace

As mentioned earlier in this chapter, the whitepaper takes also a primary focus of what AI will mean to the American Workforce. Here are some of their findings:

- AI will be used heavily across those industries where automation is heavily needed.
- AI will be used heavily in routine-based tasks, which is technically defined as a process where a specified set of rules and procedures have to be followed. It will not be used nearly as heavily in nonroutine tasks, where the rules and procedures are much more nebulous in nature. This only underscores the fact that AI can learn much more effectively in a linear path, as opposed to a curvilinear path (at least at the present time).
- There will be a huge inequality gap that exists between the demand for AI and employee labor.

- It is quite likely that neural network technology could start to learn how to do nonroutine tasks as its learning algorithms and the datasets that are fed into it become much more advanced and sophisticated.
- AI will likely see a huge increase in labor-related jobs and not so much in the professional fields. But this could all drastically change in the long term with the advent of much more sophisticated chatbots. For example, rather than having a trained, medical professional to infer the results of a medical test, chatbots could possibly do this and relay that information back to the client.
- Another key area that could see an impact of job growth could be that in data science. Although this field at the present time is very high in demand, it is quite likely that AI could potentially decrease the demand for skilled workers. The primary reason for this is that it is expected that AI will become much more sophisticated over time and be able to parse out and infer big datasets in a much faster time than a human being could.
- It is quite likely that older people could be replaced by AI in the routine-based jobs as opposed to the younger-aged workers.
- Overall, it is expected that AI, if it ever does, will take a long time to totally replace a human worker. The primary driver for this is that AI still cannot fundamentally solve complex problems or issues. So for the immediate term, it is quite likely that AI could possibly be used for staff augmentation purposes rather than total worker replacement.
- It is even quite likely that AI could even create new jobs, especially where both automation and human intervention are still needed. Consider these statistics:
  - Overall, there was an improvement of 15% in terms of job creation;
  - 41% of those organizations that adopted AI actually witnessed an increase in worker skills;
  - In Germany, it was discovered that workers who attended a vocational school greatly benefited from learning how to use AI.
- In the routine-based jobs, it is quite possible that AI could bring in high levels of redundancy, thus forcing workers who are displaced to learn new skills to make them marketable once again to the United States workforce.
- It is quite possible that AI algorithms could dictate the daily workflows of employees in general. This is an area of strong concern, as algorithms cannot define what the needs of business productivity are on a day-to-day basis. Human intervention is still and will be strongly needed in this area.
- Finally, it is also quite likely that further adoption rates of AI could lead to a greater increase in outsourcing jobs to other countries, especially when it comes to software development.

Overall more specific case studies on how AI could further impact (either positively or negatively) can also be seen in this whitepaper. Finally, the entire whitepaper can be downloaded and viewed at this link:

http://cyberresources.solutions/Cloud_Update_Book/Impacts_AI.pdf

7.3 THE UNITED STATES ARTIFICIAL INTELLIGENCE BILL OF RIGHTS

As mentioned earlier in this whitepaper, in an effort to further strike the balance of optimal usage of AI and ML in the American society, the Biden administration has also come out with what is known as the "AI Bill of Rights". In a manner that is similar to our very own constitution, this new piece of legislation spells out the rights that each and every American citizen has when it comes to this, with a special focus of how their personal information and data can be used by AI or ML system.

Some of the major components of this include the following:

- The development of safe and effective AI systems (this states that cyber safe and resilient AI and ML systems have to be created and deployed);
- Protections against algorithmic discrimination (especially that in the American workforce);
- Data privacy (this is basically your right to know as to how your PII datasets will be stored, processed, transacted, and archived by an AI or ML system);
- Notice and explanation (businesses that make use of AI and ML have to explain to you how the AI system will be used on you);
- Human alternatives, consideration, and fallback (this provision gives you the right to opt from being used by an AI system, and in its place, human intervention will be used).

The basic crux of the AI Bill of Rights is as follows:

The Blueprint for an AI Bill of Rights is a set of five principles and associated practices to help guide the design, use, and deployment of automated systems to protect the rights of the American public in the age of artificial intelligence.

The entire AI Bill of Rights can be downloaded and viewed at this link:

http://cyberresources.solutions/Cloud_Update_Book/AI_Bill_Of_Rights.pdf

7.4 AZURE AND SAFE USE OF AI

As Azure explodes into the marketplace with regards to AI and ML, Microsoft has also taken steps to ensure that end users are using the tools in a safe and proper manner, that is not harmful to the American society. In fact, even before you can launch and initiate an Azure OpenAI account, you have to digitally agree to and sign a certain agreement which spells all of this out. It is called the "Responsible AI Standard", and it can be downloaded at this link:

http://cyberresources.solutions/Cloud_Update_Book/Microsoft_Responsible_AI_Standard.pdf

7.5 CONCLUSIONS

Just like computer technology in general, AI and ML are both here to stay in American society for a very long period of time, and perhaps even beyond our own lifetimes. The technology will no doubt advance, but its pace and adoption are still yet to be determined. As it was substantiated earlier in this chapter, it has gone through peaks and valleys, and in the author's view, this trend will happen in the near future.

But one thing is for sure: The impact that ChatGPT has brought into the American society is a permanent one. Not only have we felt its technological ramifications, but the impacts on how it will be felt onto our great democracy as a whole has truly yet to be felt. In fact, many experts and social science researchers believe that a new revolution will happen in the American society, called the "Democratization of AI".

More detailed information about this can be seen at the link below:

http://cyberresources.solutions/Cloud_Update_Book/AI_NSF.pdf

But the final question still remains: Will AI ever be able to fully replicate the human brain? The answer is a quite simple "No". It is not possible, and it will never happen, from the viewpoint of the author.

Index

Note: Information in figures and tables is indicated by page numbers in *italics* and **bold**, respectively.

Printed in the United States
by Baker & Taylor Publisher Services